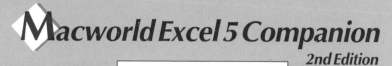

Macworld Excel 5 Companion

2nd Edition

Keyboard Shortcuts

D1477484

Editing shortcuts

Clear	Command-B
Clear-Selection (selected cell or range)	Delete
Copy	Command-C
Copy	F3 (Extended keyboard)
Copy Picture	Command-Shift-C
Cut	Command-X
Cut	F2 (Extended keyboard)
Delete	Command-K
Fill Down	Command-D
Fill Right	Command-R
Insert	Command-I
Paste	Command-V
Paste	F4 (Extended keyboard)
Paste Special	Command-Shift-V
Repeat	Command-Y
Undo	Command-Z
Undo	F1 (Extended keyboard)

File Shortcuts

Close	
New	
New-Chart	
New-Macro sheet	
New-Worksheet	Shift-F11 (Extended keyboard)
Open	Command-O
Open	Command-F12 (Extended keyboard)
Print	Command-P
Print	Command-Shift-F12 (Extended keyboard)
Quit	Command-Q
Save	Command-S
Save	Shift-F12 (Extended keyboard)
Save As	F12 (Extended keyboard)
Go To	F5 (Extended keyboard)

Formatting shortcuts

Border (remove)	Command-Option- - (hyphen)
Border-Bottom (Toggle)	Command-Option-down arrow
Border-Left (Toggle)	Command-Option-left arrow
Border-Outline (Toggle)	Command-Option-0 (zero)
Border-Right (Toggle)	Command-Option-right arrow
Border-Top (Toggle)	Command-Option-up arrow
Column width-hide (Toggle)	Command-0
Column width-unhide (Toggle)	Control-Shift-)
Font-Bold	Command-Shift-B
Font-Italic	Command-Shift-I
Font-Outline	Command-Shift-D
Font-Plain text	Command-Shift-P
Font-Shadow	Command-Shift-W

Font-Strikeout	Command-Shift-_ (underline)
Font-Underline	Command-Shift-U
Number-#,##0.00	Control-Shift-!
Number-$#,##0.00_); ($#,##0.00)	Control-Shift-$
Number-0%	Control-Shift-%
Number-0.00E-00	Control-Shift-^
Number-d-mmm-yy	Control-Shift-#
Number-General	Control-Shift-~
Number-h:mm AM/PM	Control-Shift-@
Row height-hide	Control-9
Row height-unhide	Control-Shift-(

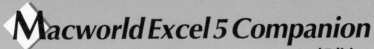

Macworld Excel 5 Companion
2nd Edition

Quick Reference Card

Excel 5's new and improved toolbars make frequently used actions just a mouse click away

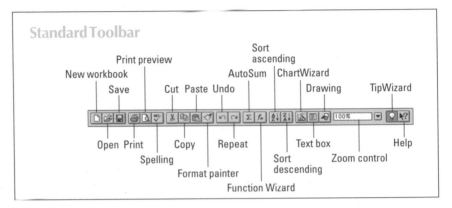

Standard Toolbar

New workbook · Save · Print preview · Cut · Paste · Undo · AutoSum · Sort ascending · ChartWizard · Drawing · TipWizard

Open · Print · Copy · Repeat · Text box · Zoom control · Help

Spelling · Format painter · Function Wizard · Sort descending

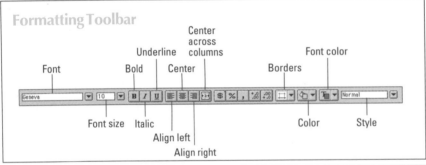

Formatting Toolbar

Font · Bold · Underline · Center · Center across columns · Borders · Font color

Font size · Italic · Align left · Align right · Color · Style

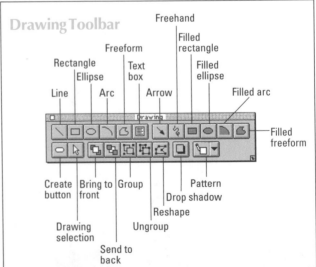

Drawing Toolbar

Line · Rectangle · Ellipse · Arc · Freeform · Text box · Arrow · Freehand · Filled rectangle · Filled ellipse · Filled arc · Filled freeform

Create button · Drawing selection · Bring to front · Send to back · Group · Ungroup · Reshape · Drop shadow · Pattern

About *Macworld Companion* Books

Macworld Excel 5 Companion, 2nd Edition, is part of the *Macworld Companion* series of books, brought to you by IDG Books, the leading publisher of computer information worldwide. This is a new kind of book designed to meet your growing need to quickly find what you want to do and learn how to do it.

These books work the way you do: They focus on accomplishing specific tasks — not learning random functions. All tasks are organized under common themes called Topics. *Macworld Companion* books are not long-winded tomes, manuals, or even quick reference guides, but are the result of drawing from the best elements of these three types of publications. These books have the easy-to-follow step-by-step sections of a manual; the comprehensive coverage you'd expect to find in a long tome; and the brevity you need from a quick reference guide — it's all here.

The designers of the *Macworld Companion* series use the following visual elements to make it easy to find the information you need:

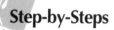

Step-by-Steps

demonstrate the concepts introduced in the Topic discussions with easy-to-follow instructions. If you're a beginner, these Step-by-Steps sections will go a long way toward getting you up to speed on unfamiliar topics.

New Feature 5 icons mark sections that bring you up-to-date on what's new in Excel 5. These icons are especially useful if you already use Excel 4.

Quick Tip sections include tips and insights on the material in each Topic; Quick Tips enable you to get the most out of your application or operating system no matter what level user you are.

Note icons point out features that you will probably use often in Excel and want to remember for future use. These items will quickly become a routine shortcut or technique that you will use in your Excel workbooks.

The authors of the *Macworld Companion* books are leading *Macworld* columnists, technology champions, and Mac gurus, who are uniquely qualified to provide you with expert advice and insightful tips and techniques not found anywhere else. We're sure you'll agree that the *Macworld Companion* approach is the best.

—David Solomon
Vice-President and Publisher, IDG Books

MACWORLD

Excel 5 Companion,

2nd Edition

MACWORLD

Excel 5 Companion,

2nd Edition

**by Christopher Van Buren
and David Maguiness**

**IDG
BOOKS**

IDG Books Worldwide, Inc.
An International Data Group Company

San Mateo, California ✦ Indianapolis, Indiana ✦ Boston, Massachusetts

Macworld Excel 5 Companion, 2nd Edition

Published by
IDG Books Worldwide, Inc.
An International Data Group Company
155 Bovet Road, Suite 310
San Mateo, CA 94402

Library of Congress Catalog Card No.: 94-77527

ISBN: 1-56884-081-0

Printed in the United States of America

10 9 8 7 6 5 4 3 2 1

2D/QZ/QR/ZU

Distributed in the United States by IDG Books Worldwide, Inc.

Distributed in Canada by Macmillan of Canada, a Division of Canada Publishing Corporation; by Computer and Technical Books in Miami, Florida, for South American and the Caribbean; by Longman Singapore in Singapore, Malaysia, Thailand, and Korea; by Toppan Co. Ltd. in Japan; by Asia Computerworld in Hong Kong; by Woodslane Pty. Ltd. in Australia and New Zealand; and by Transworld Publishers Ltd. in the U.K. and Ireland.

For general information on IDG Books in the U.S., including information on discounts and premiums, contact IDG Books at 800-434-3422 or 415-312-0650.

For information on where to purchase IDG Books outside the U.S., contact Christina Turner at 415-312-0633.

For information on translations and availability in other countries, contact Marc Jeffrey Mikulich, Director, Rights and Licensing, at IDG Books Worldwide; FAX NUMBER 415-286-2747.

For sales inquiries and special prices for bulk quantities, write to the address above or call IDG Books Worldwide at 415-312-0650.

For information on using IDG Books in the classroom, or for ordering examination copies, contact Jim Kelly at 800-434-2086.

 is a registered trademark of IDG Books Worldwide, Inc.

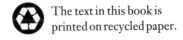 The text in this book is printed on recycled paper.

About the Authors

Christopher Van Buren (San Mateo, California) has written computer books for over ten years and has over 15 books to his credit. He is a noted Excel expert, but has also written about operating systems, graphics, and integrated programs.

Chris was a contributor to *The Illustrated Computer Dictionary For Dummies* and is a full-time writer and consultant in San Francisco's Bay Area.

David Maguiness (Carmel, Indiana) is a software consultant specializing in technical writing and training. He has written or co-written more than a dozen books on spreadsheet software for the Apple Macintosh and IBM-PC, including *PC World Excel 5 for Windows Handbook*, IDG Books, 1994. Dave contributes frequently to *PC World Lotus Edition* and was editor-in-chief of *Absolute Reference: The Journal for 123 and Symphony Users*. An alumnus of several Fortune 500 companies, Dave lives north of Indianapolis with his family.

Welcome to the world of IDG Books Worldwide.

IDG Books Worldwide, Inc., is a subsidiary of International Data Group, the world's largest publisher of business and computer-related information and the leading global provider of information services on information technology. IDG was founded more than 25 years ago and now employs more than 5,700 people worldwide. IDG publishes more than 200 computer publications in 63 countries (see listing below). Forty million people read one or more IDG publications each month.

Launched in 1990, IDG Books is today the fastest-growing publisher of computer and business books in the United States. We are proud to have received 3 awards from the Computer Press Association in recognition of editorial excellence, and our best-selling ...*For Dummies* series has more than 10 million copies in print with translations in more than 20 languages. IDG Books, through a recent joint venture with IDG's Hi-Tech Beijing, became the first U.S. publisher to publish a computer book in the People's Republic of China. In record time, IDG Books has become the first choice for millions of readers around the world who want to learn how to better manage their businesses.

Our mission is simple: Every IDG book is designed to bring extra value and skill-building instructions to the reader. Our books are written by experts who understand and care about our readers. The knowledge base of our editorial staff comes from years of experience in publishing, education, and journalism — experience which we use to produce books for the '90s. In short, we care about books, so we attract the best people. We devote special attention to details such as audience, interior design, use of icons, and illustrations. And because we use an efficient process of authoring, editing, and desktop publishing our books electronically, we can spend more time ensuring superior content and spend less time on the technicalities of making books.

You can count on our commitment to deliver high-quality books at competitive prices on topics customers want to read about. At IDG, we value quality, and we have been delivering quality for more than 25 years. You'll find no better book on a subject than an IDG book.

John J. Kilcullen

John Kilcullen
President and CEO
IDG Books Worldwide, Inc.

Acknowledgments

I would like to thank the entire staff of IDG Books Worldwide for making this book happen and for working with me on its completion. A special thanks to Andy Cummings and Janna Custer for regular support in the process as well as several other folks, including Michael Simsic, Barb Potter, Rebecca Forrest, Linda Boyer, Angela Hunckler, and Robert Simon.

Thanks also to Microsoft for providing software and beta support and for making Excel such a fabulous product.

I thank Joe and Serena Lucchesi for personal support through this project and in my entire life. Thanks also to my brother Alex for constant love and support.

(The publisher would like to give special thanks to Patrick J. McGovern, without whom this book would not have been possible.)

Credits

Publisher
David Solomon

Managing Editor
Mary Bednarek

Acquisitions Editor
Janna Custer

Production Director
Beth Jenkins

Senior Editors
Sandra Blackthorn
Diane Graves Steele
Tracy L. Barr

Associate Production Coordinator
Valery Bourke

Associate Acquisitions Editor
Megg Bonar

Production Quality Control
Steve Peake

Editorial Assistant
Rebecca Forrest

Project Editor
Andy Cummings

Editors
Michael Simsic
Barb Potter

Technical Reviewer
Howard Hansen

Production Staff
Paul Belcastro
Linda Boyer
Angela Hunckler
Carla Radzikinas
Patricia R. Reynolds
Robert Simon
Gina Scott

Proofreader
Jenny Kaufeld

Indexer
Steve Rath

Cover Design
Kavish + Kavish

Cover Illustration
Erik Adigard

Contents at a Glance

Table of Contents

Topic 3: The Excel Environment 75

Part II: Enhancing Your Worksheets 113

Topic 4: Formatting Your Work 115

Topic 5: Drawing and Annotating 149

Topic 6: Printing 169

Part III: Intermediate Excel 187

Topic 7: Formulas and Functions 189

Topic 8: Using Excel as a Database 233

Foreword

I have been testing computer products for almost 10 years, and as you may imagine, spreadsheets are a big part of my work as a Lab Director for *Macworld*. I use them to analyze test results, compare and analyze statistical functions, and graph test results. In addition, I use them to manage my home budget and balance my checkbook. Everybody I know uses spreadsheets. They have, in a quiet way, delivered as much of the early promise of personal computers for everyday people as the word processor. So much that even my Mom has called for some help on that "little spreadsheet" of hers.

Excel 5 is an extremely powerful tool. In my everyday use of Excel, I know that there are many more features than even I use. But like so many people, when I try to find that snazzy 3-D chart or the obscure statistical function, I usually end up frustrated.

This is why I'm particularly happy to introduce the *Macworld Excel 5 Companion*, 2nd Edition. It gives you step-by-step assistance, tips and tricks, and real-world examples of Excel functions. This book is the most straight-forward and easy-to-use guide I've seen. The *Macworld Excel 5 Companion* brings all of those more advanced features-like customizing Excel's charts, databases, toolbars, formulas, functions, and macros to your fingertips. Whether you're a high-powered financial analyst or the keeper of the home budget, you will find this book a useful time saver.

Like you, I need to make the most of Excel, and thanks to the *Macworld Excel 5 Companion* occupying a permanent position next to my Mac, I'll be able to tap more of Excel's power. I'm sure that this book will help you make the most of Excel.

And, Mom, your copy is in the mail.

—Lauren Black
Macworld Test Lab Director
San Mateo, California

xxiv

Introduction

Welcome to the world of rows and columns. Spreadsheets are generally used to process information that appears in rows and columns, commonly seen in financial applications. But over the years, spreadsheets have evolved from simple accounting tools for managing columns of numbers to powerful data and image management tools for all types of applications.

We find that Excel is useful for many applications in addition to accounting and financial analysis. When we need a simple database, we often turn to Excel for its simple and effective database handling. We like it because we can see everything we're doing with the data — and we have total control over it. Excel's database features don't lock you into a certain way of handling the data. In addition, we know that our database will always be transferable to other programs if the need should arise. Excel has powerful data exchange capabilities so that Excel data is compatible with almost everything else.

We also use Excel as a simple drawing package. It's excellent for creating flow diagrams or organizational charts, where objects align in rows and columns. We have created hundreds of business forms in Excel — some of them self-calculating and others merely masters for printing. And because it's easy to create row-and-column-oriented data in Excel, we always use Excel to create large tables of data for our word processing documents. Sure, many word processors have features for creating tables, but Excel is *built for creating data in rows and columns.* With its graphics, database management, data exchange, and calculation capabilities, Excel is an ideal tool for many different types of applications.

Excel 5 Adds New Power and Features

And the story gets better — Excel 5 adds more new features for creating and analyzing data. The new pivot table features let you make sense out of large amounts of raw data, such as statistical survey reports and sales data. In-cell editing makes it easier to change existing data right within the worksheet cells. And a new, revised menu and dialog structure organize commands for easier reference and access. If you are upgrading from a previous version of Excel, you may find Appendix D helpful. It details the new features in Excel 5 with special information about upgrading your old worksheets and Excel skills.

About This Book

This book provides instructions on the majority of Excel's features — those features you'll use most often, plus some more advanced features for future reference. You also learn about some special uses for Excel that you may not have thought about. An assortment of tips and special notes helps you get more from Excel than you may expect.

The *Macworld Companion* series is geared to users who want answers to Excel questions right away, with explanations and step-by-step instructions for accomplishing tasks. These books are designed to be your primary reference for your software products, without being too cumbersome or too advanced to be practical.

Think of this book as your Excel coach and personal trainer. It can teach you the fundamentals with hands-on examples and ideas. In addition, it can be there to keep you on track when you get stuck. Look up a task or Excel feature, and you'll find everything you need to know to accomplish your objective.

As you explore other new worlds in the Macintosh universe, the following books in this series can be your tour guides: *Macworld Word 6 Companion, Macworld ClarisWorks 2.0/2.1 Companion, Macworld System 7.5 Bible, Macworld Mac & Power Mac SECRETS*, and *Macworld Networking Bible*, (all published by IDG Books Worldwide.)

Who Should Read This Book

This book provides complete instructions on using Excel's primary features. If you are new to Excel or to this version of Excel, you'll find this book a valuable addition to the program's on-line help. It will help you get up and running quickly, but does not scrimp on the information. If you've used Excel before or have read an introductory book on Excel, you'll enjoy the extra detail offered in this book, including the sample worksheets and extra tips that bring Excel to life.

◆ If you're a beginner, the step-by-step instructions help you get up to speed quickly with the basic tasks.

◆ If you are an intermediate Excel user, someone who only needs the Excel essentials without the hand-holding, each topic provides overview information for each task. You can find the essentials in each section without having to work through the entire section.

◆ If you are an Excel expert, the Quick Tips, special notes, and sidebar information will help you get the most from Excel. You'll find icons that point out the new features in Excel 5, so you can move right to those explanations.

How This Book is Organized

Rather than chapters, this book is organized by topics. Each topic covers a specific area of Excel, such as creating charts, formatting charts, printing, analyzing data, and so on. When you need to perform an Excel task, scan the table of contents to locate the topic that addresses your needs.

The *Macworld Excel 5 Companion* is divided into six parts.

Part I: The Basics

This part of the book covers essential information about using Excel. After reading these chapters, you'll have the foundation necessary to create just about any Excel application you have. Highlights in this section include information on entering and editing data, making selections in the Excel worksheet, and changing the Excel environment to suit your needs.

Topic 1, "Excel's Basic Concepts," provides basic information you need to know about using Excel and other Macintosh programs, including using Help and Excel's specific instructional tools. You also learn how to open and close Excel workbook files and how to get around in Excel. If you are already familiar with Macintosh programs, you'll probably breeze through this chapter. (But make sure to note the new dialog box and help features of Excel 5.)

Topic 2, "Creating Worksheets," details the various types of information you can enter into an Excel worksheet. You learn about entering numbers, text and formulas — plus the basics of Excel's worksheet functions. Included in this topic are details about editing your work after you've entered it.

Topic 3, "The Excel Environment," shows you how to customize the basic Excel program window to suit your needs. You can change the view of your worksheets and even create your own menu commands and toolbar buttons.

Part II: Enhancing Your Worksheets

This part discusses tools for making your worksheets more attractive and presentable. If your brilliant workbooks in Excel are too complicated or confusing to read — or if you cannot print reports from your worksheet to present to others your workbooks serve very little purpose. This part gives you the details about creating reports and attractive presentations with Excel. Highlights include using fonts and styles in Excel, adding graphics to your worksheets, and customizing your printouts.

Topic 4, "Formatting Your Work," describes Excel's numerous formatting commands and options to help make your worksheets and printouts more attractive. You learn how to change fonts and type styles and, add borders and colors to your worksheets.

Topic 5, "Drawing and Annotating," explains Excel's basic drawing tools and shows you how to use them to annotate your charts and draw illustrations on your worksheets. You learn how to add text anywhere on the worksheet and format that text as you like.

Topic 6, "Printing," gives you all the details about Excel's printing features. You get special tips on formatting your printouts, as well as details about creating printed reports.

Part III: Intermediate Excel

Once you have the basics under your belt, you are ready to explore some of Excel's powerful and magical features. In this part of the book, you discover how to access and use Excel's powerful functions. In addition, you learn about some of Excel's data analysis features, including ways to perform "what if" analyses with your numbers. Excel's database features will impress you as a convenient way to store and access anything from your simple records to more complex data you may want to analyze.

Topic 7, "Formulas and Functions," explains how to use Excel's worksheet functions to build powerful, automated applications. The topic shows you how to enter functions and how to locate any function you need through the Function Wizard. You also receive detailed information about Excel's key functions.

Topic 8, "Using Excel as a Database," shows you when and how to use Excel to manage database information. This topic shows you how to set up and maintain an Excel database. Excel's database features let you search through large blocks of data for specific entries and even filter the database to show specific data you want to review.

Topic 9, "Analyzing Data in Excel," presents some of Excel's advanced features for analyzing data. This topic explains how to create "what if" analyses in your worksheets through data tables and scenarios. In addition, you learn about using array formulas to save time and space.

Topic 10, "Working with Large Workbook Applications," shows how you can manage your workbooks when they start to get large and cumbersome. Through the use of outlining and pivot tables, you can make sense out of these big workbook applications.

Part IV: Creating Informative Charts

Charting is one of Excel's strongest capabilities. Excel offers dozens of possible chart formats, plus the capability to manipulate and change every aspect of a chart. This part begins with the basics about charting and selecting the appropriate chart for the occasion. Ways to customize your charts for special needs are explained after you have the basics down.

Topic 11, "Creating Charts," offers the basics of generating charts (graphs) from your worksheet data. You learn how to use the ChartWizard to build a complete chart and format it. You also receive an introduction to the various chart types available in Excel and how to use each one.

Topic 12, "Customizing Charts," takes you into the various chart customization features of Excel so that you can manipulate specific elements of your chart presentations. After you have created a basic chart, you can use the customization features to enhance it. Tasks include changing the axis scale, adding graphics, changing chart colors, and setting up 3-D charts.

Part V: Macros and Customizing Excel

If you find yourself creating workbooks in Excel that other people use — or that you use over and over again — you will probably benefit from this part of the book. In this part, you will learn about Excel's automation powers — better known as macros. After reading this section, you will not only be able to create macros in Excel, but you will have plenty of ideas for adding this power to your existing applications.

Topic 13, "Creating and Running Macros," dispels the myth that macros are complicated. In this topic you learn how to quickly and easily create macros for your worksheets and how to attach those macros to custom toolbar buttons, custom menu items, or other worksheet objects.

Topic 14, "Creating a Custom Application," explores the world of application building in Excel. Through the use of worksheet *controls*, such as list boxes, check boxes, and option buttons, you can create a custom interface that others can use to get around in your worksheet.

Part VI: Excel Reference

A collection of appendixes combine information for your reference and interest. Appendixes cover such information as Excel's installation options and details about the new features in Excel 5. Another appendix contains workbook examples that you can study for techniques applicable to your own workbooks.

Conventions used in your Companion

Every topic contains an **Overview** at the beginning that introduces the contents of the topic and a **Quick Tips** section at the end that provides useful tips on the tasks and features covered in the topic.

In addition, the following icons are used to help streamline your learning experience:

 Step-by-Steps provides you with a hands-on opportunity to try out the tasks covered in the topic. The step-by-step instructions do not require that you perform a sample task but allow you to perform the operation on your own worksheet. So you can get the job done while you learn to use Excel 5 which represents one of the biggest advances in Excel in years.

 Quick tips give you useful information about the task under discussion. This is where you can find the inside scoop on how to accomplish an Excel task quickly and efficiently (and how to avoid those occasional pitfalls). Quick tips are spread throughout the topics as they apply and are also located at the end of each topic.

 Excel 5 shows you where new features of Microsoft Excel 5 are covered. You can scan for these icons to learn about all the newest features in Excel.

 Caution alerts you to areas that you should read before proceeding with the task at hand. Use these to avoid the hidden traps that sometimes occur when using a program.

 Note provides more information on particular features or tasks. It is information that you will use often in your Excel travels, and you may want to jot down a short note. As you become more skilled in Excel, these items will become second nature to you, and you can pass on your notebook to someone else who needs the information.

It is important to note that the term **Command** is used throughout this book and represents the ⌘ key on nearly all Mac keyboards.

What You Should Already Know

This book assumes that you know the basics behind operating an Apple Macintosh computer. Specifically, you should know how to start programs and manipulate windows (making a window active, moving and sizing a window, and zooming). In addition, you need to know how to choose commands from pull-down menus and understand pointing, clicking, double-clicking, and dragging. If all this sounds strange to you, take another look at the documentation that comes with your Macintosh, or better yet, read David Pogue's *Macs For Dummies* and *MORE Macs For Dummies* (published by IDG Books) — a fun way to learn about your Macintosh.

How to Read This Book

This book is designed to be useful on many levels. If you already have some familiarity with Excel — or if you have read through the basics in this book, you can use the book over and over again as a reference to forgotten, or little known, commands and options. In this way, the book is truly a companion to Excel.

But if you want to learn as much about Excel as you can, you can choose to follow the book in order, from beginning to end. The book is organized with the basic material first and the more complicated material at the end. While the later topics do not rely on the information covered in earlier topics, you'll find the progression used here is a natural one — with topics building on previously learned information.

You can also skip around in the book and locate information that interests you — or that you are least familiar with. Because each topic is independent of the others, you will not be required to go back and prepare any worksheets or examples before you can continue.

You should find this book easy to read on all these levels. Skim the book for its useful Quick Tips and Notes. Or find the Excel 5 icons that point out the new features and begin there. Whatever you decide...we hope you will enjoy learning about and using Excel!

Feedback, Please!

The *Macworld Companion* series team is always striving to serve its readers with the best information and presentation possible. Please let us know what you think we need to work on, and let us know what you believe worked well. You may do so by completing the Reader Response Card in the back of the book. If you are net-worked and prefer to respond through e-mail, please send a message to *The Macworld Companion Series Team* via America Online (address: IDG Books) or CompuServe (address: 74203,3412).

Part I:
The Basics

Macworld Excel 5 Companion

2nd Edition

Excel's Basic Concepts

Overview

This topic introduces you to the world of Excel and workbooks and serves as your launching pad to learning and using Excel with confidence. Specifically, you acquaint yourself with opening, creating, closing, and saving worksheets. You also discover how to select information in a worksheet.

To get the most out of this and future topics, you should have Excel running and on-screen so that you can follow along with the Step-by-Steps provided.

Important Excel Concepts

Even though Excel 5 possesses many powerful features, it is remarkably easy to use. There are some basic concepts with which you should be familiar for a complete understanding of Excel. The following sections discuss these core concepts of Excel 5. Where appropriate, these sections also make comparisons to the previous versions of Excel for those upgrading to Excel 5.

Workbooks, worksheets, windows, and files

Like many Macintosh programs, Excel lets you create individual documents and save them as files on the disk. In Excel 5, a document is called a *workbook*, which consists of 16 individual pages, or *worksheets*. Worksheet pages are labeled Sheet 1, Sheet 2, Sheet 3, and so on. You can apply your own names to these worksheets, if desired.

Excel 5 is different from previous versions of Excel, where each file on disk represents a single worksheet. Worksheets then could be *gathered together* into a workbook manually.

By contrast, when you start Excel 5, you are greeted with a workbook of 16 sheets that are already collected together for you. Each workbook can be stored on disk as a file, and you can add or remove individual pages, or worksheets, from any workbook. Workbooks appear inside the Excel program window as document windows. You can open numerous workbooks inside Excel and work with several at the same time.

You'll be creating numerous workbooks as you use Excel. Some of them will be small, independent projects, while others may be quite large, consisting of several pages of information. Whenever individual pages relate to one another — or to the same project — you may want to create them in the same workbook document. When an unrelated job comes along, you can start a new workbook. For more information about using multiple workbook windows, refer to Topic 3.

Select and then do

Many of Excel's commands and options perform actions on data in your worksheets. For example, you can change the font used for specific entries in a worksheet. The key to these commands is to *select the data first and then perform the action.* Usually, when you choose a command in Excel, the result is performed immediately on the currently selected data. This process requires you to select the data first. For example, to copy a column of numbers, you must first select the column and then use the Copy command. Details about selecting data are provided later in this topic.

Menus, shortcuts, and toolbars

Like most Macintosh programs, Excel provides several ways of accessing its commands and options. Most commands and options are available through Excel's menus. Just select the desired menu from the Excel menu bar at the top of the screen and then choose a command from within the menu. Remember that many commands require that you first highlight the data you want to modify — then select the menu command to affect the data you've selected.

Many menu commands can be invoked from the keyboard through keyboard shortcuts, or *command keys.* Keyboard shortcuts involve pressing one key and holding it (usually the Command key) while you press another key. For example, pressing Command-C is the same as using the Copy command in the Edit menu. Some keyboard shortcuts use the function keys (F1 through F12). For example, pressing F5 invokes the Go To command found in the Edit menu. (The pull-out Quick Reference card shows many helpful keyboard shortcuts.)

Besides the standard menus available in the Excel menu bar, you have access to several shortcut menus in Excel. Shortcut menus contain commands that relate to specific elements on the screen and may combine commands from two or more of the normal menus. Shortcut menus often provide easier access to frequently used commands.

You can access a shortcut menu by holding down Control while clicking the mouse button. (If your keyboard does not have a Control key, you can press both Command and Option while clicking the mouse button, and you'll get the same result.) The mouse's location determines the shortcut menu you see. Figure 1-1 shows an example of the shortcut menu that appears when you click a cell while pressing Control. This shortcut menu combines commands that appear in the Edit and Format menus — commands that you'll likely need when working with information in cells.

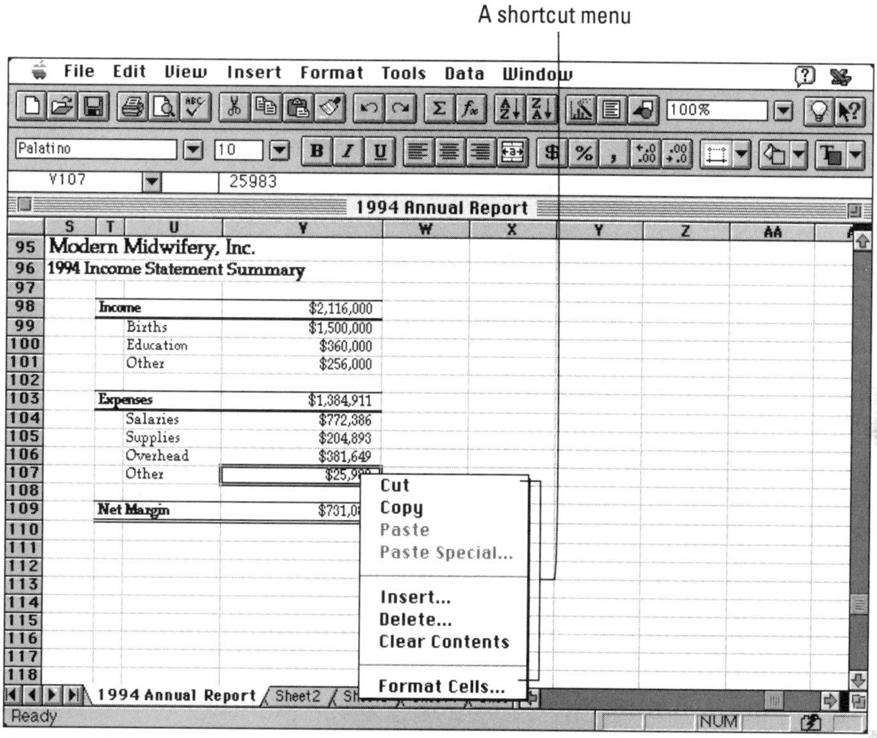

Figure 1-1: An example of an Excel shortcut menu that helps you work with cells.

Another type of shortcut available in Excel is the toolbar button. Excel provides 13 different toolbars — each containing buttons that perform specific actions. When you click the button, the action is taken. Many buttons perform actions that you can otherwise invoke through Excel's menus. But using the buttons is much easier and faster. In addition, Excel's toolbars are designed to help you with specific actions. For example, the Chart toolbar contains several buttons that pertain to creating and modifying charts. In this way, all the most important charting commands and options are available in one toolbar. Figure 1-2 shows some of Excel's toolbars.

Excel automatically places two important toolbars at the top of the screen: the Standard toolbar and the Formatting toolbar. These toolbars contain buttons that are commonly used in creating worksheets. You can access other toolbars through the Toolbars command in the View menu.

Excel toolbars

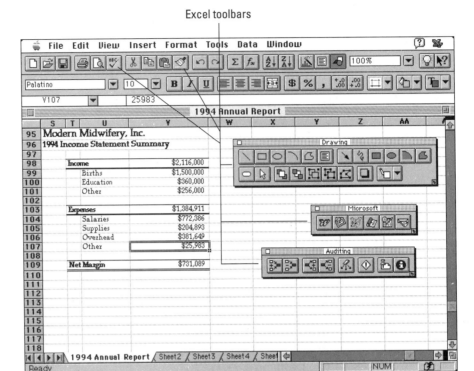

Figure 1-2: Some of Excel's toolbars.

Throughout this book, you'll see references to buttons as alternative ways of accomplishing the tasks being explained. For more information about Excel's toolbars, refer to Topic 3.

Another way to access Excel's commands and options is through *dialog boxes*. Excel 5 comes with a new style of dialog box, called a *tab dialog box*. A tab dialog box contains several pages of options that can be viewed by clicking the page's tab, as shown in Figure 1-3. In this way, one dialog box can be used to access all the options pertaining to a particular need in Excel. For example, all cell formatting options are contained in the six pages of the Format Cells tab dialog box shown in Figure 1-3.

Finally, Excel 5 offers another new way to access commands and options. *Tear-off palettes* make formatting easier.because you can leave palettes in view as you work. To tear off a palette in Excel, simply click the arrow that opens the palette and then drag to place the palette in the desired location on the screen. Figure 1-4 shows two tear-off palettes: the Color and Border pallettes.

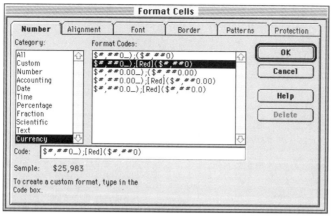

Figure 1-3: Excel 5's new tab dialog box. The example provides all formatting options for cells.

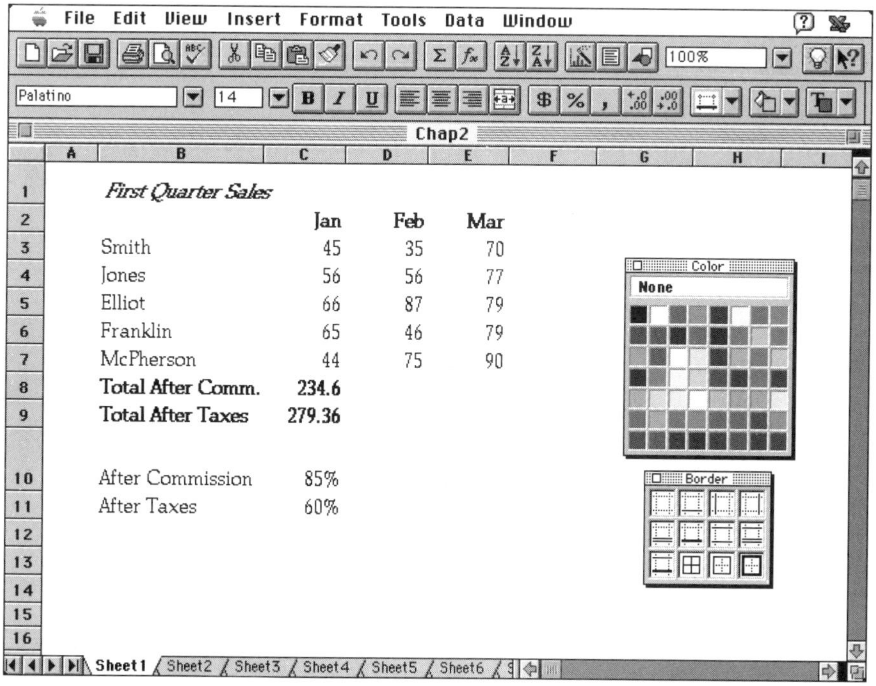

Figure 1-4: Excel 5's new tear-off palettes.

Undo and Repeat

Most Macintosh programs include an Undo command, and Excel is no exception. By selecting Undo from Excel's Edit menu, you can take back your most recent action. Often, you can select the command again to redo the action, if you so desire.

Be warned: Undo works only if you use it immediately after performing the action. Excel also provides an Undo button on the Standard toolbar.

Excel's Repeat command (and new toolbar button) lets you repeat your previous action. This command is useful if your action requires several keystrokes (or mouse movements) to perform, such as accessing a command from a tab dialog box. Click the Repeat button in the Standard toolbar, and the command is repeated automatically.

Cells and cell contents

An Excel worksheet is made up of millions of individual cells. All of the information that you enter into a workbook is entered into worksheet cells. Cells are stacked in rows and columns to make data alignment consistent. Because of this row-column orientation, spreadsheet programs lend themselves to financial applications and other projects that arrange data in tables, such as budgets, sales analysis worksheets, and expense analysis worksheets.

Cells are labeled using their column letters and row numbers, as in C5 for the cell located at the intersection of column C and row 5. This label is known as the cell's *reference* or *address*. As you learn in Topics 2 and 7, you can enter cell references in your worksheet formulas and access the information in any cell on any worksheet — provided you know its address. For example, the formula =*C5+10* adds 10 to the value in cell C5. You can enter this formula into any cell except C5. The result of this formula appears in the cell. The formula itself appears in the *formula bar* located at the top of the screen. Figure 1-5 shows an example of a formula bar displaying the formula for a cell.

To view the cell's contents in the formula bar, simply click the desired cell. If you double-click the cell, the formula bar contents appear in the cell itself. For more on this subject, refer to Topic 2.

Excel Help and Tips

Excel provides extensive help for your reference. There are several levels of help available, from quick tips to full on-line documentation. The following is a review of the various types of help available in Excel.

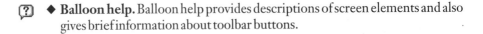

◆ **Balloon help.** Balloon help provides descriptions of screen elements and also gives brief information about toolbar buttons.

Formula   Result

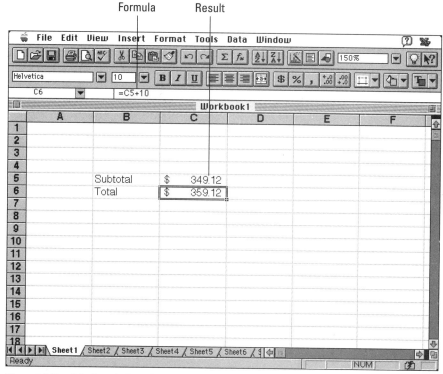

Figure 1-5: Excel displays the formula inside the formula bar and the result in the cell itself.

◆ **TipWizard.** The TipWizard is a toolbar in Excel 5 that displays brief tips as you use Excel. It follows your actions in the program and displays tips to help you perform your work more quickly and easily. If a tip is available, the TipWizard light bulb lights up, indicating that you can view a tip by displaying the TipWizard toolbar. You can also leave the TipWizard toolbar on-screen, and tips will appear inside it whenever they are available. See "Using the TipWizard" Step-by-Steps for more information.

◆ **Menu item descriptions.** As you pass the mouse across the various menu items in an Excel menu, brief descriptions of those items are displayed in the status bar at the bottom of the screen. This is a useful way of reminding yourself of the functions of various menu commands.

◆ **Point-and-click on-line help.** You can access on-line help screens for many screen elements in Excel. Just click the Help button in the Standard toolbar and then click any item on the screen, such as a cell, a chart, or a worksheet object. Excel brings up a help screen telling about the item you selected. Double-click this on-line help button to access the Excel help system.

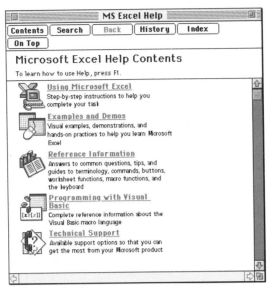

Figure 1-6: Use the Help menu to access Excel's extensive help system.

◆ **Help menu.** You can access Excel's extensive help screens through the options in the Help menu. Select the Contents option to view a table of contents for help options (see Figure 1-6). Use the Search command to search for a help topic of your choice. Use the Index command to view the index of help topics. (Note that if you are using System 6 or have a small Macintosh screen, the Help commands appear in the Window menu.)

◆ **Dialog box help.** Every dialog box in Excel contains a Help button. Click this button to access information about the dialog box, including details about each option in the dialog box (or tab dialog box).

◆ **Tool Tips.** Point at a toolbar button and wait a moment. A little yellow box appears with a short description of the button's function. This is similar to balloon help.

Using the TipWizard

1. When the TipWizard toolbar button lights up, a tip is available about the actions you've been performing.

2. Click the TipWizard button to display the TipWizard toolbar. You can also display this toolbar by using the Toolbars command in the View menu and selecting the TipWizard option from the list of toolbars. Figure 1-7 shows a TipWizard toolbar.

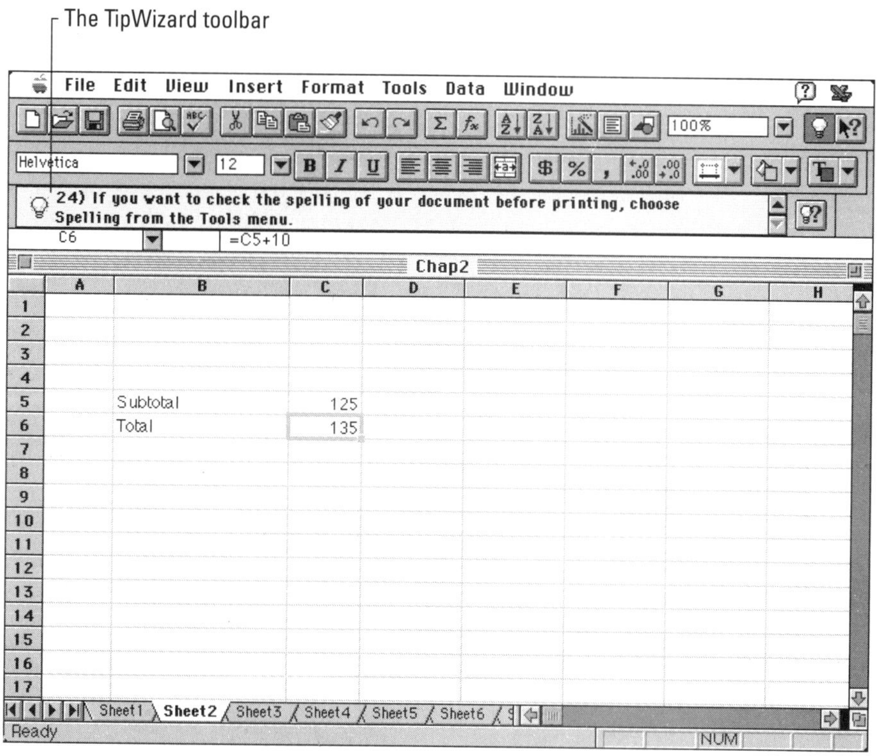

The TipWizard toolbar

| ⌘ | File | Edit | View | Insert | Format | Tools | Data | Window | | ⑦ | ✄ |

Helvetica ▼ | 12 ▼ | **B** *I* U | ≡ ≡ ≡ ≡ | $ % , | .0 .00 | ▼ | ▼ | ▼

💡 24) If you want to check the spelling of your document before printing, choose
Spelling from the Tools menu.

C6 ▼ | =C5+10

Chap2

	A	B	C	D	E	F	G	H
1								
2								
3								
4								
5		Subtotal	125					
6		Total	135					
7								
8								
9								
10								
11								
12								
13								
14								
15								
16								
17								

Sheet1 \ **Sheet2** \ Sheet3 \ Sheet4 \ Sheet5 \ Sheet6 \ S

Ready | NUM

Figure 1-7: The TipWizard toolbar provides brief tips as you work in Excel 5.

3. Leave the toolbar on-screen to view tips as they are available. You can click
the Help button on the TipWizard toolbar for detailed information about
the topic discussed in the tip. If the TipWizard tells you about a toolbar
button that is available for performing an action, it provides that button right
inside its own toolbar. ◀

Starting and Quitting Excel

Start Excel like any other Macintosh application. Just double-click the Excel
program icon. This action takes you into Excel and displays a blank workbook.

When you are through using Excel, or need to call it a day and turn off your
computer, or want to exit from Excel to free up memory, you can end your Excel
session by choosing Quit from the File menu or by pressing Command-Q.
Depending upon the other activities you've started on your computer, you are
returned to another open application or to the desktop. If you have an unsaved file
open, you are asked if you want to save it before quitting. Refer to "Opening and
Closing Worksheets" later in this topic for information about saving files.

Viewing Excel's Screen Elements

Because Excel workbooks and worksheets are so large, you can view only a small portion at a time. You view different pages of the workbook by clicking the page tabs at the bottom of the screen. Within each page, or worksheet, you view different areas by using the scroll bars, just like any other Macintosh program. The horizontal scroll bar lets you choose which columns to display, and the vertical scroll bar lets you display different rows. Refer to Figure 1-8 for a view of these elements and other elements of the Excel program.

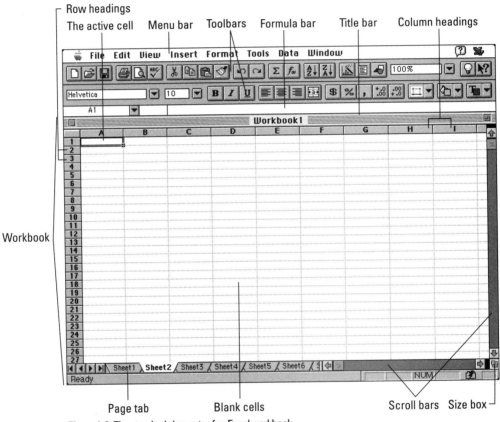

Figure 1-8: The standard elements of an Excel workbook.

When you start Excel, the screen shown in Figure 1-8 appears. This illustration shows the Excel program window, which contains Excel's menus and buttons along with a blank workbook. Details about each element follow.

The workbook

A workbook is an Excel document into which you type all your data. All the action takes place in the pages, or worksheets, of the workbook. You can create as many workbooks as you like and save them for future use.

Each workbook consists of the following elements:

◆ **The title bar.** All workbooks have a title bar that displays the name of the workbook. Also on the title bar are the standard Macintosh window elements for closing and zooming windows.

◆ **Page tabs**. All workbooks start out with 16 individual worksheets. You can add or remove worksheets as described in Topic 3. To move among the various worksheets, Excel provides you with worksheet page tabs. Clicking a page tab moves to that page. Topic 3 provides complete details about using workbook pages.

◆ **Column headings.** Each worksheet in a workbook consists of hundreds of columns, labeled A through Z, then AA through AZ, then AB through AZ, and so on, all the way to column IV. These labels are called the *column indicators* or *column headings*.

◆ **Row headings.** Worksheets consist of thousands of rows, labeled 1 through 16,384.

◆ **Cells.** Cells are the individual building blocks of worksheets. You move from cell to cell to enter your data into the worksheet. Cells are identified by their column letter and row number, as in C5. Cell C5 is the intersection of column C and row 5. This is known as the cell's *address* or *reference*.

◆ **The active cell** (or **cell pointer**). The active cell is the cell currently being used. You use the cell pointer to move from cell to cell. As you move the cell pointer (using various movement commands such as the arrow keys), the cell pointer's highlight indicates the active cell. Later in this topic you learn various ways to move the cell pointer and highlight cells. For now, just remember that the four arrow keys move the cell pointer from cell to cell in the direction of the arrow.

◆ **Scroll bars.** Scroll bars are tools that let you view portions of a window that are not currently in view. Use the worksheet scroll bars to view other parts of the worksheet.

◆ **The size box.** The size box, a small tool in the bottom-right corner of the workbook window, lets you change a window's size and shape.

Why such a large worksheet?

If you're new to Excel, you may be scratching your head — why such a large worksheet? Does anyone really create applications that require so many rows and columns? And so many different worksheet pages?

That's a fair question. For quite a long time, industry pundits have talked about the ongoing *spreadsheet war* between spreadsheet publishers, such as Microsoft and Lotus. These companies continue to fight for market share through continual one-upsmanship in their programs.

A common battlefield in this war is features. The earliest feature that drew attention was size. Each new program that came on the market boasted a larger worksheet than their competition.

Even if you could recreate an application that used every row and column in Excel (you'd run out of memory long before you did), it's not in your best interest to do so. It's much more efficient to create smaller, more compact worksheets that perform single, dedicated tasks. If you require multiple components for a single task, your best choice is to place each component onto a separate sheet in the same workbook.

Fortunately, the battle has shifted to ease-of-use features, such as the use of toolbars and worksheet functions to meet every need. The winner in all this is you — the user. As the major manufacturers continue their battle, they are providing you with a spreadsheet program that not only has great capacity, but is also becoming easier to use, more powerful, and continually improving.

The menu bar

The menu bar displays Excel's menus. Each of these menus contains several commands relating to the menu name. For example, the Edit menu contains several commands for editing data. The important Excel menu commands are discussed throughout this book.

The toolbars

Excel places several convenient buttons in toolbars that automatically appear at the top of the screen. These toolbars, known as the Standard and Formatting toolbars, are actually only two of the 13 different toolbars available for your use. Topic 3 describes how to access other toolbars, move the toolbars around the screen, and even customize them for your personal use.

The formula bar

The formula bar shows the contents of any cell in the worksheet. You can edit the cell's contents inside the formula bar, if you desire. Because of Excel's new in-cell editing features, you may find the formula bar to be a redundant screen element. You can remove it from the screen by choosing the Options command in the Tools menu and deselecting the Formula Bar option located on the View tab. See Topic 3 for more on this feature.

The formula bar includes the Active Cell reference, the Accept and Cancel icons, the Name drop-down list, and the Function Wizard button. The drop-down list in the formula bar displays the worksheets' named ranges, and the Function Wizard button provides information about Excel's worksheet functions. Both of these topics are covered in Topic 7.

The status bar

The status bar, appearing at the bottom of the Excel program window, displays messages concerning your options. Often, the status bar displays the `Ready` message, indicating that Excel is ready for your next action. Other messages appear in order to indicate the status of Excel or to explain commands.

On the far right side of the status bar are the keyboard indicators. These show whether you have activated Num Lock, Scroll Lock, or Caps Lock. You can hide the status bar by choosing the Options command in the Tools menu and deselecting the Status Bar option located on the View tab.

Creating a New Workbook

At some point, you will probably find the need to start a new, blank workbook in Excel. For example, you may need to begin a new scenario for your business, start a workbook for a new client, or create a budget for your mother-in-law. Opening a new workbook is easy. Simply choose New from the File menu or press Command-N. You can also click the New Workbook button in the Standard Toolbar (as shown in the margin).

Every time you open a new workbook, the new one is displayed smaller than the last. To enlarge the display of a workbook to its full size, click the zoom box on the title bar. (The zoom box is the small square on the far-right side of the title bar, as shown in Figure 1-9.)

Enlarging a worksheet to full size prevents you from clicking other open worksheets and making them active. To activate another worksheet, select its name from the Window menu. The currently active worksheet has a check mark to the left of its name, as shown in Figure 1-10.

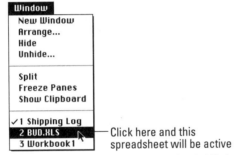

Zoom box

Figure 1-9: Resizing a worksheet using the zoom box on the title bar.

Window

New Window
Arrange...
Hide
Unhide...

Split
Freeze Panes
Show Clipboard

✓ 1 Shipping Log
  2 BUD.XLS ——— Click here and this
  3 Workbook1   spreadsheet will be active

Figure 1-10: Making worksheets active using the Window menu.

Opening Existing Workbooks

If you would like to work with a workbook you've created in an earlier Excel session, and it isn't displayed on your screen, you need to open the workbook. To do so, use the Open command in the File menu or press Command-O. Then select the name of the file from the dialog box. You can also click the Open button, which is second from the left on the Standard toolbar.

Opening a workbook

1. Select Open from the File menu. The Open dialog box appears as Figure 1-11 shows.

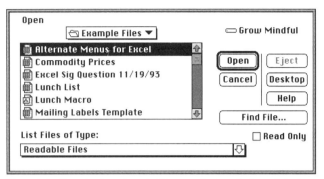

Figure 1-11: Choosing Open from the File menu displays the Open dialog box.

2. Use the various controls on the Open dialog box to locate the desired file and then double-click its name to open it. ◖

Closing and Saving Workbooks

As you become more proficient with Excel and create more advanced workbook applications, you may need to have more than one workbook displayed on the screen at the same time. To reduce screen clutter and free up memory, you can close unneeded workbooks. To close a workbook file, use the Close command in the File menu.

Closing a workbook

1. Choose Close from the File menu. The dialog box in Figure 1-12 appears.

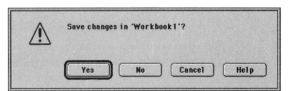

Figure 1-12: Closing a worksheet that has been modified since it was last saved.

2. If you have never saved the file and have entered or modified data in the workbook, Excel asks if you want to save the file. Press Return or click Yes to save any changes you've made since your last save operation. Click No to close this file without saving the changes, or click Cancel to abort the operation entirely. ◖

You can also save a workbook file without closing it. Saving a workbook to disk periodically is one of the most important activities you can perform. If you experience a power interruption or system problem, any work you have done since your last save will be lost permanently.

To save a workbook file to disk, use the Save command from the File menu or press Command-S. You can also click the Save button in the Standard toolbar. If this is the first time you've saved the workbook, Excel displays a dialog box that you use to name the worksheet file and to specify where to save it (which folder and disk; see Figure 1-13). After you type a name, click the Save button, and Excel saves the workbook to disk. Try to use descriptive names for your workbooks so that you can quickly identify their purposes in future Excel sessions.

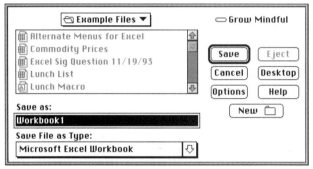

Figure 1-13: The Save As dialog box allows you to save a new file with a unique name or save an existing file under a new name.

Saving a workbook

1. Choose Save from the File menu. The Save dialog box appears,.

2. Use the various controls in the dialog box to choose a location for the file and then type a name for the file in the space provided.

3. Click the Save button to save the file. **⑴**

The next time you use File⇨Save or Command-S to save this file, Excel will save the workbook to the same disk and folder using the same name. Excel will not display the Save As dialog box this time, though you can see the progress of the save operation in the status bar at the bottom of the screen (see Figure 1-14).

Figure 1-14: The status bar displays the progress of the save operation.

If you want to save a workbook into another folder or under a different name, you can use the Save As command from the File menu. The Save As dialog box appears for you to specify a different folder, disk, and file name for the workbook.

Protecting workbooks with passwords

You can protect your workbooks with passwords, making it impossible to open the files without the proper passwords. This can be useful for sensitive information, such as salary or income information. Just use the Save As command in the File menu and choose the Options button. A dialog box into which you can enter a protection password appears. When you type the password, Excel enters only asterisks to keep snooping eyes from reading your secret code. When you click OK, you may be asked to retype the password before Excel saves the file.

When you open the password protected file, Excel asks for the password before displaying the workbook. Without the password, entered exactly as you saved it, access is denied.

Moving Around in Excel

Excel has only one active cell at any given time. Any information you type goes into this cell. The active cell is the one that is currently highlighted with the cell pointer. You can highlight any cell on the worksheet by simply moving the cell pointer to the desired cell. The following is a review of how to move the cell pointer using several different methods.

Moving around the worksheet with the mouse

To select an individual cell with the mouse, simply scroll the window so that cell is visible (use the scroll bars for this) and then click the mouse on the desired cell. Excel automatically changes the active cell to the cell you clicked. You should see a heavy border around this cell and the cell's address in the formula bar at the top of the screen.

To move to another worksheet within the active workbook, simply click its page tab. To view more page tabs, use the tab buttons located to the left of the tabs (see Figure 1-15). For more information about manipulating individual worksheets, refer to Topic 3.

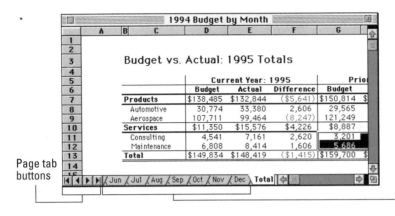

Page tab
buttons

To move to a new worksheet
quickly, click its page tab

Figure 1-15: Page tab buttons let you see tabs that do not currently fit on-screen.

Moving around the worksheet with the keyboard

To move the cell pointer using the keyboard, simply use the arrow keys to move the active cell to where you want it to be. The arrow keys work as you would expect. In addition to the four arrow keys, you can jump more quickly around the worksheet by using other keys. Table 1-1 describes each movement key.

You can hold any of the keys (or combinations) down for a *rapid repeat* of the action. For example, press and hold the down-arrow key to move continuously downward until you release the key. When you reach the edge of the screen, Excel automatically scrolls the window to keep the active cell on the screen.

The arrow keys are useful for moving the active cell in small amounts. To make larger jumps, use the mouse technique described previously or the Go To command described next.

Moving around the worksheet with the Go To command

You can make large jumps in a worksheet by using the Go To command in the Edit menu. You can specify the exact cell that you want to activate, and Excel jumps straight to that cell.

Table 1-1
Keyboard Movement Keys

Key	Moves the cell pointer this way
Down Arrow	Down one row.
Up Arrow	Up one row.
Left Arrow	Left one column.
Right Arrow	Right one column.
Tab	Left one cell.
Shift-Tab	Right one cell.
Return	Down one cell.
Shift-Return	Up one cell.
Page Up	Up one screen (about 19 rows).
Page Down	Down one screen (about 19 rows).
Command-Page Up	Left one screen (about 10 columns).
Command-Page Down	Right one screen (about 10 columns).
Home	To the first cell in the current row. If the cell pointer is in cell C15, pressing Home moves to cell A15.
Command-Home	To cell A1.
Command-End	To the bottom corner of the worksheet's used area. There is no data below or to the right of this corner cell. This location is called the *high cell.*
Command-Arrow Key	To the beginning of the next block of data in the direction of the arrow key. If there is no data in the same row or column as the cell pointer, Excel moves to the end of the worksheet in the direction of the arrow. If you are in the middle of a block of cells, this command moves to the end of the current block instead of to the beginning of the next.

Jumping around the worksheet

1. Select the Go To command in the Edit menu or press the F5 function key. The dialog box shown in Figure 1-16 appears.

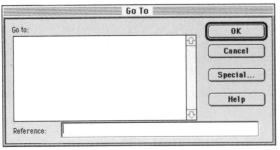

Figure 1-16: The Go To dialog box.

2. Type the address of the cell to which you want to jump.

3. Press Return. ◖

If you use the Go To command several times to jump to different locations, Excel remembers the last four locations you used and makes them available in the Go To dialog box, so you can quickly return to a previous location without entering the cell address again. If the desired cell address appears in the Go To dialog box, just double-click the address to move to that location again.

Try using the Go To command several times to set up the four locations that you jump to the most. (Note that these four Go To locations are not stored with the worksheet. They are cleared out when you close the worksheet.)

Selecting Cells

One of the most common procedures you'll use in Excel is highlighting data, or selecting the cells containing data. The golden rule of working with data in any Macintosh program is this: First you select the data and then you do something to it — select and then do. In Excel, highlighting (or selecting) cells is the first step for many different procedures. There are many additional reasons for highlighting data in Excel, including the following:

◆ To create formulas that calculate the values in a block of cells

◆ To enter data (if you want the pointer to remain in the highlighted block)

◆ To copy or move a block of data

◆ To insert or delete cells from the worksheet

◆ To name a cell or block of cells

◆ To format data (change its appearance)

◆ To specify the data you want to print

◆ To create a chart

◆ To choose any command that acts on the selected cells

You can see that highlighting data is a fundamental part of using Excel. The next few pages show you several ways in which you can highlight data in Excel.

If you are familiar with other Macintosh programs, you should pick up Excel's data-selection methods easily. Most Mac programs use similar techniques for selecting data. You can use either the mouse or the keyboard, but most Mac users find the mouse more convenient.

Selecting blocks of cells with the mouse

Selecting blocks of cells lets you perform actions on all of them at the same time. Whenever you want to perform the same action on several cells, highlight them as a block. As you'll see, they don't even have to be next to each other. Suppose you want to boldface the data in 100 cells. You will find it about 100 times more efficient to select the entire block of 100 cells and choose boldface than to select each cell in turn and make each one boldface.

To select a block of cells, click the first cell in the block and hold the mouse button. Then drag the mouse in the desired direction to highlight the cells. To select the range of cells from B5 through E12, for example, follow these steps:

Selecting ranges with the mouse

1. Move the mouse pointer to one corner of the range rectangle which corresponds to the range you want to select. For this example, point at cell B5.

2. Press and hold the mouse button and drag toward the opposite corner of the range rectangle (in this case, down and right). As you move the mouse, Excel highlights the cells.

3. When you reach the opposite corner of your desired selection (in this case, cell E12), release the mouse button. Excel selects the range. ◖

Dragging in different directions is easy with Excel. Most people have a tendency to select from the top-left corner to the bottom-right corner. You will probably find yourself selecting this way. But you may find situations where dragging from bottom to top or right to left will make things easier. Excel doesn't care which corner you start in. If you have scrolled so that you see the bottom-right corner of a table and you want to select the whole thing, by all means drag from the bottom right to the top left.

If you need to select a range that doesn't fit on the screen, simply drag the selection to the edge of the window. Excel automatically scrolls the window as you drag past the edge of the screen. As an alternative to this technique, you can click once on the first cell of the block and then hold Shift down as you click the last cell of the block. This method can be more convenient than dragging when the block of cells spans across several screens.

Excel provides a simple way to tell the size of your selection. As you drag the mouse to select cells on the worksheet, the size of the selection (number of rows by number of columns) appears in the reference area (the left portion of the formula bar).

Selecting a block of cells with the keyboard

To select a range of cells without using the mouse, you simply move to the first cell of the desired range and then hold Shift down as you press any of the four arrow keys. Here's how you would select the range from B5 to E12 using the keyboard instead of the mouse:

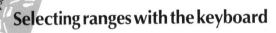

Selecting ranges with the keyboard

1. Use the four arrow keys to move the cell pointer to cell B5.

2. Press and hold Shift. Now press the right-arrow key three times and then the down-arrow key seven times. The range from B5 to E12 is highlighted. ◖

In addition to using the four arrow keys along with Shift, you can use any of the keyboard movement keys listed in Table 1-1 to select a range. For example, you can hold Shift and press Page Down to highlight from the current cell downward (about 19 rows, or one page). Press Shift-Command-Home to highlight from the current cell to cell A1. You can experiment for best results.

Selecting a range with the Go To command

You can use the Go To command in the Edit menu to select an entire block of cells—not just individual cells. Just enter the entire range reference into the Go To dialog box. The range reference should be entered using the cell address of any two diagonal corners of the range. Place a colon between the two references. For example, type in the range B2:D10 in the Go To dialog box and press Return. Excel highlights the range you specified. This technique can be useful for highlighting a range in a remote area of the worksheet.

You can enter any valid cell or range reference in the Go To dialog box, including a range name. If you have defined a name for the desired range, just type that name into the box, and Excel highlights the range. And remember: the previous four locations you specify are available for future jumps while you are working on this worksheet. Range names are discussed in more detail in Topic 7.

You can also use the Go To command to highlight cells by moving the cell pointer to the first cell in the desired range. Then select the Go To command from the Edit menu. Instead of entering an entire range reference, just enter the address of the last cell in the range and hold Shift down as you press Return. Excel highlights from the active cell to the specified cell.

Selecting multiple ranges of cells

You can select more than one range of cells at a time. A multiple range is one that contains cells in nonadjacent blocks. For example, you can highlight the range B5:E12 and the range F10:F15 at the same time. Figure 1-17 shows a worksheet with multiple ranges selected.

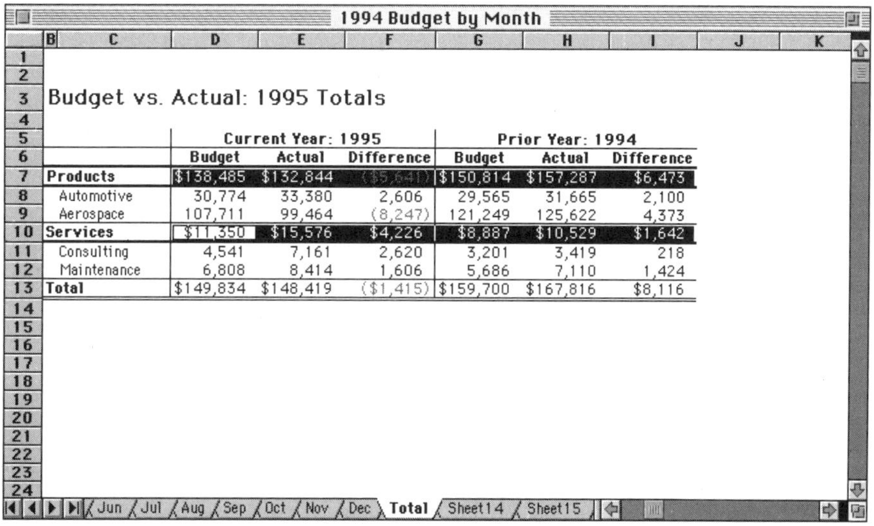

1994 Budget by Month

	Budget	Actual	Difference	Budget	Actual	Difference
Budget vs. Actual: 1995 Totals						
	Current Year: 1995			Prior Year: 1994		
	Budget	Actual	Difference	Budget	Actual	Difference
Products	$138,485	$132,844	($5,641)	$150,814	$157,287	$6,473
Automotive	30,774	33,380	2,606	29,565	31,665	2,100
Aerospace	107,711	99,464	(8,247)	121,249	125,622	4,373
Services	$11,350	$15,576	$4,226	$8,887	$10,529	$1,642
Consulting	4,541	7,161	2,620	3,201	3,419	218
Maintenance	6,808	8,414	1,606	5,686	7,110	1,424
Total	$149,834	$148,419	($1,415)	$159,700	$167,816	$8,116

Jun / Jul / Aug / Sep / Oct / Nov / Dec / **Total** / Sheet14 / Sheet15

Figure 1-17: A worksheet with multiple ranges selected.

The following are several methods of highlighting multiple blocks. These methods are all variations on the data-selection techniques described previously.

◆ Using the mouse, click and drag to highlight the first range — either one cell or a block of cells. Now press and hold down the Command key as you click and drag on the next range. Holding Command causes the first range to remain active while you select another.

◆ If your keyboard has function keys, press Shift and highlight the first range with the arrow keys. Then press Shift-F8; the word ADD appears in the bottom corner of the screen on the status bar. Now move the pointer to the beginning of the next range, press Shift and highlight the next area with the arrow keys. Press Shift-F8 again if you want to highlight another range. Repeat this procedure for as many ranges as you like.

◆ Using the Edit⇨Go To command, enter any valid multiple range reference into the Go To dialog box. Multiple-range references are individual-range references separated by commas. For example, you can enter **B5:E12,G2:G7** to highlight two ranges.

Remember that you can include range names in any multiple-range entry, assuming the ranges you want to include are named. For example, if the range G2:G7 is named ITEMS, the previous example could be entered **B5:E12,ITEMS**.

It is often helpful to select the intersection of two ranges. When you enter a multiple-range reference into the Go To command or as part of a formula, you use the comma to separate each individual range in the reference. However, if you use a space between the references, Excel selects the cells common to all the ranges. For example, the reference B5:E12 C10:G10 would result in the range C10:E10, which includes the cells located in both ranges. You can combine this type of reference (called an *intersection reference)* along with the normal combination reference by using commas.

Selecting entire rows and columns

Selecting entire rows or columns becomes important when you want to create consistent formatting or when you want to insert rows or columns into your worksheets safely—without creating problems with other data.

It may seem an unenviable task, though, to select across 256 columns to get an entire row, or worse, drag through Excel's 16,384 rows to make a complete column! Luckily, Excel has made selecting entire rows or columns a one-step process. The following list summarizes three efficient procedures to select entire rows and columns:

◆ Using the mouse, move your mouse pointer to the center of the column heading (the label A, B, C, and so on) for the column you want to select. For example, to select column E, point directly at the E at the top of the column. Now click once with the left mouse button. The entire column is selected. Drag across column labels to select additional columns. To select a row, click the row heading at the left of the screen. Note that you can hold Command down as you click to select nonadjacent rows and columns.

◆ Using the keyboard, move the cell pointer to any cell in the row or column you want to select. For example, to select row 8, place the cell pointer anywhere in row 8. To select the current row, press Shift-spacebar. To select the current column, press Command-spacebar.

◆ Using the Edit⇨Go To command, enter any valid row or column reference into the Go To dialog box. A row or column reference is simply the row number or column letter entered twice with a colon separating the two. For instance, to specify column G, enter **G:G** into the Go To dialog box. To specify row 14, enter **14:14**.

Selecting the entire worksheet

Selecting the entire worksheet is a powerful and useful technique. Once you have the entire worksheet selected, you can make global changes. For example, you can change the font of all the data in the worksheet at the same time — or preset the font on a new, blank worksheet. Want to change the color of the worksheet cells? You can do so by first highlighting the entire worksheet.

The following are the techniques for highlighting the entire worksheet:

◆ Using the mouse, locate the blank square in the top-left corner of the worksheet, where the row and column headings intersect. This square appears to the left of the A heading and above the 1 row heading. Click here, and Excel instantly selects the entire worksheet.

◆ Using the keyboard, combine the command for selecting all rows with the command for selecting all columns. The result is Command-Shift-spacebar.

◆ Using the Edit⇨Go To command, enter the reference A:IV. This action selects all columns from A to IV. You could also enter the row references 1:16384, but that may be harder to remember.

Excel provides other methods of formatting the entire worksheet. You don't have to highlight the entire worksheet in order to make global formatting changes. Topic 4 explains how to change the Excel default settings.

Quick Tips

Saving workbooks frequently

Remember to save workbooks frequently to guard against accidental errors or the loss of data as the result of a power failure.

Using the Save As command

If you have made changes to an existing worksheet but want to preserve the original version on disk, use the Save As command from the File menu. Just enter a new logical name in the filename area. This command enables you to save worksheets sequentially (Budget 1, Budget 2, and so on) so that you can keep track of previous versions.

Saving workbooks automatically

Excel includes an add-in called Auto Save that saves workbooks automatically at a time interval that you specify. See Appendix C for more information about using add-ins.

Using the Return key in dialog boxes

Remember that any time a dialog box contains a button with a bold border, you can choose that button by pressing Return. This lets you keep your fingers on the keyboard.

Saving workbooks in different file formats

Excel can save workbook files in many popular program file formats, including Lotus 1-2-3 and dBASE. If you want to save a worksheet in a file format different from Excel's standard format, use the Save As command from the File menu and then choose the format you want in the File Format box. For more information about exchanging data with other programs, refer to Topic 9.

Saving Excel Windows files

You can use workbooks created in Excel for Macintosh directly with Excel for Windows. Just use the Save As command from the File menu and then choose the Excel for Windows format in the File Format box.

Closing workbooks simultaneously

All open workbooks can be closed simultaneously by holding down the Shift key as you choose the File menu. You'll find the Close All command in the File menu, which closes all open files and prompts you to save any changes you've made.

Making automatic backups

You can have Excel automatically backup any workbook. Choose the Save As command from the File menu and then click the Options button. In the Options dialog box, check the Always Create Backup checkbox. Choose OK and Save. Excel now keeps the previously saved copy of the workbook file on your hard disk.

Finding files on your hard disk

If you want to open a file but don't remember its location or name, choose Find File from the File menu. Excel lets you search for files by name, by date, or even by contents.

Creating summary information

When you save a file, Excel asks you for summary information about it. The information includes the title, the contents, the keywords to describe the file, the author, and so on. If you don't want to have to enter this information when you save files, you can choose Options from the Tools menu and click the General tab. Now uncheck the Prompt for Summary Information checkbox. Click OK and Excel won't ask you anymore. It is important to note that summary information provides details for your Find File searches.

Jumping around the worksheet

You can jump to any cell address on the worksheet with the Edit⇨Go To command or more quickly by clicking the Name box (at the left side of the formula bar), typing the cell address, and pressing Return.

Creating Worksheets

Overview

Entering data is an essential skill in using Excel. In this topic you learn that Excel differentiates between several different types of data that you can enter — each type has its own characteristics. You also learn some basics about creating formulas to calculate totals and other values in your worksheets. (Topic 7 will complete your education of formulas and functions.) When you finish entering data, you'll probably need to make a few changes. This topic covers the basic editing procedures in Excel, including how to change entries, delete them, and copy them to other areas of the worksheet.

Entering Data

Because the data you enter into a worksheet determines the value you get out of it, a little background on the way Excel handles different types of data goes a long way. Excel handles several types of data. Text labels, numbers, formulas, and dates are the primary data types you'll enter in everyday activities.

But there's good news that simplifies the process: While there are several types of data that you can enter, there is only one way to enter that data into your worksheets. Simply move the cell pointer to the desired cell (by pressing the arrow keys or by using the mouse to click the desired cell, as explained in Topic 1). Then type the formula, number, text, or date and press Return to *accept* it into the worksheet.

Whether you are entering text, numbers, or dates, the following steps show you how to enter data into the worksheet.

Entering data into the formula bar

1. Click the desired cell. You can also use the arrow keys to move to the desired cell.

2. Type the data you want to appear in the worksheet. As you type, the information appears in the formula bar.

3. Press Return, Tab, Return, or an arrow key to accept the entry into the worksheet. The data appears in both the formula bar and the worksheet.

☒ Before you complete step 3, you can cancel your entry by pressing Escape or clicking the Reject button at the top of the screen. ❙❱

Another way of entering data into a worksheet is to type it directly into the cell itself. *In-cell* entry and editing is a convenient new feature in Excel 5. It's another example of how Microsoft's developers are trying to make Excel easier to use.

Entering data directly into a cell

1. Double-click the mouse in the desired cell. This action places the entry cursor directly in the cell.

2. Type the data you want to appear on the worksheet. As you type, the information appears in the cell.

3. Press Return to accept the entry into the worksheet. You can also press the Tab key or any arrow key to accept your entry. The data appears in the formula bar and in the worksheet. ❙❱

If you change your mind about an entry after accepting it into the worksheet, you can simply move the cell pointer back to the cell containing the entry (if the pointer has moved) and then type a new entry in its place. The new entry completely replaces the existing one. You can also press Delete or Command-B to remove the entry altogether. More information on editing your entries appears later in this topic.

As you can see, the mechanics of entering data into the worksheet are simple. How Excel treats the different types of data and what you can do with each different data type requires a little more understanding. The following sections discuss the primary data types in Excel.

Entering text and headings

Perhaps the first thing you'll enter into a new worksheet is the descriptive information, such as the worksheet title, column headings, and other text. In Excel, text consists of any information that is not a date or does not consist *entirely* of numeric values. It is important to note that text cannot begin with an equal sign because the equal sign tells Excel that a formula is coming.

In other words, just about everything you type that includes an alphabetical character is considered a text label by Excel. Here are some examples of text entries:

◆ First Quarter Sales

◆ Item 53899

◆ 223 Main Street

◆ Bob Jones

You can type up to 255 characters in a cell and expand the column's width to hold all that information, if you desire (Expanding columns is explained in Topic 4.) You can also let a long text entry exceed the width of its cell and spill into the cell to the right — provided the cell to the right does not contain information. Cell C5 in Figure 2-1 shows text spilling beyond the edge of its cell and into the next two cells. Cells C6 and C7 show the same text chopped off because the cells to the right are not empty.

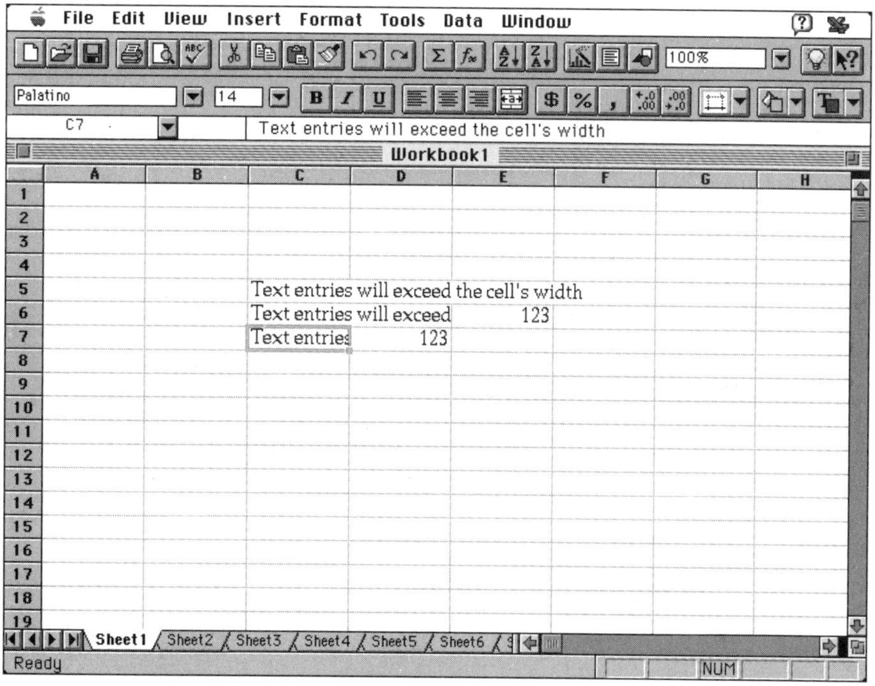

Figure 2-1: Examples of text entries that exceed cell widths.

Actually, the text is contained entirely by the original cell and only appears to spill into the next cell when the next cell is empty. If the next cell contains information, the original text entry can be seen only as far as its cell allows. You can expand the cell's width to see the rest of the entry. Notice that the cell pointer is currently on cell C7 and that you can see the entire text label in the formula bar at the top of the screen. The formula bar displays the entire contents of the cell — as you typed it — even though the worksheet does not.

In Topic 4, "Formatting Your Work," you learn how you can format your text entries to achieve different effects. You can align text with different sides of the cell (that is, push the label up against one of the four sides of the cell), make text spill in different directions (into the cells to the left rather than to the right), center a heading across several columns, and much more. You can also make long text entries wrap onto several lines within the same cell — rather than spill out of the cell. You also learn more about changing column widths.

Entering notes

Because you can enter up to 255 characters into each cell, you may be tempted to enter descriptive information about the worksheet in various cells throughout the sheet. For example, you may want to include notes that explain various parts of the worksheet, such as typing **This cell shows the total of all sales** beside a total column.

But Excel provides a better way of annotating the worksheet. Rather than entering notes right in the worksheet, which limits you to only 255 characters per cell, try using the Note command in the Insert menu.

Inserting notes

1. Choose Note from the Insert menu. The Cell Note dialog box appears.

2. Type your note into the Text Note entry box that appears in the dialog box. Press Command-Return when you want to move to a new line. (Pressing Return alone accepts the note and removes the dialog box from view.)

3. Click OK. The note is now attached to the cell. ◖◗

Although the easiest way to add a note is to first move to the desired cell, you can enter a note for any cell without moving to the cell first. Just enter the desired cell address into the Cell entry box in the Notes dialog box; then enter the note and click Add. You can continue to add notes to any cells in this manner. All notes that you add to the worksheet appear in the Notes in Sheet list. By clicking any entry in this list, you can view any note in the worksheet without having to move to a particular cell first.

Changing column widths

Allowing text to spill across other cells is one way to place headings across several columns or to create indentations in a worksheet. For example, you can deliberately reduce the first column to create a small indent (see the figure).

You can change a column width by moving the mouse pointer to the column's heading area. Now move to the line between this column and the next one (to the right).

The mouse pointer should look like this:

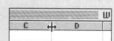

Click the mouse on the separator line and drag to the right to expand the column or to the left to reduce it.

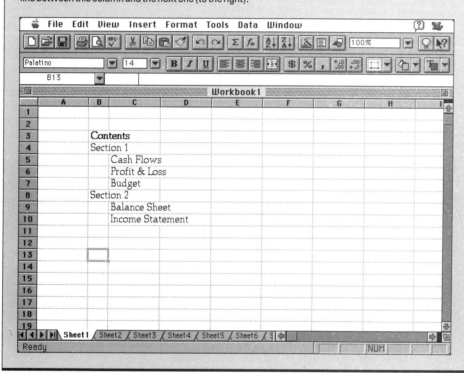

The note does not appear in the worksheet itself but is available at any time. You can view the note by moving to the cell and selecting the Insert Note command again. Or you can view the note in the Info Window. You can tell Excel to indicate which cells contain notes by displaying the *note indicator*. When the note indicator is active, Excel displays a small mark in the upper-right corner of cells that contain notes.

Displaying the Info Window and note indicator

1. Choose Options from the Tools menu. The Options dialog box appears with several tabs from which to choose.

2. Click the View tab if it's not already selected.

3. Click to place an *X* in the Note Indicator option and click again in the Info Window option. These actions tell Excel to display the Info Window and the Note Indicator.

4. Click OK. ◗

The Info Window is useful when you are reviewing a complex worksheet. The window has a number of its own commands and options for auditing a worksheet. You can arrange the windows such that the Info Window can be seen along with the worksheet window. Therefore, you can click cell after cell in the worksheet, and the Info Window follows your actions, displaying information about each cell as you click it.

Entering numbers

Numeric entries contain numerals and other numeric symbols. Numeric entries cannot contain anything other than these characters:

1, 2, 3, 4, 5, 6, 7, 8, 9, 0, $, -, +, ., (, %, /,), ,

You can *begin* a numeric entry with all but the last four (%, /,), ,), which can only be located in the middle of a numeric entry. The different numeric symbols have specific purposes. For example, you can use the slash symbol (/) to enter fractional values, such as $5^1/_4$, and you can use the dollar sign ($) to display the value as a dollar amount rounded to two decimal places. Table 2-1 provides some acceptable numeric entries.

Notice that adding the dollar sign causes numbers to round to two decimal places. This feature is an aspect of the currency number format and is described in more detail in Topic 4.

Excel normally adds leading zeros to a fractional number, so you see 0.123 when you type .123 into the cell. Again, you can change this with number formats described in Topic 4. However, you must include a leading integer value for all fractional entries or Excel may interpret them as dates. For example, the entry 1/3 is interpreted as a date (January 3 of the current year), but the entry 0 1/3 is accepted as the fractional value .333. Note that percentage values are displayed on the screen with percent signs but are stored in Excel's formula bar as decimal values. Hence the value 9% appears as .09 in the formula bar.

Table 2-1 Acceptable Numeric Entries	
You Type This	**Excel Displays This**
567	567
567.123	567.123
$567.123	$567.12
.567	0.567
567.00	567
-567	-567
(567)	-567
56,789	56,789
9%	9%
5$^1/_3$	5$^1/_3$
0$^1/_3$	0$^1/_3$

If you enter or calculate a number that's too large to fit into the cell, Excel displays ### in the cell. This message tells you that you need to widen the column, as described in the sidebar earlier in this topic (also described in Topic 4).

Entering numbers as text

Occasionally, you may need to enter a number as a text label. For example, if you are typing name and address information into a worksheet, you'll probably want to type zip codes as text entries rather than numeric entries. Doing this ensures that zip codes that begin with zero retain the leading zero. You can enter a number as text by entering the value as follows:

    ="01234"

This enters the value as a formula that produces a text result. You can also enter numbers as text by preceding them with an apostrophe (').

Entering dates and times

Excel recognizes many types of date entries and stores them as valid Excel dates. A valid Excel date can be used in date calculations. For example, you can calculate the difference between two dates or add a specified number of days (such as 130 days) to any valid date to produce a new date.

So when you type a date — such as February 1, 1904 — into a cell, Excel recognizes that this is a date and turns it into a *date serial number*, a date expressed as the number of days elapsed since January 1, 1904. In this way, the date February 1, 1904, is expressed as the date serial number 32.

In this way, every date is really a numeric value that represents days elapsed since 1/1/1904. Because every date entry is actually a numeric entry, you can make calculations using dates.

When you enter a date, it's unlikely that you'll know its serial number, so Excel automatically converts your date entry into a serial number behind the scenes. Often, Excel displays this date exactly as you typed it. However, you may see a slight change. Table 2-2 shows ways you can enter valid dates into Excel and the results supplied by Excel.

Table 2-2	
How Excel Displays Dates	
Date You Enter	*What Excel Displays*
April 30, 1993	30-Apr-93
30 April 93	30-Apr-93
30-April-93	30-Apr-93
4/30/93	4/30/93
April-93	Apr-93
Apr-93	Apr-93
4-93	Apr-93

As you can see from Table 2-2, many of these formats are simple variations on a single idea. You can abbreviate the month or use a month number. Notice that several variations produce the same date format. Don't get discouraged — these are not the only ways to format dates in Excel. These are merely the formats available when you first enter the date. Topic 4 explains how to access many other date formats to change an existing date format.

If you enter a month and a day, such as April 30, Excel assumes you are entering a month and a day value for the current year. The date value for April 30 would be 4/30/95 if the current year is 1995. However, if you enter a number that is outside the day range for the month, Excel assumes you are entering a month and year. The date April 54 produces the date 4/1/54.

Times are handled by Excel in much the same way as dates. A time entry is converted to a *time serial number*, which is a decimal fraction of a 24-hour period, beginning at midnight. In this way, the time 12:00 p.m. is exactly one-half of the day and is expressed as the time serial number .5. Excel tracks these decimal fractions to 16 decimal places. Examples of some good ways to enter times into Excel include the following:

18:35

6:35

6:35:25

18:35:25

6:35 PM

6:35 AM

It is important to note that Excel assumes the 24-hour format unless you specify AM or PM.

Timing is everything

Excel's ability to open a file in just about any format, especially worksheet files, is a terrific but under-appreciated ease-of-use feature. If you've ever had to re-enter volumes of data or formulas, you'll understand what a timesaver this overlooked capability is. But there's something you should keep in mind if you decide to forge ahead and let the computer do the work for you.

Excel uses a serial numbering system for calculating dates. In Excel for Macintosh, January 2, 1904 equals 1, January 3, 1904 equals 2, and so on. In Excel for Windows, the date system begins with January 1, 1900, so as to be compatible with Lotus 1-2-3. If you use worksheets with formulas that calculate dates, such as accounts receivable applications, Excel automatically changes to the date system used by that version. For example, if you open an Excel for Windows file with your Macintosh, Excel for Macintosh uses the 1904 date system, and vice versa. You should, however, use the 1900 date system if you develop worksheets for 1-2-3, and to be on the safe side, so should Excel for Windows users. To do so, choose

Calculation from the Options menu. When the Options Calculation dialog box appears, as shown in the following figure, unselect 1904 Date System and click OK or press Return.

Dates entered before changing date systems aren't converted to the new system; the formulas that depend on the dates return different results. The moral of the story is you should choose a date system before entering dates and thereby ensure accurate calculations.

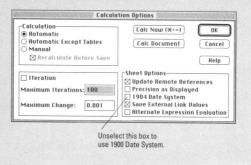

Unselect this box to use 1900 Date System.

Entering formulas

The power of an Excel worksheet is that it can perform various calculations based on the data you enter. You can make your worksheets calculate values by entering formulas into individual cells. A formula entered into cell C10, for example, may add the numbers in the range C3 through C9. Such a formula may look like this:

=C3+C4+C5+C6+C7+C8+C9

This formula begins with an equal sign and continues to list *cell references* and mathematical operations for each cell. In this case, you're adding all the cells, so plus signs are used between each reference. The equal sign is needed to tell Excel that you are entering a formula and not a text label. The simplest of formulas consists of only a cell reference:

=C3

This formula copies the value of cell C3 into the cell containing this formula and can be entered into any cell *except* cell C3.

A formula consists of three primary ingredients: an equal sign, mathematical operators, and cell references or values. To enter a formula, follow these steps:

Entering a formula

1. Move to the desired cell using the mouse or arrow keys.

2. Begin by typing an equal sign.

3. Type a numeric value or cell reference.

4. Type a mathematical operator.

5. Type another numeric value or cell reference. Repeat steps 4 and 5 until the formula is complete.

6. Press Return to accept the formula into the Worksheet. ◖◗

Calculating without a calculator

If you find yourself digging through a desk drawer for your calculator to calculate a number to use in your worksheet, or to do a quick calculation, help is only an Excel keystroke away. Make Excel the active application, type an equal sign, and then type the operators and values. Press the F9 key (or Command-=), and Excel performs the calculation in the formula bar, which you can enter into the selected cell or clear by clicking Enter or the cancel box.

You can also calculate a portion of a formula by selecting the part of the formula you want to calculate and pressing F9. Selecting the part of a formula that you want to calculate is also a way you can determine which part of a complex formula is *not* causing an error.

Generally, formulas use cell references in their calculations, making the data variable. You can change the value in any of the cells referenced, and the result of the formula changes to incorporate the new value. In this way, each cell reference is a variable in the formula.

Using the previous example of adding cells in a column, you can change the values in cells C3 through C9, and the result from the formula in cell C10 would change automatically to reflect the difference. Note that the cells being referenced may contain numbers or even their own formulas.

You can add *constant* values to your formulas, if desired. Constant values are not based on cell references but are typed directly into the formula. For example, you can add 100 to the total of cells C3 through C9 using a formula like this:

=C3+C4+C5+C6+C7+C8+C9+100

The value 100 is a constant value, while the others are variable and based on cell references. You can also calculate only constant values, as in the formula =125+13, but these kinds of formulas defeat some of the benefits of using a spreadsheet. Instead, enter these values into two cells and enter the formula using references to those cells in another cell. This way, you can change the values, and the result is automatically recalculated.

You can enter a formula by typing the cell references or by pointing to cells with the mouse or keyboard. Pointing to cells can be useful when you don't know the exact cell address you want to use in a formula because the cell is located out of view.

Pointing to cell references with the mouse

1. Move to the desired cell where you want to perform the formula using the mouse or arrow keys.

2. Type an equal sign.

3. Click the mouse in the first cell you want to reference in the formula or use the arrow keys to move to that cell.

4. Type the desired operator, such as a plus or minus sign.

5. Click the next cell you want to reference in the formula or use the arrow keys to move to that cell. Continue steps 4 and 5 until the formula is complete.

6. Press Return to accept the formula into the worksheet. ◖

If you're adding the cells, you can use a shortcut method. Begin by typing the equal sign and then click each cell — one right after the next. Excel enters the plus signs and the cell references automatically.

Mathematical operators

When you create formulas in worksheet cells, you'll most likely need to use mathematical operators to perform calculations. Operators determine the mathematical process applied to two values or references. The following is a list of the mathematical operators available in Excel:

+	Addition	=C5+C6
-	Subtraction and negation	=-C5-C6
/	Division	=C5/C6
*	Multiplication	=C5*C6
^	Exponentiation	=C5^2
%	Percentage	=C5%+C6
&	Concatenation (text)	=C5&C6

Note that the concatenation operator can be used with numbers, text values, or with references to cells that contain text values. This operation causes one value to be appended to the end of another. You can append text to text, numbers to numbers, or text to numbers. For example, if cell C5 contains the text John and cell C6 contains the text Smith, you can concatenate these entries into cell C7 with the formula **=C5&C6**. The result would be JohnSmith.

As with numbers, you can also enter text directly into a formula, thereby making the text constant. In order to make text constant, you must surround the text with quotation marks. For example, you can enter the formula **="Product "&C6** to add **Product** to the beginning of any number in cell C6. Notice that the addition of a space after Product places a space between the two entries, so that you get Product 44234 instead of Product44234. You can also enter spaces by adding a space, in quotation marks, to any concatenation formula, as in **=C5&" "&C6**.

Certain formulas, called *conditions,* do not produce numeric values. Instead, they test whether a certain condition is met and reply with TRUE or FALSE, indicating whether or not the condition was met. The values true and false are called *logical values.* For example, you may ask "Is the value in cell C5 equal to the value in cell C6?" Excel can reply true (yes) or false (no). To have a conditional test, you need to create a formula that uses a logical operator. Logical operators include the following:

=	Equal to	=C5=C6
>	Greater than	=C5>C6
<	Less than	=C5<C6
<=	Less than or equal to	=C5<=C6
>=	Greater than or equal to	=C5>=C6
<>	Does not equal	=C5<>C6

Notice that each of these examples is entered as a formula. The formula produces true or false based on the result of the text. The values true and false can be used in other tests to produce specific results. For example, you may perform one calculation if the formula =C5>C6 is true and a different calculation if it's false. To act on conditional tests requires that you use the IF function described in Topic 7.

Note that you can use the *equal to* test on text values as well as numeric values. For example, you can test whether the word Yes was entered into cell C5 using this formula:

=C5="Yes"

This formula produces TRUE if Yes appears and FALSE if it doesn't.

Using the AutoSum button to calculate totals

The fastest method of summing a column or row of values is to use the AutoSum button located on the Standard toolbar. When you click this button, Excel enters a special *worksheet function* (known as the SUM function) into the active cell. This function calculates the total of the range above or to the left of the active cell. To activate AutoSum, just click an empty cell below a column of values (or to the right of a row of values), click the AutoSum button, and then press Return.

If your active cell contains data above *and* to the left, you can specify which range to use in the SUM by highlighting the entire range plus the blank cell. Do this by clicking first on the blank cell and then dragging to highlight the rest of the range, leaving the blank cell as the active cell. Figure 2-2 illustrates this procedure.

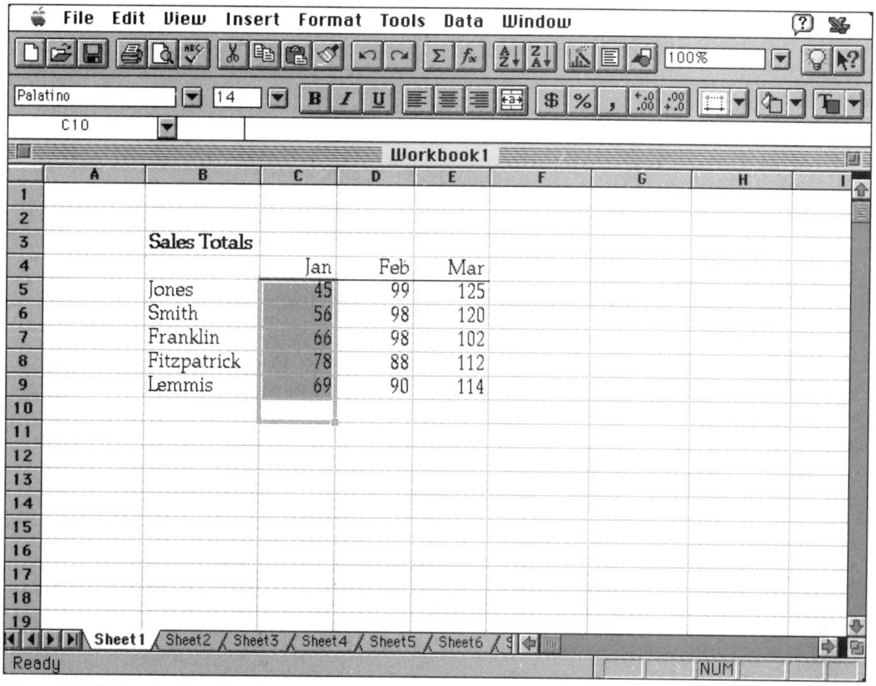

Figure 2-2: Using the AutoSum button will place the total in the blank, active cell.

There are several ways to copy a total across several cells in a row (or down several cells in a column), including the following:

◆ Highlight all the cells in the row before calculating the sum; each highlighted cell should have a column of values above it that you want to sum. Then click the AutoSum tool to enter the sums in each of the highlighted cells.

◆ Enter the formula into the first cell of the row; press Return to complete the first formula. Then click this total cell and drag across the row to highlight the remaining cells in the row. Finally, select the Edit⇨Fill Right command. Excel fills the first formula into the remaining cells to the right.

◆ Enter the formula into the first cell of the row; press Return to complete the formula. Then click the bottom-right corner of the highlighted cell and drag the mouse to *stretch* the highlighted area to the remaining cells in the row. Now release the mouse. Excel copies the formula into the remaining cells.

◆ Enter the formula into the first cell of the row; press Return to complete the formula. Then use Copy from the Edit menu to copy the first formula. Highlight the remaining cells in the row and use the Edit⇨Paste command to duplicate the formula into those cells.

◆ (For column only) Enter the formula into the first cell of the column; press Return to complete the formula. Move to the next cell down and press Command-' to copy the formula into that cell. Keep pressing Command-' until you've completed all the entries.

Controlling the order of operation

When your formulas get more complicated, and you have more than one calculation in a single formula, you may find that you need to set the order of operations. Normally, Excel calculates a formula using the following operational order:

1. Negative/Positive (-,+)

2. Percentage (%)

3. Exponentiation (^)

4. Multiplication/Division (*,/)

5. Addition/Subtraction (+,-)

6. Concatenation (&)

7. Relations (=,>,<,<=,>=,<>)

To change this natural order of operations, you can surround portions of a formula with parentheses — these are called *expressions*. Here are the results of a formula entered in two different ways (cell C5 contains 2 and C6 contains 4):

=C5*2-C6/C5+10

    2*2-4/2+10   =12

=C5*((2-C6)/C5)+10

    2*((2-4)/2)+10 =8

The results vary based on the order in which each portion of the formula is calculated.

Entering a Series of Values

Worksheets are often filled with sequential entries. You may want to enter a series of numbers down a column or a series of dates across the top of some columns. Excel makes it easy to enter a series of values or labels in your worksheets. The next three sections describe how to enter series of text labels, numeric values, and dates.

Entering a series of labels

Any label that ends with a numeric value can be turned into a sequence, or *series*. You can also begin a series with an ordinal number or the name of a month. Some examples include the following:

◆ Product 1, Product 2, Product 3

◆ Quarter 1, Quarter 2, Quarter 3

◆ Q1, Q2, Q3

◆ First, Second, Third

◆ First Quarter, Second Quarter, Third Quarter

◆ January, February, March

◆ Jan, Feb, Mar

Note that month names alone are not valid dates in Excel but are simply text labels. You can also create a sequence of dates, as described later in this Topic.

Creating a series of labels

1. Type the first two labels into two adjacent cells on the worksheet. For example, enter **Product 1** in cell C5 and **Product 2** in cell C6. If you are using names of months or ordinal numbers, you can start with only one entry if desired.

2. Highlight the entries you created in step 1.

3. Drag the *extend box* in the lower-right corner of the highlight border to extend the range (see Figure 2-3).

4. Release the mouse, and Excel extends the series into the highlighted range. Figure 2-4 shows the result. ◖

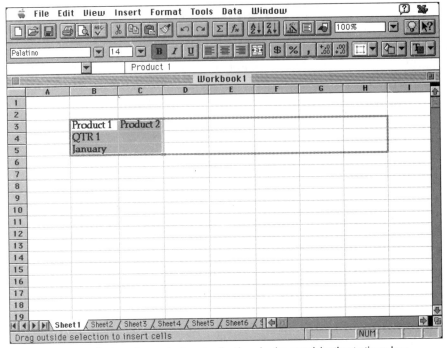

Figure 2-3: An example of creating a series by extending the selection containing the starting values.

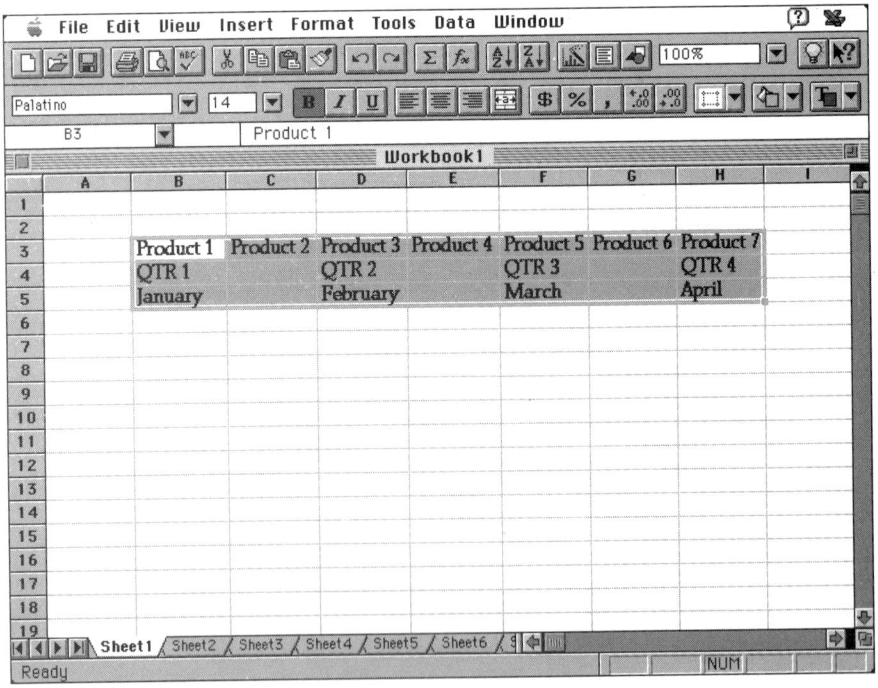

Figure 2-4: The result of creating a series.

If one of your starting cells is blank, Excel extends the blank cell into the pattern. In this way, you can leave every third cell in a series blank by highlighting two starting values and a blank cell and then extending the range.

Entering a series of numbers

You can extend any series of numbers by starting with two or three values. These starting values determine the pattern of the series. Some examples include the following:

- ◆ 1, 3, 5
- ◆ 1, 2, 3
- ◆ 100, 101, 102

Creating a series of numbers

1. Type the first two or three numbers into adjacent cells on the worksheet. For example, enter the numbers **2**, **4**, and **6** into cells C3, D3, and E3.

2. Highlight the entries you created in step 1.

3. Drag the extend box in the lower-right corner of the highlight border to extend the range.

4. Release the mouse, and Excel extends the series into the highlighted range. ◖◗

Creating a series in descending order is easy. If you drag the cell highlighter to the left or upward, Excel extends the series in the opposite numeric direction. In this way, if the series would normally increase to the right, Excel decreases the values when you drag to the left.

Entering a series of dates

To create a series of dates, you need to have two starting dates so that you can indicate whether you are increasing by days, months, or years. If you use only one starting date, Excel assumes you want to increase by days. Here are some examples:

- ◆ 4/1/93, 4/2/93
- ◆ 4/1/93, 5/1/93
- ◆ 4/1/93, 4/1/94

Creating a series of dates

1. Type the first two dates into two adjacent cells on the worksheet. Make sure that your date entries are valid dates in Excel as described earlier in this topic.

2. Highlight the entries you created in step 1.

3. Drag the extend box in the lower-right corner of the highlight border to extend the range.

4. Release the mouse, and Excel extends the series into the highlighted range. ⸙

Editing Your Work

You'll probably spend as much time modifying the data on your worksheets as you did entering it. Using simple mouse actions and commands, you can move data around the worksheet, copy data, and correct mistakes without having to retype the data.

Editing data in cells

As you type an entry into a cell (or into the formula bar), you can use the Delete and Forward Delete keys to erase characters to the left and right, respectively. However, if you have already pressed Return, you cannot use Backspace or Delete to remove individual characters. Instead, you can correct mistakes by returning to the cell and retyping the entry. The new entry replaces the old one when you press Return.

Retyping the entry doesn't present a problem when changing the number 13 to 15 — or some other small change. However, some changes are tedious to perform in this manner. Fortunately, Excel provides a simple way to make changes to the contents of a cell without a great deal of retyping.

Editing an entry in the cell

1. Double-click the cell you want to change.

2. Use the editing commands listed in Table 2-2 to make changes to the data in the formula bar.

3. Accept the changes by pressing Return. ⸙

Table 2-2
Editing Commands

Command	Moves To
Arrow	The next character in the direction of the arrow
Home	The beginning of the current line
End	The end of the current line
Command-Home	The beginning of formula bar entry
Command-End	The end of the formula bar entry
Command-Arrows	One segment of the entry at a time in the direction of the arrow

Editing an entry in the cell allows you to change data directly inside the cell itself. Double-clicking the cell places the editing cursor at the end of the entry. If you are comfortable editing your data in the formula bar, rather than inside the cell, use the following steps instead:

Editing an entry in the formula bar

1. Select the cell you want to change.

2. Press Command-U to place the cursor into the formula bar. Alternatively, you can click inside the formula bar to place the cursor there.

3. Use the editing commands listed in Table 2-2 to make changes to the data in the formula bar.

4. Accept the changes by pressing Return. ❧

Suppose you want to add the word *Inc.* to a company name you typed into cell C5. After double-clicking cell C5, simply click at the point where you want to add the text. In this case, you would click at the end of the company name.

During editing, you can instantly throw out any changes you've made by pressing Esc or by clicking the Reject button. Remember, this only works during editing. If you've accepted the changes already by pressing Return, you need to choose Undo from the Edit menu to undo the change.

You can hold Shift down as you use the commands in Table 2-2 to highlight data. If you type information while data is highlighted, the new information replaces the highlighted data.

Inserting and deleting worksheet cells

Excel gives you a great deal of flexibility in setting up and making changes to your worksheets. By inserting and deleting rows, columns, or blocks of cells on the worksheet, you can quickly make a worksheet fit onto a single page, add space for new information, or just move data around to better suit your needs.

Earlier in this topic you saw that you can delete data by pressing Delete or Command-B. These actions clear the data from its cells but do not remove the cells themselves. In the following sections, you'll learn how to actually insert and delete worksheet cells.

Inserting cells

When you insert cells into a worksheet the new cells *push* other cells out of the way, either down or to the right. To insert, you select the size of the block you want inserted into the worksheet and then choose Cells from the Insert menu. You can insert one cell in a row or column or an entire block of cells.

Inserting a cell or range of cells

1. Move the cell pointer to the location where the new cell is to appear. If you want to insert a range of cells, select the cells that currently mark the position where you want the new cells to appear. Figure 2-5 shows an example.

	A	B	C	D	E	F	G	H	I
1									
2		*First Quarter Sales*					*Sales Totals by Product*		
3									
4			Jan	Feb	Mar		RD11	44564	
5		Smith	45	35	70		PVP-6500	45646	
6		Jones	56	56	77		PVP-6501	55435	
7		Franklin	65	46	79		LARS-1	5456	
8		McPherson	44	75	90		LARS-2	89978	
9		Lucchesi	65	65	80		LARS-3	6546	
10		Green	76	66	88		SM-110	45647	
11		Olson	89	77	81		SM-120	8768	
12		Whitney	35	86	85		SM-130	45633	
13							SM-140	56567	
14							INV-110	68678	
15							INV-120	67845	
16							INV-130	45643	
17									
18									
19									

Figure 2-5: Highlighting cells for the Insert Cells command.

2. Choose Cells from the Insert menu.

3. Choose Shift Cells Right to move existing cells to the right or Shift Cells Down to move existing cells down when new cells are added.

4. Click OK. Figure 2-6 shows the result after shifting cells down. ◖

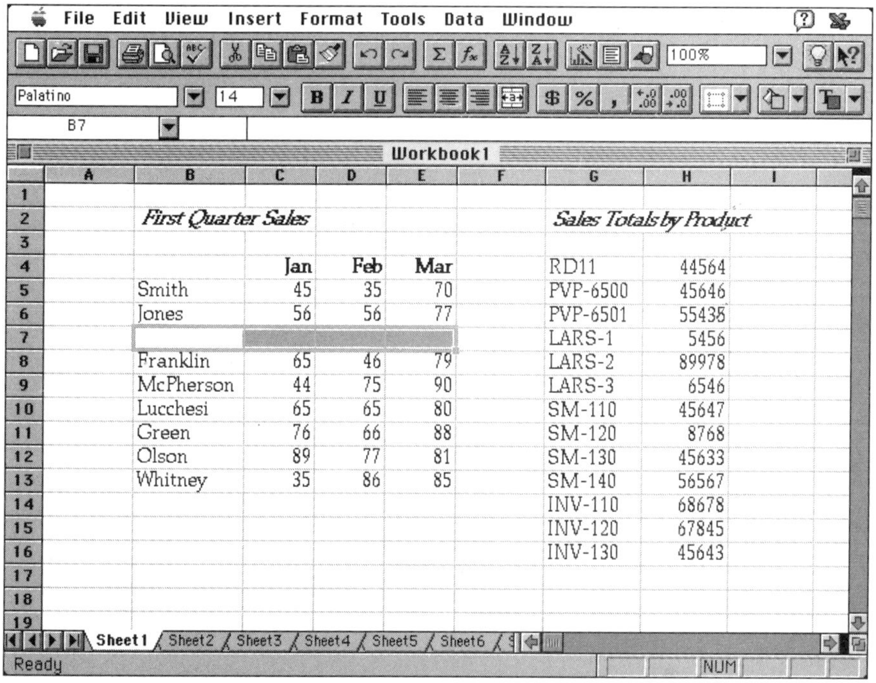

| File | Edit | View | Insert | Format | Tools | Data | Window |

Palatino 14 B I U $ % ,

B7

Workbook1

	A	B	C	D	E	F	G	H	I
1									
2		*First Quarter Sales*					*Sales Totals by Product*		
3									
4			Jan	Feb	Mar		RD11	44564	
5		Smith	45	35	70		PVP-6500	45646	
6		Jones	56	56	77		PVP-6501	55438	
7							LARS-1	5456	
8		Franklin	65	46	79		LARS-2	89978	
9		McPherson	44	75	90		LARS-3	6546	
10		Lucchesi	65	65	80		SM-110	45647	
11		Green	76	66	88		SM-120	8768	
12		Olson	89	77	81		SM-130	45633	
13		Whitney	35	86	85		SM-140	56567	
14							INV-110	68678	
15							INV-120	67845	
16							INV-130	45643	
17									
18									
19									

Sheet1 / Sheet2 / Sheet3 / Sheet4 / Sheet5 / Sheet6 /

Ready   NUM

Figure 2-6: The result after inserting new cells and moving existing cells down.

Suppose you selected D5:D7 and chose Insert Cells. The following list tells you what each option in the Insert dialog box would do:

◆ **Shift Cells Right.** Inserts blank cells at D5:D7. Moves the information from D5:D7 to E5:E7. All other information to the right of column D in rows 5 through 7 moves one column to the right.

◆ **Shift Cells Down.** Inserts blank cells at D5:D7. Moves the information from D5:D7 to D8:D10. All other information below rows 5 through 7 in column D moves three rows down.

◆ **Entire Row.** Inserts three blank rows at rows 5 through 7. Moves all information from rows 5 through 7 down to rows 8 through 10. All other information below rows 5 through 7 moves down by three rows.

◆ **Entire Column.** Inserts one blank column at column D. Moves all information in column D to column E. All other information to the right of column D will move one column to the right.

When you insert rows, columns, or blocks of cells, and push other data around, Excel updates any cell references in your formulas so they refer to the correct information. You don't need to worry about updating formulas — Excel takes care of everything.

You can quickly insert rows and columns by using the Insert Rows and Insert Columns commands instead of the Insert Cells command. You can insert more than one at a time by highlighting several rows or columns first — or cells within the rows or columns.

Deleting cells

Like inserting, you can delete cells by highlighting the cells you want deleted and then pressing the Edit⇨Delete command. Excel asks if you want to move the rest of the worksheet to the left or upward to fill the space.

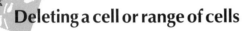

Deleting a cell or range of cells

1. Highlight the cell or range you want to delete. If you want to remove an entire row or column, you may highlight the entire row or column by clicking on the row or column heading.

2. Choose Delete from the Edit menu.

3. Choose Shift Cells Left to move existing cells to the left or Shift Cells Up to move existing cells up when cells are removed.

4. Click OK. ◊

Provided you have not removed cells that contain the precedents of other formulas on the worksheet, Excel updates all formulas to accommodate the modified worksheet. In other words, if you remove cells that are referenced in other formulas, Excel is not able to update the formula and presents you with an error message as a result. All other formulas are updated to reflect the moved cells.

Moving data

Excel lets you make nearly unlimited modifications to your worksheets, meaning that you can move data around the worksheet at will. You may find that you can move data instead of inserting or deleting cells. There are two ways to move data in a worksheet: You can use the mouse to *drag* the data to a new location and *drop* it into place; or you can use the Cut and Paste procedure.

Moving data with drag and drop

You'll find Excel's drag and drop editing to be the simplest way to move data from one place to another within a worksheet. You can move cells around the worksheet by highlighting them and then dragging the edge of the selected range. As you drag the selection, Excel shows you the outline of the cells, indicating where it will move your selection when you release the mouse button.

Using drag and drop to move cells

1. Highlight the cell or range you want to move.

2. Click the border (or edge) of the selection and hold down the mouse button. Note that the mouse pointer changes to an arrow when you have located the edge of the selection.

3. Drag the range to the desired location and then release the mouse button to drop the cells into place. Figure 2-7 shows what the screen looks like as you drag data. ◖◗

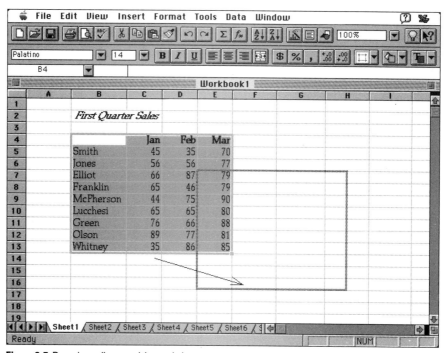

Figure 2-7: Dragging cells around the worksheet.

You need to watch the mouse pointer carefully to make drag and drop work. Normally on the worksheet, Excel displays the mouse pointer as a heavy cross. When you move the pointer to any edge of the selection, it changes to the standard arrow pointer. When you see this pointer, you can click and drag the highlighted region to another location on the worksheet.

If you drag other cells onto a location that already contains information, Excel displays the message shown in Figure 2-8.

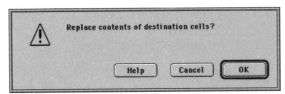

Figure 2-8: A message appears when you drop cells over the top of existing data.

If you click OK, Excel moves the cells and you lose the data in the destination cells. Clicking Cancel aborts the procedure and returns the worksheet to its previous state.

When you move cells from one place to another on the worksheet, Excel automatically maintains all connections between cells. Thus, if you move the cell that contains the interest rate in an amortization table from C3 to C5, references to C3 in any of the formulas automatically change to C5. Moving information never displays cell references, unless you drop the data onto existing cells that are used by other formulas.

Inserting as you move cells

If you don't want to overwrite existing data, you can move data into an existing range and insert new cells to make room for the data. When you drop the data into the new location, Excel pushes the existing data down or to the right to make room. You don't have to use the Insert Cells command to insert cells before moving the data.

To insert as you move, just hold Shift down before you click and drag. As you drag the selected area, you don't see an exact outline of the range. Instead, you see a special highlight bar that shows where the inserted cells containing the data will appear. As you drag across columns, the bar appears vertically, indicating that inserted cells will push existing information to the right. As you drag across rows, the bar appears horizontally, indicating that inserted cells will push existing information down.

Moving data with Cut and Paste

When you use Excel's Cut and Paste commands together, they have the same effect as using drag and drop to move information from one range of cells to another. First, you must highlight the cells you want to move and then use the Edit➪Cut command. Move the cell pointer to the new location (you can just move to the upper-left corner of the new location) and select the Edit➪Paste command. After selecting Edit➪Paste, the data moves from the old location to the new.

Using Cut and Paste to move cells

1. Select the range of cells you want to move.

2. Choose Cut from the Edit menu or press Command-X.

3. Move the cell pointer to the first cell in the new range (the upper-left corner).

4. Choose Paste from the Edit menu or press Command-V. Excel moves the cells you cut to their new location. ◖

When you use Cut in Excel, unlike most Macintosh programs, your selection does not disappear. Excel simply marks the range with a marquee and places the cells onto the clipboard. The data is moved only after you select the Edit➪Paste command. As with the drag and drop procedure, if you paste over existing data, Excel warns you first.

While drag and drop editing seems much easier and more straightforward than the Cut and Paste commands, you will find many times where cutting and pasting makes more sense. The major disadvantage to drag and drop comes with the dragging. If you have to move a range of cells a long way, it can take a long time to scroll the entire distance. Most users can move the cells much faster with the Cut and Paste commands.

Copying data

Copying data works in very much the same way as moving data, except that Excel does not delete the source data when it completes the move. Thus, when you copy data, you leave the original intact while duplicating it in another location.

As with moving data, you can use either a drag and drop technique or the menu commands (Edit➪Copy and Edit➪Paste) to copy data. The following sections explain these techniques.

Copying data with drag and drop

To copy using drag and drop, you select the range of cells you want to copy and then move the mouse pointer to the edge of the selection. When the pointer changes from the heavy cross to the arrow pointer, press Command and drag. The important thing to remember is that to copy rather than move data, you must hold Command as you drag. If this is not done, the procedure is identical to the move procedure. Note that when you hold Command and drag, Excel indicates that you are copying by showing a plus sign with the mouse pointer.

Using drag and drop to copy cells

1. Highlight the cell or range you want to copy.

2. Press and hold Command and then click the border (or edge) of the selection and hold down the mouse button. Note that the mouse pointer changes to an arrow when you have located the edge of the selection.

3. Drag the range to the desired location and then release the mouse button to drop the cells into place. ◖◗

Unlike moving data with drag and drop, you are not warned if you are about to overwrite existing information when you copy with drag and drop. Excel overwrites existing data without telling you. If you make a mistake, you can choose the Edit⇨Undo command to return the worksheet to its prior state.

If you don't want to overwrite existing data and want to insert cells to make room for the copied data, you can do this by pressing Shift as you drag and drop. In other words, press and hold the Shift and Command keys as you drag the border of the highlighted cell or range.

As with moving, this procedure displays a vertical or horizontal bar indicating the position of the inserted cells and whether existing data will move down or to the right when you drop the new data into place.

Copying data with Copy and Paste

When you use Excel's Edit⇨Copy and Edit⇨Paste commands together, they have the same effect as using drag and drop to duplicate information from one range of cells to another. To copy a range of cells from one place on the worksheet to another using Copy and Paste, follow these steps:

Using Copy and Paste to duplicate cells

1. Select the range of cells you want to copy.

2. Choose Copy from the Edit menu.

3. Move the cell pointer to the upper-left corner of the range where you wish to place the duplicate cells.

4. Choose Paste from the Edit menu. Excel duplicates the cells into their new location. ◖

When you use Copy and Paste to duplicate a range of cells, Excel applies almost all formatting information from the source to the destination (see Topic 4 for more information about formatting).

Copying data with AutoFill

If you need to copy data from a cell or cells into adjacent cells, you can use the quick and simple AutoFill feature. To use AutoFill, just highlight the cell or range containing the information you want to copy. Then expand the range by dragging the extend box in the direction you want to copy. The following steps explain the details.

Using the AutoFill feature to copy data

1. Highlight the cell or range you want to copy. You can use the AutoFill feature to copy data into adjacent cells, thereby creating a repeating pattern of data.

2. Drag the extend box in the lower-right corner of the selection. Drag in the desired direction to extend the range. Figure 2-9 shows an example.

3. Release the mouse at the desired location to extend the range. Text inside the original cells is repeated into the extended range, as shown in Figure 2-10. ◖

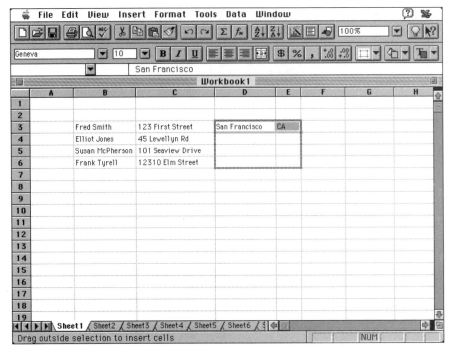

Figure 2-9: Preparing to copy data by extending the range.

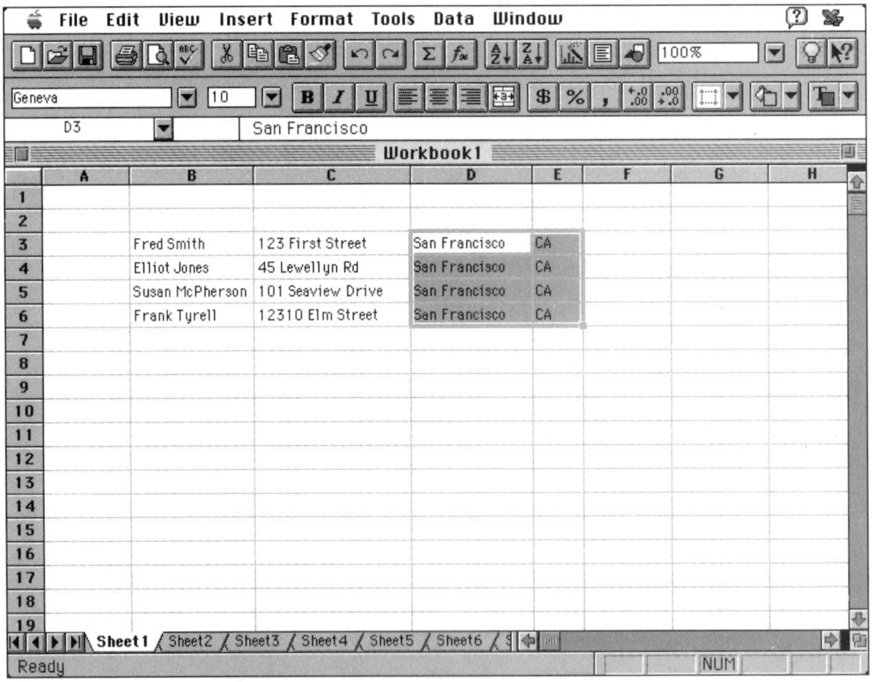

Figure 2-10: Data copied using AutoFill.

It is important to note that if numbers appear in the original cells, this procedure is identical to creating a series (explained earlier in this topic) and you will end up with a series of progressing values instead of copied values. If the original cells contain formulas, this procedure copies the formulas *relative* to their new locations.

Copying formulas

When you copy formulas from one place to another on the worksheet, you may wonder what happens to cell references within those formulas. Do they still reference the same cells? Or do they adjust to reference cells relative to the new location?

Figure 2-11 shows a simple worksheet with columns of sales figures. To obtain totals, you can use the AutoSum tool to put the total of the range C3:C7 into cell C8. There are several ways get column totals for several columns at once — each total calculating its respective column. Some methods include:

◆ Use the Copy and Paste commands. Copy the original total using Command-C, highlight the remaining cells where you want totals, and press Command-V.

◆ Use the AutoFill feature. Select the cell containing the original total and then drag the extend box to fill the remaining cells.

◆ Use AutoSum to calculate all totals at once. Highlight all the cells into which you want totals and then press the AutoSum button.

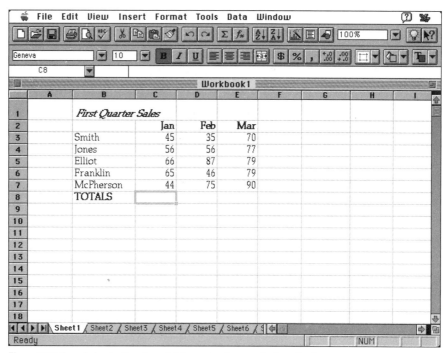

Figure 2-11: A worksheet with column totals required in several adjacent cells.

What and where is the Clipboard?

If you're new to the Macintosh, you may have heard about the Clipboard and wonder just exactly what it is. The Clipboard isn't a separate program that you have to start up like Excel. Rather, when you power up your Macintosh, the Clipboard is active and ready to go with no intervention on your part.

The Clipboard is actually random-access memory (RAM) that your Macintosh's system software sets aside to hold whatever you cut or copy to it: text, numbers, or graphics. Although there's no program icon or other indicator of the Clipboard's presence, you can access the current contents of the Clipboard by choosing Show Clipboard from the Window menu. When you do, a window similar to the one in the following figure appears.

Because the Clipboard is random-access memory, it is similar in one respect to a new unsaved worksheet file. If you turn off your Macintosh, all Clipboard contents disappear into thin air forever (if the data is large,

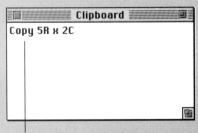

The current contents of the Clipboard

however, your Macintosh displays a warning message). If you feel you'll need the Clipboard's contents for a future Excel (to other application) session, paste the contents into a new worksheet file, and choose Save from the File menu. Or paste the contents to the Scrapbook (from the Apple menu). Either way, think of the Clipboard as one of your silent spreadsheet partners.

When you copy the formula from one cell to another, the formula changes to fit the destination columns. In other words, the range reference from the original cell (C3:C7) was made *relative* to the new cells: cell D8 contains the reference (D3:D7), and E8 reads (E3:E7). Each destination cell has a copy of the formula that is relative to its column.

Thus, copying formulas works differently than copying constant information — which remains the same across all copies of the original. You may otherwise expect exactly the same formula to copy into the other cells. If that happened, Excel would have entered the formula =SUM(C3:C7) into each cell of the total row, and all three cells would calculate the total from column C. This would be misleading to say the least.

Because you usually want Excel to adjust cell references when you copy formulas, Excel goes ahead and does it. You can take steps to prevent this relative copying from taking place. In other words, you can copy formulas so that the copy is exactly the same as the original. This procedure is known as creating an *absolute reference*.

Relative and absolute references

When you see the reference C3 in a formula, you probably see it a little differently than Excel does. Excel considers C3 a *relative* reference — it thinks of C3 in relation to the formula containing the reference. In the previous example, Excel thinks of C3 as the cell which lies five rows above and in the same column as C8.

When you think of it this way, it makes sense that the formulas change when you copy them — since everything was relative to the current cell. The range C3:C7 is relative to cell C8, just as the range D3:D7 is relative to cell D8.

When you copy a formula using the Copy and Paste commands or any other method — including drag and drop — Excel makes cell and range references relative to their new locations. However, if you move a formula using Edit⇨Cut and Edit⇨Paste (or any other method), Excel does not update the references but leaves them exactly as they are in the original cell. You are less likely to want references updated when you move them as when you copy them. If you must move formulas and want to make the references relative, simply copy them and then remove the originals.

You can tell Excel not to adjust cell and range references when you copy a formula. Just make any cell or range reference *absolute*. When you use an absolute reference, Excel uses the same cell, no matter where you copy the formula. To make a cell reference absolute, simply put dollar signs in front of the letter and the number. For example, to make cell C3 absolute, you would enter the reference as **$C$3**.

Using the previous example, suppose you entered an adjustment value into cell C10 and multiplied the column totals by this cell to get an adjusted total. Figure 2-12 shows this example with the first formula displayed in the formula bar.

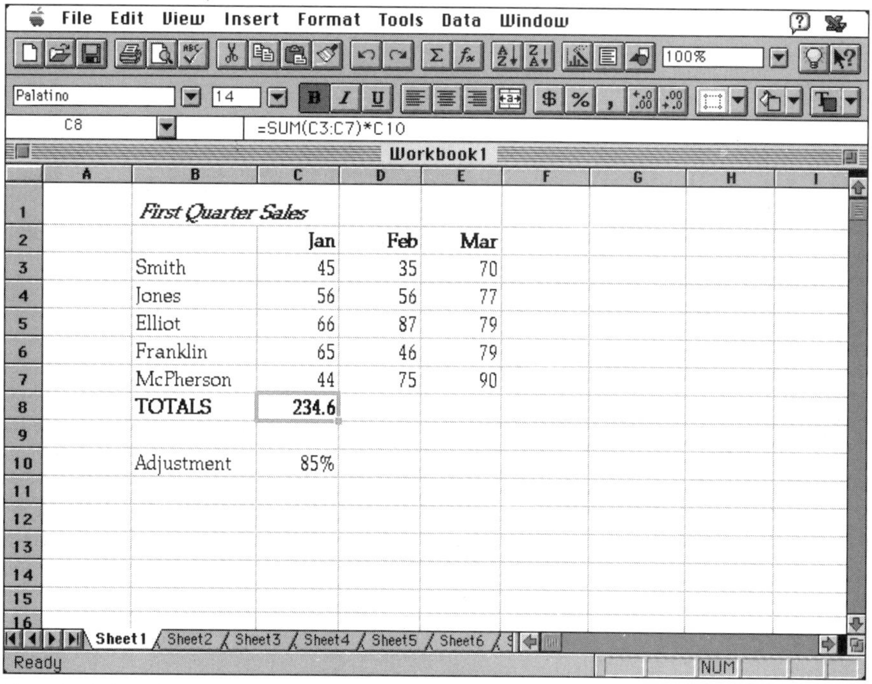

File	Edit	View	Insert	Format	Tools	Data	Window			

Palatino 14 **B** *I* U $ % , C8 =SUM(C3:C7)*C10

Workbook1

	A	B	C	D	E	F	G	H	I
1		*First Quarter Sales*							
2			Jan	Feb	Mar				
3		Smith	45	35	70				
4		Jones	56	56	77				
5		Elliot	66	87	79				
6		Franklin	65	46	79				
7		McPherson	44	75	90				
8		TOTALS	234.6						
9									
10		Adjustment	85%						
11									
12									
13									
14									
15									
16									

Sheet1 / Sheet2 / Sheet3 / Sheet4 / Sheet5 / Sheet6 /

Ready NUM

Figure 2-12: A worksheet with an absolute reference required.

If you copy the formula in cell C8 across the row, you'll get the formulas =SUM(D3:D7)*D10 and =SUM(E3:E7)*E10. The references to D10 and E10 are incorrect and should not have been adjusted; instead the formulas should both reference cell C10. In this case, the original range reference C3:C7 should be relative, but the reference to C10 should be absolute. You can enter the following formula into cell C8 to remedy this situation:

=SUM(C3:C7)*$C$10

Now copy this formula into the adjacent cells.

Notice that you can make individual cell references relative while other references in the same formula are absolute. In fact, you can do more than that. You can even divide a particular reference into its row and column reference — making the row relative and the column absolute, or vice versa.

Suppose you add another adjustment to the example worksheet. This time, you'll subtract taxes from the totals, adding a second row of totals (see Figure 2-13).

	A	B	C	D	E	F	G	H	I
1		*First Quarter Sales*							
2			Jan	Feb	Mar				
3		Smith	45	35	70				
4		Jones	56	56	77				
5		Elliot	66	87	79				
6		Franklin	65	46	79				
7		McPherson	44	75	90				
8		**Total After Comm.**	**234.6**						
9		**Total After Taxes**	**138.6**						
10		After Commission	85%						
11		After Taxes	60%						
12									
13									
14									

Figure 2-13: A worksheet with mixed references required.

In this case, the formula in cell C8 will be copied into rows 8 and 9. The totals in row 8 should deduct the Commission percentage in cell C10, and the totals in row 9 should deduct the Commission + Taxes percentage in cell C11. The formula in C8 reads:

=SUM(C3:C7)*$C10

Notice that the reference to cell C10 is now partially absolute; the column reference is absolute, but the row reference is relative. In this case, the row will adjust when you copy the formula, but the column will stay the same. This will cause row 9 to use the percentage in cell C11 instead of C10. Try this yourself to see the results.

Proper use of relative and absolute references can simplify the task of creating worksheets. When you create formulas, think of how you will be copying them into other cells on the worksheet, what type of relativity is required, and how you may save some steps by combining relative and absolute references.

Use Command-T to toggle among the different references. Excel provides a quick method of making references absolute or relative. Just highlight the cell reference in the formula and then press Command-T repeatedly until the desired relative mix is found.

Copying one cell to many

Did you notice in the previous example that Excel let you copy one cell into many other cells at one time? If you select more than one cell as the destination range before pasting, Excel automatically fills in all of the cells. (This applies to copying with the Copy and Paste commands.)

This feature can work when you copy an entire range, too. However, Excel restricts the destination range to ranges which are even multiples of the source range. You can copy a 2-by-3-cell range and paste it into a 4-by-6 or a 8-by-12, but Excel won't let you paste it into a 5-by-9 range. If you try to paste into an inappropriate range, Excel gives you the `Copy and Paste references are different shapes` error message.

Reselect the destination range or just select one cell — the top-left cell in the destination — to copy the data exactly as it appears in the original.

Transposing data

When you analyze data in Excel, you often want to look at it in different ways and move things around. Drag and drop moving can work well for simple movements. But what if you want to completely transpose a range of cells, switching rows for columns? Even with a small range of cells, you can have problems — to say nothing of a large job.

Fortunately, Excel allows you to transpose even the largest ranges quickly and easily using the Edit⇨Paste Special command.

Transposing a range

1. Select the range you want to transpose.

2. Copy the range with the Edit⇨Copy command (or Command-C).

3. Move the cell pointer to the top-left corner of the destination range. This range is where you want the transposed range to show up.

4. Choose Paste Special from the Edit menu.

5. Select the Transpose option.

6. Click OK, and Excel pastes the transposed range into the destination cells. ⁑

If you want to remove the original data, you should go back and delete by pressing Command-B.

Converting formulas to values

Excel's formulas do wonderful things and can make your life much easier. But you may find the need to remove the formulas from a series of values and leave just the values. Or you may want to copy some data to another part of the worksheet (or to another worksheet), but want only the values and not the formulas copied.

Excel provides you with a way to copy formulas and paste just the values returned by those formulas. If you paste the values back over the original formulas, you essentially end up converting the original formulas to the values. Otherwise, you can place the copies in another area of the worksheet or into another worksheet.

Stripping away formulas behind the values

1. Select the range of cells you want to convert. Not all of the cells have to contain formulas.

2. Choose Edit⇨Copy.

3. Move to your destination range. You may choose to paste the values over the original formulas. If you want to do this, simply skip this step.

4. Choose Paste Special from the Edit menu.

5. Select the Values option.

6. Click OK or press Return. Excel pastes the values from the source range into the destination cells. ⁑

Converting formulas to values can be useful for finding errors in large formulas. You can convert a portion of a large formula — any complete expression — into its value to see if that portion is correct.

Calculating portions of a formula

1. Double-click the cell containing the desired formula.

2. Highlight part of the formula that you would like to calculate. The highlighted portion must be a complete expression.

3. Press Command-=. ◖

Use the ditto feature to get a value from a formula. The ditto command (Control-") has the ability to copy the value from the cell above. You can use this command to produce the value from a formula if you don't want to destroy the original formula.

Quick Tips ▪ ▪ ▪ ▪ ▪ ▪ ▪ ▪ ▪ ▪ ▪ ▪ ▪

Highlighting for data entry ease

When you enter data into the worksheet, try highlighting the range of cells into which you want to enter data. To move among the cells, press Tab or Return (Shift-Tab and Shift-Return to move backward). The cell pointer stays within the highlighted range, making data entry easier. Press an arrow key to remove the highlight.

Using date and time quickies

You can quickly enter the current date or time into a cell by using the following keyboard commands:

◆ Control -;   Enters the current date

◆ Command-;   Enters the current time

You can also enter the current date or time with the worksheet function =NOW(). This function enters the serial number for the current date and time and can be formatted into either a date or a time or both. See Topic 4 for details about formatting dates and times. Note that the NOW() function is updated each time you open or calculate the worksheet. Hence, the date/time in the cell containing this function is continually updated. This feature may be inappropriate for some applications. If you want the date/time to remain "frozen" use the normal keyboard commands. See Topic 7 for more information about worksheet functions.

Noting that numeric format goes with copy

Excel copies the numeric format of the cell reference. When you use a cell reference in a formula, Excel not only refers to the value in that cell but also its numeric format. For example, if you enter the value **$45.1254** into cell C5, it appears in the currency format as $45.13. Any formula that refers to this cell, such as =C5-25, displays its result in the same numeric format (in this case, currency). If you use more than one cell reference in a formula, Excel uses the format of the last cell referenced. For more on number formats see Topic 4.

Filling one formula into many cells

To enter a formula or data into a range of cells, select the target cells and then type the formula or data into the active cell. Hold down the option key and press Enter to accept the entry. Excel immediately fills your cell entry into all selected cells.

Making automatic column widths

If you need to widen or narrow a column so that all data will show up, just point at the right edge of the column header. Double-click the mouse and Excel automatically resizes the column so that all data in the column fit.

Employing custom AutoFill patterns

You can customize Excel's AutoFill feature by creating your own patterns. For example, if your company has four divisions — North, South, East, and West — you can turn the divisions into a custom list. Choose options from the Tools menu and click the Custom Lists tab. Type in the pattern of North, South, East, and West, and Excel will remember the pattern. Now type North into one cell, press Enter, and drag the AutoFill handle. Excel automatically enters South, East, and West into the neighboring cells.

One-step inserting

You can insert entire rows and columns into your worksheet by holding down the Option key and clicking any row or column heading.

The Excel Environment

Overview

Your environment plays an important role in how well you work. Some people like their workspace neat and free of clutter, while others seem to thrive on disarray. You may prefer a certain type of visual environment in Excel, too. You can change, or tailor, the Excel environment to fit your needs by using a number of commands and options.

Changing the Excel Environment

Changes to your Excel workbook's environment can affect both the way the individual worksheets and the workbook itself operate. Some of the changes that affect individual worksheets include the following:

◆ Turning off the worksheet gridlines that outline the cells

◆ Changing the color of the gridlines that outline the cells

◆ Displaying or hiding the row and column headings

◆ Displaying or hiding values of zero on the worksheet

◆ Zooming to enlarge or reduce the worksheet window

◆ Changing the arrangement of worksheet windows

Because these changes affect worksheets individually (they affect whichever worksheet is active when you make the changes), Excel assumes that you may want to store the changes along with the worksheet data and automatically save the changes along with the worksheet.

Besides these worksheet-oriented changes, you can make a host of changes to the overall Excel environment. These changes apply to Excel in general and affect each and every worksheet that you use in Excel. Such environment changes include the following:

◆ Changing the number of decimal places shown for numeric values

◆ Hiding or displaying the worksheet scroll bars

◆ Hiding or displaying the formula bar

◆ Hiding or displaying the status bar

◆ Changing whether pressing Return moves the cell pointer down to the next cell

◆ Displaying toolbars other than the Standard toolbar, including several at the same time, or removing toolbars altogether

Figure 3-1 shows a sample worksheet with some of these changes. Notice that the example has been resized to fit into the corner of the program workspace. Also, the gridlines and the row and column headings have been removed, as have the scroll bars, the formula bar, and the status bar.

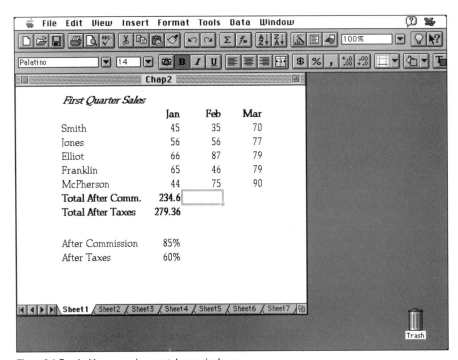

Figure 3-1: Excel with some environment changes in place.

Understanding Workbooks

Topic 1 covers some basic concepts about using workbooks in Excel, including details about moving around within a workbook. This section provides more details about workbooks in Excel, such as how to arrange the individual worksheets in a workbook, how to name worksheets, and how to insert and delete worksheets.

Moving between worksheets

You can easily switch to another worksheet within the current workbook by clicking its page tab at the bottom of the screen. Although Excel provides 16 blank worksheets with each new workbook, you can see only the first six tabs on the screen. To view more of the tabs, you can click the tab buttons that appear to the left of the tabs. These buttons permit you to move forward or backward through the tabs or to quickly jump to the beginning or end of the tabs. When the desired tab comes into view, click it to activate that worksheet. Figure 3-2 shows the tab buttons and other tabbing tools.

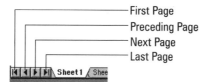

Figure 3-2: Excel offers several tools to help you work with worksheet tabs.

To view more tabs on the screen at one time, slide the horizontal scroll bar to the right. This action shrinks the scroll bar but makes room for more tabs. Likewise, you can expand the scroll bar and view fewer tabs.

You can also move through the worksheets in your workbook by using the keyboard. Press Option-right arrow to move forward through the pages and Option-left arrow to move backward.

Finally, the Go To command lets you move among the worksheets in your notebook. Enter the worksheet name (listed on the tab), along with the desired cell in the worksheet, in the Go To entry. For example, press F5 (or choose Go To from the Edit menu) to activate the Go To dialog box and then type **Sheet5!A1** to move to cell A1 of Sheet 5. Remember to include the exclamation point whenever you enter a worksheet reference. (You must surround the worksheet name with apostrophes if it contains spaces, as in 'Sheet Five'!A1.)

Naming worksheets

As you begin to use the various worksheets in your workbook, you may find it convenient to name the worksheets with more memorable names than Sheet1, Sheet 2, and so on.

Naming your worksheets

1. Double-click the worksheet's tab. The Rename dialog box appears.

2. Type the new name and click OK. Figure 3-3 shows an example. **◖◗**

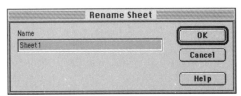

Figure 3-3: Name pages by double-clicking the page tab.

To make worksheet references easier to enter in your formulas, try to keep your worksheet names concise. You can rename a worksheet at any time. Excel updates any 3-D references you may have entered by using the old name.

Rearranging worksheets

As you begin to use the 16 worksheets in your workbook, you may find the need to change their arrangement—especially if you are creating 3-D formula references, as described in Topic 7. (The order of your worksheets is important when creating 3-D formulas.) To move a worksheet, simply drag its page tab to the desired location as described in the following steps.

Moving worksheet pages

1. Click the tab of the worksheet that you want to move and hold down the mouse button. You may have to scroll the pages to get the desired worksheet tab into view.

2. Drag the worksheet tab to the desired location. As you move the tab, an arrow appears above the tabs, indicating where the page will be inserted (see Figure 3-4).

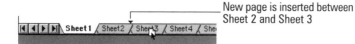

New page is inserted between
Sheet 2 and Sheet 3

Figure 3-4: Drag the page tab into place to rearrange the pages.

3. Release the mouse button to insert the page in the new location. ◖

Inserting and deleting worksheets

If you need additional worksheet pages in your workbook, just insert a blank page between two existing worksheets. You can do this through the Worksheet command in the Insert menu.

Inserting a worksheet

1. Click the tab of the worksheet that you want to follow the inserted worksheet.

2. Select the Worksheet command from the Insert menu. ◖

You can also use the shortcut menu to insert a worksheet. This menu provides access to all the possible worksheet types that you can insert. Press Control as you click the desired page tab. Then choose Worksheet from the list that appears.

You can tell Excel to start your workbooks with more than or less than 16 worksheets. Just choose Options from the Tools menu and click the General tab. The Sheets in New Workbook option lets you determine how many blank worksheets appear in your workbooks. Change this number to suit your needs.

Grouping worksheets

Excel's worksheet grouping feature allows you to perform actions to several worksheets at the same time. This feature can be useful when you have multiple worksheets that have similar structures, and you want to format, or change, them all at once. For example, you may have a budget workbook that consists of 12 separate worksheets for each month of the year. All 12 worksheets have the same basic structure and layout, with different data. You can quickly change all 12 worksheets by grouping them before making the changes. Changes you then make to one worksheet in the group automatically appear on all worksheets in the group.

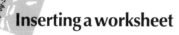

Creating a group of worksheets

1. Click the tab of the first worksheet that you want in the group.

2. Hold down Command and click the next worksheet that you want in the group. Continue holding down Command and clicking all the tabs that you want to group together. If the worksheets are sequential, you can click the first worksheet, hold down Shift, and then click the last worksheet (see Figure 3-5).

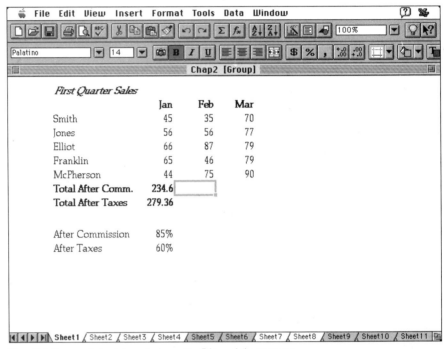

Figure 3-5: Group worksheets to apply changes to all the worksheets at once.

3. Make any desired changes or additions to the active worksheet. Changes affect all grouped worksheets.

4. Remove the group by clicking any worksheet tab that is not currently in the group. If all worksheets are grouped, access the shortcut menu by holding Control as you click any of the grouped page tabs. Then select the Ungroup Sheets command.

Grouping worksheets is a method of selecting ranges that span across several sheets. If you select a range on one worksheet in a group, the same range is selected in all the grouped worksheets. In this way, grouping can be a handy way of creating 3-D references.

You can also copy information from one worksheet onto several at one time. Just copy the desired information and then create a group of the worksheets onto which you want the information copied. Then paste the data onto any of the grouped worksheets, and it appears on all of them.

Moving and Copying worksheets between workbooks

You can easily copy your worksheets between two workbooks in Excel, which can be useful for duplicating important worksheet pages in unrelated workbook applications. For example, a form that is used in one workbook application may also be useful in a completely different one.

Copying worksheets between workbooks

1. Open the workbook into which you want the worksheet page to appear. Then open the workbook containing the worksheet that you want to move or copy.

2. Press Control and click the worksheet tab of the worksheet that you are moving or copying in order to activate the worksheet and display the shortcut menu.

3. Choose Move or Copy from the shortcut menu.

4. Use the To Book drop-down list to specify the workbook into which you want the page moved or copied. This list displays all open workbooks.

5. Use the Before Sheet list to determine where inside the destination workbook you want the sheet inserted.

6. Click the Create a Copy box to copy the worksheet or leave the box unchecked to move the worksheet.

7. Click OK. ◖

If the worksheet that you copy has formulas that refer to other pages of the workbook, those formulas attempt to locate similar data in the new workbook. You may have to update these references after copying the worksheet. For example, if you copy a worksheet page named "January Sales" that has a cell that contains a reference to a page called "Product Info," the copy will attempt to locate the same page reference in the new workbook. If such a reference does not exist, then you'll have to update the cell containing the external reference.

Changing the Work Environment

Excel gives you the power to change all sorts of screen elements. You can change the look and feel of Excel to suit your needs. Want to get rid of the cell gridlines? No problem. Or how about displaying them in green? You can access and change dozens of Excel environment settings through the Options dialog box. Choose the Options command from the Tools menu to display the Options dialog box shown in Figure 3-6.

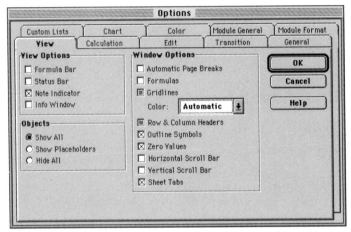

Figure 3-6: The Options dialog box provides access to numerous environment settings.

The following sections explain the various options in the Options dialog box. These options include View, Edit, and General, and are grouped by the tab names that appear in the Options dialog box. Other tabs in this dialog box are explained in different topics, as applicable.

View options

The Options dialog box includes a page of View options. These options control various ways that you can view data and worksheets. You may find some of these options useful when you are constructing complex worksheets. Others are useful for viewing worksheets that have elaborate formatting needs. Table 3-1 provides a list of the view options.

The View and Objects options (listed in Table 3-1) affect all worksheets in your workbook — and even other workbooks. The Window options listed in Table 3-2 affect only the current worksheet page or workbook.

Table 3-1
Workbook Viewing Options

Option	What It Does
Formula Bar	Displays or hides the formula bar that appears in the Excel program window. You may not need this formula bar if you perform most of your editing inside worksheet cells by double-clicking the cell. Remove the X to hide the formula bar.
Status Bar	Displays or hides the status bar that appears at the bottom of the screen. Remove the X to hide the status bar.
Note Indicator	Displays or hides the note indicator symbols that appear inside cells that contain cell notes. Cell notes are described in Topic 2.
Info Window	Displays or hides the Info Window, which contains information about worksheet cells and their notes. Use the Info Window to help you debug your complex worksheets. See Topic 2 for more information.
Show All	Displays and prints all objects (charts, buttons, drawings, and so on) on the worksheet as they appear on the screen.
Show Placeholders	Displays a gray box in place of all the charts, pictures, and text boxes on the worksheet. Other objects appear normally. This option can improve the performance of Excel, especially for worksheets that contain many complicated charts that can take a long time to update.
Hide All	Hides all objects (arrows, rectangles, charts, text boxes, and so on) from the worksheet. Excel leaves them in their prior positions but does not display them. Choosing either of the other two options (Show All or Show Placeholders) immediately brings the objects back. At print time, objects on the worksheet do not print if this option is selected.

You can selectively hide objects from printing. You may find the need to eliminate certain individual objects from the printout but not all the objects on the screen. For instance, you may have added a button to the worksheet that performs some action when you click it. This button may be useful, but you don't want it to show up on the printout. To eliminate an object from the printout, select the object, choose Object from the Format menu, and then choose the Properties tab. Click to uncheck the Print Object check box. Finally, click OK to return to the worksheet. Now the object does not print — although it does normally appear on the screen. For more information on changing object properties, see Topic 5.

Table 3-2
Window Viewing Options

Option	What It Does
Automatic Page Breaks	Displays or hides Excel's page break indicator lines. These lines appear on the worksheet when you print and show where each printed page begins and ends. You can hide these indicator lines if you don't want them to appear on the worksheet. Remember that turning off the display does not affect where pages break, nor does it keep Excel from displaying a manual page break. See Topic 6 for more information about page breaks and printing.
Formulas	Displays the values returned by your worksheet formulas or the text of the formulas. For example, if cell B4 contains the formula $=2+2$, checking this option shows $=2+2$ in the cell; leaving the option unchecked displays 4 in the cell. This option is useful when you want to check your worksheet formulas for errors or when you are first constructing a worksheet. Note that this option is normally unchecked for new worksheets because most people want to see the results of formulas in their worksheets. This option is also useful if you have removed the formula bar from view.
Gridlines	Displays or hides the gridlines between cells. Gridlines can make it easier to read crowded worksheets or complicated tables. They help you see how data lines up in rows and columns. However, gridlines can be distracting, especially if you add graphics to your worksheets or use borders to outline sections of a worksheet. In such cases, you will want to turn the gridlines off to make the borders easier to see. Remember, this has no affect on the printout — only the screen. Use the Color drop-down list to set the color of the gridlines when they are displayed.
Row & Column Headers	Displays or hides the column and row headings on the worksheet. Unchecking this item removes the 1, 2, 3,... row headings and the A, B, C,... column headings from the worksheet. You can only directly change column widths or select entire rows or columns with the mouse if you have Row and Column Headings displayed.
Outline Symbols	Displays or hides Excel's outlining symbols above and left of the column and row headings. The Show Outline Symbols tool has the same effect. You find the Show Outline Symbols Tool on the Utility toolbar, along with the other tools specific to outlining. For more information about toolbars, see "Using Toolbars" later in this topic.

Option	What It Does
Zero Values	Displays or hides values of zero on the worksheet. Unchecking this item causes any cell that contains a zero to display nothing. Often, values of zero are not input from the keyboard but are calculated by formulas. In these cases, you may not want to display the zeros in the cells but instead leave the cells blank. Hiding zeros is also useful in many financial worksheets where values of zero are better left blank. If checked, Excel displays all zeros — whether typed into a cell or produced from a formula.
Scroll Bars	Displays or hides the scroll bars from the screen. You can create more space for your page tabs by removing the horizontal scroll bar. Of course, scroll bars make it easier to move around the worksheet.
Sheet Tabs	Displays or hides the worksheet page tabs within the current workbook.

Quickly switching between formulas and values is relatively simple. To *toggle* the display between formulas and values (or vice versa) without using the Options dialog box, simply press Command-' (the Command key plus the single left quote), and the Formulas display changes to the opposite setting. Press Command-' again to restore the original setting.

If you don't want to display zero values for a portion of the worksheet but you do want to see them somewhere else on the same worksheet, don't turn off zeros by using the Options dialog box, because this changes the entire worksheet at once. To suppress zeros on only part of the worksheet, you can use a custom number format.

Remember that environment settings can be saved with the workbook to which they apply. This excludes the View and Objects options, which apply to Excel generally and not to individual workbooks.

Edit options

Edit options affect the way you edit and manipulate worksheet cells and data. The Edit options apply to the entire workbook, not just to the active worksheet, and the settings are saved with the workbook so that you don't have to repeat them each time you use the same workbook. Figure 3-7 shows the Edit options in the Options dialog box.

Table 3-3 lists the Edit options and their purposes.

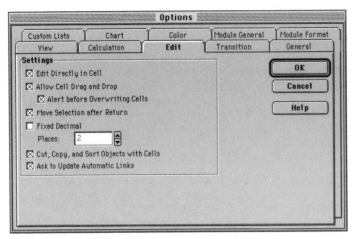

Figure 3-7: The Edit options.

Table 3-3
Edit Options in the Options Dialog Box

Option	What It Does
Edit Directly in Cell	Allows or prohibits in-cell editing features. If you like being able to double-click a cell to edit its contents, leave this option checked. If you never use this feature or don't like it, remove the check mark.
Allow Cell Drag and Drop	Allows or prohibits the ability to drag cells around the worksheet to move or copy data.
Alert before Overwriting Cells	Enables or disables the alert message that occurs when you drag cells over the top of other information, resulting in the old information being replaced. You can eliminate this warning by removing the check from this option.
Move Selection after Return	Determines whether the cell pointer moves down one cell after you press Return. Check this option to make entering columns of numbers easier.
Fixed decimal places	Determines the number of decimal places that automatically appear on your numeric values. This makes Excel work like some adding machines so that you don't have to enter a decimal point. Turn this option on when you want to enter a lot of currency values.
Cut, Copy, and Sort Objects with Cells	Determines whether worksheet objects are affected by worksheet cut, copy, and sort operations.
Ask to Update Automatic Links	Determines whether Excel asks you if you would like to update links between this workbook and other workbooks.

General options

The General options in the Options dialog box consist of a collection of miscellaneous environment changes. General options tend to affect Excel's default parameters, such as the font used as the default for worksheet cells and the assumed location of data files. Some of these options are rather esoteric and may not apply to your worksheets. Figure 3-8 shows the General options.

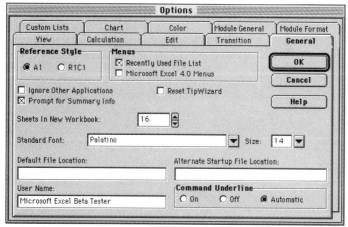

Figure 3-8: The General options in the Options dialog box.

Table 3-4 provides a list of the General options.

Table 3-4	
General Options in the Options Dialog Box	
Option	**What It Does**
Reference Style	Lets you choose A1 or R1C1-style referencing in Excel. R1C1-style references can be useful in macros to create relative references. R1C1 means "row 1, column 1," which is the same as cell A1.
Menus	Lets you choose between the new Excel 5 menus and older Excel 4 menus.
Ignore Other Applications	Lets you turn off remote activity from other applications through Microsoft's Visual Basic language or Apple Events. When checked, this option tells Excel not to respond to remote requests from other applications.
Prompt for Summary Info	Tells Excel to ask you for summary information when you save a file for the first time.

(continued)

	Table 3-4 *(continued)*
Option	**What It Does**
Reset TipWizard	Sets the TipWizard back to the beginning of its queue. The TipWizard displays tips in order, noting which ones have already been displayed. Checking this option starts the TipWizard at the beginning again.
Sheets in New Workbook [1]	Sets the number of worksheets that automatically appear in new workbooks.
Standard Font and Size [1]	Sets the font and point size of the workbook's standard font. This affects all sheets in the workbook and all workbooks that you open in Excel.
Default File Location [1]	Sets the folder in which Excel automatically looks for existing files. You can change the default location in the File⇨Save As or the File⇨Open dialog boxes, but the default location is the first place that Excel looks.
Alternate Startup File Location	Sets the location of the alternate Startup file, which contains startup data and formats for Excel.
User Name	Establishes the user name that automatically appears in the worksheet summary information.

[1] New with Excel 5.

Choosing colors

Your company or neighborhood no doubt has a few resident Excel gurus. If you've peeked over their cubicle walls or hedge rows, you've probably been dazzled by their Excel displays — rainbows of colors, windows, and toolbars! If you yearn for such special but useful effects, this is the section for you. This portion of the discussion shows you how to select colors for various Excel screen regions.

You have wide latitude on the regions and colors you can display in Excel. You can change the color of the following:

- ◆ Cell contents
- ◆ Patterns of shades
- ◆ Ranges
- ◆ Gridlines
- ◆ Borders
- ◆ Row numbers and column letters

The following section discusses how to select the color of each of these items.

Choosing colors for cells

You can add color to the contents of cells in two ways: by a predefined or custom numeric format or by changing the color of the font.

Setting colors by numeric format

Creating a custom numeric format can display a particular color based on a condition, such as when results are above or below expectations. You can use a numeric format that includes color for date formats as well as values.

For example, if you have a range of values that are positive and negative, and you want to display negative values in red (and both positive and negative values with a dollar sign and two decimal places), you'd use the following Excel format:

$#,##0.00_);[Red]($#,##0.00)

You can change the color red to something else by selecting from one of the eight available colors listed in Table 3-5.

Table 3-5 Color Coding Options	
Color name	**Color number**
Black	1
White	2
Red	3
Green	4
Blue	5
Yellow	6
Magenta	7
Cyan	8

You can change the format by adding a color symbol at the point in the format that represents what you want to color. In the preceding example, suppose that you have a holiday version of your worksheet, and you want to display positive values as green. The new format would be the following:

[Green]$#,##0.00_);[Red]($#,##0.00)

If you prefer another color set to work with, you can customize one or more of the colors on the color palette. This process is explained later in this Topic.

Changing the color of a font

You can change the color of fonts by choosing the Format⇨Cells command and clicking the Font tab, which is shown in Figure 3-9.

Pull down this list to select a color
for the font in the selected range

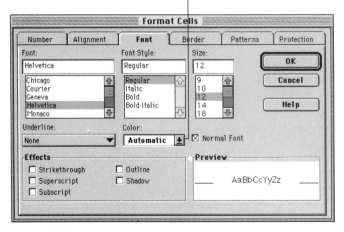

Figure 3-9: The Font tab of the Format Cells dialog box.

To select another color, simply select a range, choose Cells from the Format menu and then click the Font tab. The Color pull-down list is your ticket to changing colors. Select a color from the list and evaluate how the color looks with the font type and size shown in the Sample box. If you're satisfied with your choice, choose OK or press Return, and the data in the range you've selected now sports the new color.

Choosing colors for borders

Choosing a color for borders is similar to choosing a color for fonts. The Border tab shown in Figure 3-10 also has a Color pull-down list from which you can select a color. You can add a color to borders as you're applying them to spreadsheet cells or after you have the lines the way you want them. In either case, select the range of cells that contains borders, choose Cells from the Format menu, choose Color, and select the color for the lines. When you choose OK or press Return, Excel displays the borders around the selected cells with the color you selected.

Pull down this list to select a color
for the border in the selected range

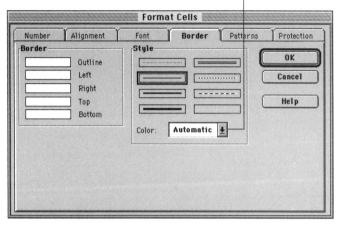

Figure 3-10: Adding color to borders using the Border options in the Format Cells dialog box.

Choosing colors for ranges

You may also decide to use colors for ranges. After you select a range, choose Cells from the Format menu and select the Patterns tab, which is shown in Figure 3-11. Choose a background color for the cells by using the color palette in the Cell Shading area. Then pull down the Pattern drop-down list to select the type of pattern (horizontal, vertical, diagonal lines, and so on) and choose a color for the pattern. Make sure that you select colors that won't cause the data to become illegible. Watch the Sample box to preview how the colors look before you choose OK or press Return. If you pull down the Patterns list a second time, you can see how the various patterns appear with the color combination you've chosen.

Select the color and pattern from these lists

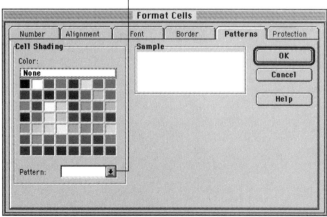

Figure 3-11: The Patterns tab of the Format Cells dialog box.

Choosing the gridline and headings colors

Two more areas of the worksheet for which you can control the color are the gridlines and the headings. Headings are the row numbers and column letters along the left side and on top of the worksheet, respectively. To change a heading's color, choose the Tools⇨Options command and click the View tab. Then pull down the Color list in the Window Options area, as shown in Figure 3-12.

Select the color you want and then choose OK or press Return. That's all there is to it. Excel displays the worksheet's gridlines and headings with the selected color.

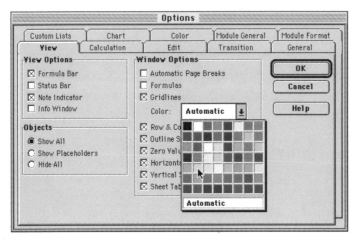

Figure 3-12: Changing the color of a heading by using the View tab of the Options dialog box.

What is an automatic color?

The Automatic color found on all Color pull-down lists is based on the color selected from Control Panels. You can easily select another Automatic color by selecting Control Panels from the Apple menu. When you do, the Control Panels window shown in the following figure appears.

Double-click Color.

Double-clicking the Color icon displays the window shown in the following figure.

Select another color by pulling down the Highlight color list. Watch how the color appears in the Sample text box. In addition, you can customize the color by selecting Other from the pull-down list. You can also select a color for windows from the Window color pull-down list.

When you're finished changing or customizing colors, choose OK or press Return. You'll be returned to the Control Panels window. Close the window, and Excel displays the color you selected.

Modifying colors

Excel comes with 16 standard colors that you can customize or use out-of-the-box plus several more colors for special purposes, such as chart fills. If you use a different set of 16 colors, you can keep this modified set in a template worksheet for use in other Excel models. Creating your own custom set of colors is a relatively painless process, as you will see. First, activate the worksheet that contains the color palette you want to modify. Next, choose the Tools⇨Options command and click the Color tab. You see the options shown in Figure 3-13.

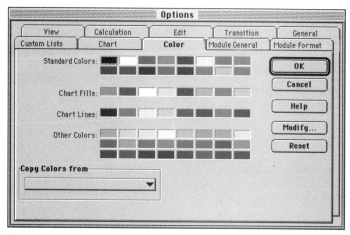

Figure 3-13: The Color tab of the Options dialog box.

Now, choose the color you want to change by clicking on it or by using the arrow keys. When you've selected the one you want, choose Modify. The dialog box in Figure 3-14 appears.

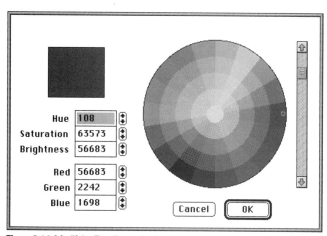

Figure 3-14: Modifying Excel's standard colors.

Move the mouse pointer over the small circle contained in the color wheel. When the pointer resembles a circle, click and drag the mouse around the color wheel while watching the square in the upper-left corner of the dialog box. As you drag the mouse, the upper half of the square changes color according to the location of the mouse pointer on the wheel (the lower half of the square remains the same for purposes of comparison). When the color appears the way you want, choose OK; you return to the Color Palette dialog box where you can choose OK to implement the color or edit another color.

You can also copy color palettes from one worksheet or chart to another, so only once will you need to modify a palette that contains colors you like. Copying color palettes from one worksheet to another is similar to copying named styles among worksheets.

Copying color palettes

To copy color palettes between worksheets, do the following:

1. Open the source and target worksheets (or charts).

2. Make the target worksheet the active worksheet.

3. Choose the Tools⇨Options command and click the Color tab.

4. Select the name of the source worksheet from the Copy Colors From pull-down list.

5. Choose OK. ⁌

When you choose OK or press Return, the target (active) worksheet (or chart) receives the source worksheet's color palette. Fonts, borders, ranges, gridlines and headings, and objects in the target worksheet display colors based on the new palette.

Zooming the Worksheet

Another display setting that affects individual worksheets is the worksheet magnification, or *zoom*, setting. You can reduce or enlarge the worksheet on-screen so that you can see more of the worksheet or get a closer look at a specific part of it. This new feature makes it easy to see details of worksheets set in very small fonts and allows you to see the overall design of a worksheet at a glance. Figure 3-15 and 3-16 show a worksheet in two different magnification settings.

To change the worksheet magnification, use the Zoom command in the View menu or the Zoom tool in the Standard toolbar.

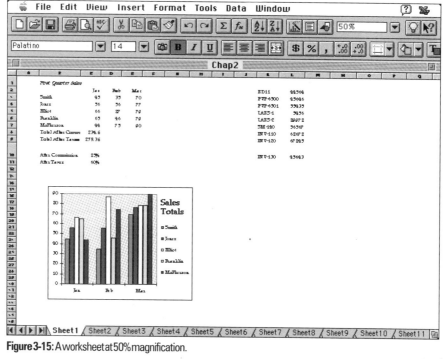

Figure 3-15: A worksheet at 50% magnification.

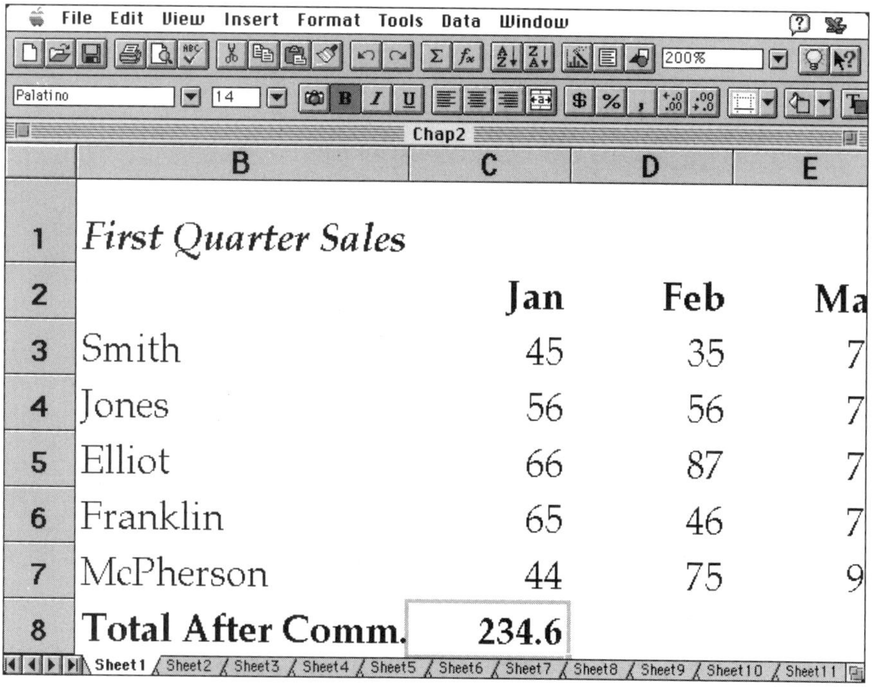

Figure 3-16: A worksheet at 200% magnification.

Magnifying the worksheet

1. Choose Zoom from the View menu. Alternatively, you can click the Zoom tool in the Standard toolbar. The Zoom dialog box (Figure 3-17) appears.

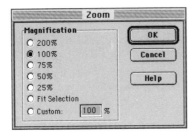

Figure 3-17: The Zoom dialog box appears when you choose the Zoom command from the View menu.

2. Click one of the levels of magnification. Note that values under 100 percent reduce the worksheet, and values over 100 percent enlarge it. The Fit Selection option (or just Selection in the Zoom tool) enlarges the currently selected range to the full size of the screen.

   If you are accessing the Zoom dialog box, you can also type any value between 10 and 400 percent into the Custom entry box.

3. If you are using the Zoom dialog box, click OK to accept the change. The worksheet is displayed at the new magnification.

Excel offers five built-in zoom settings, most of which reduce the worksheet view. The Fit Selection option tells Excel to reduce or enlarge the worksheet so that a particular section fills the window. Just highlight a block of cells on the worksheet and choose the Fit Selection option from the Zoom dialog box or the Selection option from the Zoom tool.

Note that you can also highlight a large area that must be reduced to fill the entire screen. When you get a large, unfamiliar worksheet, you can spend a lot of time simply trying to get around the worksheet and figure out what it contains. With Excel 5, you can use the Zoom command to create an instant view of the worksheet. Use these steps to view the entire worksheet on-screen.

Viewing the entire worksheet

1. Open the worksheet that you want to view.

2. Choose the Go To command from the Edit menu and click Special. Choose the Last Cell option and click OK. You are at the outermost corner of the worksheet.

3. Again, choose the Go To command from the Edit menu and type **A1** as the destination cell. Hold down Shift as you click OK to select all the cells between the last and first cells on the worksheet.

4. Choose Zoom from the View menu. Click on the Fit Selection option and click OK. Now the entire active area of the worksheet should fit on your screen. From this vantage point, you should see everything in the worksheet. ◖◗

Because Excel can zoom down only to 10%, trying to fit a very large worksheet onto a small screen may not work.

When you decrease the magnification of a worksheet, everything starts to look muddy, especially if you have gridlines turned on. Turn them off so that you can see your worksheet more clearly. Instructions for removing cell gridlines appear earlier in this topic under "View options."

Here are some guidelines for using the Zoom command and its various options:

◆ **Zooming does not affect Excel's worksheet features.** You can use all of Excel's features at any level of Zoom; you can select cells, edit their contents, copy and paste, apply formatting, and so on.

◆ **Zooming does not affect the printout.** The level of zoom magnification you see on the screen has nothing to do with the reduction or enlargement that occurs when your worksheet prints. This depends on your printer and Excel's Page Setup options. For more information on enlarging or reducing when you print, see Topic 6.

◆ **You can use toolbar tools to zoom.** Excel offers two tools for zooming worksheets incrementally. Clicking the Zoom In tool increases the magnification, and clicking on the Zoom Out tool reduces the magnification. Hold down Shift while you click on either of these, and each tool has the opposite effect. These tools can be added to any toolbar through Excel's toolbar customization features explained later in this topic under "Customizing toolbars." The Zoom In and Zoom Out tools appear in the Utilities tool category within the Customize dialog box. (You get to this dialog box by selecting Toolbars from the View menu and clicking Customize.)

◆ **Zooming applies to individual worksheet windows.** You can change the zoom factor for each worksheet in your workbook or change several at once by grouping the worksheets before zooming. When you save the workbook file, the zoom settings are saved along with the workbook.

◆ **Use the View Manager command to save different zoom settings for a single worksheet.** You can save zoom settings with the View Manager command in the View menu and then switch between your saved settings. Refer to "Saving Worksheet Views" later in this topic for more details.

◆ **Use the Full Screen command to see more of the worksheet.** You can select the Full Screen command from the View menu to remove unnecessary screen elements and display more of the worksheet cells on the screen. Combine this command with the zoom settings.

Changing the Workbook Window

Each Excel workbook is displayed in a window inside the Excel program window. You can alter these "document" windows to enhance the Excel environment and make your work easier. By maximizing, minimizing, or otherwise changing the size and shape of a window, you can organize your Excel program workspace.

When the information you store in a worksheet grows larger than what will fit on your screen, you can have a difficult time determining where each portion of the worksheet is located. Also, you may want to view different sections of a worksheet at the same time. Excel lets you open several different windows to your workbook so that you can view different areas of the workbook in each window. In this way, you can view the balance sheet worksheet and the income statement worksheet of your bookkeeping workbook at the same time.

Another interesting feature of Excel is that it lets you split a single window into *panes*. This feature can be similar to using two different worksheets, but it is often more useful when you want to keep column or row headings in place at the top and left side of a worksheet. The following sections describe these and other window-oriented changes that you can make in Excel. These changes, like other environment changes discussed so far, affect individual worksheets and can be saved with the worksheets to which they apply.

Splitting the worksheet window

Splitting a window in Excel divides it into separate *panes*. Each of these panes has its own set of scroll bars that allows you to scroll independently of the other panes. Figure 3-18 shows an Excel window with split panes. Notice that the window has two horizontal scroll bars: the left one controls panes 1 and 3, and the right one controls panes 2 and 4. Similarly, there are two vertical scroll bars.

To split a window into four separate panes, just select the Window⇨Split command after highlighting the cell that marks the intersection of the four panes.

Creating window panes

1. Select the cell that will be the top-left corner of pane 4 on your worksheet. In Figure 3-18, E8 is the selected cell. If you want to split the worksheet into four equal panes, move the cell pointer to cell A1.

2. Choose Split from the Window menu. The window splits into panes at the top-left corner of the cell that you selected. ◖◗

To split a window into only two panes (one on top of the other) select an entire row and then choose Window⇨Split. Excel splits the window into two horizontal panes just above the row you highlighted. Selecting an entire column splits the window into two side-by-side (vertical) panes.

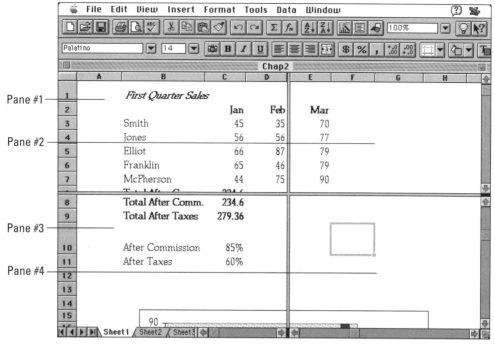

Pane #1

Pane #2

Pane #3

Pane #4

Figure 3-18: A worksheet window split into panes.

Use the split screen markers to create panes. You can split a window into panes by dragging the split screen markers rather than using the Window⇨Split command. Just click a split screen marker and drag it into position on the worksheet. Excel provides both a horizontal and a vertical split screen marker.

Note that splitting windows applies only to the current worksheet and does not affect other worksheets in the workbook.

If you don't like the current position of the window split, you can choose Window⇨Remove Split, and Excel returns the window to normal. To change the position of the current split, follow these steps.

Changing the position of a split

1. Move the mouse pointer on top of the split line that you want to change.

2. The pointer changes to a double arrow. Click and drag the mouse to move the split line to the new position. ◖

If you point at the intersection of the two split screen markers, the pointer turns into a four-sided arrow, and you can change the position of both splits at the same time. If you drag the split to the top or the left edge of the window, Excel removes that split from the window. You can also remove the split screen marks by choosing the Window⇨Remove Split command.

Moving between panes is easy. You can move between window panes by simply clicking on the desired pane or by pressing F6.

Freezing window panes

Although splitting a window makes working with large tables a lot easier, you will often find the extra set of scroll bars annoying and difficult to work with. Splitting the screen is an excellent way to display headings along the top or left side of the window — and keep those headings in place as you scroll through the worksheet. After you have set up the panes, and the headings are in view, you may not want to move or adjust the panes again.

Excel lets you *freeze* the top and left window panes so that you cannot move or adjust them. Use this feature when you want to display headings at the top and/or left side of the worksheet and keep those headings in place as you scroll through the rest of the worksheet.

Notice that the scroll bars for each pane disappear. You can now scroll the bottom-right pane while the other panes remain intact. Because you cannot adjust the placement of the frozen panes, you should make sure that the panes are properly placed before you freeze them.

To freeze the panes, choose the Freeze Panes command in the Window menu. If you have two panes, Excel freezes the top or left pane. If you have four panes, Excel freezes all panes except the bottom-right one.

Using multiple windows for a worksheet

Excel lets you have a virtually unlimited number of windows that show the same worksheet. Although worksheets normally appear in a single window, you can add new windows to the screen — each one showing the same worksheet. Actually, each new window can show a different portion of the same worksheet. So you can display an important table or database in one window and data entry in another.

To add new windows to the current worksheet, just use the New Window command in the Window menu. Each new window has the same name as the original, with a colon and the window's number added. For example, if you have the file REPORT open and then create a new window, Excel titles the new window REPORT:2 and retitles the original window REPORT:1. If you save the file, Excel remembers that you have two windows; when you open the file again, both windows will be there.

When you have a worksheet with more than one window open, Excel allows you to close the extra windows by clicking their close boxes or selecting the File⇨Close command. Because Excel has another window to the worksheet open, it does not actually close the file until you close all the windows to the worksheet. Be careful when you close the extra worksheet windows. You may have done a lot of work making display changes to the window (removing gridlines, changing the magnification, and so on). If you close the file without saving it, you lose those changes.

Hiding windows and worksheets

You may have one or more windows that you want to hide from casual or deliberate snooping, such as a salary planning worksheet or an income projection worksheet. You can keep confidential windows and worksheets from being displayed by hiding them.

To hide an entire workbook window, including all the worksheets in it, choose the Hide command from the Window menu while the workbook is active. If you want to redisplay the hidden window, choose Unhide from the Window menu and select the name of the window you want to display from the list box. Press OK to display the hidden window.

To hide a worksheet, choose the Sheet⇨Hide command from the Format menu while the desired worksheet is active. You can redisplay the worksheet by choosing the Sheet⇨Unhide command and selecting the worksheet name from the list provided.

Saving Worksheet Display Settings as Views

You may find that you frequently switch between two or three different display settings for a worksheet. For example, when you are constructing a large worksheet, you may like to view the worksheet at 75% magnification and display the row and column headings. But when you actually use the worksheet — or give it to someone else to use — you may want to display the worksheet at 100% and remove the gridlines and row and column headings.

In the preceding discussion of using multiple windows for a single worksheet, you learned that you can use different display settings on each window. You can then switch between the different windows to view different display settings. But Excel provides another method of saving different display settings that permits you to switch settings instantly: the View Manager available through the View menu. This command lets you store display options under unique names and then move between these named sets at any time.

The View Manager Add-in remembers the following information about your worksheet:

◆ The current number of windows active for the worksheet and their positions on the screen

◆ Which windows are split into panes

◆ The current environment settings (that is, the status of gridlines, zero values, and so on)

◆ Which cells are currently highlighted

◆ The current print area set for the worksheet (See Topic 6 for more information about print areas.)

◆ Which rows and columns are hidden (if any)

You create a worksheet view by simply setting up the worksheet with the desired display settings. Then use the View Manager command in the View menu to save the current settings under a unique name. Change the display settings and save another view. Save as many as you like. The following steps provide the details.

Creating a view

1. Apply any worksheet display settings you want, including using multiple windows, arranging the windows, zooming the worksheet, and using the Options command in the Tools menu.

2. Choose View Manager from the View menu. The dialog box in Figure 3-19 appears.

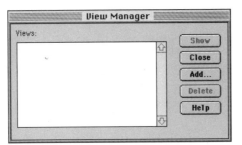

Figure 3-19: The View Manager dialog box.

3. Click Add to add a named view. The dialog box in Figure 3-20 appears.

Figure 3-20: Adding a new view name to the View Manager list.

4. Type a name for the view into the Name edit box. Choose whether you want to save the current print settings with the view and whether you want to hide the currently hidden rows and columns when you come back to the view.

5. Choose OK to save the view. ◖

Repeat these steps to add more views to the worksheet. Be sure to change the display options before saving the next view. Notice that you can include the current print settings in the view by checking the Print Settings box in the Add View dialog box, or you can omit the print settings by removing the check mark. Print settings are established through the Print Setup command in the File menu and are discussed in Topic 6.

Another option in the Add View dialog box is the Hidden Rows and Columns check box. When checked, the view remembers which rows and columns are hidden in the current setup. Then when you return to the view later, those rows and columns will be hidden again — even if they were showing before you selected the view.

This option can be useful all by itself. Suppose that you have a worksheet that contains employee records. Some of the data is private, so you hide certain columns when you produce reports. But when you are entering new employee records, you display all the columns — including those containing the sensitive data. You can store each of these displays as a different view, one showing the columns and one hiding them. Switch between the two displays instantly by selecting the desired view from the View list.

After you have created views on your worksheet, you will find it simple to return to those views. When you do, Excel restores the display and other settings you have chosen for that view. To return to an existing view, follow these steps.

Returning to a view

1. Choose the View Manager command from the View menu.

2. Choose the view that you want to show from the list box and then choose the Show button. The worksheet changes automatically. ◖

Remember that the views you add to the View list are saved only after you save the worksheet. Be sure to use the File⇨Save command to make your View settings permanent. The next time you open the worksheet, the views you created will appear in the Views list.

Using Toolbars

By now you are familiar with Excel's toolbars that appear at the top of the program window. These toolbars contains several point-and-click buttons that help you accomplish tasks more quickly. By clicking the button, you can avoid using the equivalent menu commands.

Toolbar buttons are so useful that Excel doesn't stop with the two toolbars that appear at the top of the screen. Excel gives you 13 different toolbars from which to choose. Each toolbar contains the tools best suited for a specific task. For example, the Chart toolbar contains five tools that are handy when creating charts. You can use as many of these toolbars at the same time as you like — although you'll probably find that two or three is about as many as you'll ever need at any one time.

Excel's toolbars were created for some specific activities as well as general Excel use. The Standard toolbar is great for general purposes, while the Chart toolbar is useful only when you're creating charts. But because the built-in toolbars can't anticipate all your needs, Excel lets you customize the toolbars by removing some tools and adding others. You can even create your own toolbars completely from scratch.

To create a new toolbar or to add to an existing one, Excel offers a palette of tools. These tools are primarily shortcuts to menu commands and options; that is, they duplicate the command or option when you click them. However, it's important to note that some of the tools offer unique capabilities and are not duplicates of menu commands, such as the drawing tools.

The next few sections show you how to access Excel's 13 toolbars and how to create your own custom toolbar. You also discover how to determine the purpose of any tool in Excel.

Excel's built-in toolbars

To access any of the built-in toolbars in Excel, simply use the Toolbars command in the View menu and select the desired toolbar from the list that appears. After selecting the Toolbars command, the Toolbars dialog box appears (see Figure 3-21).

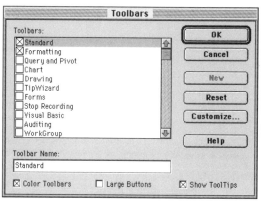

Figure 3-21: The Toolbars dialog box presents the 13 different toolbars.

Click to check the box beside the name of any toolbar and then click OK to display your choices. Those toolbars marked with an X are already on the screen. To remove a toolbar, remove the X from its check box in the Toolbars dialog box and click OK. Another way to remove a toolbar is to click its go-away box in the upper-left corner of the toolbar itself.

Using the shortcut menu should save you time. You can access Excel's toolbars through a shortcut menu. Just press Control as you click on any open toolbar and the shortcut menu appears. Click any toolbar title in the shortcut menu to add or remove the toolbar from the screen.

Table 3-5 provides a brief explanation of Excel's built-in toolbars.

In addition to these toolbars, the Toolbars dialog box offers options for displaying the toolbars in color or with large buttons. The Large Buttons option makes the tools easier to see, as shown in Figure 3-22.

Finally, the Tooltips option in the Toolbars dialog box provides or eliminates the instant descriptions that appear when you move the mouse over a button. If you no longer require this feature, or find it annoying, remove the X from the Tooltips option.

When you show a toolbar in Excel, it remains in view at all times. You can click the worksheet and work normally in Excel, even though the toolbar is in view at top of the worksheet. Because some toolbars cover a portion of the worksheet, you may want to move the toolbar or change its size and shape. After a toolbar is on the screen, you can move it around and change its size and shape as you can any Macintosh window.

Table 3-5
Excel's Built-In Toolbars

Toolbar	What It Can Do
Standard	The toolbar that appears automatically at the top of the program window and contains tools for general use, including some file management tools and formatting tools.
Formatting	Buttons to help you format the information on a worksheet, such as changing fonts, adding boldface, and applying shading.
Query and Pivot	Buttons that help you work with pivot tables and database queries. For more information, refer to Topic 9.
Chart	Buttons that make charting easier. Includes buttons for changing chart types and formatting charts.
Drawing	Buttons you can use to draw pictures onto the worksheet. These are discussed in Topic 5.
TipWizard	Displays or hides the TipWizard, which is discussed in Topic 1.
Forms	Buttons that let you create dialog boxes and create controls for your worksheets. For more information, see Topic 12.
Stop Recording	A button that stops your macro recorder. This toolbar automatically appears when you start the macro recorder.
Visual Basic	Buttons to help you create and run macros in Excel. See Topic 13 for more details.
Auditing	Buttons that help you locate and correct errors in your worksheets.
Workgroup	Buttons for connecting with other users in a network. Includes tools for sending and receiving e-mail.
Microsoft	Buttons for moving instantly to other Microsoft applications.
Full Screen	A single button that toggles between full-screen mode and standard viewing. Full screen mode eliminates many screen elements to maximize your view of the worksheet.

To move a toolbar, simply click its title bar and drag to another location on the screen. Release the mouse when you've reached the desired location. To prevent a toolbar from overlapping the worksheet, you can move it to any of the four sides of the program window. The toolbar adjusts to fit into the window and the worksheet fits within the remaining workspace. Figure 3-23 shows an example with toolbars on the buttom.

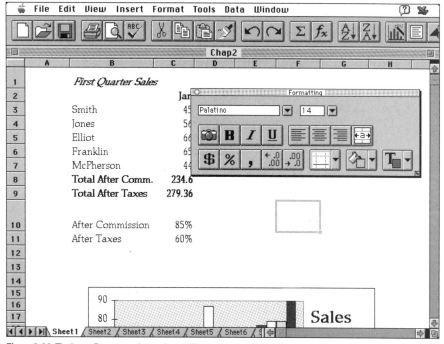

Figure 3-22: The Large Buttons option makes toolbars easier to read.

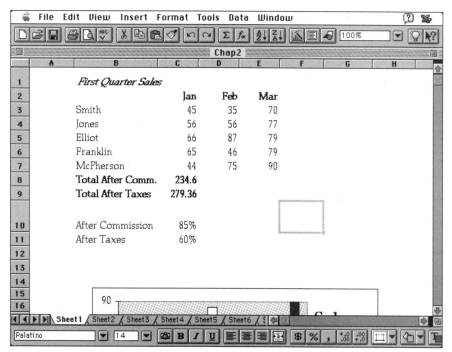

Figure 3-23: Toolbars can be positioned on the bottom (shown above) or sides of the screen.

Note that some toolbars contain more tools than can fit in the vertical position along the side of the window. Therefore, some tools cannot be seen. To move a toolbar from the side of the screen, click a blank area of the toolbar (that is, anywhere on the toolbar itself, but not on a tool) and drag it to the middle of the screen.

Remember that toolbar changes are saved with Excel; when you exit Excel, the toolbars and their positions are recorded. The next time you use Excel, the toolbars will be just as you left them.

Customizing toolbars

You can add or remove buttons from a toolbar, and you can create your own toolbars from scratch. Excel provides numerous tools that you can use for this purpose — some of which do not appear on any of the built-in toolbars. Use the following steps to create a new toolbar.

Creating a toolbar

1. Select the Toolbars command from the View menu. The Toolbars dialog box appears.

2. Press Tab until you highlight the Toolbar Name entry box.

3. Type a name for your new toolbar into the Toolbar Name entry box. The new name you type should replace the name currently showing.

4. Click New. A small, empty toolbar appears on the screen in the upper-left corner of the program window (see Figure 3-24). ◖

You can now add buttons to your new toolbar. You can even add buttons to one of the built-in toolbars if you like. The following steps show how to add and remove buttons from any toolbar showing on the screen.

Adding buttons to a toolbar

1. Create the new toolbar as described in the preceding steps or, if you want to modify an existing toolbar, just display it on the screen by using the View➪Toolbars command.

2. Activate the Customize dialog box (if you just created the toolbar, this dialog box is already active). Do this by selecting the View➪Toolbars command and clicking Customize in the Toolbars dialog box. You can also access the Customize option from the shortcut toolbar menu.

3. Click one of the tool categories on the left side of the Customize dialog box. The tools for that category appear in the Buttons area of the dialog box. Figure 3-25 shows the Text Formatting tools.

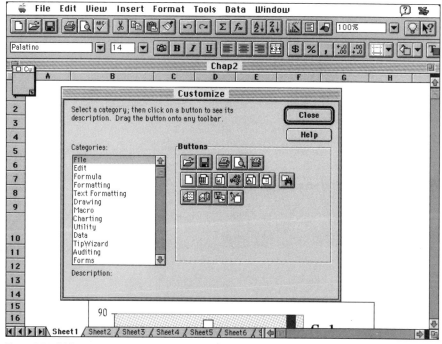

Figure 3-24: Adding a new toolbar to the screen.

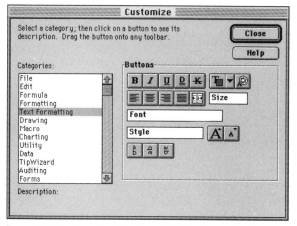

Figure 3-25: The Customize dialog box contains tools for customizing your toolbars.

4. Click any tool in the Buttons list (or any tool showing on the screen) to view a description of its purpose. The description appears at the bottom of the Customize dialog box.

5. Click the desired tool, drag it to the toolbar, and then release the mouse. The tool should appear inside the toolbar.

6. To remove a tool from a toolbar, click the tool inside the toolbar, drag it back into the Customize dialog box, and then release the mouse. ◀

Table 3-6 summarizes the customization options.

Table 3-6 Toolbar Customization Options		
Desired Task	**Steps to Take**	**Excel's Result**
Add a tool	Select a tool category and then drag a tool from the Tools box to the location on the toolbar.	Adds the tool and resizes the toolbar.
Delete a tool	Drag the tool off the toolbar to anywhere other than a toolbar or the dialog box.	Deletes the tool and resizes the toolbar.
Move a tool	Drag the tool to its new location on the existing toolbar or another displayed toolbar.	Changes the order that the tools are displayed on the toolbar and closes up any extra space.
Copy a tool	Press Control and drag the tool to its new location on the existing toolbar or another displayed toolbar.	Inserts a copy of the tool and resizes the toolbar to accommodate the duplicate.
Create space between tools	Drag the tool half-way towards the tool to its right and release the mouse.	Moves the tool over slightly, creating space between it and the tool to its left.

After you are satisfied with the changes, close the Customize dialog box. The new toolbar appears in the Toolbars list when you next use the View⇔Toolbars command. Your changes are permanently in Excel. Remember the following points about customizing toolbars:

◆ **Don't overcrowd a toolbar.** If you put too many tools on a toolbar, you may not be able to see them all when the toolbar is placed at the top or the bottom of the screen.

◆ **You can add the same tool to several different toolbars.** Many tools appear on two or three of the built-in toolbars. You can add any of the built-in tools to your custom toolbars.

◆ **You can create custom tools.** If you don't find a tool for the task you need to accomplish, you can create your own tool for that task. Excel provides a number of custom tools that you can use to store your own procedures. To create a custom tool, refer to Topic 13. After you create a custom tool, you can add it to any toolbar.

◆ **You can restore a built-in toolbar to its original state.** If you've modified a built-in toolbar and want to return it to normal, select the View⇨Toolbars command and click once on the toolbar you want to restore. Then click Reset.

Quick Tips ▪ ▪ ▪ ▪ ▪ ▪ ▪ ▪ ▪ ▪ ▪ ▪ ▪ ▪ ▪ ▪ ▪

Using the More Toolbars command

If you've caught toolbar mania and have created more toolbar names than the toolbar shortcut menu can display, the More Toolbars command appears on the shortcut menu. Choosing More Toolbars displays the Toolbar dialog box, where you can see all existing toolbar names.

Understanding unlockable toolbars

You cannot place the Standard, Formatting, and Workgroup toolbars in the left or right toolbar docks (or positions) because of their pull-down list boxes.

Returning a toolbar to its former location

Double-clicking the background of a previously moved toolbar returns it to its former location.

Double-click auditing

Turning off in-cell editing in the Edit tab of the Tools⇨Options dialog box changes what happens when you double-click a cell. Instead of editing, a double-click will now select all of the cells used in the cell's formula.

Part II:
Enhancing Your Worksheets

2nd Edition

Macworld Excel 5 Companion

Formatting Your Work

Overview

Now that you've successfully created Excel worksheets and workbooks, you may want to spruce them up a bit. For example, wouldn't it be nice if the text lined up over the values? If you're used to working with dollar amounts, you may prefer to display a dollar sign in front of each number. Or you may want a comma to separate the thousands in each number. Perhaps you'd like both.

With Excel you can change the display of text and numbers, otherwise known as formatting your data. You can choose from various data alignments to adjust how columns line up. You can even add shading and color to your text. This Topic shows you how to format your data using Excel's powerful formatting commands, which appear primarily in the Format Cells dialog box.

Changing Column Widths and Row Heights

You can type up to 255 characters in each cell, but the standard cell displays only eight or nine characters at a time. Text entries can spill into adjacent cells but only if those cell do not contain data. Numeric entries simply revert to #### when the entire number does not fit into the current cell width. Excel lets you change the width of each column on the worksheet. You can also change the height of each row as described in the following sections.

Changing column widths

Besides displaying more data in each cell, you may want to change your worksheet's column widths to help make your data fit onto one page or on one screen. By reducing column widths (without chopping off data), you can reduce the overall space those columns take up on the page or screen.

Changing column widths

1. Move the mouse pointer to the column divider at the right edge of any column. As you move the mouse pointer from the worksheet to the column heading area, it changes from a heavy cross to an arrow. When you point directly at the column divider within the heading area, it changes again to the column width changing pointer (see Figure 4-1).

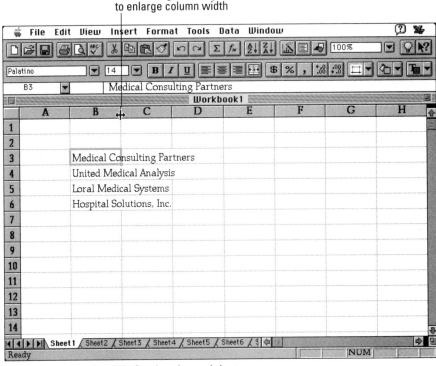

Figure 4-1: Changing the width of a column in a worksheet.

2. With the column width changing pointer showing, click and hold the mouse button down and drag to change the column width (left to narrow, right to widen).

3. As you drag the mouse, you see a gray line down the column indicating the proposed column width. The reference area to the left of the formula bar also displays the numeric width of the column. Release the mouse button and the column width changes. ◭

You can also choose Column Width from the Format menu to change the column's width. When the Column Width dialog box appears, enter an integer or decimal fraction representing the number of characters (in the current font) you want the column to contain.

You will probably find that you change column widths many times as you create and edit your worksheets.

Simultaneously changing the width of multiple adjacent columns is just as easy as changing the width of a single column. To change the widths of many columns to the same width, select the columns by dragging across the column header. Then drag on the line separating any two selected columns in the column headings area. When you finish, Excel changes all selected columns to the new width.

Excel lets you set a standard column width to use as the default width for all columns that have not been set individually. In other words, all columns whose widths have not been adjusted are automatically set to the *standard* width. If you change the standard width setting, all these columns adjust accordingly. Just choose the Column⇨Standard Width command from the Format menu and enter a new value into the Standard Width entry box. All standard columns change to reflect the new standard. Remember that columns whose widths you have changed manually are unaffected by the standard width setting unless you have cells in the changed column selected at the time you change the standard width.

While changing column widths works fairly intuitively (especially with the mouse), you may still find it tedious to get every number in a column to show up properly. You need to look down the column, find the widest number, and then widen the column to fit that number.

Excel automates this process with its best-fit column width and row height techniques. The best-fit technique automatically fits the row or column to its largest data.

Automatically changing column widths

1. Point at the column divider in the column heading area. If you want to change the row height, point at the separator line below the row's heading. The mouse pointer changes shape when you move it to the correct area.

2. Double-click the mouse, and the column width automatically changes to fit its data. ◖

You can also apply the Best-Fit technique by choosing the Column⇨Autofit Selection command from the Format menu.

You can reduce the width of a column to zero by dragging the column border to the left, past the column's own left edge. You can also select the Column⇨Hide command in the Format menu to hide any selected columns. Hiding columns can be useful for keeping sensitive data out of view — and out of your printouts. For example, you may want to hide a column containing employee salaries so that wandering eyes cannot see them as you work on the worksheet. If these salaries are used in other calculations throughout the worksheet, hiding the column will have no effect on those formulas.

Hidden columns do not appear in printouts and cannot be selected for graphs or other worksheet procedures—they are inaccessible. You can restore a hidden column by clicking the column heading to the left of the hidden column and dragging the column to its right—you have surrounded the hidden column. Then select the Column Unhide command from the Format menu. The hidden column returns to view.

Changing row heights

Changing row heights works exactly the same as changing column widths. When using the mouse, you simply point to the row divider below the row you want to change (in the row heading area) and then drag the mouse up or down to change the height of the row. Excel adds extra space to the top of the row so that any existing data in the row appears toward the bottom of the cell. Note that you can change the vertical placement of data within a cell by using the alignment options described later in this topic under "Changing Data Alignment."

From the keyboard, select a cell in the row you want to change and then choose Format Row Height. (You can also select multiple cells to change many rows at the same time.) The number Excel assigns to column widths roughly corresponds to the number of characters the cell holds (because each character has a different width, Excel approximates). Excel measures the height of a row in points (or 72nds of an inch), the same measure that Excel uses for font size.

When you change the point size of your data, Excel automatically adjusts the height of the row to accommodate the larger (or smaller) font. Note that if you have several different point sizes for the data appearing in the same row, Excel automatically sets the row height to fit the largest size. The height is the point size used for the data, plus one extra point for spacing. For example, if your row contains data in 12-point, 14-point, and 18-point type, Excel sets the row height to 19. You can reduce this height or increase it to create extra space by using the mouse or keyboard procedures.

To make a worksheet easier to read, many people skip every other row on the worksheet, leaving a blank row between data. Unfortunately, the blank rows can cause problems when creating formulas or working with databases. Because you can change the height of rows, you can get the best of both worlds. Just expand all the rows at once. Leave the point size of the data about half the size of the row height to create the extra space. This arrangement gives you more flexibility because it is much easier to alter the spacing between rows of data by changing the height of the rows than it is by skipping every other row. You can also add borders to all rows, rather than every other row.

Using Fonts

Excel lets you access all of the fonts available on your Macintosh computer. You can apply up to 255 different fonts to each Excel workbook. A *font* or type *face* is the graphical appearance of characters. Some fonts are very businesslike, others are casual and friendly. Still others use fancy flourishes to grab attention. The fonts you use in your worksheets affect how the information is perceived. Figure 4-2 shows a worksheet with a selection of fonts in use.

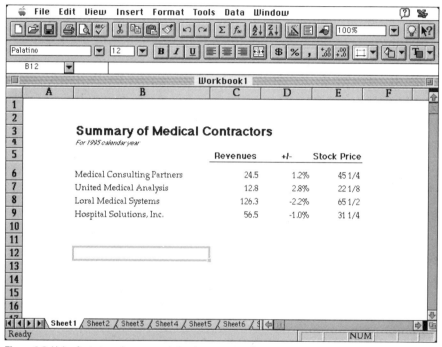

Figure 4-2: Using fonts to make your worksheets more attractive.

Besides type *faces* — the graphical style of type — you have control over the type size and style. Type size is measured in *points*; a point is about $^1/_{72}$ of an inch. Type styles are the special enhancements you can apply to fonts, such as boldface, underline, italics, and so on. By combining fonts, sizes, and styles, you can create a wide variety of type effects in your worksheets.

You can change the font, size, and style of each cell individually in Excel, and you can also change a block of cells at the same time. In addition, Excel 5 allows you to apply different fonts to different parts of the data within one cell. That is, you can change the font of individual characters in a cell's text.

Changing the font of a cell or range

1. Select the cell or range that you want to change.

2. Click the drop-down font list in the Formatting toolbar and choose the desired font from the list.

 3. Click the drop-down size list in the Formatting toolbar and choose the desired point size from the list.

 4. Click the Bold, Italic, or Underline button to apply any of these styles to the selected range.

 5. Click the Type color palette to change the color of the type within the selected cells. Remember that this is a tear-off palette, so you can keep it available for more coloring tasks. ⏴

Formatting individual characters within cells

1. Double-click the cell containing the entry that you want to format.

2. Drag the mouse to highlight the portion of the entry that you want to change. Figure 4-3 shows an example.

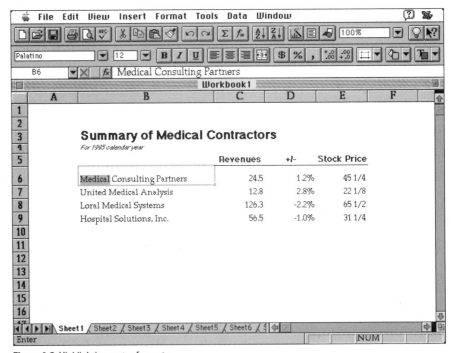

Figure 4-3: Highlighting parts of an entry.

3. Use the drop-down lists and formatting tools in the Formatting toolbar or choose the Cells command from the Format menu and select the Fonts page tab to access formatting options.

4. When finished with the formatting, press Return to accept your changes in the cell. ◖

You can access additional font formatting capabilities by using the Format Cells dialog box instead of the Formatting toolbar. Just highlight the desired cells and choose the Cells command from the Format menu. Then click the Font tab within the dialog box. The options in Figure 4-4 appear.

Format Cells

| Number | Alignment | **Font** | Border | Patterns | Protection |

Font:
Palatino

Geneva
Helvetica
Monaco
New York
Palatino

Font Style:
Regular

Regular
Italic
Bold
Bold Italic

Size:
12

9
10
12
14
18

OK
Cancel
Help

Underline:
None

Color:
Automatic

☐ Normal Font

Effects
☐ Strikethrough ☐ Outline
☐ Superscript   ☐ Shadow
☐ Subscript

Preview

AaBbCcYyZz

Figure 4-4: The Font options in the Format Cells dialog.

Here you can access fonts, sizes, and styles from separate lists. You also have access to several underlining options, including double-underlining for accounting applications, as well as font colors and special effects. Combine any of these formatting options for various results, if desired.

The Normal Font option lets you change the default, or standard, font used throughout the worksheet. If you want your font selections to be used as the default font, click to place an X in this option.

Remember, you don't have to change everything in the dialog box. For example, if you have selected a range of cells that has many different sizes, styles, and so on, and you only want to change the font for each cell, don't change anything in the Format Cells dialog box but the font. Excel makes any change you tell it to and leaves everything else alone.

Note that changing the color of your fonts can affect the printout — even on black-and-white printers. For more information on printing in color and shades of gray, refer to Topic 8. Other ways of changing the color of data are covered later in this topic under "Adding Shading and Patterns."

In the Toolbar Customization dialog box (choose View⇨Toolbars and then click the Customize button) is a host of additional text formatting tools. Two of these let you change the font size incrementally. Just click the Size Increase tool (large A) to increase the active cell's font by one point size. Click the Size Decrease tool (small A) to reduce the font. If you Shift-click the Size Increase tool, it decreases the font size. Shift-clicking the Size Decrease tool increases the font size.

Changing Data Alignment

Excel provides an assortment of alignment commands for your worksheets. Alignment controls how data appears inside cells. Data can appear flush with the left side, flush with the right side, or centered. Also, Excel lets you adjust the vertical placement of data in a cell so that the data can be flush with the top, bottom, or center of the cell.

Excel uses its *general* alignment when you first enter data into a cell. General alignment pushes text to the left edge of the cell, numbers to the right edge of the cell, and error values to the center, between the right and left edges of the cell. Vertically, the general alignment leaves data at the bottom of the cell. Hence, if you reduce the point size of one cell in a row, you'll notice that the type in that cell lines up with the bottoms of the other cells' data. Figure 4-5 shows a variety of alignment settings.

Aligning data within cells

1. Select the cell or range that you want to align.

2. Choose the Cells option from the Format menu.

3. Click the Alignment tab in the Format Cells dialog box.

4. Choose from the Horizontal and Vertical alignment options, in addition to the data Orientation options. (Details on these options are provided below.)

5. Click OK when finished. ⋀

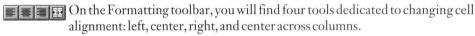 On the Formatting toolbar, you will find four tools dedicated to changing cell alignment: left, center, right, and center across columns.

 Changing cell alignment with the toolbar works as you may expect it to — you select the cells you want aligned and then click the appropriate alignment tool. Excel changes the alignment of the selected cells. Centering a label across several columns is described in the following section, "Horizontal alignment options."

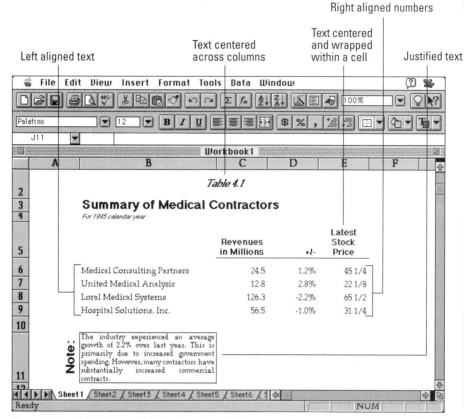

Figure 4-5: Use Excel's alignment options for various effects.

Horizontal alignment options

The first set of Alignment options in the Format Cells dialog box affects the horizontal position of data. You can use simple left, right, and center alignment, plus a host of special options for aligning data within the left and right sides of the cell's walls. Table 4-1 presents a description of these options.

Justification aligns data along both the left and right sides of the cell and is often considered an attractive effect for paragraphs of data. The Justify option is one way to create justified paragraphs on your worksheet. When you want to justify a cell's entry into a paragraph of data, choose both the Justify option and the Wrap Text option in the Alignment options of the Format Cells dialog box. Note that the justified type fills the current width of the cell. For more information about wrapping text within a cell, refer to "The Wrap Text option" later in this Topic.

You may find that you need more than 255 characters for your justified paragraphs. To overcome this limitation, add a text box to the worksheet and enter the data into the text box. The text box can then be moved around the worksheet and formatted with various commands and options. Refer to Topic 5 for more information on creating and formatting text using text boxes.

Excel provides an alignment option that lets you center a heading across a group of columns. If the column widths change, the heading adjusts itself to return to the exact center of the columns. This tool is useful for formatting your worksheets.

	Table 4-1 Data Alignment Options	
Option	**What Is the Result**
General	Aligns text left, numbers right, and errors center. This is the default alignment used for all cells.
Left	Aligns the cell entry to the left edge of the cell.
Center	Aligns the cell entry between the left and right edges of the cell.
Right	Aligns the cell entry to the right edge of the cell.
Fill	Repeats the contents of the cell as many times as needed to fill the entire cell. If adjacent cells to the right have this alignment, Excel extends the fill through those cells as well. This tool is sometimes useful for adding special borders and lines onto the page, but its usefulness is rare.
Justify	Aligns the cell entry to both the left and right edges of the cell; Excel extends the spaces within the entry to achieve this effect. If the entry contains no spaces, Excel uses left alignment. This option is useful for creating a small paragraph of information on the worksheet when the cell contains a lot of text. Use this option along with the Wrap Text option to justify a large amount of data in a cell.
Center Across Selection	Centers the cell entry across all cells adjacent on the right which are empty and have the same alignment. Details on this option appear later in this section.

You may be tempted to use a text box to center a heading across columns, but you should resist the temptation. Text boxes do not adjust when you change the column widths, and they cannot contain values that come from cells in the worksheet or any numeric values. Hence, they cannot contain formulas, numeric entries, or dates. (You can type numbers into text boxes, but they are considered text entries to Excel.)

To align a heading across several columns, just type the heading above the first column. Then highlight the heading plus all other cells to the right (see Figure 4-6). After highlighting the heading and columns, select the Center Across Selection option in the Format Cells dialog box (Alignment page). Alternatively, you can just click the Center Across Selection tool in the Standard toolbar. Figure 4-7 shows the result.

Remember that you can change the width of any column in the selection and Excel will adjust the position of the heading so that it remains centered.

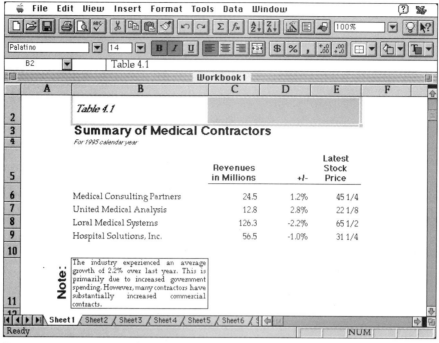

Figure 4-6: To center across a selection, highlight the entry plus the cells to the right.

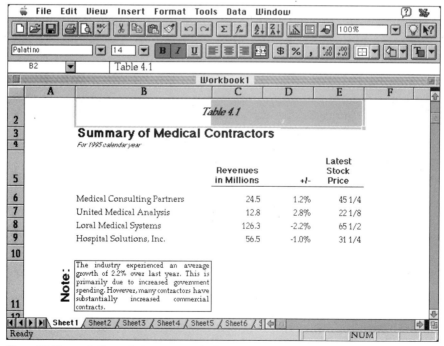

Figure 4-7: The result after centering across a selection.

Note that the cells adjacent to (to the right of) the heading must be empty, or Excel centers the heading only as far as the next entry. Also, the next entry will be centered across the following cells as well. You can use this aspect of the command to center several headings at once. For example, you can enter headings above every other column and then use the Center Across Selection to center each heading above two columns.

Vertical alignment options

The Alignment options in the Format Cells dialog box provide several ways of aligning data vertically within a cell. Vertical alignment changes the position of data relative to the top and bottom of the cell. Table 4-2 provides an overview of the options.

These options are easy to understand. But remember that they can be combined with the horizontal orientation options for various effects as seen in Figure 4-4.

Table 4-2 Vertical Alignment Options	
Top	Excel aligns the cell entry to the top of the cell.
Center	Excel aligns the cell entry midway between the top and bottom of the cell.
Bottom	Excel uses this as a default, aligning the cell entry to the bottom of the cell.
Justify	Excel spaces the text in even rows vertically.

Orientation options

Orientation options in the Format Cells dialog box change the way data *reads* within a cell. You can read data from left to right, top to bottom, bottom to top, and so on. Combine these options with the vertical and horizontal alignment options for additional effects. See Figures 4-8 to 4-11 for examples of each option.

Left-to-right   Displays data horizontally in normal left-to-right fashion. Excel uses this setting by default (see Figure 4-8).

Note:

Figure 4-8: An example of the left-to-right orientation option.

Top-to-bottom   Displays data in a stacked manner. Excel displays the
(characters vertical)   characters in the cell upright, one character per line, with the first character at the top of the cell.

Figure 4-9: An example of the top-to-bottom (characters vertical) orientation option.

Bottom-to-top   Displays the contents of the cell tipped sideways, so the text reads from the bottom to the top. This option acts as if Excel rotated a standard left-to-right cell 90 degrees counterclockwise.

Figure 4-10: An example of the bottom-to-top orientation option.

Top-to-bottom   Displays the contents of the cell tipped sideways so the text reads from the top to the bottom. This option acts as if Excel rotated a standard left-to-right cell 90 degrees clockwise.

Figure 4-11: An example of the top-to-bottom orientation option.

When you select one of these orientation options, Excel automatically adjusts the row height to fit the data. This may have adverse effects on the worksheet. If you want to display text using one of the special orientations but don't want to increase the row height, use text boxes to display the text. Refer to Topic 5 for information on using text boxes.

The Wrap Text option

Simply changing row heights does not wrap the cell entry onto more than one line. If a cell contains a long text entry, you may consider using the Wrap Text option in the Format Cells dialog box to split the text onto several lines within the cell.

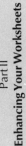

Wrapping text within a cell

1. Select the cell(s) containing the long entries.

2. Adjust the column widths of the cells to determine the length of each line.

3. Choose the Cells command from the Format menu and then click the Alignment page tab.

4. Check the Wrap Text check box.

5. Choose OK. Text which runs beyond the edge of the cell now wraps onto a new line. ◖◗

Although the Wrap Text command uses the current column width to measure each line, you can adjust the column's width, and Excel will change the lines to fit the new width. For example, you may begin with three lines, but by increasing the column width you may end up with only two.

Note that Excel does not change the row height again when you adjust the column width of the cells. So after adjusting the column width, you may want to manually adjust the row height using the best-fit technique described earlier in this Topic under the heading, "Changing column widths."

Formatting numbers

When you create worksheets, you may use many different types of numbers: the current month's sales figures, the prime interest rate, the number of units sold, and so on. If you entered these numbers on paper, you would put a dollar sign in front of the sales figures, show the interest rate as a percentage, and put commas between every third digit of the sales count.

Excel offers many number formats that display numbers in various ways. By applying a number format, you can change the way a number looks in the cell. For example, if you apply the standard currency format to a cell containing the number 45678, you would see $45,678.00 displayed in the cell. When you look in the formula bar, you'd simply see 45678, because number formatting has no effect on the underlying number.

Excel applies the General number format to all cells in a worksheet as the default. You can change any cell's number format by using the Number options in the Format Cells dialog box.

Choosing a number format

1. Select the cell or range containing the numbers that you want to format.

2. Choose the Cells command in the Format menu and then click the Number tab to access the number formats. The dialog box in Figure 4-12 appears. On

the left edge of the dialog box is the Category list box. This box gives a list of different categories of number formats already created for you by Excel. At the right of the dialog box, you see the Format Codes list box. This box lists all of the formats in the category selected on the left. At the bottom of the dialog box, the Sample tells you what the active cell will look like if you apply the currently selected number format.

3. Choose the desired number category from the list on the left. If you're not sure which category to use, select All.

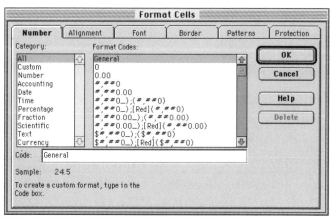

Figure 4-12: The Number formats in the Format Cells dialog box.

4. Select the desired format code from the list on the right. Format codes and their effects are shown in Table 4-3.

5. Click OK. ⏴

After selecting one of the number formats in the list — and before clicking OK — examine the Sample at the bottom of the dialog box. You can flip through various formats and watch the sample change if you want to *shop* for the right format. Note that if the active cell does not contain an entry, the Sample display will be blank. Refer to Table 4-3 for details about each number format in the list.

Some of the more common number formats are available through various shortcut methods, such as shortcut keystrokes and toolbar tools. Also, the styles list provides access to several of these formats. (The styles list is a custom toolbar tool and is discussed later in this topic.)

Using number formats on your worksheet may at times appear to round your numbers. This rounding is for appearances only. The actual value stored in the cell is the original, unrounded value. Therefore, any calculations you prescribe use the entire value, not the rounded value. If you want to round the actual values in cells, you should use the ROUND function.

Table 4-3
Available Number Formats

Display format	Positive	Negative
General	1234.5	-1234.5
0	1235	-1235
0.00	1234.50	-1234.50
#,##0	1,235	-1,235
#,##0.00	1,234.50	-1,234.50
#,##0_);(#,##0)	1,235	(1,235)
#,##0_);[RED](#,##0)[1]	1,235	(1,235)
#,##0.00_);(#,##0.00)	1,234.50	(1,234.50)
#,##0.00_);[RED](#,##0.00)[1]	1,234.50	(1,234.50)
$#,##0_);($#,##0)	$1,235	($1,235)
$#,##0_);[RED]($#,##0)[1]	$1,235	($1,235)
$#,##0.00_);($#,##0.00)	$1,234.50	($1,234.50)
$#,##0.00_);[RED]($#,##0.00)[1]	$1,234.50	($1,234.50)
0%	123450%	-123450%
0.00%	123450.00%	-123450.00%
0.00E+100	1.20E+103	-1.20E+103
#?/?	1 2/3	-1 2/3
#??/??[2]	1 2/3	-1 2/3

[1]   Displays negative values in red.
[2]   Left aligned in cell.

Menus vs. tools vs. shortcut keys

You've undoubtedly discovered by now that there's more than one way to accomplish a task with Excel. For example, you can format numbers using the Numbers page in the Format Cells dialog box, the style list, toolbar tools, or shortcut keystrokes.

Actually, it comes down to personal preference. If you're a Macintosh veteran, you're probably accustomed to using the mouse, so that is probably the most efficient way for you to apply commands. If you're new to graphical computing or would rather keep your hands on the keyboard, you may want to use shortcut keys. Of course, there's nothing that says you can't use a combination of the keyboard and mouse. You need both to enter text and values anyway.

Don't let the multiple ways of performing Excel operations confuse you. Look at it as an opportunity to select what works for you. Use the advice in this book to help you decide what's best.

Creating custom formats

The scores of number formats you see in the Format Cells dialog box serve only as suggestions. Excel lets you create new number formats for special needs.

Many industries require more (or less) precision in their numbers. You may want to display the figures in a company balance sheet in thousands or show a product cost down to the hundredth of a cent. If you couldn't create custom number formats, you may find yourself at a loss.

You may have noticed that while some number formats seem brief and simple, others can take up an entire line. In long number formats, values which fall into different numeric ranges often get formatted differently. For example, a format may display positive numbers one way, negatives another way, and zeros yet another way.

Number formats in Excel can contain up to four different types of formatting for different sets of values. Excel uses semicolons to separate the different types of number formatting, as illustrated here:

```
format for positive numbers;format for negative numbers;format
for zero;format for text
```

The first section, which ends at the first semicolon, affects positive numbers. In other words, if the number in the cell is positive, the formatting determined by this section will be used on the number. The second section determines the format of negative numbers; the third section determines the format of the value zero. The last section determines the format of text. By entering special formatting symbols into these four groupings, you can account for all kinds of values. The following sections review the procedure for creating custom formats and then review some of the formatting symbols.

Building a custom number format

1. Select the range of cells you want formatted with your custom number format.

2. Choose the Format Cells command and then click the Number page tab.

3. Enter the new formatting code into the Code entry box near the bottom of the dialog box. If the new format is a simple variation on one of the built-in formats, you may consider starting with the built-in format and modifying it. When you choose the existing format, Excel enters the code in the edit box, after which you can modify it. Otherwise, just enter your format from scratch.

4. When you have finished typing in the formatting codes, choose OK. Excel applies the new format to the cells you selected. If Excel detects a problem with the number format you created it brings up a dialog box and prompts you to change the format. Unfortunately, Excel doesn't tell you what it doesn't like — just that it has a problem.

After you add the custom format, Excel adds it to the list in the Number options. If Excel cannot place it into one of the categories, you'll see it at the bottom of the All category.

Number format symbols

Before you can design your own custom formats, you should be familiar with the formatting symbols. Study the symbols in Table 4-4 along with the built-in formats to see how they actually perform.

Some custom formats

You should now create an example of a custom number format. You will design this number format for a data entry range that requires the user to only enter numbers. You also want positive numbers to show up with commas at each thousand and two decimals. Negatives will print in red, and zeros should be displayed as -0-. If the user enters text, you want Excel to show an error message — in magenta.

To break this down, each part of the formatting codes should look like the following:

Group	Code Entry
Positive Values	#,##0.00
Negative Values	[Red]#,##0.00
Zero Values	-0-
Text Values	[Magenta]"Error"

Now we simply combine these into the following format:

#,##0.00;[Red]#,##0.00;-0-;[Magenta]"Error"

Some additional number formats you can create are listed in Table 4-5.

Table 4-4
Number Format Symbols

Symbol	Definition
0	Digit place holder. If the entry does not contain as many digits as specified by the number format, zeros are used as place holders. The number format 0000.000 displays the value 5.5 as 0005.500
#	Digit place holder. Add no extra digits or place holders to the value. The format #####.### displays the number 5.5 as 5.5.
?	Digit place holder. If the entry does not contain as many digits as specified by the number format, spaces are used as place holders. The format ????.??? displays the value 5.5 as _ _ _5.5_ _ (underscores indicate spaces in Excel).
.	Decimal point.
%	Percent sign. Add this to the end of percent formats.
,	Comma symbol. Add this to the thousands position in numbers to add commas to thousands.
$ - + ( ) / : [space]	Special symbols. Insert these anywhere in a custom format to add the symbol to the format.
"text"	Text insertion. Enter text in quotation marks to insert it into the format. The format #.## "Dollars" displays the value 5.5 as 5.5 Dollars.
*	Repeat symbol. This character causes the character immediately following it to fill the cell.
—	Adds space to the number format. Enter this character followed by any other character to add space to the format. The format #.##_) adds the space of a ")" symbol to the right edge of the value. This format is useful for controlling right-alignment in cells.
[BLACK][BLUE][CYAN] [GREEN][YELLOW][MAGENTA] [RED][WHITE][COLOR n]	Applies the specified color to the group.
m, mm, mmm, mmmm	Adds month digits to the format. Use this for date formats only. The symbols m and mm add one and two digit month values. The symbols mmm and mmmm add an abbreviated and full month name.
d, dd, ddd, dddd	Adds day digits to the date format or the day name in abbreviated or long versions
yy, yyyy	Adds a two- or four-digit year to a date format.
@	Placeholder for text. Apply this only to the fourth grouping if you want to display any text entry into the cell. Leaving the fourth group out makes Excel display the text as entered.

Table 4-5
Examples of Custom Number Formats

Code	Definition
$#,##0_);[red]($#,##0);	Hides zero values as a modification of a currency format. By eliminating the zeros section, but including the semicolon, you tell Excel to display nothing if the value in the cell is zero.
0000	Displays zip codes without dropping the leading zero. zip codes that begin with zero display properly. (Ideally, you should enter zip codes as text labels.)
000-00-0000	Displays social security numbers without having to type the dashes.
;;;	Hides data completely.
#.##*.	Adds dot trailers to a number, as in 53.5...........
*.#.##	Adds dot leaders to a number, as in 53.5
;;;@*.	Adds dot trailers to text.
;;;*.@	Adds dot leaders to text.
##0.00,	Displays values in thousands.
##0.00,,	Displays values in millions.

Applying number formats when creating formulas

Excel can do some of your number formatting for you. When you enter a formula into a cell which does not have any number formatting applied (that is, it has the General number format), the cell takes the number format from the cells that make up the formula.

Any cell reference used in a formula draws the value and the number format from the cell being referenced. For example the formula =A5 pulls the value and the number format from cell A5. If you use two or more cell references in a formula, Excel pulls the format from the last one in the formula.

As you can see, if you want to use this shortcut, you need to give some attention to the order in which you create the formula and how you format the cells you will use in the formula. Format copying only applies to number formats. None of the other format attributes, such as fonts or alignment, transfer when you create a formula.

Using Borders and Lines

You can make your worksheets much more readable by adding borders and lines to highlight totals or other important data. You can also use borders and lines to create forms and other input sheets for your data. You can put a border on the top, bottom, left, and right edge of any cell or group of cells on the worksheet. In addition, you can quickly outline a range to create a simple box.

Excel makes applying borders simple by giving you a tear-off border palette. This palette provides 12 preset borders from which you can choose — including a quick way to remove borders entirely.

Adding borders to a range

1. Select the cell(s) to which you want borders attached.
2. Click and drag to *tear off* the border palette, making it available for your formatting.
3. Click any of the border options in the palette. You can repeat the last border you set by clicking the button's face. ◖

Choose the first tool in the palette to remove borders or any of the last three to apply borders to a range of cells — as a grid pattern, a thin outline, or a thick outline.

Note that the border palette provides only a few of the options available in border design. By using the Format Cells command with the Border options, you have access to all of Excel's border powers. For example, Excel provides many more line styles for your borders, including the ability to add color to the border lines. Excel's Border options are shown in Figure 4-13.

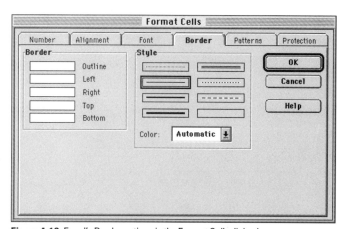

Figure 4-13: Excel's Border options in the Format Cells dialog box.

You may need to use the Border options several times to get all the border effects you want. When combining borders in a table-oriented worksheet, try to use a variety of line thicknesses to make the information easier to read.

Making Drop Shadows

Drop shadows let you highlight worksheet titles or other selected ranges in a dramatic way, as shown in Figure 4-14. A drop shadow is a kind of cell border, but it's applied differently than the other border options.

Adding a drop shadow to a range

1. Select the cell or range to which you want to add the drop shadow.

2. Choose the Toolbars command from the View menu.

3. Select the Drawing toolbar and click OK to display the drawing buttons.

4. Click the Drop Shadow button.

When you add a drop shadow like this, you are actually adding a rectangular object to the worksheet. You learn more about worksheet objects in Topic 5.

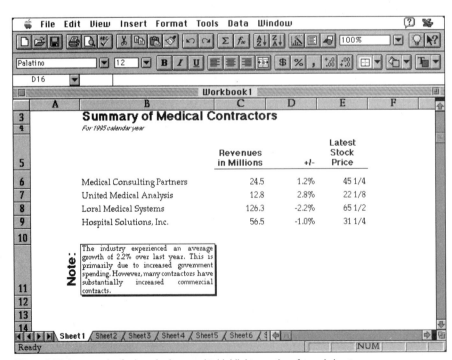

Figure 4-14: An example of a drop shadow used to highlight a portion of a worksheet.

Adding Shading and Patterns

Excel allows you to add a wide variety of colored or patterned backgrounds to cells. These backgrounds can be useful for highlighting areas of the worksheet or defining different sections of a form. Shading can often be combined with font styles — such as boldface — and font colors for best results.

Shading or coloring cells

1. Select the cell or range of cells you want to shade.

2. Click the color palette located in the Formatting toolbar. You can tear off this palette if you want to leave the color options on the screen as you work. Choose any color from the palette.

3. Remember: To repeat the previous color, you don't have to locate it in the palette again; just click the button's face. ◖◗

In addition to these color options, you can add a number of patterns to your worksheet cells. These patterns can appear in various colors — on top of the cell color you've selected. To apply a pattern choose the Cells command in the Format menu and then choose the Patterns tab. Click the Patterns drop-down list to view the 18 different patterns and 56 different colors in which the patterns can appear. Figure 4-15 shows these selections.

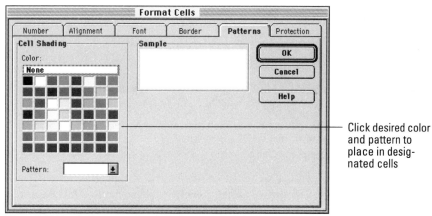

Figure 4-15: Excel's Patterns options in the Format Cells dialog box.

Remember that the pattern and the color you choose are displayed on top of the cell's overall color.

Applying a cell pattern can help you create attractive worksheets — and some extremely unattractive ones if you go too far. When formatting your worksheets, think about its purpose and try to use appropriate formatting. Some patterns make the worksheet more difficult to read and should be avoided. In general, if you're in doubt as to the appropriateness of the pattern or shading effect you are using, don't use it! It's better to make your worksheets simple and clean than to over-design them.

Select colors carefully if you're printing in black and white. Remember that colors print as shades of gray on black-and-white printers. Select colors that print in the shades you like — or don't use them at all. Sometimes colors that look great on the screen look terrible in black-and-white. Refer to Topic 8, "Printing," for more information.

Protecting Data in Cells

When you set up your worksheet and apply various formatting options to the cells, the last thing you want is for someone to come along and mess with your handy work. You can protect the data and formatting of your cells by using Excel's simple cell protection system.

Applying protection to the entire sheet

1. Choose the Tools⇨Protection⇨Protect Sheet command. The dialog box in Figure 4-16 appears on the screen.

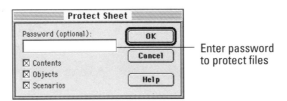

Figure 4-16: The Protect Sheet dialog box.

2. By default, Excel assumes that you want to protect all cell Contents, Objects, and Scenarios. *Contents* protects data inside cells and cell formatting. *Objects* protects the placement and formatting of objects on the worksheet. *Scenarios* protects the scenarios you've established. For more information about scenarios, refer to Topic 9.

   If you want to leave any of these unprotected, remove the check mark from the specific option.

3. Enter a password into the space provided if you want to prohibit anyone else from turning off the protection you've set. You don't have to worry about entering a password if you are simply protecting the worksheet from accidental mistakes. To forgo the password, simply leave the space blank.

4. Click OK to protect the sheet. All cells, objects, and scenarios are protected (unless you have indicated otherwise in Step 2). ⁾⁾

If desired, you can protect certain cells in the worksheet while leaving others open for change. This is useful when you want to keep formulas from being changed or accidentally erased, but you want to leave entry areas open for raw data. To allow specific cells to remain editable while the worksheet is protected, you can use the Protection options in the Format Cells dialog box.

To turn protection off again, simply use the Tools⟹Protection⟹Unprotect Sheet command. If this command does not appear in the Tools⟹Protection menu, then the sheet is already unprotected.

Removing protection from specific cells

1. If you have protected the worksheet, make sure that the worksheet is unprotected by using the Tools⟹Protection⟹Unprotect Sheet command.

2. Select the cells that you want unprotected, or editable.

3. Choose the Format Cells command. Then select the Protection page tab.

4. Click the Locked option to remove the X. This unlocks the selected cells.

5. Click OK.

6. Turn protection back on by using the Tools⟹Protection⟹Protect Sheet command as described in the previous Steps-by-Steps, "Applying Protection to the Entire Sheet." ⁾⁾

If you try to change the entry or its format settings in a protected cell, Excel presents a message telling you that the cell is protected. You have to remove protection before you can make the change. Remember that by adding a password to the Protect Sheet dialog box, you can prevent anyone else from turning off the protection.

When you leave some editable cells in a protected worksheet, pressing Tab moves the cell pointer among the editable cells. This can be useful for quick data entry within a protected worksheet. By protecting all cells that are not data entry cells, you can speed the data entry process.

When you protect a worksheet, Excel deactivates certain commands that could be used to modify the sheet. You may notice that some commands turn gray when the worksheet is protected.

Establishing Worksheet Styles

Excel lets you duplicate combinations of formatting options throughout your worksheet—without having to repeat all the options again and again. By setting up formatting styles, you can repeat these formatting combinations whenever you like. Styles are then stored by name in the Styles list, which can be added to any of the toolbars, or to a custom toolbar.

Each Excel style contains information about the same six formatting categories you find in the Format Cells dialog box: Number, Font, Alignment, Border, Patterns, and Protection. With any style, you can specify what formatting to change and what not to change. The easiest way to create and apply styles is through the use of the Style button. You can add this button to any toolbar in Excel.

Accessing the Style tool

1. Choose the Toolbars command from the View menu.

2. Click the Customize button.

3. Click the Text Formatting category.

4. Drag the Style tool to the desired toolbar. Figure 4-17 shows the tool on a modified Formatting toolbar.

5. Click the Close button. ◗

The Style button contains some preset styles for you. These include the Normal style, plus a host of numeric formatting styles, which were described earlier in this Topic under "Formatting Numbers." Note that the settings applied to the Normal style affect the default formatting for the entire worksheet. So if you want the worksheet to automatically appear with a different font, change the font associated with the Normal style. Details on modifying a style appear later in this section.

Applying a style to selected cells

1. Select the desired cell or range on the worksheet.

2. Choose the desired style from the Style drop-down list. ◗

If the selection contains cells that already have styles or formatting options applied to them, Excel asks if you want to modify the current style using the style of the selected cells. If you choose "Yes," Excel modifies the style to match that of the cell. Choose "No," and Excel applies the chosen style to the selected range, changing the style currently in use there.

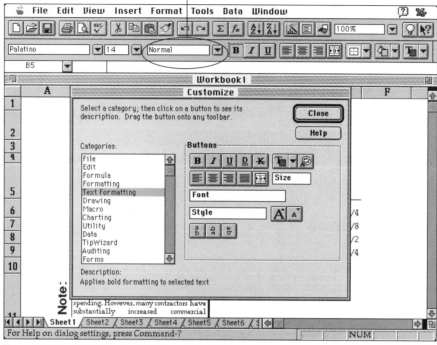

Figure 4-17: The Style tool added to the Formatting toolbar.

Creating a style

You can create a style in Excel by showing Excel what the formatting looks like on the worksheet. This method is called *style by example*.

Creating a style by example

1. Format a cell with all of the attributes you want for your style. Include any fonts, cell shading, borders, alignment, number formats, or protection options that you want. Now move the cell pointer to that cell.

2. Click the style name displayed in the Style button (which probably says Normal), and it darkens. (Don't click the down-arrow next to the name — Excel would then merely present you with a list of styles which already exist.)

3. Type in the name of the new style. Once you start typing, Excel replaces the current style name.

4. Press Return and Excel creates the style that includes the attributes of the active cell. ◖◣

Excel offers an additional way to create styles —*by definition*. Creating a style by definition is accomplished with the Style command in the Format menu.

Creating a style by definition

1. Choose the Style command from the Format menu.

2. Double-click the Style Name entry box to highlight the existing style name.

3. Type a name for your new style, replacing the highlighted name.

4. Click the Modify button. Excel presents the Format Cells dialog box.

5. Use the various page tabs and option in the Format Cells dialog box to establish the formatting you want in this new style. Click OK when finished.

6. Click Add to add the new style to the Style list. ◑

Now that the style has been created, you should save the worksheet to make the change permanent. When you display the Style list in the Standard toolbar, you will now see the name of your new style listed. You can apply this style to any cell in the worksheet by moving to that cell (or highlighting the desired range) and selecting the style's name from the Style list.

Modifying an existing style

Excel gives you an easy, *by example* way to modify a style. When you modify an existing style, all cells formatted using that style instantly reflect the changes you made. In this way, you can make sweeping changes to your worksheet's formatting without having to repeat your changes over and over. For this reason, it's a good idea to always use styles to format your worksheets.

Modifying a style by example

1. Select a cell that has been formatted with the style that you want changed.

2. Make the formatting changes you want to the cell itself. Use the Format Cells dialog box to apply the various changes to the cell. When finished, click OK to return to the worksheet.

3. Choose the same style from the Style tool on the toolbar — that is, choose the style name from the Style tool that is already applied to the cell. In this way, you'll be reapplying the style back to the same cell again.

4. Excel brings up a dialog box that asks if you want to redefine the style based on the current selection. Choose OK to redefine the style. (Choosing No reapplies the old style back to the cell, and you lose all of your formatting modifications). ◑

To modify an existing style by definition using the Style command, simply choose the Style command from the Format menu and choose the desired style from the list. Then click the Modify button to change the style's settings.

After you change an existing style, all cells formatted with that style are automatically updated. Therefore, you can make changes throughout the worksheet without repeating the same options over and over again.

Note that Excel does not reformat cells to which you have applied more formatting. Suppose you have a cell styled as Headline and then decide to bump the point size up to make it a little larger. When you change the definition of Headline, the cell does not change to reflect the modified style. So to assure that the formatting of all cells changes when you change style definitions, make sure you make all formatting changes through styles.

You can delete a style by using Delete in the Style dialog box. This button deletes the style currently displayed in the Style list. When you delete a style from the worksheet, Excel finds all the cells which you have formatted with that style and changes them to the Normal style. Excel takes you at your word when you choose the Delete button. It just goes ahead and deletes the style — no questions asked, and no second chance. You cannot choose Undo after you have deleted a style, so tread carefully.

Copying styles between workbooks

When you define a new style in Excel you can only use it in the workbook in which you created it. Excel doesn't provide a method to create a global style sheet available to all workbooks. You can, however, take styles created in one workbook and merge them into another.

Merging styles between workbooks

1. Open both the source and destination workbooks in Excel.

2. Activate the destination workbook.

3. Choose the Style command from the Format menu.

4. Choose the Merge button in the bottom-right corner of the expanded dialog box.

5. Excel presents you with a list of open workbooks — choose the source workbook and click OK.

6. Excel automatically copies all style definitions from the source workbook to the destination workbook. ◖◗

If you have any styles with the same name but different definitions in two workbooks (for example, you may have redefined the Normal style), Excel asks you if you want to merge styles with the same names. If you say yes, Excel globally redefines styles in the *destination* worksheet with those from the *source* worksheet.

To take a few styles from one worksheet and move them to another, simply copy cells which you have formatted with those styles and paste them into an inconspicuous place in the other worksheet. Excel adds the new styles to the worksheet. If any styles conflict, Excel asks you, style-by-style, if you want to use the new or old definition.

Using Templates for Formatting

You may already be aware that you can use the File⇨Save As command to save a copy of a worksheet under a different name or in a different folder from the original. This feature lets you make a number of formatting changes to a master worksheet and then save those changes under a new name.

Unfortunately, users often find themselves inadvertently saving the specific changes they make to the master file on top of the master file, which overwrites material they want to keep. To combat this problem, Microsoft created a new file format for Excel — the Template.

Worksheets created from templates cannot be inadvertently saved over the original template. Also, templates act as the starting point for your worksheets. These templates may contain the skeleton of a worksheet, customized number formats, customized styles, and more. All these things will be available in the worksheets you create from the template. Information saved with templates includes:

◆ Outline settings

◆ Data Consolidate settings

◆ Styles

◆ Display settings

◆ Calculation settings

◆ Defined Names

◆ Print Area/Print Titles

◆ Database settings

Start by creating a normal worksheet that contains the elements you want to repeat over and over in other worksheets. These elements can be anything from styles to actual data and calculations. Then follow these steps for turning the worksheet into a template:

Creating a template

1. Activate the worksheet you want to make into a template.

2. Choose Save As from the File menu.

3. Choose Template from the Save File As Type drop-down list.

4. Type the name of the new template and choose OK. Excel saves the file as a template. ◀

When you open a template you have created, Excel automatically makes a copy of the file and won't allow you to save over the old one (unless you follow the same steps as above).

You may have noticed that Excel's File⇨New dialog box lets you pick from a scrolling list of file types to create. You can add to that list by saving a template in the Excel Startup folder located in the System folder. If you use a template often and don't want to have to navigate through folders to find it, copy or move it into the Excel Startup folder. The next time you choose File⇨New, Excel will let you open the new template worksheet you want.

Using Automatic Table Formats

Microsoft has built a lot of *smarts* into Excel when it comes to formatting data. These new features makes Excel easier to use. One example is the AutoFormat command. This command applies any of a number of predefined table formats (including font sizes, font styles, borders, and shading) to a table in just one step, which can save you a tremendous amount of time. To use the AutoFormat command, follow these steps:

Applying automatic table formats

1. Select a cell somewhere within the table. Make sure that the table contains headings at the top. It may or may not contain totals along the bottom or sides.

2. Choose AutoFormat from the Format menu. The dialog box in Figure 4-18 appears.

3. Choose the format you want to apply from the Table Format list box. Click OK button to apply that format. ◀

It's that easy. Note that you can eliminate certain aspects of the AutoFormat command by choosing the Options button and removing the check mark from any formatting options that you don't want to apply to the selected table.

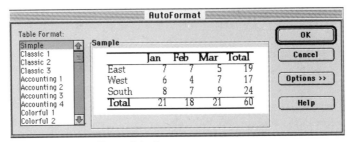

Figure 4-18: The AutoFormat dialog box.

*Q*uick Tips

Using restraint when selecting fonts

When you select fonts for your worksheets, try to choose no more than three different type faces. Instead of using different faces to emphasize the different parts of your worksheets, use variations of size and style within the same face. Try to establish a font scheme that you apply throughout an application. The scheme should include three or four *levels* of data, including three styles for headings, one style for the body, and possibly another for special data, such as footnotes.

Creating instant access to the Format Cells dialog box

You can quickly bring up the Format Cells dialog box by holding Control (or Command-Option) and clicking any cell. Then select Format Cells from the shortcut menu.

Other shortcuts include:

Command-Shift-B	Boldface
Command-Shift-I	Italics
Control-Shift-P	Point size change (with Formatting toolbar active)
Control-Shift-F	Font change (with Formatting toolbar active)
Command-Shift-U	Underline

Previewing your work

Choose Print Preview from the File menu to view how a worksheet will appear with fonts and other attributes before it is printed.

Clearing up your printout

Colors added to a worksheet print as patterns on black-and-white printers. To avoid having these patterns show up in the cells of a worksheet, choose the Black and White Cells check box from the Page Setup dialog box. Choosing this option results in text printed in black-and-white (regardless of the actual color on the worksheet) and text boxes printed with a white background.

Drawing and Annotating

Overview

Excel is not just a spreadsheet program to crunch numbers; it has some powerful drawing capabilities as well. Using these drawing features, you can annotate your worksheet data, enhance the appearance of charts and reports, and even create simple illustrations, such as logos, forms, and diagrams. Figures 5-1 through 5-3 show some examples of Excel's drawing features.

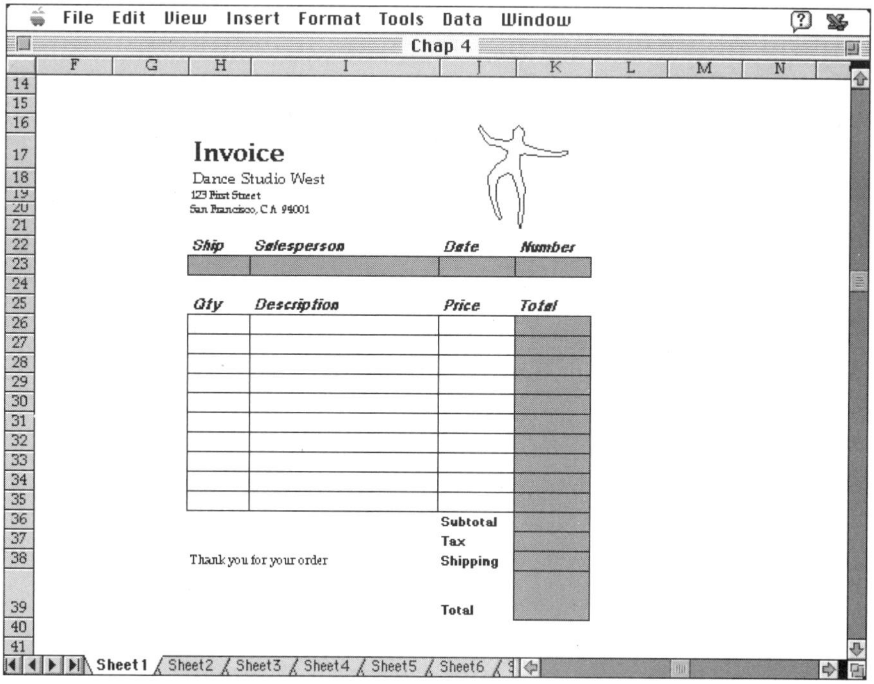

Figure 5-1: Create attractive business forms by adding imported art, text boxes, and picture objects (using the camera tool).

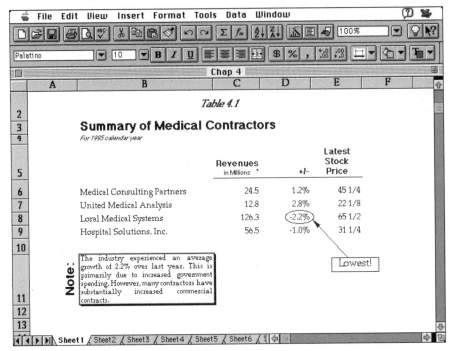

Figure 5-2: Adding annotations to your worksheets and charts.

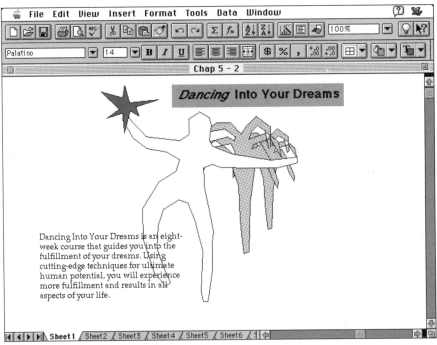

Figure 5-3: Using Excel as a simple drawing package.

Excel's drawing features are *object oriented*, which means that illustrations are created from a series of objects that combine to form the image. Objects consist of circles, squares, polygons, and lines, as well as freehand lines and shapes. Even simple objects placed together on the worksheet, overlapping each other in precise ways, can form some intricate and compelling images.

Excel's Drawing Tools

Excel's drawing tools appear on the Drawing toolbar, available through the View Toolbars command or by holding Command-Shift as you click any toolbar and select Drawing from the list that appears. The Drawing toolbar appears as follows:

Using these tools you can create logos, simple illustrations, and graphic enhancements for spreadsheets and charts. Excel's drawing tools are no match for a high-end graphics program, but you'll probably be surprised at just how useful and flexible they are. When you exceed Excel's drawing capabilities, you can always import images from other drawing packages, as described later in this topic. Here are descriptions of Excel's drawing tools:

- ◆ **Line.** Select this tool and then click and drag on the worksheet to draw lines. Hold Shift as you draw to create horizontal lines, vertical lines, or lines at a 45-degree angle.

- ◆ **Arrow.** Select this tool and then click and drag on the worksheet to draw arrows. Hold Shift as you draw to draw horizontal arrows, vertical arrows, or arrows at a 45-degree angle. You can change the arrow style by double-clicking the finished arrow and selecting from the Pattern options.

- ◆ **Freehand.** Select this tool and then drag the mouse on the worksheet to draw curved lines.

- ◆ **Rectangle.** Select this tool and then drag on the worksheet to create squares and rectangles. Hold Shift down to draw perfect squares.

- ◆ **Ellipse.** Select this tool and then drag on the worksheet to create ellipses. Hold Shift down to draw perfect circles.

- ◆ **Arc.** Select this tool and then drag on the worksheet to create semicircles, or arcs. Semicircles are exactly one-quarter of an ellipse. Hold Shift down to draw perfect quarter-circles.

- ◆ **Freeform.** Select this tool and then click several times to create each side of the polygon; double-click to finish the shape. You can also connect the beginning and end of the freeform to create complete shapes.

◆ **Text Box.** Select this tool and then drag on the worksheet to create text boxes into which you can type text. Text boxes can be formatted with various fonts and character attributes; you can place floating text boxes on the worksheet or a chart.

◆ **Selection.** Select this tool and then drag to surround, or select, other objects. Use this tool when you're through drawing and want to manipulate objects on the worksheet.

◆ **Reshape.** Select this tool and then click a polygon to modify the sides of a polygon or freehand shape. You can move or extend any side to change the shape of the object.

◆ **Group.** Select several objects and then click this tool to unite the separate objects into a single object that behaves as one.

◆ **Ungroup.** Select a grouped object and then click this tool to separate the grouped object into individual objects again.

◆ **Bring to Front.** Select an object and then click this tool to move it to the front of the others. This tool is useful when objects overlap each other and you want to bring one of them to the forefront.

◆ **Send to Back.** Select an object and then click this tool to move it to the back of others.

◆ **Color Changer.** Select an object and then click this tool to access colors and patterns for the object.

◆ **Shadow.** Select an object and then click this tool to add a shadow to the object, including lines and freehand shapes.

◆ **Drawing toolbar.** Select this tool (which appears on the Standard toolbar) to show or hide the Drawing toolbar.

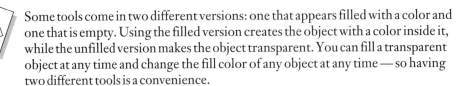

Some tools come in two different versions: one that appears filled with a color and one that is empty. Using the filled version creates the object with a color inside it, while the unfilled version makes the object transparent. You can fill a transparent object at any time and change the fill color of any object at any time — so having two different tools is a convenience.

Besides these tools, which appear on the Drawing toolbar, Excel includes a few other tools for drawing on the worksheet. Figure 5-4 shows some additional drawing tools.

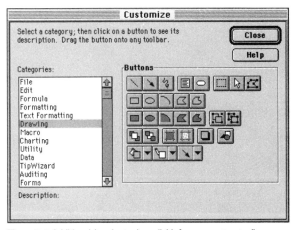

Figure 5-4: Additional drawing tools available for your custom toolbars.

Basic Drawing Techniques

Most of Excel's drawing tools work the same way. You first click the tool and then click and drag on the worksheet to draw the object inside a box. This procedure applies to rectangles, ovals, text boxes, charts, buttons, arcs, lines, and arrows. Figure 5-5 illustrates the drawing procedure.

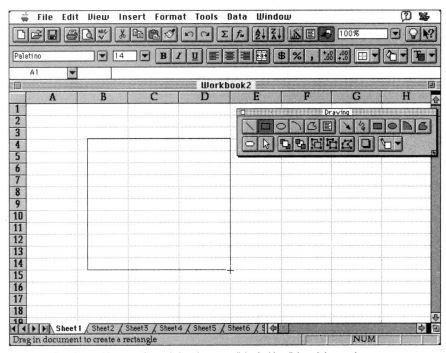

Figure 5-5: Drawing an object onto the worksheet is accomplished with a click-and-drag motion.

If you're drawing freehand lines, the procedure is the same, but the line follows each and every movement of the mouse as if you were drawing with a pencil.

Polygons and freehand polygons require a slightly different approach. To draw a polygon with straight sides, just click on the tool and then click once on the worksheet to pinpoint the first side. This action is called *anchoring* the side. Now click again in another spot to place the side between the first and second spots. Continue to click to position each side. When finished, double-click to complete the shape. You can double-click back at the beginning of the first side to close the shape or anywhere else to leave the last side open.

Technically, an open polygon is really not a polygon at all but a combination of straight lines. These objects are extremely useful in drawings.

You draw text boxes just as you would draw a rectangle, except that after drawing the object you can type text into it. Just begin typing immediately after drawing the text box. Excel automatically wraps each line when you type past the end. Press Return to start a new line. (More on editing text boxes later in this Topic under "Working with Text Boxes".)

Drawing restrained shapes

By holding Shift down as you draw certain objects, you can create perfect circles, perfect squares, and other *restrained* shapes. Just click on the tool, press and hold Shift, and then draw the object. Be sure to release the mouse button before releasing Shift to complete the procedure.

The Oval tool creates perfect circles; the Arc tool creates perfect quarter-circles; and the Rectangle tool creates perfect squares. Also, the Text Box tool creates a perfect square when restrained with Shift. Restraining lines and arrows makes horizontal, vertical, or 45-degree lines.

Drawing along the cell grid

If you hold Command as you draw an object, Excel makes it fit into the current cell grid. In other words, the object fits inside a range of cells, which can be useful for keeping lines and boxes aligned with worksheet data.

You can always edit an object later if you no longer want it to adhere to the worksheet grid, and you can move an object off the grid while retaining its exact size and shape. For details on moving and sizing objects, refer to the section, "Modifying Objects" later in this topic.

Using the Camera button

The Camera button, located in the Utility toolbar, is unique among the drawing tools. Its purpose is to take a snapshot of any highlighted range of cells in the worksheet. The resulting picture can be placed in the same worksheet or any other worksheet and behaves as a single graphic object. In addition, the picture is linked to the original data. So if you change the original in any way, the picture changes right along with the original (see Figure 5-6).

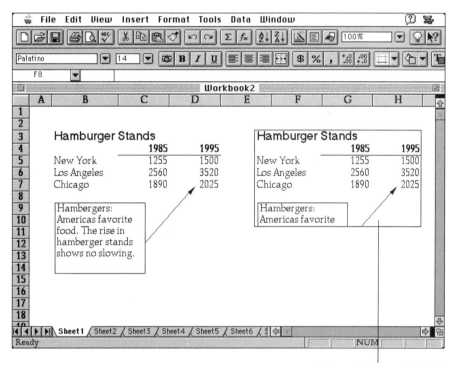

Picture of the range B3: DID

Figure 5-6: Creating a picture of a worksheet range. Anything inside the range becomes part of the picture.

Notice that the picture includes not only the text and data from the image area but also the graphics from the area. Anything appearing inside the image area becomes part of the picture. Some uses for these snapshots include the following:

◆ If you want to use a date, value, or formula as a heading over several columns and find that it will not spill over into adjacent cells, try creating the heading in a remote area of the worksheet, taking a picture of it, and moving the picture over the columns. The picture can be a composite of text and graphics plus any cell formatting you've applied.

◆ You can take a picture of a form or display area that contains data you don't want changed. The picture shows the current data but does not allow it to be changed (unless you change the original).

◆ You can take a picture of any entire print area if you want to enlarge or reduce the image for printing, viewing, or any other desired purpose.

◆ You can use pictures to copy Excel data into other programs, such as a word processor. The picture will be copied into the program as a single graphic object rather than as a table of values. The picture will still be linked to the original data and all formatting and graphics in the image area.

◆ You can use pictures to create forms to overcome column-width limitations. You can think of pictures as worksheet cells that can be placed anywhere on the worksheet — rather than in a row-column structure. This feature can be valuable for creating forms. For example, you can create pieces of the form in different areas of the workbook and then combine these pieces into the final form using pictures.

To create a picture, you must first add the Camera button to any toolbar by entering the toolbar customization dialog box, as described in Topic 3. With the Camera button displayed on a toolbar, just highlight any range of cells on the worksheet and then click the Camera button. Click once on the worksheet to place the picture. You can click a different workbook to move the picture into a different file if you like.

Modifying Objects

Once you have drawn an object you can still change it size, shape, and location on the worksheet. You first select the object(s) you want to modify, and then you can use the mouse to make the changes. You can change the size and shape of an object, its location on the worksheet, copy and delete objects, and even protect objects from being moved or changed. The following sections provide the details.

Selecting objects

Before you can modify objects, you must know how to select them. Selecting objects tells Excel which objects you want to work on — change the size, shape, or border, add color, and so on. You can select a single object or several objects in a group.

To select an object, just click the object. Small black squares, called *size boxes*, appear around its edges. When the size boxes appear, you know the object is selected. You use these to modify the size and shape of the object.

To select more than one object, hold Shift down as you click each object. You can also click the Selection button and then click and drag in the worksheet to surround the desired objects. All objects completely inside the selection box will be selected.

The drawing shortcut menu

When an object is selected, the shortcut menu contains several Edit and Format menu options, as well as several new options relative to drawings, as shown in the following figure. Remember, to display the shortcut menu, press Ctrl (or Option-Command) and click the mouse on the object.

See if you can locate other shortcut menus throughout Excel. Just press and hold the Ctrl key (or Option-Command) and click on various parts of Excel. You'll find shortcut menus all over the place.

Cut
Copy
Paste
Clear
Edit Object
Format Object...
Bring to Front
Send to Back
Group
Assign Macro...

Moving and sizing objects

You can move any object around the worksheet by clicking it and dragging it to another location. If you want to make large jumps, you may find it easier to use the Cut and Paste commands. If you are moving several objects, try grouping them as a single object before moving them. Then you may wish to separate them again to move them individually.

Changing an object's size and shape.

1. To change the size and shape of an object, select the object by clicking it. You know that the object is selected if it has size boxes around its edges.

2. Now click and drag on any of the size boxes to change the size and shape of the object. Dragging a corner size box lets you change two sides at the same time. Of course, straight lines contain only two size boxes — one on each end of the line. ◖

If you hold Command down as you drag on a size box, the sides you are moving adhere to the worksheet grid. Also, you can enlarge or reduce an object without changing its overall proportions by holding Shift down as you drag on a corner size box. This technique is especially useful for pictures and grouped objects. Be sure to release the mouse button before you release Shift.

Besides changing the overall size and shape of an image, you can make modifications to all sides of a polygon or freehand shape. Just select the object (any freehand line, polygon, or freehand polygon) and click the Polygon Editing tool. Figure 5-7 shows a freehand line at this point. You can now drag on any of the size boxes to change the shape, as shown in Figure 5-8.

Topic 5
Drawing and Annotating

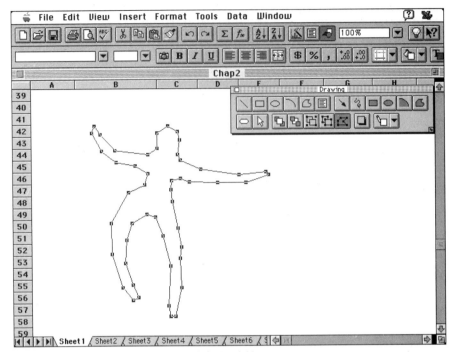

Figure 5-7: The Reshape tool highlights all sides of a freehand object.

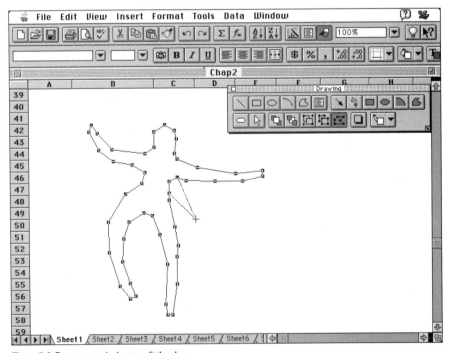

Figure 5-8: Drag on any size box to edit the shape.

Copying and deleting objects

The Copy and Paste commands in the Edit menu apply to any selected objects. You can Copy an object by selecting it and choosing Copy and Paste. You can delete an object by selecting it and choosing Cut.

Both the Copy and Cut commands place the object on the clipboard until you remove it. So you can always use the Paste command to duplicate or restore the object.

Copying an object

1. Select the object you want to copy.

2. Place the mouse pointer on an edge of the object, but not on a selection handle.

3. Press Option. The mouse pointer appears as a black arrow with a plus sign.

4. Drag the copy of the object to the desired location and then release the mouse button. **◖**

As with moving, pressing Shift as you drag the object limits movement to horizontal and vertical directions. Pressing Command while you drag the object aligns the copied object to the worksheet gridlines.

Protecting and hiding objects

You can protect an object from being moved or changed by accessing the protection options in the Format Cells dialog box.

Protecting an object

1. Select the object.

2. Choose the Object command from the Format menu.

3. Click the Protection tab.

4. Make sure the Locked option is chosen for the object.

5. Choose the Tools⇨Protection⇨Protect Sheet command.

6. Make sure the Objects option is selected and click OK. **◖**

If you don't want to activate the protection for the worksheet cells, just uncheck the Cells option in the Protect Document dialog box (but make sure to leave the Objects option checked).

Note that objects and cells are automatically locked by Excel when you create them—but the worksheet itself starts out unprotected, so you don't notice that your cells and objects are locked. In other words, all objects and cells are marked and ready to be locked from the start. Just enable worksheet protection with the Tools⇨Protection⇨Protect Sheet command, and they will all be locked. You may want to use the Format Cells dialog box to *unlock* some objects.

Displacing objects with inserted cells

Even if you've protected objects, you can still displace them when you insert rows, columns, or blocks of cells into the worksheet. In addition, if you change the widths of columns or the heights of rows, you will affect the size and shape of the object on top of those changed columns and rows.

To control the relationship between an object and the worksheet cells, use the Properties options in the Format Object dialog box. The Properties page of the Format Object dialog box offers four options:

◆ **Move and size with cells.** Allows changes to cells to affect the objects on top of them. For example, expanding a column's width expands the width of the object overlapping that column. Inserting a column moves the object aside to make room.

◆ **Move but don't size with cells.** Prohibits an object from expanding or contracting when you change row heights or column widths. However, inserting rows or columns above or to the left of an object still displaces it.

◆ **Don't move or size with cells.** Completely locks the object with regard to column widths and row heights; inserting rows and columns will not change the object.

◆ **Print object.** Includes the object in the printout of the worksheet. Uncheck this option to eliminate the object from the printout.

Figure 5-9 shows three objects with a different option from the Format Object dialog box applied to each. Figure 5-10 shows these objects after inserting a new column and changing some column widths and row heights. The column was inserted at column C and moved the top two objects over. Only the object using the *Don't move or size with cells* option remained in place. Similarly, when columns F, G, and H were narrowed, only the object using the *Move and size with cells* option was narrowed.

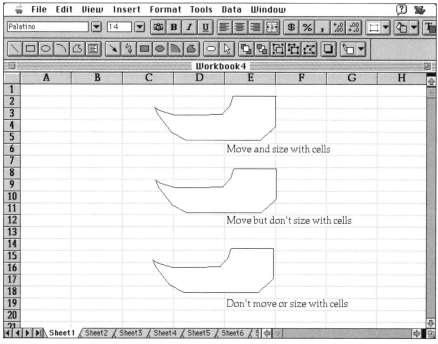

Figure 5-9: An object with various Object Properties applied.

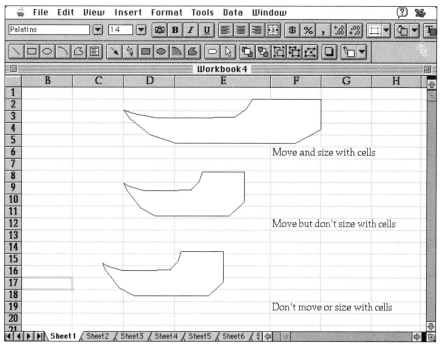

Figure 5-10: Objects after inserting a column and changing row heights and column widths.

Formatting objects with patterns

Many object formatting options appear in the Patterns page of the Format Object dialog box. This page offers formatting options for the interior — fill — and border of your objects (depending on the object selected). To change a pattern, first select the object you want to format and then select the Format Object command. Now click the Patterns page tab. Alternatively, you can double-click the object to bring up the Patterns dialog box for that object. Figure 5-11 shows the Patterns options dialog box for lines and arrows; Figure 5-12 shows the Patterns options dialog box for all other objects.

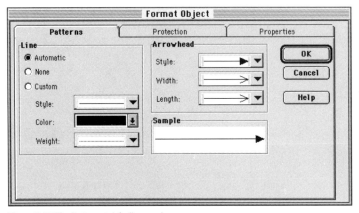

Figure 5-11: The Patterns tab for lines and arrows.

Choose None for the fill to make an object transparent. Choose None for the border to remove the box (border) surrounding the object. For example, if you select None for both the border and fill of a text box, you can make the text appear to float on the worksheet.

When selecting a text box for formatting, be sure to click the border of the box to select it. Then choose the Format Object command. Or you can double-click the edge of the text box to bring up the Format Object dialog box. Text boxes can be formatted like any rectangular object. Double-clicking in the middle of the text box does not produce the Format Object dialog box; rather, it allows you to enter text into the box.

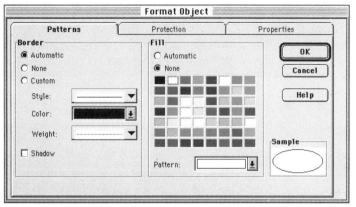

Figure 5-12: The Patterns tab for polygons, ovals, and rectangles.

Grouping and Overlapping Objects

Excel's drawing tools may not rival sophisticated drawing software, but you can create some interesting things with them—particularly when you combine and overlap many objects into one composite drawing. A composite drawing may consist of several individual objects. By overlapping these objects in a precise order, you can achieve various effects. Figure 5-13 shows an example of overlapped objects.

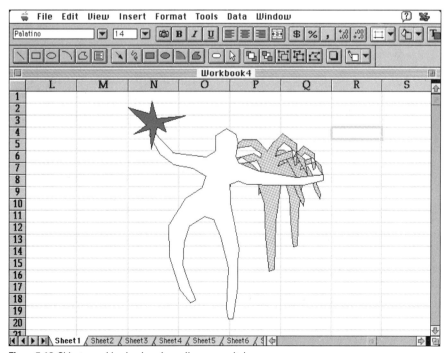

Figure 5-13: Objects combined and overlapped in a composite image.

To overlap objects, you'll need the Bring to Front and Send to Back buttons on the drawing toolbar. (The Bring to Front button is pictured at the top in the margin.) These buttons move the selected object to the front of all other objects or behind them (respectively). To achieve the proper overlap order, you may need to send objects to the back several times. Once the overlap order is established, you can move the objects around without changing the order.

Note that all objects are "in front of" data that appears in cells on the worksheet. If you want text to appear in your drawing, consider using a text box.

When you combine objects in a composite image, you may find it easier to work with several objects at the same time. Manipulating objects in groups saves time and makes your work easier. Earlier you learned that you can select several objects at the same time by using the Selection tool or by holding Shift as you click each object. After you have selected several objects, you can move them together as a unit.

You may find it convenient to group objects together more permanently. Several objects can act as a single object — making it easier to modify their sizes and shapes uniformly. To combine objects into a group, follow these steps:

Grouping objects

1. Select all the objects that you want to combine, pressing Shift as you click each object.

2. Select Placement Group command from the Format menu or click the Group Objects button in the Drawing toolbar. The objects are now grouped together. **⋒**

You can now add this combined object to others to form another group if you like, or you can format the object as a single unit. To remove grouping, select the object and then use the Placement Ungroup command in the Format menu. You'll have to ungroup objects in the same order in which you grouped them if you have used grouped objects inside other groups.

Note that objects can overlap each other. The order in which you draw objects determines which one is "on top." Objects drawn first are at the bottom, although all objects are above the worksheet. You'll find that the way objects overlap can have an important effect on your images. If an object is beneath another, you can bring it to the top by selecting it and using the Placement⇨Bring to Front command in the Format menu (or by clicking the Bring to Front tool in the Drawing toolbar). Send an object to the back of others using the Placement⇨Send to Back command in the Format menu (or the Send to Back tool).

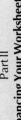

Working with Text Boxes

Placing text inside text boxes gives you total control over the appearance of the text. Because the text box is "detached" from the worksheet grid, you can move the text anywhere within the worksheet. You don't have to make the text fit into the worksheet grid. This feature is useful for placing notes and titles into your worksheets.

Creating a text box is identical to creating a rectangle object on the worksheet, except that you begin with the text box button. Click this button and then drag on the worksheet to create the text box. You can then immediately type information into the box. When you are finished typing into the box, click anywhere in the worksheet, and the edit cursor is removed from the text box.

To edit the text inside a text box, you must first place the cursor into the box. Do this by clicking once on the text box to select it and then again to place the cursor inside the box. After the cursor is inside the text box, you can move it around using the arrow keys or other text editing commands discussed in Topic 2. When finished, click outside the text box.

You can change the size and shape of the text box by clicking the text box to select it. Then you can drag on the selection boxes that appear around the text box. Double-clicking the text box brings up the Object Properties dialog box, but two slow clicks places the edit cursor into the box. You can change the font of specific text inside the box by highlighting the text and then choosing the Format⇨Object command. The font settings you select apply only to the highlighted text. See Figure 5-14 for an example of font changes within a text box.

Remember that the text box itself is a worksheet object, just like a rectangle or oval. You can change its color, pattern, and border properties through the Object Properties dialog box. Just double-click the text box to view these properties. Figure 5-14 shows text boxes with different box properties in view. Note that you can change the font of the text inside the box through the Object Properties dialog box. Likewise, the alignment settings in the Object Properties dialog box change the alignment of all text inside the box.

You can use various toolbar buttons to format the text inside a text box. Just highlight the desired text inside the box and click the desired button. Some buttons, such as the alignment buttons, format the entire text box at the same time.

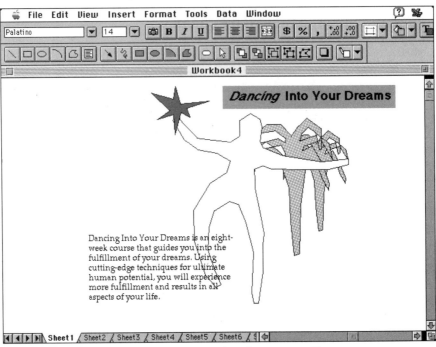

Figure 5-14: Placing text inside text boxes gives you control over the appearance of the text.

Using External Art with Excel

If Excel's drawing capabilities do not meet your needs, you can import art from outside sources, such as Illustrator, MacDraw, and other programs. The procedure is simple, requiring that you copy the image from the outside source and then paste it into Excel.

Using external art

1. Start the program that contains the art you want to use in Excel. Get the desired image onto the screen.

2. Copy the image using the program's Copy procedure. Usually, you can use Command-C.

3. Switch to Excel using the System 7 program switching procedure. Alternatively, you can quit the program and start running Excel.

4. Choose Edit⇨Paste inside the desired Excel worksheet to paste the image into the worksheet. ◖◗

Note that the original structure of the image determines the quality of the imported picture. For example, bitmapped images may appear jagged when you import them into Excel. However, object-oriented art retains its proper shape. As an alternative, you can use the Publish and Subscribe features of System 7 to use outside art inside Excel. In such a case, the image is dynamically linked from Excel to the originating program, such that changes that you make to the original are updated in the copy in Excel.

 You can convert imported images or text into bitmapped pictures by pasting the object into Excel as a picture. Do this by holding the Shift key down when you click the Edit menu. Then choose the Paste Picture command.

Quick Tips

Understanding that charts are objects

When you create an imbedded chart on a worksheet, you can use the same moving and resizing techniques that you used for text boxes, lines, or other graphic objects on the worksheet. For more information on creating imbedded charts, turn to Topic 11.

Selecting an object with no border or fill

When you format an object with no border or fill, you can sometimes have a hard time selecting it. Clicking in the middle usually doesn't work. You need to move the mouse pointer around at the edge of the object. When you hit the edge of the elusive object, the mouse pointer changes from the standard heavy cross to a black arrow. When you see the arrow, click the mouse, and you'll see the object's selection handles.

Instant formatting

To format an object instantly, just point at it and double-click. Excel selects the object and brings up the Format Object dialog box, so that you can make the desired changes.

Printing

Overview

This topic explains Excel's printing features and how to get the most from your printed documents. Excel offers numerous printing enhancement features that help make your printouts more professional and easier to read. Excel takes full advantage of your printer's capabilities by letting you access the printer's built-in fonts, resolution modes, and other settings. Here's what you learn in this topic:

◆ The basic printing process

◆ How to print different parts of a worksheet

◆ How to control long printouts

◆ Details about the Page Setup options

◆ Details about the Print options

◆ How to preview the printout on the screen before printing

The Basic Printing Process

Printing involves a simple four-step process. First, this basic process is described. Later, the various printer and page setup options are detailed.

1. **Select the correct printer using the Chooser utility in the Apple menu.** As with all Macintosh Applications, you must choose the desired printer from the Chooser utility before printing. If you use the same printer in all your applications, chances are, the correct printer is already selected in the Chooser. For more information on installing and selecting printers on your Macintosh, see *Macs For Dummies* and *MORE Macs For Dummies* (published by IDG Books).

2. **Choose File⇨Page Setup to specify the worksheet range you want to print along with any other enhancements.** In the Page Setup dialog box, you can specify exactly what range you want to print. You can also add headers, footers, page numbers, row and column headings, and gridlines to your printouts. In addition, you can change the page margins and even the magnification of the final report.

3. **Preview the printout with the File⇨Print Preview command.** (Or you can choose the Preview Printout button in the Page Setup dialog box.) This option gives you an on-screen version of the final printout, including any fonts and special formatting. The preview feature even simulates any printer-specific results, such as gray shades and patterns. If you like what you see in the preview, you can print directly from the preview screen, or you can change the page margins right on the preview. You can also make changes to the Page Setup options by moving to the Page Setup dialog box directly from the preview screen.

4. **Print the report using the File⇨Print command — or print directly from the preview screen.** Make sure that the printer is connected and ready. Before printing, Excel gives you the opportunity to set the number of copies, the page range, and other print options.

Of course, some of these steps are optional. You don't have to preview the printout before printing, and you don't have to use Page Setup options to enhance the basic printout. Still, you'll find this basic procedure worth following. The next few sections in this topic describe each of these steps.

You can quickly print a highlighted range without using the Page Setup command. Just highlight the range you want to print on the desired worksheet page and then choose the File⇨Print command. In the Print dialog box, choose the Selection option under the Print options in the bottom-left corner. Choose OK to print the selection. You can use the Selected Sheets option to print highlighted worksheets.

Selecting Items for the Printout

With the correct printer installed and selected, you're ready to begin printing. Begin by telling Excel what you want included in the printout. Besides choosing the worksheet range you want to print, you can add row and column titles to the printout, headers and footers, and worksheet elements (gridlines, column and row indicators, and so on).

Selecting the area to print

To set the print area and other elements of the printout, choose the File⇨Page Setup command and select the Sheet tab (see Figure 6-1).

```
                          Page Setup
 ┌──────────┬──────────┬───────────────┬──────────────┐
 │   Page   │ Margins  │ Header/Footer │    Sheet     │
 └──────────┴──────────┴───────────────┴──────────────┘
 Print Area:  [                              ]    ┌─────────────┐
 ┌─Print Titles───────────────────────────┐       │     OK      │
 │ Rows to Repeat at Top:    [          ]  │       └─────────────┘
 │                                         │       ┌─────────────┐
 │ Columns to Repeat at Left: [         ]  │       │   Cancel    │
 └─────────────────────────────────────────┘       └─────────────┘
 ┌─Print──────────────────────────────────┐       ┌─────────────┐
 │ ☐ Gridlines    ☐ Black and White        │       │   Print...  │
 │ ☐ Notes        ☐ Row and Column Headings│       └─────────────┘
 │ ☐ Draft Quality                         │       ┌─────────────┐
 └─────────────────────────────────────────┘       │Print Preview│
 ┌─Page Order─────────────────────────────┐        └─────────────┘
 │ ◉ Down, then Across                     │        ┌─────────────┐
 │ ○ Across, then Down      [📄→📄]         │        │  Options... │
 └─────────────────────────────────────────┘        └─────────────┘
                                                    ┌─────────────┐
                                                    │    Help     │
                                                    └─────────────┘
```

Figure 6-1: The Sheet tab in the Page Setup dialog box.

Type the desired range reference into the Print Area box to specify a print range. You can use a range name and include a page reference if desired (for example, Sheet 2!SALES to print the range named SALES on Sheet 2 of the workbook). You do not need a worksheet reference if the range is located on the active worksheet.

Specifying the print area

1. Choose the Page Setup command in the File menu.

2. Select the Sheet tab from the Page Setup dialog box (see Figure 6-1).

3. Type the desired range into the Print Area box. Alternatively, you can click to place the cursor inside the Print Area box and highlight the range on the worksheet itself. Excel enters the reference of the range you highlight into the Print Area box. You may want to move the Page Setup dialog box to the corner of the screen while you do this. ◖◗

If you don't choose a print area, Excel automatically prints the entire active worksheet — that is, the worksheet that is currently in view. If desired, you can print the entire workbook or a selected range by choosing the File⇨Print command and selecting from the Print options in the bottom-left corner of the dialog box. These settings override the print area specified in the Page Setup dialog box.

You can switch among different established print areas by using the reporting features in Excel, which are explained later in this topic, under "Printing Reports."

You can print specific selections from several worksheets at the same time by setting up a group. Hold down Command and click all the pages you want to include in the printout. Using the File⇨Print command, select the print area on the top sheet. Choose the Selection option in the Print dialog box, and the same range is printed from all the sheets.

Hiding rows and columns from the printout

You can hide rows or columns if you don't want them to appear in the printout. By hiding certain rows and columns, you can condense a worksheet to a much smaller, contiguous range of cells for printing — when you may otherwise have to select noncontiguous ranges. You can hide rows or columns using the Column Width and Row Height commands in the Format menu or by dragging on the column and row separator lines. Refer to Topic 3 for more information on changing (and hiding) columns and rows.

Adding print titles

When you print long tables of data, you may find it helpful to add titles to the top or left side of every page of the printout. Rather than add them to the worksheet, you can have Excel print these titles from the main column titles on the page.

To set the titles for the printout just select the File⇨Page Setup command and choose the Sheet tab. Place the cursor inside the Rows to Repeat at Top box and then click the worksheet to select the rows containing the titles. Note that Excel lets you select only entire rows. As you highlight rows, they are entered into the dialog box.

You can also have titles along the left edge of each page on the printout by using the Columns to Repeat at Left entry box and indicating the desired columns.

Note that if you add column titles to the printout, you should not include the same rows inside the print area. Otherwise, the titles print twice on the first page — once as part of the data range and once as column titles.

Note that your print titles don't actually have to be located above the columns; they can, in fact, be taken from any row on the worksheet. When you print any column in the worksheet, Excel prints the corresponding cell from the title row.

Print titles or column text?

Generally, this choice depends on the nature of your worksheet. Using a header to display the title of a report makes several extra rows available for data to be displayed on screen. A header, however, cannot be used to describe the data in your columns. In most cases, use a header (or footer) to display information about your printouts—date, time, page numbers, and so on.

Adding worksheet elements to the printout

Excel lets you add worksheet elements to the printout, including the worksheet gridlines, row and column indicators, and more. These options are located on the Sheet tab of the Page Setup dialog box. Five check boxes let you add or remove specific elements from your printout (see Table 6-1).

Table 6-1
Worksheet Elements for Printing

Option	What It Does
Gridlines	Adds or removes the worksheet gridlines from the printout. Note that the status of gridlines displayed on the screen has no affect on this option.
Notes	Includes or excludes cell notes in the printout. For information about creating cell notes, refer to Topic 2.
Draft Quality	Prints the report in draft mode when selected. This option can be useful for quick, text-only printouts.
Black and White	Determines whether the printout will be in black and white or color.
Row and Column Headings	Adds the worksheet row and column indicators to the printout. This option can be useful for troubleshooting your worksheets.

Printing in black and white vs. color

If you've added a lot of color to your worksheets, such as displaying fonts in different colors and adding background colors to cells, you may find the results less than pleasing on a black-and-white printer. As a result, you may decide to remove the colors and print data in black on a white page.

You can remove the colors from the printout without having to remove them from the worksheet. Just select the Black and White option in the Printer Setup dialog box. When this option is active, your printer ignores the color settings.

On the other hand, you may want to print colors as shades of gray on your black-and-white printer. You can apply different shades to your worksheet to add contrast and interest. When colors are printed on a black-and-white printer, they are translated into various gray shades. However, the colors that look best together on the screen may not produce the best gray shades. Consequently, you should select colors in your worksheet specifically for their black-and-white results.

Adding headers, footers, and page numbers

Among the most important options in the Page Setup dialog box are the Header and Footer options located on the Header/Footer tab. These options let you add a line of text to the top and/or bottom of each page in the printout. Headers and footers are often used to display the name of the report, the page number, the date, and other pertinent information.

Excel automatically prints a header and footer onto your reports unless you remove or change them. The default header is simply the name of the file; the default footer contains only the page number. To remove the default header and footer or change them to your own information, click the Header or Footer tab in the Page Setup dialog box. The Header/Footer options are shown in Figure 6-2.

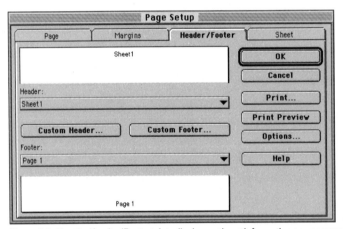

Figure 6-2: Use the Header/Footer tab to display pertinent information on your report.

To choose a different header and footer, click the drop-down lists containing the built-in formats. Numerous preexisting header and footer styles are available to choose from. Figure 6-3 shows the footer list.

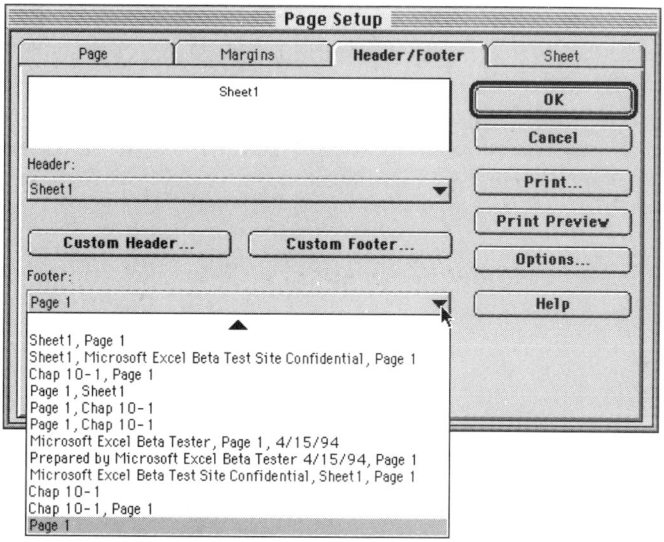

Figure 6-3: The built-in footer styles.

You can also create custom headers and footers by clicking the Custom Header and Custom Footer buttons (see Figure 6-4).

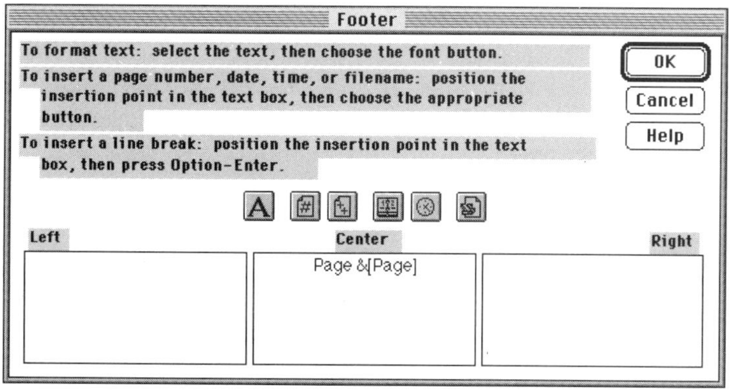

Figure 6-4: You can create a custom header and footer.

Notice that the footer (or header) consists of three sections. You can enter data into any or all of these three sections, depending on the desired result. Information in the left section begins at the left margin and extends to the right; information in the right section begins at the right margin and extends to the left; information in the center section is centered in the final printout.

Note that information entered into these sections can overlap. If the information you enter into the Left Section extends too far to the right, it may overlap with the information in the Center Section, and so forth.

Once you've entered the data, you can select from the option buttons to add special elements to the header or footer. The following is a summary of the header and footer options:

A	Font	Lets you change the font and character attributes of the header/footer text. First select the text you want to change and then click this button to produce the Font dialog box.
#	Page Number	Adds the page number at the location of the cursor. **&P** is added to the text.
	Total Pages	Adds the total number of pages. **&N** is added to the text at the cursor location. For example, you can number pages like this: "Page 1 of 12." The entry would appear as **Page &P of &N**.
	Date	Adds the current date. **&D** is added to the text.
	Time	Adds the current time. **&T** is added to the text.
	File Name	Inserts the name of the worksheet at the cursor position. **&F** is added to the text.

Normally, Excel begins page numbers with page 1, but you can change the starting page by using the Start Page No's At entry in the Page Setup dialog box. This option makes it easy to include your Excel printouts as part of a larger document. Of course, you must add the &P entry into the header or footer to print the page numbers. Note that the starting page you set does not affect the total number of pages. Therefore, you're better off avoiding the Total Pages button when you change the starting page number.

Fitting Data Onto the Page

If the print range spans more than one page, Excel automatically splits the data based on the amount of data that can fit on each page. Excel indicates where each page breaks if you select the Automatic Page Breaks option in the Tools⇨Options dialog box (see Figure 6-5).

You can influence the way Excel splits the pages by changing the amount of data that fits onto a single page. You can do this by adjusting the page margins within the Page Setup dialog box (see "Changing the page margins" later in this topic) or by changing the row heights and column widths on the worksheet. Sometimes just reducing a column or two can make a print range fit when it is otherwise too large. You can also influence the amount of data that fits onto a page by reducing or enlarging the point sizes used for the type.

Dotted lines indicate
where Excel breaks the page

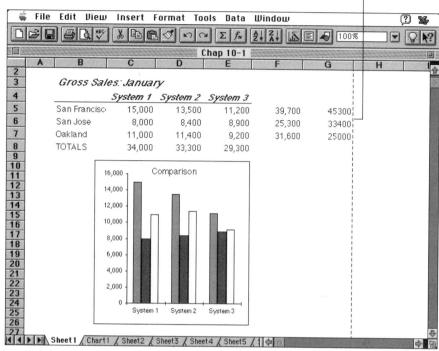

Figure 6-5: Excel breaks the page based on your margins and other settings.

Another way in which you can influence how much data fits onto a page is by reducing or enlarging the entire printout through the Scaling options in the Page Setup dialog box. By reducing the page, you can fit more on each sheet and effectively increase the amount of data in the print area. Note that if you use the Scaling options, you should return to the worksheet before printing (as opposed to printing directly from the Page Setup dialog box) so that you can give Excel a chance to show you the new page breaks. The following sections explain these data-fitting possibilities.

Setting page breaks

If you are still not happy with the way Excel breaks the pages in your print area, you can tell Excel exactly where you want the breaks to occur by setting the breaks manually. Set the bottom of each page by highlighting the row above which the break should occur. In other words, highlight the row with which you want to start the next page. Then select the Page Break command from the Insert menu. Excel marks your manual page break with a slightly different dotted line than the one used for the automatic breaks (see Figure 6-6).

A manual page break

An automatic page break

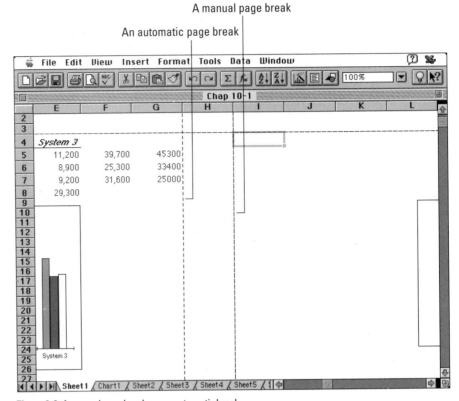

Figure 6-6: A manual page break vs. an automatic break.

To mark the right edge of a page, highlight the column with which you want to start the next page and select the Page Break command from the Insert menu. The break occurs to the left of the column you highlight.

If you want to mark the row and column in one shot, just highlight the cell that intersects the desired row and column and then select Insert⇨Page Break. Excel places the row break above the cell and the column break to the left of the cell.

Remember that page breaks mark pages all the way across and down the worksheet. If a page break occurs at column H, then all pages in the worksheet break at column H.

If you set manual page breaks, your pages can contain only as much data as fits onto the page — given the current margin and magnification settings. If your manual breaks encompass too much data, Excel adds automatic breaks within your manual breaks.

You can remove a manual page break by highlighting the row below the break or the column to the right of the break and selecting the Insert⇨Remove Page Break command. If the command does not appear, you have not selected the correct row or column. (Note that you cannot remove an automatic page break, you can only create a manual break ahead of it to move it).

Changing the page margins

Your page margin settings — especially the Top and Left margin settings — play a large role in your printouts. The Top and Left margin settings determine where the selected data begins on the page. A left margin of two inches bumps the data two inches from the left edge of the page. As a result, fewer columns of data fit on your page than if you used a one-inch left margin. Hence, it's a good idea to return to the worksheet after making margin adjustments, so you can view the changes in page breaks before printing.

If your print area does not fill an entire page, your right and bottom margin settings may not have an impact on the printout, because the data will fall short of the right side and bottom.

To change the margins, choose the File⇨Page Setup command and click the Margins tab (see Figure 6-7).

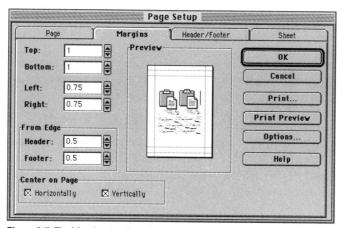

Figure 6-7: The Margin tab in Excel's Page Setup dialog box.

Note that the margin settings also affect the placement of headers and footers. Headers are printed below the Top margin setting and to the right of the Left margin setting.

If you want to center your printout on the page, click the desired Center on Page options in the Margins tab of the Page Setup dialog box. These options automatically center the data within the margins you establish. If you want your printout to be in the center of the paper, make sure that all four margin settings are equal. The smallest margin setting on most printers is 0.25, or ¼ inch.

Setting the orientation: printing sideways

The Orientation options let you print vertically or horizontally on the page. To view these options, choose the File⇨Page Setup command and select the Page tab. Selecting the Landscape (horizontal) option causes Excel to recalculate the page breaks and display the new breaks on the worksheet. This option can be useful for getting more columns of data on a single sheet of paper, as in large tables and lists. You can preview the selections to see the results before printing.

In addition to printing with the Landscape orientation, you may try reducing the page margins to squeeze more onto the page. On dot matrix printers, you can select the No Gaps Between Pages option in the Print dialog box. This option lets you print continuously onto multiple pages. For laser printers, try using the Larger Print Area option. To find this option, click the Options button from the Print dialog box and then press Options again to find the LaserWriter Options dialog box.

Scaling the printout

In the Page tab of the Print Setup dialog box are a number of options for scaling the printout. The print scaling options let you enlarge or reduce the printout. Just select the desired percent value from the drop-down list. The value 100% normal size prints normally, and any number greater than 100% enlarges the worksheet (for example, 200% prints the worksheet at twice the size). This setting affects the automatic page breaks on the worksheet.

You can also make the print area fit onto a single page or any number of pages by allowing Excel to choose the reduction value that best matches your desired result. To fit the print area onto one page, set the Scaling option to read: **Fit to 1 pages wide by 1 pages tall.** For long, wide tables of data, you may set the values to **Fit to 1 pages wide by 99 pages tall.** The value 99 simply anticipates as many pages as are needed to print the entire range.

Setting the page order

Print order is a simple setting that lets you specify whether pages are printed from the top of the worksheet down or from the top of the worksheet to the right. The difference can affect the way multiple pages and multiple copies come out on the printer and can save you from having to manually collate the resulting printouts.

Locate the print order options by selecting the Sheet tab in the Page Setup dialog box.

Previewing Your Worksheet On-Screen

Before you print your report, you should consider previewing it on-screen. Excel shows you a small replica of each page in the final printout — including the headers, footers, page breaks, and margin settings. Excel also simulates the fonts and graphics features of your printer.

To preview the printout, select the File⇨Print Preview command. Alternatively, you can check the Preview option in the File⇨Print dialog box and then click OK. The resulting preview looks like Figure 6-8.

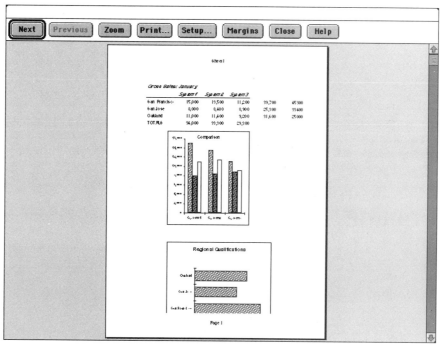

Figure 6-8: The Print Preview screen.

The preview screen offers numerous options for manipulating the preview. You can even print directly from the preview screen if you like what you see, or you can return to the Page Setup options. One of the most useful features is the ability to change the page margins and column widths right from the preview screen. Table 6-2 provides a list of the Print Preview options.

Table 6-2
Print Preview Options

Option	What It Does
Next	Displays the next page in a multiple-page printout.
Previous	Displays the previous page.
Zoom	Enlarges the preview to full size. This option helps you see the details of the printout and view the fonts more accurately. You can zoom by clicking the sample page with the magnifying glass pointer.
Print	Brings up the Print dialog box from which you can print the report.
Setup	Brings up the Page Setup dialog box, so that you can change the setup options.
Margins	Lets you change the page margins and column widths by dragging the margin and column lines. Click this button and then click and drag the indicator lines that appear. Changing the column widths affects the worksheet as well as the printout.
Close	Returns you to the worksheet.

It's a good idea to preview your printouts before wasting paper on mistakes. The preview reflects all your Page Setup and Print options.

Printing

When you are ready to print, select the File⇨Print command. You can also print by selecting the Print button in the Page Setup dialog box or by choosing the Print button from the preview screen. Regardless of the method you use, the Print options appear on the screen, as shown in Figure 6-9.

Each different printer you use produces a different set of options. Among the standard options you find are the number of copies to print and the page range you would like to print. Note that the page range sets the specific pages from the print area that you want to print.

You can print to a file on disk by specifying the PostScript File option. Upon printing, you have the chance to enter a file name for the resulting file.

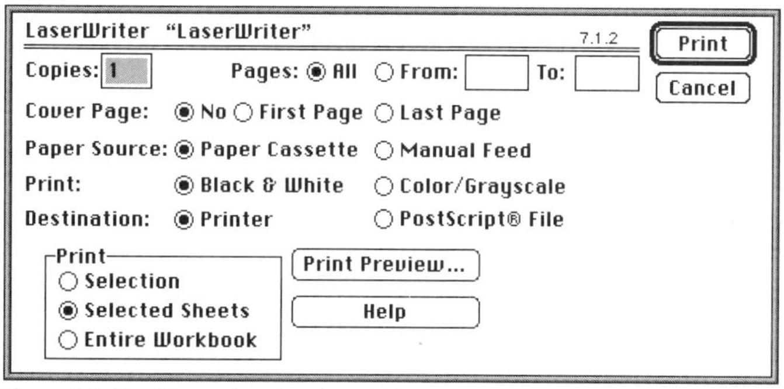

```
┌─────────────────────────────────────────────────────────────┐
│ LaserWriter  "LaserWriter"              7.1.2    ┌─────────┐  │
│ Copies: 1          Pages: ⊙ All  ○ From:    To:  │  Print  │  │
│                                                  └─────────┘  │
│ Cover Page:   ⊙ No ○ First Page  ○ Last Page     ┌─────────┐  │
│ Paper Source: ⊙ Paper Cassette  ○ Manual Feed    │ Cancel  │  │
│ Print:        ⊙ Black & White   ○ Color/Grayscale└─────────┘  │
│ Destination:  ⊙ Printer         ○ PostScript® File           │
│  ┌─Print──────────┐   ┌──────────────────┐                   │
│  │ ○ Selection    │   │ Print Preview... │                   │
│  │ ⊙ Selected Sheets   └──────────────────┘                   │
│  │ ○ Entire Workbook  │   ┌──────────────────┐               │
│  └────────────────┘   │      Help        │                   │
│                       └──────────────────┘                   │
└─────────────────────────────────────────────────────────────┘
```

Figure 6-9: The Print options for a LaserWriter. Each printer will have a dialog box that you to use all the options available for that printer.

Printing Reports

Excel lets you combine different worksheet views and scenarios into a single report for printing. You can build many different reports within a workbook to print your information in various ways — depending on the need. For example, in a Cost Estimate worksheet, you may want to print certain pages of information as a client estimate form and a different set of pages as an internal work order form. Each different report may be printed with different options.

To understand and appreciate this feature completely, read about views in Topic 3 and scenarios in Topic 9. The reports feature enables you to print a back-to-back sequence of views and scenarios so that you can create a large report without printing the individual pieces or repeating the setup and view settings. To use the reports feature, therefore, you must already have saved different views or scenarios (or both) for the worksheet.

Suppose that you have saved two different worksheet views. The first view, called PrintLarge, uses a 150 percent enlargement setting in the Page Setup dialog box. The second view, called PrintSmall, uses a 50 percent enlargement setting in the Page Setup dialog box. (Remember that Page Setup settings are stored as part of a view.)

Now suppose that you want to print both views back-to-back. You don't have to select the first view and print the worksheet and then select the second view and print the worksheet again. This process would be tedious. Instead, you can use the Reports feature to print these views in tandem while you do something else.

To expand this example, suppose that you have two different scenarios *and* two different views for this worksheet. You want to print four pages, with each scenario printed using each view. You want a PrintLarge view and a PrintSmall view of Scenario A and the same kinds of printouts for Scenario B.

With the Report Manager, you can combine a scenario with a view and print both sets of information together. This combination is referred to as a *section* of the report. In this case, you have four sections to comprise all four combinations of the scenarios and views. You can save this combination of four pages as a single report. You then can save other combinations. Now you can easily print the four pages by printing the stored report.

Use your imagination to see how this feature can add significant power to Excel's reporting capabilities. The Report Manager is ideal for large applications that produce different kinds of reports from the same data.

If the Print Reports option does not appear in the File menu, you may not have installed the option into Excel. Choose the Add-Ins command from the Tools menu to locate the add-in called Report Manager. If you locate this add-in, install it through the Add-In Manager. If you cannot find the add-in, then you will have to return to the Excel Setup program and install the Report Manager from there.

Building a report

1. From the File menu, choose the Print Report command. All previously created and saved reports are listed in the Print Report dialog box. You can select one of these reports for the current report, or you can create a new report, as explained in the remaining steps.

2. Click the Add button. Figure 6-10 shows the dialog box that appears.

3. Type a name for the report then select the desired worksheet name from the Sheet option. You can combine different worksheets with your views and scenarios.

4. Select a view from the View list and select a scenario from the Scenario list. These lists display views and scenarios that you have saved previously. Your two selections, along with the specified worksheet, comprise the first section of this report.

5. Click the Add button.

6. Repeat steps 4 and 5 to combine other scenarios with other views for this report.

7. Use the Move Up and Move Down buttons to change the order of the sections. (Simply highlight a section and click Move Up or Move Down.) Sections are printed in the order in which they appear in the Current Sections list. Pages are numbered accordingly.

8. When the order of the sections is satisfactory, click OK.

Figure 6-10: The Add Report dialog box.

You now can select the report from the list and click the Print button to print. You don't have to establish Page Setup or Print options because these page and print procedures are controlled by the views you are printing.

The following is a summary of guidelines and ideas for using the reports feature:

◆ **Create your views and scenarios first.** Use the Window Views command and the Formula Scenario command to store any desired views and scenarios for the worksheet. You cannot create a report unless you have stored views and/or scenarios. If you select a view and a scenario together as a section, the scenario values are printed with the view's page setup settings. If you select a scenario without a view as a section, the scenario values are printed using the current page setup settings. If you select a view without a scenario as a section, the currently defined print area is printed using the view's page setup values.

◆ **A report consists of a collection of sections.** All the sections you define under a single report name are printed when you print the report. You should build reports based on how you usually print the worksheet. Remember, you can create as many different reports as you like.

◆ **You can rearrange the sections of a report.** To change the order in which the sections are printed, select a section in the Add Report dialog box and click the Move Up or Move Down buttons until the section moves to the desired spot in the list. Sections print in the order presented in the list.

◆ **Reports are saved with the worksheet.** When you save the worksheet, all reports you have created are saved with it.

◆ **You can edit any existing report.** To edit an existing report, choose the

Print Report command from the File menu and then click the report you want to change. Now click the Edit button. You can now rearrange sections, delete sections, or add new sections to the report.

◆ **Page numbers can start over with each section or continue through the report.** If you check the Continuous Page Numbers box for a report, each section continues after the previous section's page numbers. Of course, page numbers print in each section only if the views used in those sections include page numbers in their headers or footers. If the Continuous Page Numbers option is unchecked, each section begins at page 1.

Quick Tips

The print area can consist of multiple ranges

If you highlight two or more ranges as the print area, Excel prints each range on a separate page. This feature is useful if you want to split the data onto several pages or control page breaks in a large printout, but you may want to print noncontiguous ranges onto the same page. See the next tip for one solution.

Printing noncontiguous ranges on the same page

Printing two or more ranges onto the same page is easy. Just take pictures of each range using the Camera button that you can add to any toolbar through the toolbar customization feature. Then place these pictures side-by-side in a remote area of the worksheet and highlight the range containing all the pictures as the print area. The pictures can come from any part of the worksheet and will be updated when the original data is updated. See Topic 10 for more information about the Camera button and pictures.

The print area can be a range of columns or rows

If you highlight several entire rows as the print area, Excel prints all the data in the rows and stops when there is no more data to print. You do not receive blank pages.

Part III:
Intermediate Excel

2nd Edition

Macworld Excel 5 Companion

Formulas and Functions

*O*verview

Formulas are the engines of Excel worksheets. Formulas enable you to change the data in a worksheet and instantly produce updated results. Because Excel gives you the power of formulas to complete simple to complex calculations quickly and accurately, it is another reason yesterday's analysis tools — pencil, ledger paper, and an adding machine — have ended up on the scrap heap.

Topic 2 provides essential information about entering formulas into your worksheet cells. This topic also goes further into the world of formulas, explaining how to create, document, and troubleshoot formulas. You also learn about functions — formulas that are built into Excel — and how functions can be used in conjunction with other calculations in your worksheets. Finally, you learn some techniques for making formulas and functions easier to work with, such as naming cells and ranges.

Introduction to Formulas

A formula is a mathematical relationship among the cells in a worksheet. On a basic level, you can use formulas to perform arithmetic on your worksheets' values (add, subtract, multiply, or divide), much like you did in grade school. On a more advanced level, you can combine functions and values in your formulas, arrive at results, and even have Excel take a specific action based on a calculation.

Defining your problem or need so that you can express it mathematically as an Excel formula is the first and most important step in setting up a formula. For example, do you need to total a range of sales values? Or do you need to subtract total expenses from total sales? Or perhaps you'd like to know how much that $30,000 sports coupe will set you back monthly at nine percent interest over five years. Determining where the numbers are located in the worksheet that will be required in your formula is the first step in building the formula. Next, determine the mathematical operations required for the formula. For example, you may need to add some numbers or subtract one number from another. You may need a division of values or a special financial function that calculates a value (such as the Net Present Value of a series of investments). In any case, after you've defined your needs, entering a formula into Excel that fulfills your needs is easy. And when formulas fall short, Excel provides functions that can do your work.

Entering formulas

1. Select the cell in which you want the formula (and its answer) to appear. This cell should currently be blank.

2. Type an equal sign.

3. Enter a value by doing *one* of the following:

   ◆ Typing the value.

   ◆ Clicking the cell that contains the value.

   ◆ Typing the address (or reference) of the cell that contains the value.

   ◆ Moving the cell pointer to the cell containing the value by pressing arrow keys or other keyboard movement commands.

4. Type an operator (+, -, *, /). (Refer to Topic 2 for information on operators.)

5. Repeat steps 3 and 4 until you've completed the formula (but don't end your formula with an operator).

6. Click the Enter box in the formula bar or press Return, Tab, or an arrow key.

That's all there is to it. Figure 7-1 shows a formula in an Excel worksheet. Note in the figure that a formula can have one or a combination of values, cell references, and worksheet functions. If you want to reference a cell in a formula, use the mouse or the arrow keys to select the cell containing the value you need, and then continue building the formula by entering the next operator. If you try to compute values and text, however, Excel displays the #VALUE error message in the cell.

Correcting errors in formulas

If you make a mistake entering a formula or function, Excel beeps and displays the message box shown in Figure 7-2. After you click OK or press Return, Excel highlights a possible cause for the error in the formula. Most errors are the result of typing errors, missing arguments, or mismatched parentheses within a formula, such as those errors shown in Table 7-1.

Table 7-1 Typical Errors in Formulas	
Formula	*Explanation of Error*
A1+B1	Missing equal sign
=((A1+B1)*(C1+D1)	Extra (left) parenthesis
=RAND	Missing argument in function (left and right parenthesis)

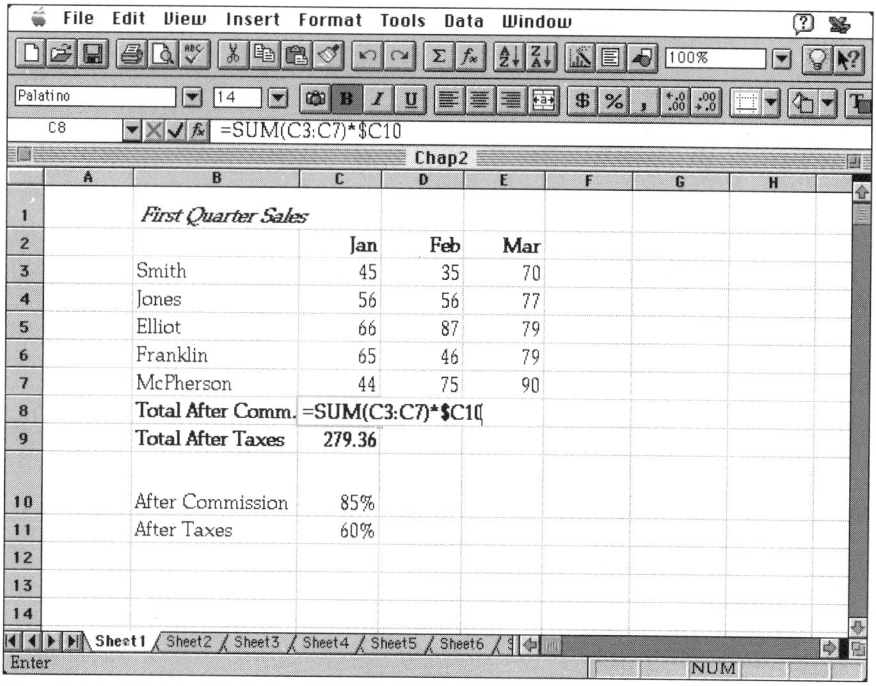

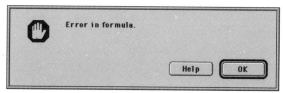

Figure 7-1: Sample formula in an Excel worksheet.

Figure 7-2: This message box alerts you to errors you have made when entering a formula or function.

If you have trouble finding the error in the function or formula, delete the equal sign and press Return. Excel accepts the function or formula as text. When you do this, you won't have to reenter the formula, and you can correct the formula after you've had an opportunity to mull it over. Clicking the Cancel box or pressing Esc clears the formula bar so that you can start over from square one.

In addition, some formula entries may not produce the error message in Figure 7-2, but they may produce an error value inside the cell. An error value is a message that Excel returns to the cell in place of a numeric result. The message explains what caused the formula to fail. Table 7-2 shows some typical error values.

Table 7-2 Typical Error Values	
Error Message	**Explanation**
#DIV/0	Attempt to divide by zero. This error value may appear if you have referenced a blank cell or a cell that contains a zero or text as the divisor in a division formula.
#NAME?	Cell or range name unknown. This message occurs when you type a range name that does not appear in the worksheet or if you type something that Excel thinks is a range name. Expect to receive this message for formulas in which you have forgotten the quotation marks around text entries.
#VALUE!	Value unknown. This message occurs when your formula expects a value but receives text. Check your references to make sure that they don't point to cells that contain text.
#NUM!	Invalid number. This error message occurs when your worksheet functions receive improper numeric arguments. Check the function's requirements or use the Function Wizard to help you.
#REF!	Reference unavailable. This error message occurs when you remove cells from the worksheet that are referenced in formulas.

Finally, your worksheet can have errors that don't produce error messages. These are the insidious problems in worksheets that occur due to poor formula design and execution. The only way to locate such errors is to double-check your work by entering simple values into cells and checking the formula results against your manual calculations.

Understanding circular reference errors

You may come across a special type of error when you enter a formula into a cell in which the formula refers to that cell's address. For example, by entering the formula **=A1+A2+A3** into cell A3 you receive the circular reference error message box.

Whenever a formula depends upon itself for a result, there is a circular reference. Besides displaying the message box, Excel attempts to pinpoint the problem by listing a cell address in the status bar. In a case like this one, you can easily spot the error and remove the circular reference.

However, not all circular references are so easy to catch. A circular reference can occur through a large network of formulas—where one formula refers to another, which refers to another, which refers back to the first cell.

Choosing when to calculate: automatically or manually

Excel normally calculates the formulas in a worksheet when a value, function, or other formula it depends on changes. Excel also begins calculating at the bottom of a worksheet's formula hierarchy. That is, the less a formula depends on other cells for information, the sooner it's calculated. In these ways, all formulas reflect the most current results. Excel also temporarily suspends calculation if you're busy with another worksheet task and resumes when you're finished.

If creating a single, monster worksheet is unavoidable (as opposed to creating a set of smaller, linked worksheets), you may want to change to manual calculation. Manual calculation enables you to choose when you want the worksheet updated, which is useful if you have a lot of data to enter or complex open charts that depend on new or edited data. It is also helpful if your worksheets have many links to other worksheets that require updating each time you calculate the sheet.

To change to manual calculation, choose Options from the Tools menu and then click the Calculation tab. When the Calculate dialog box appears, as shown in

the following figure, choose Manual. Manual calculation will be in effect until you either change back to Automatic or close the worksheet without saving to disk.

To calculate a worksheet while in Manual mode, press Command-= or choose Calc Now from the Calculate options. Alternatively, you can press F9. Be sure that the worksheet has been calculated before you print so that the printout reflects the most current information.

Working with Ranges

When you use functions in Excel, you'll probably be required to enter range references. A range reference is simply a way of identifying a group of cells on the worksheet. Rather than indicating each cell, you simply enter the first and last cell, separated by a colon. For example, to identify the group of cells C3 through C7, you enter **C3:C7.**

You can actually identify a range using any two corners of the range. For example, the range C3 through C7 could be identified as C7:C3. If your range includes a block of cells spanning several rows and columns, you have four ways of entering the range: C3:F7, F7:C3, F3:C7 and C7:F3. One thing to keep in mind is that the formula uses the number format of the last cell identified in the range. Hence, the reference C7:F3 uses the format of cell F3, and the reference F3:C7 uses the format of cell C7. For more information on this type of formatting, refer to Topic 4.

There are two other ways of entering range references. First, if you want to identify more than one range, such as the ranges C3:C7 and M3:M7, you must enter a *multiple-range reference*. A multiple-range reference simply includes all range references separated by commas. For example, C3:C7,M3:M7 identifies the two ranges C3:C7 and M3:M7 as a single reference. The reference C3:C7,A5 also identifies two ranges — one of which is a single cell (a single cell is just a small range).

A final way to enter range references is to use a *combination reference*. A combination reference is a reference to cells that are common to two or more ranges. For example, the ranges C3:C7 and A5:G5 have cell C5 in common — that is, cell C5 appears in both ranges. To identify the cells that are common to two or more ranges, enter all ranges separated by spaces (using the spacebar). In the previous example, you would use the reference C3:C7 A5:G5 to identify cell C5.

Naming cells, ranges, and values

Excel makes it easy to identify commonly used cells and ranges in your worksheets by allowing you to name ranges and cells. A named cell or range can be identified by name in a formula or function. For example, if you name the range C3:C7 as January, then you can use January to refer to that range like this:

=SUM(January)

Naming a cell or range

1. Highlight the desired cell or range. The easiest way to highlight a range is to click and drag the mouse on the worksheet.

2. Select the Name⇨Define command in the Insert menu. The dialog box shown in Figure 7-3 appears on the screen.

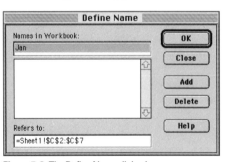

Figure 7-3: The Define Name dialog box.

3. Type a name into the Names in Worksheet entry box. Make sure that the Refers to box correctly identifies the range you've highlighted. (If you want to identify a different range, just type the range reference into the Refers to box.)

4. Click OK.

When specifying a range name, be sure to begin with a letter and to not use spaces in the name. You can enter names in uppercase or lowercase letters — Excel does not distinguish between the two. You can enter up to 255 characters for a range name, but you should keep the name to about 20 characters for easy readability.

Excel assumes that the range reference should be absolute, so it enters dollar signs between each part of the cell addresses in the reference. You can change the reference to make portions of it relative if you like. The range name will then apply to a relative range reference, which will affect the way the name (reference) adjusts when it's copied. For more information on relative and absolute references, see Topic 2.

Note that Excel may suggest a name for the range you've highlighted. If the first cell of the range contains text, Excel suggests this text as the name for the range. You can accept this suggestion by clicking OK or by retyping the name. This feature is useful when you are naming columns (or rows) of data that contain column headings; the column headings can easily be used as the range names.

If you want to name several columns and/or rows of data located in a table, you can use the Name⇨Create command from the Insert menu instead of the Name⇨Define command. Highlight the entire range of data (including row and column labels) and choose the Name⇨Create command. The Create Names dialog box appears.

Choose the location of the range names you want to use. If you choose Top Row, each label in the top row identifies its column. If you choose Left Column, each label in the left column identifies its row. Figure 7-4 illustrates these features.

Figure 7-4: The Name⇨Create command from the Insert menu uses row and column labels to apply names to the rows and columns in the highlighted range.

In the example in Figure 7-4, you end up with three named columns (January, February, and March) and six named rows. In addition, Excel applies the label in the upper-left corner (if one appears there) to the entire range. In this example, SALES applies to the entire highlighted range.

The following are some guidelines for creating and using range names:

◆ Excel doesn't accept names it can interpret as cell addresses, such as A2 or EE1.

◆ Existing names appear in the Define Name dialog box. You can view a list of existing names in your worksheet by using the Name⇨Define command from the Insert menu.

◆ You can use two or more different names for the same range. Excel stores each unique name and the range reference to which it refers.

◆ You can use the same cell or range in two or more named ranges. In fact, a cell or range can appear as part of any number of other ranges.

◆ You can apply a name to a multiple-range reference to identify all the segments together. This method can be useful for naming all the areas in a worksheet that must be filled out by a data entry operator. You can name such a range ENTRY_AREA. The best way to identify a multiple-range reference is to highlight the first range and select the Name⇨Define command from the Insert menu. Click the cell pointer inside the Refers to box (after the first reference). Type a comma and then click and drag on the worksheet to highlight the next range (you can move the Define Name dialog box out of the way if needed). Press another comma and highlight the next range. When finished, type a name for the range and then press Return or click OK.

◆ Use the Name⇨Define command to remove a range name. To remove a range name, select the Name⇨Define command from the Insert menu and click once on the range name in the list that appears. Then click Delete and press Return.

◆ You can enter any range name into the active cell by using the Name⇨Paste command from the Insert menu and double-clicking the desired name in the list that appears. To paste a list of all the range names, click the Paste List button in the Paste Name dialog box.

◆ You can name important values and formulas. If you use a formula or value frequently, you may consider naming it. Just select the Name⇨Define command from the Insert menu and enter a name into the Name entry box. Then press Tab to highlight the data inside the Refers to box. Type the formula or value you want to name; this entry should replace the existing data in the Refers to box. Press Return. For example, in the Define Name dialog box, type **Total,** and in the Refers to box, type the SUM function with the range of cells that you want to total as the argument, such as **SUM(A3:A10),** for January's budget total. You then type or paste the name **=TOTAL** for each of the other eleven months of the year.

◆ When using range names in formulas, do not surround them with quotation marks as you would a text label.

◆ You can jump to any named range by pressing F5, the Go To command (or Go To in the Edit menu), and selecting the range name from the list provided, or by choosing the range name from the name list that appears on the formula bar.

Referencing ranges from other pages

You can create formulas that refer to ranges on other sheets in the same workbook. For example, you may want cell C5 on the first page to calculate the sum of cells from some of the other pages. To create such a reference, simply add the sheet name to the cell reference, followed by an exclamation point. For example, to add the contents of cells C5 on the second, third, and fourth sheets of the workbook, you would enter the following into cell C5 of the first page:

=Sheet2!C5+Sheet3!C5+Sheet4!C5

Of course, if you have named the pages you would use the new page names, instead of the default Sheet# names. By referencing cells across several sheets like this, you are creating *3D references*. 3D references can be useful when you are working with ranges that span across several sheets. The above example is actually a 3D range that is one column wide, one row long, and three sheets deep. Such a range can be given the reference Sheet2:Sheet4!C5. This reference specifies that the range of sheets is Sheet2 through Sheet4 and that the cell or range on those sheets is C5. A formula that uses this 3D reference would look like this:

=SUM(Sheet2:Sheet4!C5)

Note that you can sum more than a single cell across multiple sheets. For example, you can refer to the range C5:D8 across three worksheets with the formula:

=SUM(Sheet2:Sheet4!C5:D8)

This formula produces the total of all the cells (18 cells). You can use range names in these 3D references also. By default, Excel defines all names globally for the entire workbook. In order to use the same name on different worksheets within the same workbook, you have to define it as a worksheet-specific name.

Creating worksheet-specific names

1. Choose Define Name from the Insert Menu.

2. Type **'January Sales'!Totals** in the Names in Workbook box. Put the worksheet name in single quotes; the exclamation point separates the sheet name from the range name.

3. Type the reference range in the Refers to box.

4. Choose OK. Excel creates the name. You can use this name in the current worksheet or (by specifying the sheet name) other sheets in the workbook. ◊

To select a 3D range, simply click on the first cell in the first page of the reference and hold Shift as you click the page tabs to move to the last page. Click the ending cell on the last page of the reference.

Understanding Functions

You can do many things with creative use of formulas. You can sum the values in a column or receive an average of those values. But some things are difficult to manage with standard formulas and worksheet logic.

Excel provides a set of special functions that help you calculate special values with your data. Some functions are simple and perform calculations that could otherwise be accomplished with formulas. For example, the SUM function simply totals the values in several cells and the PI function simply represents the value . Other functions are rather complex and perform calculations that cannot be accomplished with normal formula-building logic. A good example is the IF function, which lets you perform one of two actions based on the outcome of a conditional test.

Depending on how you installed Excel, you may have several categories of functions from which to choose. Table 7-3 provides a description of these categories.

Table 7-3 Excel's Function Categories	
Function Category	*Description*
Engineering	Functions that calculate engineering values, such as working with complex numbers and unitary conversions. These functions are available only if you have installed the Analysis ToolPack.
Financial	Functions that perform financial calculations, such as figuring various parts of a loan or calculating depreciation.
Date and Time	Functions that help you perform date and time math, such as adding dates, calculating the difference between dates, and more.
Information	Functions that return information about cells and the data in them. You can determine whether a cell is blank or whether it contains an even number.
Math and Trig	Functions that perform mathematical and trigonometric calculations, such as finding the absolute value of a number, calculating the factorial of a number, and figuring the SINE of a value.
Statistical	Functions that perform statistical analysis on your data. You can determine the covariance of a set of values, perform trend analysis, calculate the number of permutations for a given set of objects, and more.
Lookup and Reference	Functions that help you locate values from tables. You can search a table of values to locate information for your worksheets by using these Lookup and Reference functions.

Function Category	Description
Database	Functions that process information stored in an Excel database range, including database statistical analysis — such as counting certain entries in a database.
Text	Functions that manipulate text labels, such as converting numbers to text, displaying text in all uppercase letters, and more.
Logical	Functions that work with logical operators and conditional tests, including the IF function and many others that work with IF to provide worksheet logic.

How to Enter a Function

All functions must contain three main parts: the equal sign, the function name, and the arguments (in parentheses). If the function begins a formula entry (or is the only thing in a cell), then it must also begin with an equal sign. For example, the SUM function can be entered as a formula itself, or as part of a larger formula:

◆ =SUM(C3:C7,C9)

◆ =C1*SUM(C3:C7,C9)

Worksheet functions can be entered in one of two ways: either by typing (manually) or by using the Function Wizard.

Entering functions manually

1. Select the cell that you want to hold the function.

2. Type an equal sign.

3. Type the name of the function, followed by a left parenthesis. You have to provide some information (arguments) between the parentheses for the function to operate properly. Some functions, such as SUM, require only one piece of information, which is the address or name of the range to total. Other functions require many more arguments. You supply these arguments by entering a value or reference, which you can type or *point to*, or by entering a name. If you use a function that requires several arguments, separate the arguments with commas. How do you know which arguments are required by a given function? Try using the Function Wizard for starters.

4. Type a right parenthesis.

5. Click Enter or press Return. ◖

Using the Function Wizard

1. Select the cell that you want to hold the function.

f_x

2. Click the Function Wizard button that appears in the formula bar.

3. Choose a function category from the Categories list and then choose the desired function name from the Function Name list. Excel provides a brief description of the function at the bottom of the dialog box (see Figure 7-5).

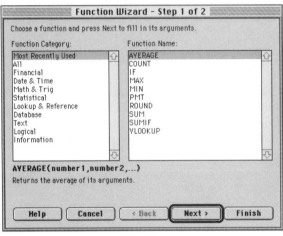

Figure 7-5: The Function Wizard dialog box.

4. Click Next. Excel provides information about the function's arguments. See Figure 7-6 for an example.

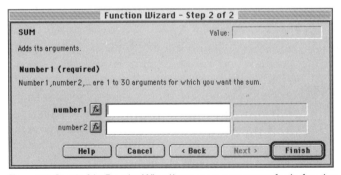

Figure 7-6: Step 2 of the Function Wizard lets you enter arguments for the function.

5. Fill in values or type cell or range references for the arguments listed. You can click the worksheet to point to a cell that contains the desired value. Note that some arguments require text entries, in which case you should type the

text in quotation marks or point to a cell that contains the text (more on argument types later). If you want to insert another function where the argument requires a value, then click the Function Wizard tool beside the argument entry box.

6. Click Next if applicable or Finish when you are done.

Most functions perform operations on data that you enter into the function's parentheses. These sets of data are called *arguments*. The arguments for the preceding SUM example (=SUMC3:C7,C9) include the range C3:C7 and the cell C9. Therefore, the SUM function produces the sum of those cells. Some functions have no arguments — just empty parentheses, such as PI(). Others require several arguments. Although you will probably have to learn the syntax requirements of each function you want to use, here are some tips to help make things easier:

◆ **Arguments must be separated by commas.** If a function requires more than one argument, use commas between them. Arguments are sometimes described with two or three words, such as *lookup_range*. In these cases, an underline character is used between the words to indicate that these words represent only one argument.

◆ **Some arguments require that you enter a range.** Many functions use range references as arguments. These are usually identified with the word *range*. When entering a range argument, you may enter any range reference (such as C3:C7) or range name (such as SALES). For example, the SUM function uses a range, as in SUM(C3:C7).

◆ **Value arguments can be any numeric values.** When a function calls for a value, you can enter any constant value, any reference to a cell containing a numeric value, or any expression that results in a value. For example, the function SQRT(*value*) indicates that you can enter any numeric value as the argument. Some examples include the following:

SQRT(9)

SQRT(C5)

SQRT(C5+21)

Value arguments are not always listed with the word *value*. Some functions try to be more descriptive, with names like *decimal_places* and *row_offset*. These names help describe the purpose of the argument. Chances are, you'll have to refer to the Excel Function Reference or the function help screens for more details about these special values.

◆ **Some arguments let you list values or ranges.** A *list* argument indicates that you can enter a series of values. For example, the SUM function uses the *list* argument, which means that you can enter any values or ranges, separated by commas. For example, SUM(C3:C7,C9,D4:D8,25) indicates four separate items in a list argument — two ranges, a cell reference and a constant value. The syntax of this function is simply SUM(*list*).

◆ **Text arguments can be entered as constants or references.** If a function specifies the *text* argument, you can enter any text label in quotation marks or a reference to a cell containing the desired text. If you use a reference, then don't use quotation marks. Here are two examples using the function UPPER(*text*), which converts a text label to all uppercase letters:

UPPER("john doe")

UPPER(C5)

◆ **When entering functions manually, you can enter function names in uppercase or lowercase letters.** Excel does not care if you use uppercase or lowercase letters for the function, but it converts your lowercase letters into uppercase letters for you. You can use this feature to your advantage. By typing functions in lowercase letters, you will get visual feedback that you've entered the function correctly when Excel converts it to uppercase letters. If Excel leaves your entry in lowercase letters, you know the entry is incorrectly typed.

◆ **You can use functions to convert arguments among the different types.** Excel includes a host of functions that convert data between text, numbers, dates, and other types of arguments. If your data is in the wrong form for the function that you want to use, you can probably convert it. Conversion functions include the following:

DATEVALUE	Text to a valid date serial number
DOLLAR	Numbers to text (text is displayed as dollar values)
TEXT	Numbers to text
TIMEVALUE	Text to a valid time serial number
VALUE	Text to a numeric value

Function List

The following is a list of Excel functions that you may find useful in your workbooks. This is not a complete list of Excel's functions (Excel has over 200 of them!), but it covers some of the most commonly used functions for general purposes. Experiment with these functions. If you find the need for more power, seek additional functions from the Excel Function Wizard.

Database functions

Database functions apply to information found in a database. A *database* is a table of information in which the rows correspond to records and the columns correspond to fields. The structure of an Excel database is discussed in Topic 8. The following function descriptions don't provide details about how to set up an Excel database, so before you use these functions, you should have a general understanding of Excel databases. The first function, DAVERAGE, includes a full explanation and an example that applies to all the functions.

DAVERAGE

The DAVERAGE function calculates the average of particular fields, over a database subset, that are determined by search criteria. The field used for the average is determined by an offset value; the actual database is determined by the database range. The following line shows the correct syntax for DAVERAGE:

DAVERAGE(*database,field,criteria*)

database	is the range of cells that contains the database information. The database range must include field names (column labels) over each column.
field	is the field that serves as the operand for the DAVERAGE function; here, *field* is the field to be averaged across the database subset. This variable can be any number from 1 to the number of fields in the database, where 1 represents the first field, 2 represents the second, and so on.
criteria	is the range of cells that contains the search criteria for the database. This reference must adhere to the rules for criteria ranges described in Topic 8 — namely, that the criteria range contains the required field names and search formulas beneath these names.

In the example database in Figure 7-7, the database contained in the range AZ8:C7 holds information about salaries for a set of workers. The criteria range contains the formula <35, which establishes a subset of all workers under the age of 35. The DAVERAGE function is set up to calculate the average income of all workers under 35 when you specify the database range, the criteria range, and the field.

The field should point to the third column in the database, which contains the income figures. The third column's field is offset. Therefore, the formula for the DAVERAGE function is as follows:

=DAVERAGE(AZ:C7,C2,A9:A10)

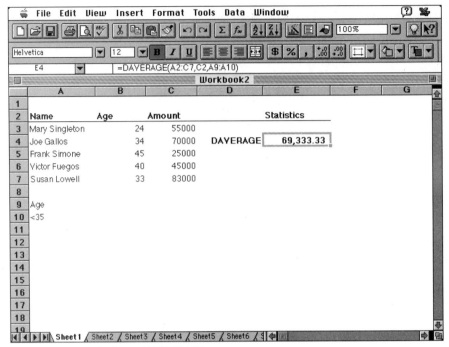

Figure 7-7: A sample database with DAVERAGE.

Unless the database range or criteria range changes, you don't have to alter this formula to calculate other salary averages; simply enter new criteria for the search. You can, for example, find the average income of all workers who are 35 and over by changing the criteria formula to >=35. The DAVERAGE formula recalculates its value according to the new criteria.

DCOUNT, DCOUNTA

The DCOUNT function counts the number of records that match the criteria established for a database search. Only records that contain numbers are counted. The DCOUNTA function counts database records and all matching records that are not blank. The following is the correct syntax:

DCOUNT(*database,field,criteria*)

DCOUNTA(*database,field,criteria*)

database   is the range of cells that contains the database information.

field   is the field that serves as the operand for this function; here, the field is insignificant because the function is counting the number of records that match the criteria, with no regard to any particular field. In fact, you can leave this argument blank. If you specify a field offset and some records don't have information in this field, those records are not counted.

criteria   is the range of cells that contains the search criteria for the database. This reference should adhere to the rules for criteria ranges described in Topic 8.

DGET

According to criteria you establish, the DGET function extracts a field from a database range. You can string together several DGET functions to extract an entire record or just a few fields. The following line shows the syntax for DGET:

DGET(*database,field,criteria*)

database   specifies the database range on the worksheet. This range reference should indicate a block of data that adheres to the basic rules for databases.

field   indicates the column heading of the field to be extracted from the database. Type the text of the column heading (for example, *"Name"*) or the number of the field in the database. Fields are numbered from left to right starting with 1.

criteria   specifies the range of cells that contains the criteria for the search.

If the database contains no matching records, the DGET function displays the error #VALUE!. If the database contains more than one matching record, DGET returns the error #NUM!.

DMAX, DMIN

The DMAX and DMIN functions find the maximum and minimum values in a database subset. The functions require offset values to determine the field used for the search. The following lines show the syntax for DMAX and DMIN:

DMAX(*database,field,criteria*)

DMIN(*database,field,criteria*)

database   is the range of cells that contains the database information.

field   is the field that serves as the operand for this function; here, the offset is the field through which the function searches for the maximum value.

criteria   is the range of cells that contains the search criteria for the database.

DSUM

The DSUM function commonly is used to calculate the total of a particular field in a database subset, as shown in the following syntax:

DSUM(*database,field,criteria*)

database   is the range of cells that contains the database information.

field   is the field that serves as the operand for this function; here, *field* is the numeric field for which the sum is calculated.

criteria   is the range of cells that contains the search criteria for the database.

Date/Time Functions

Date and time functions perform date and time math calculations and conversions. Date and time math includes calculating elapsed time, adding time to a given date or time, and calculating the difference between two dates or times. This kind of math is useful for creating payment schedules or determining payment delinquency. The following sections discuss the functions used for these purposes.

DATE

The DATE function creates a date from individual values for the day, month, and year. This function is used primarily in macros when a date specification must be variable; DATE enables you to enter variables as the arguments for the date by using the following syntax:

DATE(*year,month,day*)

year   can be any value from 1904 to 2040.

month   can be any value from 1 to 12.

day   can be any value from 1 to 31.

If a variable is invalid, the function returns an error. Otherwise, the function returns a number that corresponds to the number of days elapsed since January 1, 1904. The Format⇨Number command enables you to format this number as a date.

DATEVALUE

The DATEVALUE function converts a text string into a valid date. Use the following syntax for the DATEVALUE function:

DATEVALUE(*text*)

text   must contain text data recognizable as a date.

The function recognizes text entered in all date formats available through the Number command on the Format menu. You can specify any date from January 1, 1904 to February 6, 2040. Consider the following example:

=DATEVALUE(B5)

If cell B5 contains the text string ="1/25/91", this function returns 31801 — the number of days between 1/1/04 and 1/25/91. You can format this date value by using any date format available through the Format⇨Number command.

DAY, MONTH, YEAR

The DAY, MONTH, and YEAR functions return the respective day, month, or year that corresponds to a specified date, breaking a date into separate portions. Use the following syntax:

DAY(*date*)

MONTH(*date*)

YEAR(*date*)

date   can be any valid date, entered as the number of days elapsed since January 1, 1904; a reference to a cell that contains a valid date; or any date expression that results in a valid date.

You can combine the YEAR function with IF to test the value of a date. To determine whether a person is within a certain age limit, for example, check whether the birth date entered falls before a minimum date, as in the following formula:

=IF(YEAR(B2)<=1973,"OK","Must be 21 or older")

This formula tests whether the year portion of the date in cell B2 falls before or is equal to 1973.

NOW

The NOW function pulls the current date and time from the Macintosh internal clock, returning the value as a number with a decimal, as in 2245.2025. The integer portion of this number represents the date (in days-elapsed format), and the fractional part represents the time (in time-elapsed format).

The syntax for NOW, shown in the following line, has no argument:

NOW( )

You can format the value into a date or time by using any date or time format from the Format⇨Number command. You also can separate the two portions with the TRUNC function, as the following line illustrates:

=TRUNC(NOW( ))

This formula strips off and converts the decimal portion of the date/time serial number to a date. You then can format this date or use the DAY, MONTH, and YEAR functions to split the value even further.

Each time the worksheet recalculates the values, the NOW function updates the current date and time. To stop the date and time or to archive the date and time with a worksheet, convert the NOW function to the value of the NOW function by following these steps:

Freezing the NOW function

1. Move the pointer to the cell that contains the NOW function.

2. Copy the contents of the cell by pressing Command-C. Then move to a blank cell and choose the Paste Special command from the Edit menu.

3. Select the Values option and press Return. The value of the NOW function is pasted into the cell but not recalculated. ◖

You also can convert the =NOW( ) function by highlighting =NOW( ) in the formula bar and pressing Command-=. You should perform either method immediately after you enter the =NOW( ) function.

TODAY

The TODAY function returns the date serial number of the current date. You then can format this value with a date format. The TODAY function contains no arguments:

TODAY( )

Each time you calculate or open the worksheet, the TODAY function recalculates the value. If you want the date you entered to remain, don't use the TODAY function or freeze the calculation of the function as described in the previous step-by-step instructions.

WEEKDAY

The WEEKDAY function returns a value from 1 to 7 to indicate the day of the week of any valid date. The value 1 equals Sunday, 2 equals Monday, and so on. Use the following syntax:

WEEKDAY(*date*)

date   is a valid Excel date.

To format the returned value as the appropriate day name, choose the Format⇨Number command and specify the custom date format *dddd*. The following function, for example, returns 4:

=WEEKDAY("1/1/92")

You can format the 4 as the name Wednesday by using the *dddd* format. See Topic 4 for more information on date formats.

Financial functions

Financial functions are used for numerical calculations, such as interest rates, loan terms, present values, and future values. Financial functions are essential for performing detailed financial analyses for purchases, investments, and cash flows.

DDB, SLN, SYD

The DDB, SLN, and SYD functions use three different methods to calculate depreciation. The DDB function uses the double-declining balance method, which allows for an accelerated rate of depreciation for the initial period and can also accelerate depreciation by a specified rate. The SLN function uses the straight-line method, and the SYD function uses the sum-of-the-years digits method. With each function, when the book value depreciates to the salvage value, depreciation stops. The following lines show the syntax for these functions:

DDB(*cost,salvage,life,period,factor*)

SLN(*cost,salvage,life*)

SYD(*cost,salvage,life,period*)

cost	is any numeric value representing a dollar amount.
salvage	is any numeric value representing a dollar amount.
life	is an integer value representing the life (in units of time) of the asset.
period	determines the period in the asset's life for which depreciation is calculated.
factor	is an integer value representing the rate of depreciation.

You provide the initial *cost*, the *salvage* (value after the life), the *life* of the asset, and the *period* for which depreciation is calculated. The *life* and *period* arguments should be given in the same terms; that is, these arguments should indicate years, months, days, or any other period you choose. Optionally, you can enter a factor for the rate of depreciation (DDB only). If you don't enter a factor, the function assumes a standard DDB factor of 2 (double-declining).

To see depreciation for all periods requires multiple copies of the function — a copy for each period. *Period* should be equal to or smaller than *life*, and both variables must be integers. *Cost* and *salvage* can be any numbers. Figure 7-8 shows a worksheet that uses the three depreciation methods.

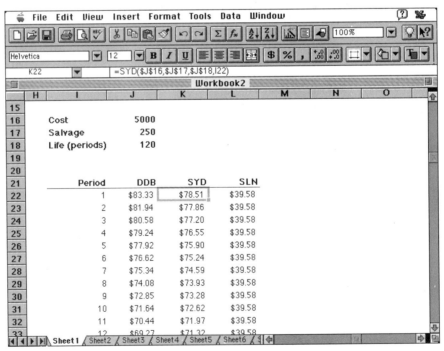

Figure 7-8: A comparison of depreciation functions.

FV

The FV function calculates the *future value* of an investment—the value after payments have been made at a specified rate over a period of time. This function can determine the amount of money you have after the term of an investment ends. FV uses a regular payment amount over a period of time, the interest rate, and the number of payment periods. Use the following syntax for FV:

FV(*rate,periods,payment,present_value,type*)

rate	is the interest rate per period, which you specify as any numeric value.
periods	is an integer indicating the life of the investment in units. Specify *periods* in the same units used for the *interest_rate* (months, years, and so on) because FV figures interest earned per period. Both arguments must be integers.
payment	is the income from the loan or outflow from the investment.
present_value	is the starting value of the investment.
type	can be 1 or 0. If you enter 1, Excel assumes that payments occur at the beginning of the period. If you enter 0, Excel assumes that the payments occur at the end of the period. If you omit this argument, the default of 0 is used.

Remember that you must show cash paid out as a negative number and interest or cash received as a positive number. If you are calculating the future value of an investment, such as a savings account, the *present value* (amount deposited) and the *payment amount* (monthly deposits) are negative numbers because these amounts are paid out to the investment. If no starting value exists, you can enter 0 as the *present_value* argument or omit the argument altogether.

IPMT

The IPMT function calculates the interest paid for a particular payment, given the interest rate, the number of periods in the term, and the present value. Use the following syntax for the IPMT function:

IPMT(*rate,period,periods,payment,present_value,future_value,type*)

rate	is the interest rate per period, which you specify as any numeric value.
period	is an integer indicating the period for which you want to calculate the result.

periods	is an integer indicating the life of the investment in units. Specify *periods* in the same units used for the *rate* (months, years, and so on) because FV figures interest earned per period. Both arguments must be integers.
payment	is the income from the loan or outflow from the investment.
present_value	is the starting value of the investment.
future_value	is the final value of the investment.
type	can be 1 or 0. If you enter 1, Excel assumes that payments occur at the beginning of the period. If you enter 0, Excel assumes that the payments occur at the end of the period. If you omit this argument, the default of 0 is used.

NPER

The NPER function determines the amount of time (number of payment periods) required for a payment amount to equal an investment, given a specific interest rate. Alternatively, you can calculate the number of periods required for a payment amount to build to a specified future value, based on a present value and an interest rate. This function is useful for playing "what if" with interest rates to see how the rates affect the term of an investment. The following shows the correct NPER syntax:

NPER(*rate,payment,present_value,future_value,type*)

rate	is the periodic rate of interest. You can calculate *rate* by dividing the annual interest rate by the number of periods; to calculate monthly interest, for example, divide the annual rate by 12. This value should be consistent with the *payment* argument, which is the periodic payment amount. If, for example, you enter a monthly payment amount for the *payment* variable, *rate* should be the monthly interest rate.
payment	is the income from the loan or outflow from the investment.
present_value	is the starting value of the investment.
future_value	is the final value of the investment.
type	can be 1 or 0. If you enter 1, Excel assumes that payments occur at the beginning of the period. If you enter 0, Excel assumes that the payments occur at the end of the period. If you omit this argument, the default of 0 is used.

NPV

The NPV function returns the net present value of an investment. Use the following syntax:

NPV(*rate,range*)

The net present value (NPV) is the present value of an investment's cash flow, minus the initial cash outlay. The interest rate used to compute the NPV is known as the *discount rate*, or the return that you can earn on investments of equivalent risk.

rate   is the interest rate of the loan and can be any value or expression.

range   is the range of cells that contains the monthly payments and can be any valid worksheet range.

The concept of present value is based on the premise that one dollar today is worth more than one dollar a year from now because you can invest this money. (If you invest one dollar today at 10 percent annual interest, for example, you have one dollar and 10 cents in a year.) The present value of a dollar paid to you in a year can be said to be worth approximately 90 cents at a 10 percent interest rate.

NPV enables you to consider the future value of your money and helps you determine whether an investment is worthwhile. To calculate the NPV of an investment, you need a list of the payments to be made to you for the use of your investment as well as the current interest rate that you can earn on investments of equivalent risk.

Because the function returns the present value, you have to calculate the net present value by using a formula that subtracts the original investment from the present value. Note that the values of the payments don't have to be the same. Remember that cash out is represented as negative and cash in is represented as positive.

PMT

The PMT function calculates the payment amount required to pay off an investment, given a specific term and interest rate. This function is useful for playing "what if" with the term or interest rate of an investment to see how a change affects the amount of the payment. Use the following syntax:

PMT(*rate,periods,present_value,future_value,type*)

rate   is the periodic rate of interest. You can calculate *rate* by dividing the annual interest rate by the number of periods; to calculate monthly interest rate, for example, divide the annual rate by 12. This value should be consistent with the *payment* argument, which is the periodic payment amount. If, for example, you enter a monthly payment amount for the *payment* variable, *rate* should be the monthly interest rate.

periods   is an integer indicating the life of the investment in units. Specify *periods* in the same units used for the *rate* (months, years, and so on) because FV figures interest earned per period.

present_value   is the starting value, or principal amount, of the investment.

future_value   is the final, ending value of the investment.

type   can be 1 or 0. If you enter 1, Excel assumes that payments occur at the beginning of the period. If you enter 0, Excel assumes that the payments occur at the end of the period. If you omit this argument, the default of 0 is used.

You enter *rate* as the periodic interest rate, matching the period you want for the payment result. To calculate a weekly payment amount, for example, *rate* should be a weekly rate (the annual rate divided by 52). *Periods* is the number of periods you want for the term of the investment. *Present_value* is the principal amount of the investment. To determine the amount of the payment for the investment to equal a specified future value (after interest), enter this value as the *future_value* argument.

PPMT

The PPMT function is similar to the PMT function. PMT returns the payment amount required for a given investment over a given time at a given rate; PPMT, however, returns the amount of principal paid in any given period under the same conditions. Use the following syntax for PPMT:

PPMT(*rate,period,periods,present_value,future_value,type*)

rate   is the periodic rate of interest. You can calculate *rate* by dividing the annual interest rate by the number of periods; to calculate monthly interest, for example, divide the annual rate by 12. This value should be consistent with the *payment* argument, which is the periodic payment amount. If, for example, you enter a monthly payment amount for the *payment* variable, *rate* should be the monthly interest rate.

period   is an integer indicating the period for which you want to calculate the result. You have to create a new PPMT formula for each period you want to view.

periods is an integer indicating the life of the investment in units. Specify *periods* in the same units used for the *rate* (months, years, and so on) because FV figures interest earned per period.

present_value is the starting value, or principal amount, of the investment.

future_value is the final, ending value of the investment.

type can be 1 or 0. If you enter 1, Excel assumes that payments occur at the beginning of the period. If you enter 0, Excel assumes that the payments occur at the end of the period. If you omit this argument, the default of 0 is used.

PV

The PV function calculates the present value (principal) of an investment, given the payment amount, interest rate, and number of payment periods. You can supply the argument *future_value* to base the present value on a specific future value. The following line shows the PV syntax:

PV(*rate,periods,payment,future_value,type*)

rate is the periodic interest rate.

periods is an integer indicating the life of the investment in units. Specify *periods* in the same units used for the *rate* (months, years, and so on) because FV figures interest earned per period.

payment is the income from the loan or outflow from the investment.

future_value is the intended resulting value expressed as a numeric value.

type can be 1 (payments occur at the beginning of the period) or 0 (payments occur at the end of the period). If you omit this argument, Excel uses 0.

Information functions

Special functions serve various purposes that don't fit the other categories. Many of these functions are designed primarily for macros. This section lists the most common of these functions.

ERROR.TYPE

The ERROR.TYPE function enables you to determine what kind of error a given cell is reporting. The following line shows the syntax for ERROR.TYPE:

ERROR.TYPE(*error_val*)

error_val   is usually a cell reference, but it can be a formula representing the cell that you are checking for an error.

Table 7-4 shows the *error_val* and the values that are returned.

Table 7-4 ERROR.TYPE Error Values	
Values Returned	**error_val is...**
1	#NULL!
2	#DIV/0!
3	#VALUE!
4	#REF!
5	#NAME?
6	#NUM!
7	#N/A
#N/A	any nonerror

Suppose that cell A3 contains the formula =3/0, which returns a #DIV/0! error. The following formula would then return the value of 2:

=ERROR.TYPE(A3)

The ERROR.TYPE function returns a number that corresponds to the kind of error to which the function refers. Unfortunately, these number codes are relatively unclear. Use the following formula to give you more precise feedback:

=CHOOSE(ERROR.TYPE(A7),"Null Error Message","Divide by Zero Error Message","Value Error Message","Reference Error Message","Name Error Message","Number Error Message","N/A Error Message")

This formula returns the #N/A error if cell A7 evaluates to anything other than an error.

By using this kind of formula, you can indicate specifically what may have gone wrong in the worksheet and suggest a course of action to make the correction.

NA

The NA function uses the following syntax:

NA( )

This function returns the message #N/A to a cell, which indicates that the information needed to produce a result isn't yet available. Excel doesn't know when information isn't available; you must program this logic into worksheets by using the NA function.

As you can see, this function has no arguments. If a cell produces the value #N/A, all calculations that access this cell produce the value #N/A. Later, you can convert the #N/A value to a meaningful message by using an IF statement.

Suppose that, based on the number you enter into cell B1, the formula in cell B2 calculates this cell's value. In cell B2, you may want to use the NA function in a formula to test whether data was entered into B1, as in the following formula:

=IF(ISBLANK(B1)=TRUE,NA(),B1*2)

This formula means *if cell B1 is blank, return #N/A; otherwise, calculate B1*2*. (See the ISBLANK function for more information about this function's syntax.)

Now suppose that a formula in cell B3 calculates the related value based on the value of cell B2. To have the formula test whether the value of B2 is #N/A before making the related calculation, use the following formula:

=IF(ISNA(B2)=TRUE,"Amount not entered in cell B1",B2+100)

This formula means *if the value of B2 is #N/A, print the message 'Amount not entered in cell B1'; otherwise, calculate B2+100*. The formula converts the #N/A value into a message more useful to the operator.

TYPE

The TYPE function tells you the kind of information a cell contains. The following shows the TYPE function's syntax:

TYPE(*cell*)

cell   can be a range or a constant value. If *cell* is a range, the function returns the kind of information contained in the first cell of the range.

Table 7-5 shows the values that this function returns; the values correspond with the type of information in the cell.

Table 7-5	
TYPE Function Values	
Values Returned	*Cell Contents*
1	Numeric value
2	Text
4	Logical value (TRUE or FALSE)
16	Error
64	Array

The formula =TYPE(B5) returns 2 if cell B5 contains "January" and returns 16 if B5 contains the error message #VALUE!.

Logical functions

Logical functions create logical tests that enable a formula to account for more data. A test may determine, for example, whether a particular value is greater than 25. The formula that carries out the test then performs one function if the value is true and another function if the value is false. In short, logical functions enable formulas to branch according to particular values. The most common logical function is IF, which enables you to develop several kinds of tests based on the operators used in the test statement. IF is often combined with other logical functions for more variety.

AND, OR

Although you can nest IF functions to make multiple tests in one formula, Excel also provides two important logical functions for this purpose. You can add more power to the IF function by adding the logical functions AND and OR. When added to an IF function, AND adds a second test to the condition. The following line shows the correct syntax for AND:

AND(*condition1,condition2...*)

If all conditions are true, the AND function returns TRUE; otherwise, it returns FALSE. An example may appear as follows:

=IF(AND(A1=A2,A1=A6), "Right","Wrong")

This function adds a second test to the condition and means *if cell A1 equals the value of A2 and cell A1 equals the value of A6, display 'Right'; otherwise, display 'Wrong'.* Notice that two conditional tests appear before the first comma in the IF function. Both tests fall in the parentheses of the AND function, so the AND function and the two related tests replace the single test used previously.

The OR function also adds a second test to the IF function. If one or more conditions are true, the OR function returns TRUE; otherwise, it returns FALSE. Use the following syntax for OR functions:

OR(*condition1,condition2...*)

Consider the following example:

=IF(OR(A1=5,B1=25),"Right","Wrong")

This function is similar to the preceding example but means *if the value of A1 equals 5 and/or if the value of B1 equals 25, display 'Right'; otherwise, display 'Wrong'*. Note that the OR function serves as an and/or condition, which means that, for the statement to prove TRUE, both conditions can be true. You can stack several tests into one AND or OR statement, as in the following line:

=IF(AND(A1=5,B1=25,G5=G6),"Right","Wrong")

If all three conditions are true, this statement is true.

IF

The IF function is probably the most powerful of all worksheet functions, providing most of the logic you need for evaluating information. The IF function tests whether a condition is true or false. If the condition is true, one value is returned; if the condition is false, another value is returned. The syntax for IF appears in the following form:

IF(*condition,value_if_true,value_if_false*)

condition   is a mathematical expression representing a test condition.

value_if_true is the resulting value if the condition proves true.

value_if_false is the resulting value if the condition proves false.

Proving a condition true or false requires a comparison operator. Table 7-6 shows which operators Excel offers.

In the following examples, you can substitute any of the operators for the operators given in the preceding listing. Consider the following example:

IF(A1=A2,"Right","Wrong")

	Table 7-6
	Excel's Operators

Operator	Definition
>	Greater than
<	Less than
=	Equal to
>=	Greater than or equal to
<=	Less than or equal to
<>	Not equal to

This formula means *if the value of A1 is equal to the value of A2, then return 'Right';
otherwise, return 'Wrong'. Value_if_true* and *value_if_false* can be any constant value,
cell reference, or formula that results in a numeric value or text. Consider this
example:

=IF(D3=1,1500,IF(D3=2,2000,0))

This formula contains a nested IF statement. The second IF statement is entered
as the "else" of the first statement. If D3 doesn't contain 1 or 2, cell E3 displays 0.

ISBLANK

The ISBLANK function tests for a blank cell. Use this syntax:

ISBLANK(*cell*)

cell   is the cell reference you want to test.

If the specified cell is blank, the function returns TRUE; otherwise, the function
returns FALSE. The referenced cell can be any valid cell in the worksheet. The
function commonly is used with the IF function to test for a blank cell and then
perform an action based on the outcome of the test. You can combine ISBLANK
with IF, for example, to print a message next to cells that need to be filled in; you
can remove the message after the data is entered.

=IF(ISBLANK(B5)=FALSE,"","Enter your ID number in cell B5")

The IF function tests whether the result of the ISBLANK test is FALSE. If so, the
blank string is returned. Otherwise, the message appears.

The ISBLANK function can also determine whether a value was entered before
you use the cell reference in a formula. Consider the following formula:

=IF(ISBLANK(B5)=TRUE,NA(),B5*B6)

This formula means *if B5 is blank, return #N/A; otherwise, multiply B5 by B6 and return the result.* The formula suspends calculation until the number is entered.

ISNA

The ISNA function tests whether a cell contains #N/A. Use the following syntax:

ISNA(*cell*)

cell   is the cell referencing you are testing.

The value #N/A may appear because a function is unable to find data or because a formula has specifically returned the #N/A message. #N/A implies that information that the function needs to continue is not available. You can convert #N/A into a more meaningful statement through a formula that contains ISNA.

=IF(ISNA(B5)=FALSE,B5*B6,"Unable to complete this calculation")

If #N/A is discovered in cell B5, this formula returns the message: `Unable to complete this calculation.`

ISNONTEXT, ISNUMBER, ISTEXT

The functions ISNONTEXT, ISNUMBER, and ISTEXT have the following syntax:

ISNONTEXT(*cell*)

ISNUMBER(*cell*)

ISTEXT(*cell*)

These functions test whether a cell's value is a number or a text string. This kind of test can help determine whether a cell contains a number before you reference the cell in a formula. Blank cells are considered text. You really don't need all three functions; if you use ISNUMBER to determine that a cell doesn't contain a number, you already know that the cell must contain a text string. The only reason for using ISNONTEXT is to distinguish between text and blank cells.

NOT

The NOT function causes the function to return TRUE if a condition doesn't match your criterion. The following line shows the syntax for NOT:

NOT(*condition*)

condition   is a mathematical expression that you are testing.

Consider the following example:

=NOT(A5>B5)

This formula asks, *is A5 not greater than B5?* The answer is TRUE if A5 is not greater than B5 (rather like saying *Yes, it is not true*). You can use the NOT function with any of the comparison operators listed previously, as in the following example:

=IF(OR(C5=25,NOT(A5=B5)),TRUE(),FALSE())

Lookup functions

Lookup functions search for values within tables or lists. Each lookup function follows a different method for searching and returning values. Each method is suited for a particular task. Whenever a worksheet places values in tables (such as tax tables or price tables), you can employ a lookup function for added power in the application.

CHOOSE

The CHOOSE function uses a value to look up another value in a specified set. The following line shows the syntax for CHOOSE:

CHOOSE(*value,list*)

value   can be any number, formula, or cell reference that results in a value and designates which item from *list* is to be returned.

list   is a series of values to be returned. If the value is 1, the first item in the list is returned; if the value is 2, the second value is returned, and so on.

Suppose that you enter the following formula:

=CHOOSE(A1,"primero","second","trio")

If the value of cell A1 is 3, the formula returns t r i o because this item is third in the list. Here, the list contains text references; however, numbers, cell references, formulas, or any combination are also acceptable. You must supply the values as a list, however; a range reference isn't acceptable. If *value* is a blank cell or text, Excel assumes that the argument is 0.

You probably already can see some limitations to this function. What if *value* is 141? Must you have 142 values in the list? The answer is yes. Remember that the

CHOOSE function, however, is meant to be used when the first value is sequential (as in 141, 142, 143, 144, and so on), not variable. Because the possible values are sequential, not variable, you can convert them to 1, 2, 3, 4, and so on, by using the following formula:

=CHOOSE(A1–140,"primero","second","trio")

Notice that the first value consists of the formula A1–140, which converts the values to a more manageable range for the function — the values 1, 2, 3, and 4.

The CHOOSE function is much like HLOOKUP and VLOOKUP, which are described in the following section. A major advantage of CHOOSE is that this function can choose parameters randomly, and HLOOKUP and VLOOKUP require parameters to be in a range of cells. CHOOSE, for example, may appear as follows:

CHOOSE(A5,C4,G25,H2,B33,F2)

The listed items aren't adjacent cell references. If the value in the CHOOSE function is larger than the greatest item in the list, the function returns #VALUE!.

HLOOKUP, VLOOKUP

The HLOOKUP and VLOOKUP functions search for values in tables, basing the search on a specified lookup value. A *lookup value* is a value you are trying to match in the table. In a tax table that contains tax rates based on income, for example, income is the lookup value. VLOOKUP searches vertically in a column of values and returns a corresponding value from the table. HLOOKUP searches horizontally in a row of values and returns a corresponding value from the table. The syntax of the two functions is shown in the following lines:

HLOOKUP(*value,range,row_offset*)

VLOOKUP(*value,range,column_offset*)

value　　　is any valid number, text string, or expression that results in a valid number or string, which includes formulas and cell references.

range　　　is the worksheet range that contains the table.

row_offset　determines the value to be returned.

column_offset　determines the value to be returned.

The VLOOKUP function takes the search variable and looks down the first column of the table for a match. When a match is found, the function maintains the row position of the matched value but moves across the table to return one of the columns, determined by the offset value that you specified.

Suppose that a worksheet contains the table of values shown in Figure 7-9. In the figure, cell B16 contains the following formula:

=VLOOKUP($A$1,$A$7:$D$14,2)

Also in the figure, cell B17 contains the following formula:

=VLOOKUP($A$1,$A$7:$D$14,3)

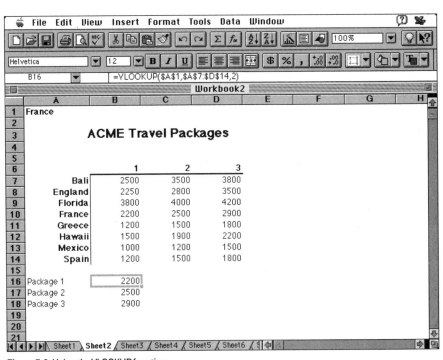

Figure 7-9: Using the VLOOKUP function.

The first formula (in cell B16) tries to match the value in cell A16 to the first column of the range A7:D14, column A7:A14. This column is known as the *lookup column*. In a VLOOKUP statement, this column always is the first column in the specified range; in an HLOOKUP statement, the *lookup row* is the first row.

When the formula finds a match, the function returns the corresponding value from the table column specified by *column_offset*. (The lookup column offset value is 1.) Because the offset value in the formula is 2, the corresponding value in the first column to the right of the lookup column (column 2) — 5.50 — is returned. The second formula (cell B17) performs the same operation but returns the value from the third column of the table.

Several rules apply to performing lookups with HLOOKUP and VLOOKUP. First, if the search variable is numeric, the values in the lookup column (or row) should be numeric. Moreover, these values should be in ascending order. If the lookup column isn't in ascending order, the functions may return incorrect values. Excel searches the lookup column until a match is found; if a match isn't found, Excel uses the value closest to — but smaller than — the search variable. If a lookup value is greater than all values in the table, the last value in the table is used because this value is the largest.

If the lookup value is smaller than all values in the table, the function returns the error message #N/A. Remember that if no match is made, Excel returns the first value that is smaller than the search variable.

If the lookup range within the specified table range contains text strings, the search variable also must be a text string. In these cases, the lookup function must be able to find a match for the specified information. If no match is found, the function returns the error #N/A. The data in the table (that is, the value to be returned) can be numeric or text.

INDEX

The INDEX function returns a value from a table according to the row and column offsets specified. Rather than matching a value in the table, INDEX goes directly to the row and column offset values you specify and returns the contents of the intersection. The following line shows the syntax for INDEX:

INDEX(*range,row_offset,column_offset*)

range   is a range reference that indicates the range containing the table.

row_offset and *column_offset*

                   must be equal to or less than the number of rows (or columns) in *range*. If either argument is too large, the function returns an error. If either argument is 0, the function returns the error #VALUE!.

Mathematical functions

Mathematical functions apply to general mathematical needs, such as finding the absolute value of a number or rounding a number. These functions also include some logarithmic functions. The following sections describe Excel's mathematical functions.

ABS

The ABS function returns the absolute value of a number or cell reference. The *absolute value* of a number is the number without positive or negative status. (The absolute value of –34, for example, is 34.) The following line shows the syntax of ABS:

ABS(*value*)

value   can be a number, formula, or cell reference — any expression that results in a value.

Consider the following examples:

ABS(–354)

ABS(A5)

ABS(TOTAL)

ABS(TOTAL – (A5*4))

CEILING, FLOOR

The CEILING function returns the value of a number or cell reference, rounded up to the nearest incremental amount (known as the *multiple of significance*). The FLOOR function rounds down to the nearest incremental amount. The following lines show the syntax of each function:

CEILING (*number, significance*)

FLOOR(*number, significance*)

number   is the number or cell reference that you want rounded.

significance   is the increment or step by which you want the rounding done.

Here are some examples:

=CEILING (3.1415,0.1)

=FLOOR(3.1415,0.1)

The CEILING function calculates the value of rounded up to the nearest increment of 0.1 and returns 3.2. The FLOOR function calculates the value of rounded down to the nearest increment of 0.1 and returns 3.1.

INT

The INT function rounds down a number to the nearest integer, which results in a positive or negative number without decimal values. The INT value of 829.98, for example, is 829; the INT value of –829.98 is –830. This function is commonly used in financial worksheets. Use the following syntax for the INT function:

INT(*value*)

value   is a number, formula, or cell reference.

Here's an example:

=INT(B5)

If cell B5 contains 45.55, the function returns 45.

PI

You can use the PI function wherever the value is required. Excel calculates to 14 decimal places and keeps track of all 14 places. The PI function uses the following syntax:

PI( )

Be sure that you include the empty parentheses, even though the function has no argument. To calculate the area of a circle, for example, enter the following formula:

=PI()*B5^2

Cell B5 contains the radius of the circle.

PRODUCT

The PRODUCT function calculates the product of the specified values. Use the following syntax:

PRODUCT(*list*)

list   a list of references, values, or formulas that you want to multiply together.

Excel ignores references to blank cells or cells that contain text. You can list the values in the function or enter a range reference to specify the values. For example, =PRODUCT(5,3,7,8) produces the result of 840.

RAND

The RAND function produces a random number between 0 and 1. Each time you calculate the worksheet, this function produces a new random number. Although the function requires no arguments, parentheses must follow the function name, as shown in the following syntax:

RAND()

To calculate a random number between any two numbers, use the following syntax:

=*start*+RAND()*(*end–start*)

Substitute the starting number for *start* and the ending number for *end*. To calculate random numbers between 4 and 24, for example, use the following formula:

=4+RAND()*(24–4)

Note that this formula produces the decimal values between two numbers. You may want to remove the decimals. Removing the decimals, however, can distort the beginning and ending values. Often, you end with numbers equal to or greater than the starting value but less than the ending value. To remove the decimal values, try the following formula, which produces numbers from the *start* to the *end* values, inclusive:

=*start*+INT(RAND()*(*end–start*)+.5)

To choose a random number from a list of numbers, try the following formula:

=CHOOSE(1+RAND()*5,33,35,39,45,60)

In this formula, the 5 in the random-number calculation indicates the number of items in the list.

ROUND

The ROUND function rounds a value to a specified number of places. The difference between using this function and formatting the cell to display a specified number of places (using the Format⇨Number command) is that the ROUND function permanently changes the number to the rounded version. Any subsequent calculations based on this number are made with the rounded number. A number rounded with the Format⇨Number command displays a number in a certain format but doesn't change the number. Calculations that include the number use the original number, not the formatted version.

The following line shows the syntax of the ROUND function:

ROUND(*value,precision*)

value   is the number to be rounded.

precision   is the number of places to which the number is rounded.

If the value 5.2573 appears in cell A1, for example, you can use the following formula to round this number to two decimal places:

=ROUND(A1,2)

The result of this formula is 5.26.

The standard for rounding monetary values is to two decimal places. This procedure also can be termed *rounding to the nearest penny*. You can round an amount to the nearest dime by entering 1 in place of 2 in the formula, as in the following example:

=ROUND(A1,1)

When 0 is the precision argument, the formula rounds to the nearest dollar. When –1 is the argument, the formula rounds to the nearest 10 dollars; when –2 is the argument, the formula rounds to the nearest 100 dollars.

SUM

SUM, the most commonly used function, is an easy way to add values. SUM uses the following syntax:

SUM(*range*)

range   can be a row or column (or portions thereof) or a block of cells.

To add values that are not in a row or a column, enter a list.

You also can add the numbers in a block of cells by entering the entire range as the argument for the SUM function. The formula =SUM(C1:D5) adds the numbers in a two-by-five block of cells. You can specify any valid range in the SUM function.

Note that the AutoSum button in Excel's Standard toolbar automatically enters an appropriate SUM function for you. Refer to Topic 2 for more information on using AutoSum.

Statistical functions

Statistical functions work on groups of numbers. Common statistical tasks include calculating the average of a group, finding the minimum and maximum value of a group, and adding the numbers in a group. Statistical functions also include more advanced functions, such as standard deviation and sample statistics calculations.

AVERAGE

The AVERAGE function calculates the average of a group of numbers. Usually, the numbers you average fall in a row or a column, but AVERAGE also can average randomly plotted values. Use the following syntax for the AVERAGE function:

AVERAGE(*list*)

list   is a list of cell references, values, formulas, or functions that you want to average.

Remember that unwanted values of 0 destroy the accuracy of an average. When used with a range reference, the AVERAGE function skips blank cells and text.

COUNT, COUNTA

COUNT and COUNTA count the number of cells in a range or list of references. The COUNT function counts only numeric values; the COUNTA function counts all cells that are not blank. The COUNT and COUNTA functions use the following syntax:

COUNT(*range*)

COUNTA(*range*)

Suppose that the range A1:A7 contains the following values:

A1: 1

A2: 0

A3: text

A4: 983

A5:

A6: 298

A7: 2

The COUNT and COUNTA functions return the following results when you enter this range:

COUNT(A1:A7)   5

COUNTA(A1:A7)   6

MAX

The MAX function returns the maximum value in a group of cells. Use the following syntax:

MAX(*range*)

range   can be a range of cells, random cell references, a formula, direct entries, or a combination of these items, as in the following examples:

MAX(A1:A5)

MAX(A1,25,C23*3)

If range A1:A5 contains the values 1, 25, 3, 6, and 13, the first function returns 25. If cell C23 contains 100, the second function returns 300. The MAX function ignores text cells and references to blank cells. If a maximum value isn't found, the function returns 0.

MEDIAN

MEDIAN calculates the median of a group of values (the middle value among the values, such that half the values are greater and half the values are lesser). You can enter a range or include up to 14 values in a list. Use the following syntax:

MEDIAN(*range*)

range   is a range or list of cells for which you want the median.

MIN

The MIN function returns the minimum value in a group of cells. Use the following syntax for MIN:

MIN(*range*)

range   can be a range of cells, random cell references, a formula, direct entries, or a combination.

The MIN function ignores text cells and references to blank cells.

You can calculate the span of numbers, but when evaluating a column of numbers, you may need to determine the span between the smallest and largest numbers. Suppose that you have the list 25, 49, 33, 120, 101, and 40. The span is 95 because the difference between the smallest number (25) and largest number (120) is 95. The following formula calculates this value:

=MAX(*range*)–MIN(*range*)

Quick Tips

Matching parentheses in a formula

Excel helps you match left and right parentheses in a formula when Excel is in Edit mode. When you move the blinking cursor across a formula in the formula bar, Excel momentarily bolds the matching set of parentheses. Excel also does this if you add a missing parenthesis in response to a formula error.

Navigating through formulas

If you double-click a formula, Excel automatically moves the cell pointer to the first cell referenced in that formula (called the *precedent* cell). In this way, you can move backward through cell references and take a "tour" of your spreadsheet logic. This is called worksheet navigation.

Duplicating a formula and its results

Press Command-' or Command-" in the cell immediately below a cell containing a formula to duplicate the formula and the result of the formula, respectively. Note that if you use this method to copy a formula, the cell references do not change.

Using Excel as a Database

Overview

Although Excel is not engineered specifically to be a sophisticated database management program, it contains some powerful database management tools. You can enter individual records in your worksheets and manipulate the records in groups or perform other database management tasks with the records. Many spreadsheet-oriented applications lend themselves to database management, including applications that must store and retrieve individual records, such as employee records, payroll applications, income and expense management, checkbook management, and so on. You'll find that databases are a common element in advanced worksheets.

In this topic, you learn why and when to use a database in Excel, how to set up your Excel databases, how to add and remove information from a database, and how to find specific information in a database.

What Is a Database?

A database is a collection of similar data stored in a structured manner. You use databases, such as the white pages of a telephone book, a Rolodex, or your checkbook, every day of your life. A database is organized so that you can easily analyze, list, sort, or search its contents for data that meets certain requirements.

Databases store their information as *records*. Each record contains separate items of information, or *fields*. In a telephone book, for example, each entry is a record, and each record contains three fields of information (name, street address, and telephone number). You can create similar databases in Excel. Figure 8-1 shows a spreadsheet that functions like a database.

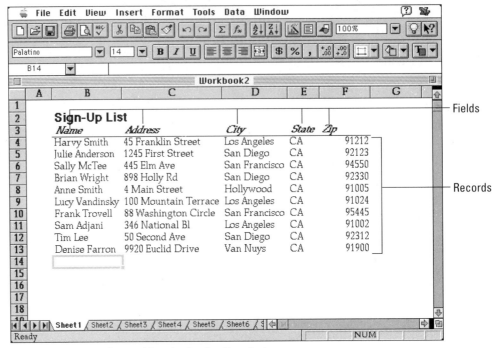

Figure 8-1: An example of a spreadsheet that functions like a database.

Excel database ranges are not much different than any worksheet ranges that contain column headings and data beneath the headings. In fact, you can turn any worksheet range into a database range, provided that you adhere to a few simple rules that are detailed later in this topic, under "Database Setup."

Why Use a Database?

Why use a database? What advantages are there to turning a worksheet range into a database range?

Setting up a database range gives you access to Excel's database management tools. These tools can help you do the following tasks:

◆ Easily adding and removing data from a range

◆ Easily finding and changing existing data in a range

◆ Viewing subsets of an entire database

◆ Performing statistical analysis on groups of records from a database

If you frequently perform any of these tasks on your worksheet data, you may benefit from setting up a database. To help you in these database management tasks, Excel gives you access to your data through the *data form*. The data form is a dialog box that displays your database records and provides easy access to database management tasks. Refer to "Using the Data Form" later in this topic for more information on the data form.

In short, you should set up a database if you need to store data in the form of records, in which all the records contain the same basic types of data, and if your data changes frequently or you frequently need to find and view subsets of the data. Some examples of when setting up a database may be helpful include:

◆ Calculating sales statistics

◆ Analyzing stock market information

◆ Monitoring accounts receivable

◆ Targeting direct mail promotions

The good news is that you already have Excel and don't need to spend the time or money researching, comparing, shopping, and buying another computer program. You can find out whether you need database capabilities by trying Excel's database features before you go and plunk down a considerable amount of your life savings on a database program.

The not-so-good news is that Excel's database capabilities may be limiting. Because Excel loads a copy of your spreadsheet into memory from disk, your Macintosh's memory may limit the size of the database you can run. Most dedicated database management programs read and write records to and from the hard disk and therefore don't face this limitation.

But if your database needs are relatively simple, what you lose in capacity is more than made up for in speed and flexibility. You won't have to wait around while your database is performing intensive disk operations. Because your database is in your computer's memory, you'll enjoy very fast calculation and short task-completion times. Chances are, you can manage as many as 5,000 to 8,000 records easily in Excel, depending on the number of fields you use and your Mac's memory.

Database Setup

An Excel database is simply a range of cells on the worksheet. The first row of the range should contain headings for the columns that indicate the fields contained in each record. Each row of data, entered under these headings, is a record. As you can see, databases use a common structure for spreadsheet data. Chances are, you already have data arranged in rows and columns with headings above each column.

If you plan to access this data often, search the data for information, or add new information to the existing entries, then you can benefit from Excel's database features.

Note that the fields you choose for your database are of paramount importance, as they determine the information in each record and, ultimately, the usefulness of the database. You should decide what information you want in your database before jumping in and creating the headings. Consider the following guidelines when setting up your database and choosing field names (column headings):

◆ **Make sure your field names (column headings) are all unique text entries.** Each column heading must use a unique text label. If two column headings are identical, Excel may be unable to perform certain database functions on the data. For best results, use single words. If you must use numbers, enter them as text labels using the form *="1993"*, as explained in Topic 2. You can use formulas as your column headings, provided that they calculate text strings.

◆ **The maximum length of a database field name is 255 characters, but you should keep the names down to a readable size.** In general, shorter field names are easier to understand and permit you to display more fields on the screen at the same time. You should also note that Excel is interested only in the row of field names directly above the first row of data. You can have two or more rows of names to help you understand a field, but it's the single row above the data that counts with Excel. Any extra rows above this one are for your convenience.

◆ **Enter each record as a new row.** Each row under the column headings represents a new record in the database. Although you can leave some cells blank within a record, avoid leaving entire rows blank as this can throw off Excel's data query commands. Also, each record in the database should be unique. A record is unique if one or more fields contains exclusive information. For example, your Orders database may contains two orders from the same company that are identical in every way except for the date. Note that you can use a special field to sequentially number your records that automatically makes each record unique (see Figure 8-2).

◆ **Format the field names and records differently.** Excel 5 has the new capability of being able to identify your database range automatically. As your database grows and shrinks, Excel can follow the bottom of the database range without your help. However, to do this, Excel expects the field names to be formatted differently than the record rows. For best results, make the headings stand out by using boldface type or a special font for them.

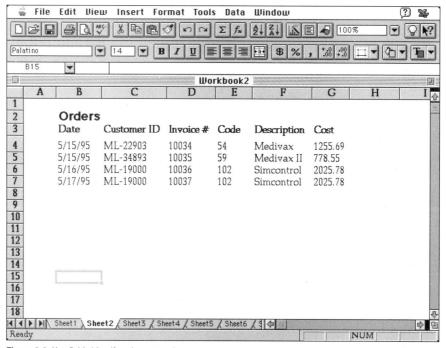

Figure 8-2: Key fields identify unique records.

◆ **Leave plenty of room below the headings for new records.** Because databases commonly expand to include new data, you should make sure that your database range has plenty of room at the bottom for new entries. For best results, place the database range in a separate worksheet in your workbook or in the lower-right corner of a worksheet where other data will not interfere with it. If other worksheet data appears to the right or left of the database range, it could be destroyed when you add or remove records from the database.

Entering database records

In Excel, there are two ways to enter records into a database. The first way, with which you should be familiar, is to type the desired information into rows below the column headings. The second method is through the use of Excel's data form, which displays each record one at a time, on the screen in a dialog box. For an explanation of the data form, turn to "Using the Data Form" later in this topic.

Adding records to the database

1. Highlight a range under the existing database records (or under the field names if no records exist yet) that includes all the columns of the database, plus as many rows as you plan to enter. Figure 8-3 shows an example of a highlighted range.

Figure 8-3: Begin by highlighting a range in which you plan to enter new records.

2. Type the first piece of information into the first cell of the highlighted range. Press Tab when you are finished.

3. Continue to fill out the fields, pressing Tab after each one. The cell pointer will remain inside the highlighted area. **◊**

Turn calculation off when entering new rows. If your database range contains calculated fields (fields whose values are the results of calculations), you may find it faster to temporarily suspend recalculation in the worksheet until you're finished entering records. Use the Manual option in the Tools⇨Options⇨Calculation command to suspend recalculation. Set this back to Automatic when you're finished.

Editing and deleting data

One common database task is to modify or update records as the data changes. You can change your Excel database records by modifying the data on the worksheet or by using the data form. Both methods are quite simple. Details about using the data form appear later in this topic, under "Using the Data Form."

To modify the worksheet data, simply locate the row containing the data you want to change, move to the appropriate cells, and edit the contents of those cells. Refer to Topic 2 for more information about editing the contents of cells. To remove a record, simply delete the entire row from the database by highlighting all the cells in the unwanted record and selecting Delete from the Edit menu. Choose the Shift Cells Up option when prompted.

Sorting the Database

One of the advantages of entering your database records in Excel (or any computer database system) is that you can sort and re-sort the data whenever you like. Sorting the data is simply the process of arranging them alphabetically, chronologically, or numerically. Generally, you choose a *key field* by which the data is sorted. For example, an address list database would typically be sorted by either the Last Name field or the Zip Code field. In fact, you can sort the records by Last Name and then re-sort them by Zip Code whenever you like. Excel sorts instantaneously.

Quick sorting your database

1. Place the cell pointer in the column by which you want to sort the data. For example, if you want to sort by the Last Name field, place the cell pointer anywhere in the Last Name column below the field name and within the data.

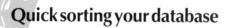

2. Click the Sort Ascending tool to sort from A to Z or the Sort Descending tool to sort from Z to A. Of course, if the field is numeric, Excel sorts the records numerically — from negatives to positives (ascending) or positives to negatives (descending). ♦

You may find that sorting by a single key field is not detailed enough. Perhaps you have an address list that you want to sort by the Last Name field. What if the database contains two entries with identical last names, such as Fred Jones and Mary Jones? In such cases, you may want to use a second key field, such as the First Name field, to break the "tie." Using the First Name field as the second key field would place Fred Jones before Mary Jones. You can use up to three key fields for sorting your database records. The first key is used as the main sort, and the second and third keys are used as the tie breakers.

Sorting records by multiple keys

1. Place the cell pointer in the column by which you want to sort the database.

2. Select the Sort command from the Data menu. Excel selects the entire database range, and the Sort dialog box appears as shown in Figure 8-4.

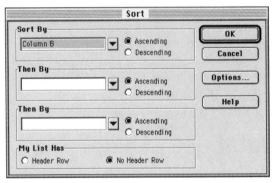

Figure 8-4: The Sort dialog box lets you choose key fields for the sorting procedure.

3. Choose the first sort field from the drop-down list that appears in the Sort By dialog box.

4. Select either Ascending or Descending to determine the order of the sorted records.

5. If you want to add a second key for additional sorting detail, choose the desired field from the second drop-down list provided. Select Ascending or Descending for this key (generally the same as the first key, but not always). Repeat this step if you want to add a third key.

6. Determine whether your database has a header row (column headings) and choose the appropriate option at the bottom of the dialog box.

7. Click OK to sort the data.

When sorting the database, consider the following points:

◆ **Sort formulas, provided they refer to cells inside the same row (record).** If your database uses formulas to produce certain columns of data, you can include those calculated columns in the sorted data, provided the formulas refer to other cells in the same row. For instance, one cell may be the sum of two other cells within the same record.

If the formulas refer to cells in other rows or outside the sorted data range, you should perform a test sort to determine if the formulas are corrupted by the sorting procedure. Use the Undo command to return the database back to normal. Generally, formulas that refer to cells inside the data range are not changed when you sort the data. In other words, the references remain the same after you sort the data.

◆ **Don't sort totals or column headings with the data.** If your database includes column totals, don't include them in the sort range. Also, exclude the column titles at the top of the database. To ensure that Excel automatically chooses the database range correctly, make sure that you have a blank row of cells above the column headings.

◆ **Excel sorts numerically, chronologically, and alphabetically at the same time.** Excel sorts information in the following order:

  ◆ Numbers from negative to positive

  ◆ Text in ANSI order (spaces, symbols and numerals first, then alphabetically)

  ◆ Logical values FALSE then TRUE

  ◆ Error values

  ◆ Blank cells

◆ **Note that dates are really just numeric values or *serial numbers*.** Dates then appear chronologically, which could cause problems if you are sorting dates along with other numeric values.

◆ **You don't have to sort all the records, but you should sort all the fields.** You can sort a portion of the records if you don't mind that records excluded from the sort range will be out of order. However, you should include all columns (fields) in the sort. If you don't, records will be split up and, perhaps, impossible to piece back together.

◆ **Filter the records before sorting if desired.** If you filter your database before you sort it, you will be able to sort only those records showing through the filter. Filtering is discussed in the next section.

You can sort any worksheet data. The sorting procedure can be applied to any data on the worksheet, not just database data. Just follow the sorting procedure described at the beginning of this section to sort any list of items.

You can sort columns of data instead of rows. To sort the columns of your database (i.e., to rearrange the columns), select Options in the Sort dialog box and choose the Sort Left to Right option. The first key should point to any cell in the row containing the column headings. As an alternative, you can use a row above the column headings to sort the columns. Just type a number above each column heading to determine the column's placement. The arrangement of these numbers determines the order of the columns.

Filtering Your Database

Excel's new database filtering capabilities make it easy to locate specific information in the database and to display groups of records that meet certain criteria. *Filtering* is a way of viewing subsets of the entire database.

As your database grows you'll find it more and more difficult to locate specific records by looking through a sorted list. Excel provides the filtering procedures to help you narrow down the options and display groups of records that share similar data. For example, you can view all the records that have a zip code entry of 92123. Or you can view all the records for Sam Jones. The more specific you are with the filtering criteria, the fewer records that will match the criteria. For example, you may have several records with a zip code entry of 92123, but only one *also* contains Jones in the Last Name field. By specifying Jones and 92123, you filter the matching records down to only one.

Displaying a filtered subset of your database

1. Place the cell pointer anywhere inside the database range.

2. Choose the Filter⇨AutoFilter command from the Data menu. Excel adds drop-down list arrows to the cells containing your field names, turning each of these cells into a drop-down list. Figure 8-5 shows an example.

3. Choose the desired information from the drop-down lists by clicking the down arrow and choosing the criteria that you want. Excel narrows the database records, showing only the records that match your selected criteria. Each of the drop-down lists contains a summary of the items inside the respective database column — eliminating duplicates. If you want to display records that contain CA in the State field, choose CA from the drop-down list above the State column. Choose from additional drop-down lists to narrow the selection even further. Figure 8-5 shows the example database filtered to display records with CA in the State field.

4. Return the database to normal (displaying all records) by choosing the Filter⇨Show All command from the Data menu. Also, you can return specific columns to normal by selecting the (All) option from the drop-down field list within the desired column. ◖◗

Each of the AutoFilter lists contains unique entries from the column of data it represents. Therefore, you will find only one state of CA, even though you may have numerous records with CA in the State field. In addition to the data, Excel provides the options described in Table 8-1 in each drop-down AutoFilter list.

Figure 8-5: Excel's Data⇨Filter⇨AutoFilter command turns your field names into drop-down lists.

Table 8-1
AutoFilter Options

Option	Description of What It Does
All	Displays all the records in the chosen column. Other columns that you have filtered may still be in effect. To quickly display all records in the database, choose the Filter⇨Show All command from the Data menu.
Custom	Lets you establish custom criteria for filtering, such as all records that begin with certain letters, or values that are between certain limits (such as order amounts between 100 and 500 dollars). Details about custom autofiltering appear later in this section.
Blanks	Displays all records that have blank cells in the associated field, allowing you to go back through your database and fill in missing information.
Nonblanks	Displays all records that have information in the associated field, allowing you to exclude records that have blank cells in the chosen column.

Using custom criteria

The Custom option in Excel's AutoFilter lists lets you filter the database in a number of special ways. You can filter records by the conditional operators, >, <, <=, >=, and <>, to specify records that meet your conditions. For example, rather than selecting a specific zip code to filter your records, you can view records that contain zip codes greater than 90000. The Custom AutoFilter option also allows you to choose two separate items by which to filter a single column. For example, you can view records that have CA or NY in the State field. Finally, the Custom AutoFilter option lets you specify a range in which numeric values can appear. For example, you can filter records containing prices greater than 100 and less than 1000.

Establishing custom criteria

1. Select Custom from the AutoFilter list in the desired column. The dialog box shown in Figure 8-6 appears.

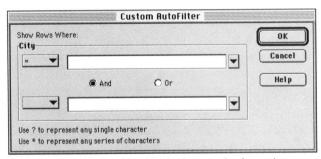

Figure 8-6: The Custom AutoFilter dialog box lets you select from various criteria options.

2. Choose an operator from the first drop-down list provided. Use the conditional operators on numeric fields to establish conditions, such as zip codes greater than 90000.

3. Choose the desired data from the next drop-down list or type the desired entry into the entry box. For example, you may type **90000** to establish the criterion of zip codes greater than 90000.

4. Select the And or Or option if you want to add more conditions to the criteria. Use the And option when you want to establish a numeric range between two values. For example, if you want to view records with zip codes between 94000 and 95000, the dialog box should look like Figure 8-7. Use the Or option when you want to match two different pieces of data in the same field, such as CA or NY in the State field.

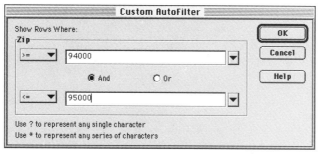

Figure 8-7: Establishing two criteria entries for a numeric range.

5. Enter or choose the second set of criteria in the dialog box, using the two drop-down lists provided.

6. Click OK. ♦

Remember that you can use custom filtering on several of the fields in the database or mix custom criteria with standard filtering selections.

Extracting Records

At times you may want to locate specific records in your database and then copy those records to another worksheet or workbook. For example, you may want to copy (or *extract*) a specific group of customers from your customer database into your accounts receivable database for billing purposes.

There are several ways to extract records from a database. The simplest is to use the Copy and Paste procecures as described in the following steps.

Using wildcards to help locate records

You can specify records that begin with certain characters or that contain certain information. Do this by choosing the equal sign operator in the Custom AutoFilter dialog box and then typing the desired information into the entry box, using wildcards. For example, you may enter S* to establish records that begin with S, or you may type *Mac* to locate records that contain Mac. Here are the most common wild cards:

* The asterisk stands for any number of characters. For example, entering **M*** locates all entries that begin with *M*. Entering ***m** locates entries that end with *m*.

? The question mark stands for any single character. For example, entering **M?** locates entries like *Me, My, Mr,* and *Ms* — but not *Mike* or *Miss*. Enter **M?d** to locate *Mad, Mod, Mid* and so on.

When dealing with text criteria entries, Excel always assumes that a * wildcard appears after each entry. Therefore, Excel assumes that your entry includes words that begin with your entry.

Copying records from the database

1. Use the filtering technique (see "Filtering the Database" earlier in this topic) to display those records you want to extract. The With specific records should be showing in the database list.

2. Highlight the records showing in the database. Do not highlight the field names.

3. Select the Edit⇨Copy command or press Command-C.

4. Move to the destination worksheet and press Command-V to paste the records. ◖◗

Finding and extracting data with a criteria range

You can automate the extract procedure so that you don't have to copy and paste each time. Automating the extract procedure also lets you choose sets of database records based on data that you enter, rather than selections you make from the drop-down filter lists. This procedure is useful for databases that will be used by other people — people who may not know much about using Excel's filtering tools. For example, an operator can locate the record for *Frank Smith* in *California* by typing **Frank, Smith** and **CA** into the database. Excel can then use this information to automatically extract the proper record — the operator doesn't have to use the filtering features.

The key to automatically finding and extracting records (without filtering) is the criteria range. A *criteria* range is a range of cells that includes the names of the fields in which you are searching and the specific data for which you are searching. Figure 8-8 shows a typical criteria range.

Notice that the criteria range consists of a row containing the database field names (column headings) and another row below it for the criteria entries. In this example, the criteria range specifies that you are looking for all records in the 92123 zip code. You can be more specific in the criteria entries by adding additional entries. Figure 8-9 specifies records that have 92123 in the Zip Code field and Jones in the Last Name field. When you activate the find or extract procedure, Excel looks for records that match both criteria entries.

Here are some guidelines for creating a criteria range:

◆ **Headings used in the criteria range must match the database's column headings exactly.** For best results, copy the headings from the database range to the criteria range to make sure they are exact copies. Any differences cause Excel's searching commands to fail.

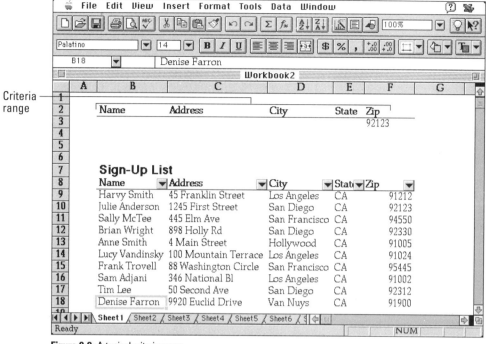

Figure 8-8: A typical criteria range.

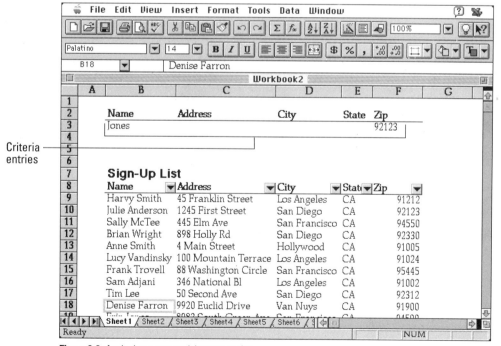

Figure 8-9: A criteria range containing two entries.

- **You don't have to include all the column headings in the criteria range or even enter them in the same order.** Copy only the headings that you need in the criteria range; you don't have to copy them all. If you have an address list database and you will be searching in the Last Name and Zip Code fields, then you don't need to use the First Name field. However, it's never a problem if you include all the headings and just leave some unused.

- **Enter the criteria range above the database range.** To provide room for expansion in the database range, make sure the criteria range is above the database.

- **Enter the criteria for each field under the appropriate heading.** After copying the headings from the database range, enter your search criteria under each appropriate heading as shown in Figures 8-8 and 8-9. For more information about entering criteria, see the next section, "Entering search criteria".

- **You can use conditional operators in your criteria entries.** You can find groups of records that meet a certain condition by using the conditional operators >, <, <=, <=, and <>. For example, entering **>90000** under the Zip Code heading finds all records whose zip codes are above 90000. For more information on criteria entries, see the next section, "Entering search criteria."

Once you have entered the desired criteria, you can either filter the database or extract the specified records by selecting the Data⇨Filter⇨Advanced Filter command. The Advanced Filter dialog box appears (see Figure 8-10).

Figure 8-10: Use the Advanced Filter dialog box to filter a database or copy specific records to another worksheet.

Choose the Filter List In Place option if you want to use the criteria entries to simply filter the database. You can also use the filtering drop-down lists with the AutoFilter command (see "Filtering the Database" earlier in this topic). Choose Copy to Another Location if you want to extract the specified records to another worksheet.

After selecting the desired action, enter the range reference of the criteria range you created. To make this easier, try naming the criteria range first; then you can enter the range name in this dialog box. If you are extracting the records, also enter the range to which you want the records copied. For example, enter **Sheet5!A1** to extract the records to Sheet 5, beginning with cell A1.

Click OK when you are finished making your dialog box selections.

Entering search criteria

Search criteria entered into your criteria range can be very simple or somewhat complex. A simple database search may consist of an exact match. In this case, you would enter the information that you want to match under the appropriate heading in the criteria range. For example, to locate records with 1993 in the Date column, you would simply type **1993** under the Date heading in the criteria range.

If you add another entry to the criteria range, you can narrow the search to fewer matching records. For example, you can enter **1993** under the Date heading and Smith under the Last Name heading to locate records that match *both* criteria — that is, records that have both 1993 in the Date column *and* Smith in the Last Name column. The more specific you are, the more you narrow the search down to a few records.

If your criteria entry is text, you can include *wildcards* in the entry. A wildcard takes the place of a character or several characters, so you can locate groups of records that share common naming conventions. For example, with wildcards you can find any entry in the Last Name column that begins with *M*. Excel offers two different wildcards that you can use in your criteria entries (see the sidebar entitled "Using wildcards to locate records").

You can also specify value ranges for the search, such as all records whose dates are later than 1993. In this case, you would employ a conditional operator. You should use conditional operators with numeric fields for best results. For example, entering **>1990** locates all records with a date later than 1990.

Here are some additional points to remember about entering criteria:

◆ **Make sure you blank all entries before typing new entries.** If any of the criteria cells contain data of any kind, it will be included in the search, including spaces entered by pressing the spacebar. If Excel cannot find records to match your criteria (and you are certain that some records match the criteria), consider blanking all the entries and starting over. This action may remove unseen spaces in the criteria range. Highlight the criteria entries, press Delete, and click the (All) option to blank all data from the range.

◆ **Blank cells in the criteria range indicate all possible entries.** Leaving a criteria entry blank makes all entries in that column eligible to be included in the search.

◆ **You can change the criteria entries at any time and repeat the search.** After you have defined the criteria range, you don't have to define it again. Just blank out the current entries and type new entries to perform a new search.

Using AND and OR searches

If you type more than one entry into the criteria range, you are specifying multiple conditions which must all be met for a record to match the criteria. Such an entry constitutes an *AND* expression. An AND expression says that criteria A *and* criteria B must be met before a record is considered a matching record. For example, the Zip Code field must be greater than 90000 *and* the Last Name field must contain Smith.

You can also create *OR* expressions. An OR expression specifies that criterion A *or* criterion B can be met. For example, the Zip Code field can be greater than 90000 *or* the Last Name field can contain Smith. An OR expression actually increases the likelihood of finding records that match the criteria because you've eased the restrictions to two possible conditions — either of which can be met. Actually, you can enter more than two OR expressions, depending on how many fields you use in the criteria range.

To specify an OR expression you must increase the size of the criteria range to include more rows; you need a new row for each OR expression you want to add. For example, to indicate that the Zip Code field can be greater than 90000 *or* the Last Name field can contain Smith requires two rows. Type each criterion entry into a different row (see Figure 8-11).

Figure 8-11: Entering an OR expression into the criteria range.

Using OR expressions, you can repeat entries for the same field. For example, you can locate records that contain Smith in the Last Name field *or* Jones in the Last Name field. In addition, you can include AND expressions along with OR expressions by adding entries to the respective rows.

Don't use Or expressions to specify ranges within the same field. You cannot use an OR expression to search for a range of values for a single field. For example, if you want to find all zip code entries that are between 80000 and 90000, you must use *calculated criteria* rather than OR expressions because the span of zip codes between 80000 and 90000 is really the AND expression: Zip Code is >= 80000 *and* Zip Code is <= 90000.

Using calculated criteria

Calculated criteria are useful for establishing a range of values within a single field. For example, you may want to locate all records that have zip codes in the range 80000 to 90000. This requires a calculated criteria entry. Calculated criteria are entered as a formula that uses a conditional operator. The formula should test the value of the first cell in one of the database columns. For example, the formula for the zip codes would be:

=AND(G8>80000,G8<90000)

Notice that the formula refers to the first cell in the Zip Code column of the database range. It uses a conditional formula to ask "is the value of G8 greater than 80000 *and* less than 90000?" The result of the formula will produce a TRUE or FALSE value in the criteria range. Ignore this value. The point is that the formula is used by Excel to evaluate every record in the database when you perform the Data/Find command.

When using calculated criteria, note that you must change the name of the criteria heading to a temporary name, such as "Calc." You cannot use the regular column headings or Excel will be unable to find matching records. When you're finished with the calculated criteria, you can return the heading back to normal.

Using the Data Form

The data form is a data entry dialog box for your database that lets you enter and manipulate database records using a fill-in-the-blanks form. Select the Form command from the Data menu to see the data form for your current database. Figure 8-12 shows the data form for an example database.

Figure 8-12: An example of a database data form created by choosing Form from the Data menu.

The data form simply lists the database fields and shows the first record of the database. The data form also includes several command buttons along the side. Using these buttons and other commands, you can add new records, edit existing data, find specific records, flip through the records one by one, and remove records. First, here are a few things to note about the data form:

◆ **The data form can exceed the size of the screen.** If your database has more than 15 fields, you may find that the data form is too long to fit onto the screen (the actual limit is determined by your video device).

◆ **The data form shows one record at a time.** Each piece of data (field) within a record is displayed in a box, called an edit box. You can change the information in these boxes if you like. In addition, you can flip through the database and view other records by using the scroll bar on the data form.

◆ **Calculated fields cannot be modified in the data form.** Your database may contain calculated data, such as a column of totals calculated from other information in the database. An entire column of values in the database may be calculated with formulas. Calculated fields cannot be edited; in other words, calculated data does not appear in edit boxes and cannot be changed. When you add a new record to the database using the data form, Excel automatically duplicates the calculation for the calculated field.

◆ **Click Close to remove the data form from view.** You can call the form back up again with the Form command in the Data menu.

Adding records with the data form

Now that you know a bit more about the data form and how it applies to the database range, you can start using it to add records to your database. Adding records with a data form helps you enter data properly so that you don't need to worry about data going into the wrong field (cell). Forms are especially useful for data entry operators who may not be well versed in spreadsheets.

Adding records

1. Make sure the cell pointer is located somewhere inside the database data. Now open the data form using the Form command in the Data menu. Excel automatically displays the data form using the correct field names from your database.

2. Click New.

3. Enter the new record into the blank data form that appears. Press Tab to move from field to field. (If you press Return, you will add the record to the database, creating a new row in the database range.)

4. When you're finished with all the entries, click New to add another record or click Close to exit the data form. ◖

You can continue to add record after record by clicking New after each completed entry. Excel adds the new records as you complete them. In fact, when you select a button on the data form, Excel automatically adds any new records to the database before proceeding with the button's action.

Remember that calculated fields cannot be entered from the data form. Instead, Excel duplicates the calculation in the new record. The result is the same as if you had copied the formula down the column into the new rows of the database.

Editing records with the data form

After you've found the record you're searching for, you can make changes to it. Move to the text box by clicking it or by pressing Tab. Edit the contents of the record in the data form with the mouse and keyboard as you would any worksheet cell entry. If you change your mind about the edits you've made, make sure you click Restore before pushing on to the next record.

Editing records

1. Activate the data form using the Form command from the Data menu.

2. Flip through the database until you locate the desired record. You can flip one record at a time by clicking the scroll bar arrows. You can make larger jumps by clicking the scroll bar itself or by moving the scroll box to a different position in the scroll bar. If your database is sorted, you'll find these large jumps save you a lot of time. You can jump to a general area of the database and then use the arrows to flip through the records until you locate the one you want. You can also use the Find option (explained in the next section, "Finding records with the data form").

3. Press Tab to highlight the field (data) you want to change and then retype the information. If you don't want to retype the entire entry, press the left arrow key after highlighting the field to move the cursor inside the entry. Use the editing commands for formula bar editing (listed in Topic 2) to change the entry.

4. Click Close to return to the worksheet or click any button to perform another action. Excel updates the database with your changes before starting the next action. ❮❮

To delete a record using the data form, just follow the first two steps to get the desired record in view and then click Delete.

Finding records with the data form

The data form provides a quick and easy way to locate specific records or groups of records in a database. You can simply enter your search criteria directly into the data form and then move among the records that match the criteria.

Finding records

1. Activate the data form with the Form command in the Data menu.

2. Click Criteria. The form goes blank so you can enter your criteria for one or more of the fields.

3. Using Tab to move among the fields, enter the desired criteria into the spaces provided. Type a specific entry to locate a specific piece of information or use conditional criteria (criteria with conditional operators, such as >90000) to locate groups of data.

4. Click Find Next to view the first matching record.

5. Continue to click Find Next to flip through the matching records. Or use Find Previous to locate previous records that match. ❮❮

Note that Find Next and Find Previous display only records that match the criteria currently active. You can change the criteria (or view the currently active criteria) by clicking Criteria again. While viewing the criteria, click Clear to return to normal. While you are viewing records that match your criteria, you can still use the scroll bar to view any record in the database.

Deleting records with the data form

Deleting records is simple with the data form. Just find the desired records using the find procedure described in the previous section. With the unwanted record showing in the data form, click the Delete button to remove it.

You can delete a group of records at one time by filtering the database to display only the unwanted group. Now highlight all the records and press Command-B to remove them.

Performing Database Statistics

Excel provides a number of statistical functions for analyzing database data. These database functions let you calculate values from specific records in a database range. The database function uses your criteria entries to select certain records from the database to make its calculation. For example, suppose you have a database of financial transactions; each transaction shows an income or expense item, its date and amount. You may want to have the sum of all expenses for a certain period, such as the first quarter of the year, which would consist of the sum of the Amount column for a specific subset of records that indicate expense transactions for the first quarter.

Excel's DSUM function provides an easy way to perform this task. Other database statistical functions let you produce different results. The following is a list of the database statistical functions offered by Excel. Notice that they all share the same syntax:

◆ **DSUM(***database,field,criteria***)** provides the total of all values in the *field* that match the specified *criteria*. Use this function to provide totals of specific subsets of the database.

◆ **DMAX(***database,field,criteria***)** finds the maximum value in the specified *field* within the records that match the *criteria*. Use this function to locate the largest entry within a specific group.

◆ **DMIN(***database,field,criteria***)** finds the minimum value in the specified *field* within the records that match the *criteria*. Use this function to locate the smallest entry within a specific group.

◆ **DPRODUCT(***database,field,criteria***)** produces the product of the values in the specified *field*. The product is calculated by taking each value and multiplying it by the previous value in the database. Use this function to find the product of all records that match a specific criteria.

◆ **DSTDEV(***database,field,criteria***)** calculates the standard deviation among the subset of records identified by the *criteria*. Note that this function uses sample statistics and assumes that the records are a sample of the entire population. Use DSTDEVP to calculate the standard deviation for a total population.

◆ **DSTDEVP(***database,field,criteria***)** calculates the standard deviation for an entire population. See DSTDEV for more information.

◆ **DVAR**(*database,field,criteria*) shows the amount of variance across the database subset identified by the *criteria*. This function uses sample statistics, assuming that the subset is a sample of the total population. Use DVARP to calculate variance for an entire population.

◆ **DVARP**(*database,field,criteria*) shows the amount of variance for an entire population identified by the criteria.

To use a database statistical function, simply move to a blank cell and activate the Function Wizard. (One way to activate the Function Wizard is to choose the Insert⇨Function command.) Now choose the Database function category and locate the desired database function in the function list. Double-click the desired function to display the dialog box for step 2 of the Function Wizard (see Figure 8-13).

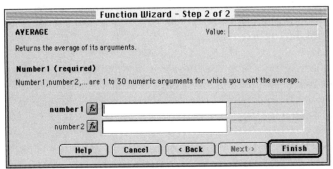

Figure 8-13: Step 2 of the Function Wizard lets you specify the specific data for the function.

You simply identify the database range, the criteria range, and the column that you want to sum. Enter the reference of the database range into the *database* argument. This reference should include the field names at the top of the database data.

Next, identify the field that you want to calculate. Just click on the desired field in the database range to enter its address into the appropriate space.

Finally, enter the reference of the criteria range that you want to use as the criteria for the calculation. You can select the criteria range to enter its reference into the space provided.

Note that your database and criteria ranges can be external references. That is, the database function can appear on a worksheet other than the one containing the database and criteria ranges. In this case, you would enter an external reference to the database and criteria ranges—to specify the worksheet name and the cell or range reference.

Quick Tips

Anticipating your database design

Before creating your database fields, examine the data you'll be working with. Create the fields for your database based on the type of data that appears most often and consider whether you need to separate fields into smaller units or add additional fields for calculations or other database operations.

Using multiple databases in a workbook

You can use as many databases as you like within a single workbook. Chances are, you'll find it easier to separate the databases onto separate worksheet pages, however.

Understanding criteria in a data form

Criteria you set in the data form works independently of criteria used in the AutoFilter lists.

Creating cross-tabulation reports

Excel offers the powerful PivotTable Wizard feature to help you create cross-tabulation reports and other summary information for your database data. Refer to Topic 9 for more information on pivot tables.

Part III
Intermediate Excel

Analyzing Data in Excel

Overview

Once you have a general understanding of Excel, including how to create formulas and functions, you are ready for the next step. Excel provides a host of data analysis features that help you make sense of complex data and present that data in a readable fashion. This topic discusses Excel's data analysis features, including advanced "what if" analyses and the new PivotTable Wizard. Each of these tools lets you look at your worksheet data in various ways, so you can develop a better picture of the meaning of your data.

Performing What If Analyses

One of the most useful features of a worksheet is that it lets you perform what if tests based on variable information. By changing the values referenced in formulas, you can view different results in the formula cells. For example, you may use a formula to calculate the future value of a series of deposits over time. By substituting various monthly deposit amounts, you can determine how your savings will accumulate as you deposit more or less of your income.

At times, you may want to compare several what if tests, but this would require that you change the variable cells over and over again, once for each test. If you are changing several cells each time, this could become cumbersome rather quickly. Besides, you may want to view the results of these various tests side by side. Or you may want to automatically cycle through the various *sets* of values, so that you can view each what if scenario in sequence and then quickly return to any of them without having to retype the values.

Excel provides a number of powerful tools for playing "what if" with your workbooks. You can choose the tools that best fit your needs. The following is a brief description of these tools and the advantages of each.

Data tables

Data tables let you see how one or two variables can change the results of a formula. You can create a *matrix*, or table, showing the different results based on the variables you want to substitute. This capability is handy for viewing the different results in a table, side by side.

Suppose, for example, that you want to start a savings plan for your children's college education. You start with a formula that calculates the future value of a savings investment using a monthly deposit of $100 at an annual interest rate of, say, 5.2 percent.

You want to know what the future value would be if you increased the monthly deposit to $125, then to $150, then to $200, and so on. And what if the interest rate were different? The results of calculating these two variables in the formula would create a matrix of outcomes, called a *data table*.

Single-variable data tables

If you want to see quickly how a single variable can change the outcome of a calculation, you can use a single-variable data table. This data table can show you the result of the calculation using several different values for one of the variables.

Suppose you want to examine the result of saving part of your income each month for five years at 9.6 percent interest. You want to see how much you will save after five years, specifying different monthly deposit amounts. The Future Value function (FV) performs the basic calculation. The following are the steps for creating a single-variable data table.

Creating a single-variable data table

1. Enter the desired formula, or calculation, into a cell of the worksheet. In this example, we're using the FV function. Use sample figures for each of the variables in the table. Make sure that the formula uses cell references for each of the variables and that the cells being referenced are located in the same worksheet. One of these variables will be used as the what if value. Figure 9-1 shows an example, where the formula in cell D4 uses the input cells B3, B4, and B5 to calculates its result.

2. List the variables that you want to use for the what if tests. List these variables in a column, leaving a blank column to the right for the results. You can include as many values as you want. Figure 9-2 shows ten values.

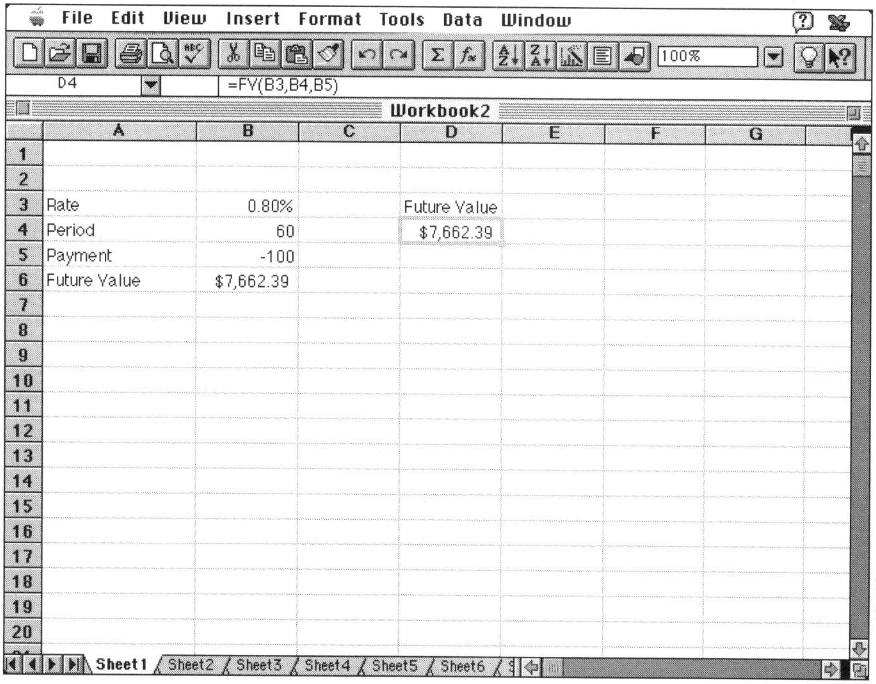

Figure 9-1: Starting the data table with a function.

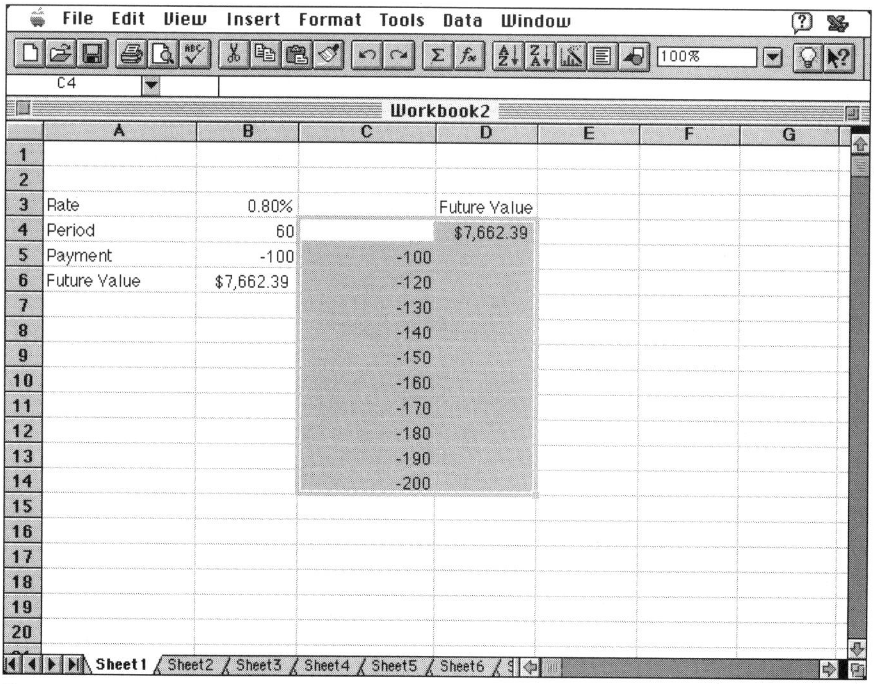

Figure 9-2: Entering the variable values for a single-variable data table.

3. Enter the formula (or a reference to the formula) into the cell just above the empty column of the data table. In the example, the formula has already been entered into cell D4, which is above the second column of the table range. However, if the formula appears elsewhere, you can simply refer to the cell containing the formula. Think of this formula as a heading for the column that will contain the resulting values.

4. Highlight the column of variables and the adjacent blank column, including the row containing the formula you entered in Step 3.

5. Choose the Table command from the Data menu and enter the input cell into the dialog box by clicking the cell or typing the cell reference (use an absolute reference, as in $B$4). Enter this reference into the entry box marked Column Input Cell if the table is vertical (as in our example), or use the Row Input Cell entry box if the table is horizontal. Figure 9-3 shows an example. Figure 9-4 shows the completed table.

Note that the input cell you specify is one of the original cells used in Step 1 of this procedure. In the example, it's the Payment input cell listed in B5. ◖

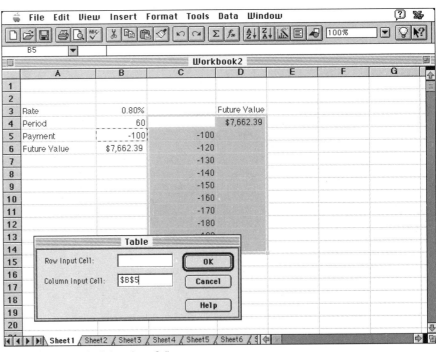

Figure 9-3: Entering the Column Input Cell.

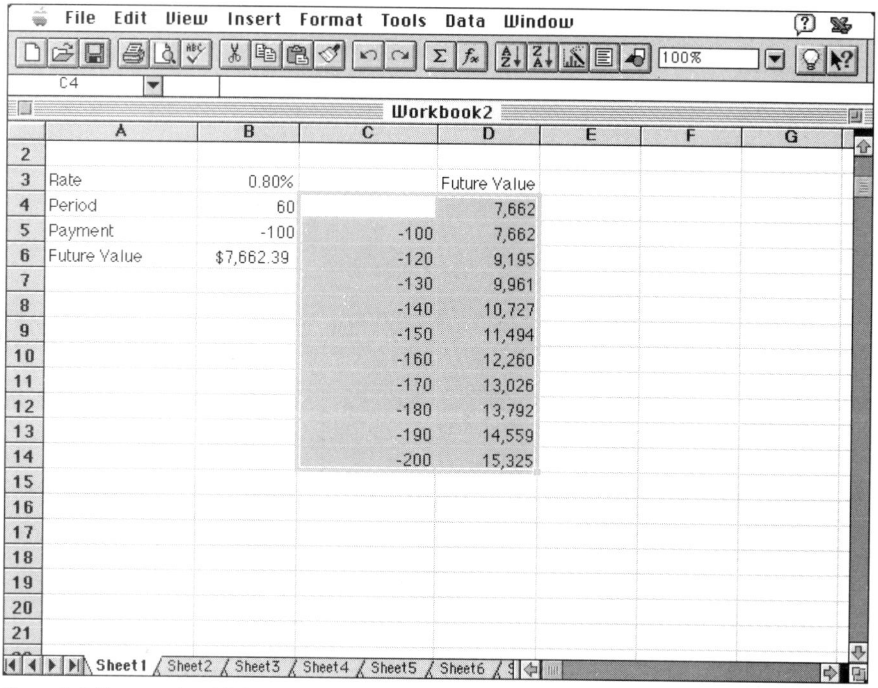

	A	B	C	D	E	F	G
2							
3	Rate	0.80%		Future Value			
4	Period	60		7,662			
5	Payment	-100	-100	7,662			
6	Future Value	$7,662.39	-120	9,195			
7			-130	9,961			
8			-140	10,727			
9			-150	11,494			
10			-160	12,260			
11			-170	13,026			
12			-180	13,792			
13			-190	14,559			
14			-200	15,325			
15							

Sheet1 / Sheet2 / Sheet3 / Sheet4 / Sheet5 / Sheet6 /

Figure 9-4: The completed data table.

You can set up the input table in rows instead of columns. In this case, you would enter the input cell into the space marked Row Input Cell in the Table dialog box. The top row should contain the variables, and the bottom row should be empty and ready to hold the resulting calculations.

Double-variable data tables

The data table described in the previous example is relatively simple. You can create more complex data tables. Suppose you want to calculate what if results using two of the input cells in a formula. The result would be a matrix of values that corresponds to combinations of the two variables. A double-variable data table requires that you enter variable amounts in a row above the table and in a column to the left of it.

Creating a double-variable data table

1. Enter a series of what if values for the first variable of the formula into a column on the worksheet.

2. Enter a second series of what if values for the second variable of the formula in a row above the table area. The result is a blank range of cells with variables along the top and left side.

3. In a different area of the worksheet, enter the formula that calculates the desired result. For each number or variable in the formula, use a cell reference and enter a value into the referenced cell. Do not refer to any of the cells in the data table within this formula — although you may duplicate values from the table. Figure 9-5 shows the worksheet at this point. The formula in cell B5 is =FV(B2,B3,B4).

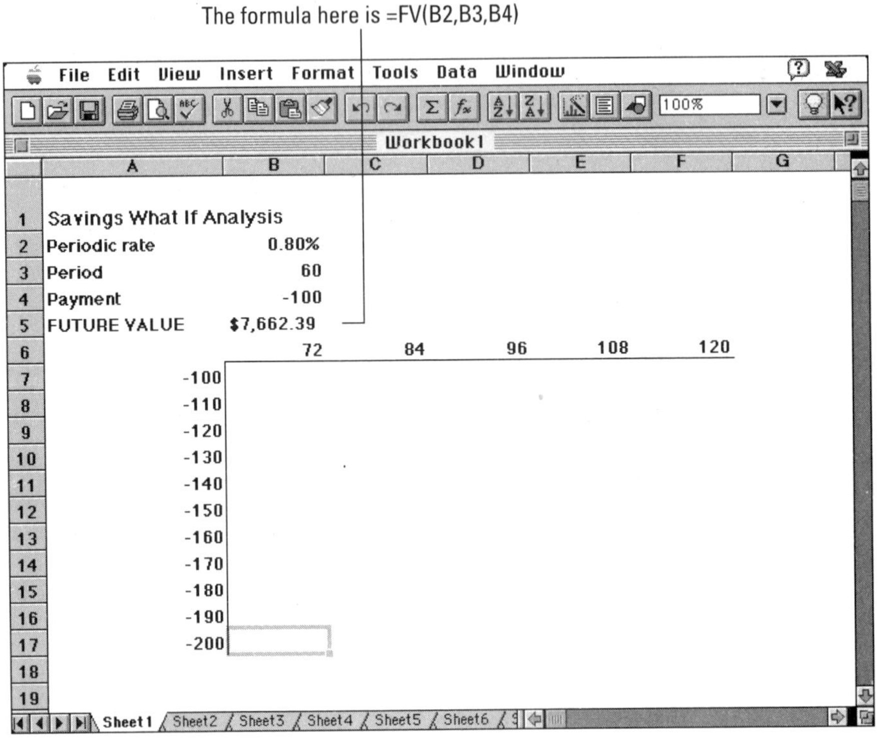

The formula here is =FV(B2,B3,B4)

Figure 9-5: A double-variable table setup.

4. In the upper-left corner of the data table, enter a formula that refers to the formula you entered in Step 3. This formula can be a simple cell reference, such as =B5.

5. Highlight the entire table and choose the Table command from the Data menu.

6. Locate the first input cell for the column of the data table. The first input cell is the cell located outside the data table (you created in Step 3) that corresponds to the column of the table. In Figure 9-5, this is cell B4, which is the Payment amount. The left column of the table lists alternative Payment amounts. Now enter this cell address into the Column Input Cell of the Table dialog box.

7. Enter the Row Input Cell into the Table dialog box. The Row Input Cell is the cell that corresponds to the top row of the data table. In Figure 9-5, this is cell B3 because the top row of the table lists alternative periods.

8. Press Return to complete the table. Figure 9-6 shows the completed data table. ◖◗

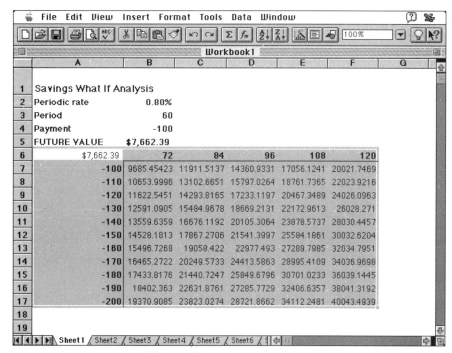

Figure 9-6: A completed two-variable data table.

If you change the data table's row and column input values, the table recalculates its values. Using the previous example, you can change the values in row 7 and column A to calculate a new table. You can also change any other variables used in the formula in cell B5, such as the value in cell B2. However, do not change individual results within the table as this will create errors throughout the table. Data tables use *array formulas* to produce their results; array formulas must all be changed together to create new results. For more information on array formulas, see "Working with Arrays and Array Calculations" later in this topic.

Scenario Manager

The Scenario Manager add-in lets you cycle through different values for several variables in your worksheets, which may be useful when a data table is too confining for your needs. Scenario Manager lets you use any worksheet and does not require a table-oriented approach. In addition, you can modify more than two variables using the Scenario Manager.

Suppose you have a worksheet that calculates job quotations for your event planning company. The worksheet takes your subcontractors' fees into consideration, as well as the cost of materials, labor, and general expenses. You want to view the quotation using several different amounts for the basic costs and expenses. These different views require that you change numerous cells, maybe three or four times, depending on how many different scenarios you want to view. The Scenario Manager lets you store input values for each scenario of the application.

If you have three different subcontractors you can use for the catering portion of an event, you can store each contractor's prices in a separate scenario and calculate the quotation using each of the different caterers. If you have other elements of the job that you want to analyze in this way, you can create more scenarios for those elements. You can also combine these values to produce even more possibilities. You can then print a quotation that includes Mr. Big Catering along with ACME Lighting and another quotation that uses two different subcontractors.

Creating a scenario

1. Open the workbook that contains the application you want to use.

2. Choose Scenarios from the Tools menu. The dialog box in Figure 9-7 appears. This dialog box displays the names of existing scenarios for this worksheet and lets you create new ones. Click the Add button to create a new scenario.

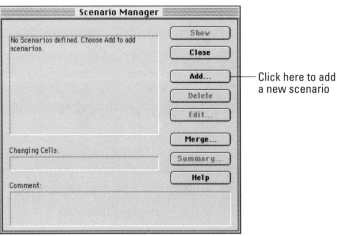

Figure 9-7: The Scenario Manager dialog box.

3. Enter a name for the scenario you want to create. For example, you may use the name BEST to create a "best-case" scenario, or use the name OUTSIDE for a scenario that uses all outside contractors.

4. Press Tab to move into the Changing Cells entry box. Then highlight the cells on the worksheet that will be changing for this scenario. You may have to move the dialog box aside while you click the worksheet. Hold down the Command key to select multiple cells that are not adjacent. If the cells are named, you may enter the cell names into the Changing Cells entry box. Names should be separated by commas. Note that cells you specify should not contain formulas.

5. Press Tab to enter any notes for the scenario you are creating.

6. Click OK and the Scenario Values dialog box appears, showing you the cells you specified as changing cells, along with their current values. Figure 9-8 shows an example.

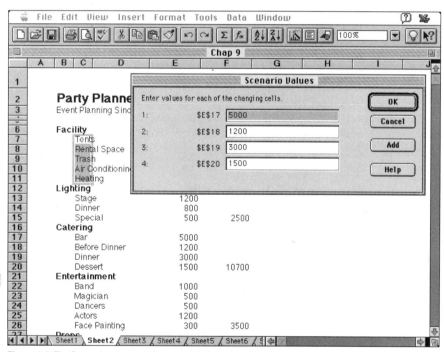

Figure 9-8: The Scenario values you have established.

7. Using Tab to move among the values, type the desired value for each of the cells listed. This set of values constitutes one scenario.

8. Click OK to accept your scenario, or click Add to create a second scenario. If you click Add, return to step 3. ◗

It's a good idea to start by creating a scenario using the values that you've already entered into the worksheet (the values that automatically appear in the Scenario Values dialog box). You'll probably want these values to appear as one of the scenarios. By just accepting these values as the first scenario, you won't have to re-enter them again later.

Using the quotation worksheet example, suppose that you want to create different scenarios to compare the different subcontractor costs. These scenarios will enable you to compile the best quotations for your clients.

Figure 9-9 shows a part of the quotation worksheet that pertains to catering work. Many of these cells will be included in the different scenarios. Entries for Mr. Big Catering appear in Figure 9-10.

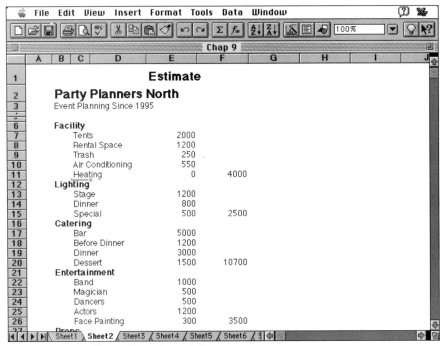

Figure 9-9: The Event Planning Estimation worksheet.

You can continue to build new scenarios for each major component of the worksheet and then combine them like pieces of a puzzle. Or you can create one large scenario that includes all the variable cells in the entire worksheet. You can create worksheet scenarios from small pieces by applying each desired scenario to the worksheet to achieve one complete version of the estimate. You can then create a scenario from this complete version if you like, so that you can automatically return to the particular combination of pieces you've created. Just add a new scenario and establish all the input cells and changing cells. Then use the existing values as the scenario values.

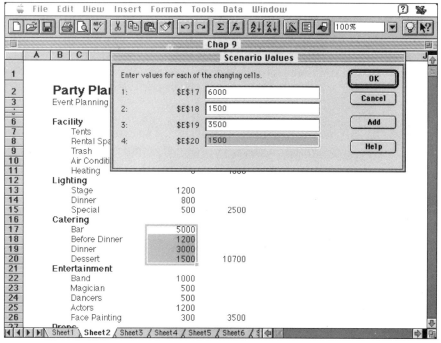

Figure 9-10: Scenario Values for one catering scenario.

You can edit an existing scenario by returning to the Changing Cells box in the Add Scenario dialog box and adding or removing cell references. If you add references, you have to modify each named scenario that includes that cell. If you remove a reference, Excel automatically deletes the reference and the scenario values from each named scenario. You can also change the scenario values at any time to modify an existing scenario.

Using a scenario

After you have created several scenarios, you can quickly return to any one by selecting its name from the Scenario Manager dialog box. Just choose the Tools⇨Scenarios command and double-click the desired scenario name in the dialog box. Excel instantly updates the worksheet with the scenario values.

To cycle through scenarios you can highlight a name in the list and click the Show button; then highlight another name and click Show again.

The Workgroup toolbar contains a drop-down list that displays all existing scenarios for the active worksheet. Just open the Workgroup toolbar and select the worksheet page that contains your scenarios. Instantly, the Scenarios list in the toolbar displays the scenario names for that sheet. You can switch among the different scenarios by choosing a name from the list.

Creating a summary report

One of the most powerful features of the Scenario Manager is its ability to create summary reports that summarize and compare different scenarios. This feature helps you see, at a glance, how the different values affect your totals. Otherwise, you would have to compare individual printouts of the worksheet.

A summary report includes the variable values and any totals in your worksheet that you want to include. Generally, you will want to compare the totals that are affected by the changing variables. The summary report is created on a new worksheet in the workbook. You can print this worksheet to view the report on paper.

Creating a summary report

1. With the model worksheet open and in view, choose the Scenarios command from the Tools menu.

2. Click the Summary button. The Summary dialog box appears.

3. Choose between a summary report and a pivot table. Pivot tables are explained later in this topic.

4. Make sure that the Result Cells entry box contains the desired cells for your summary worksheet. If not, replace the entry with the desired selection of cells.

5. Click OK and Excel creates a summary table for you, as shown in Figure 9-11. ◐

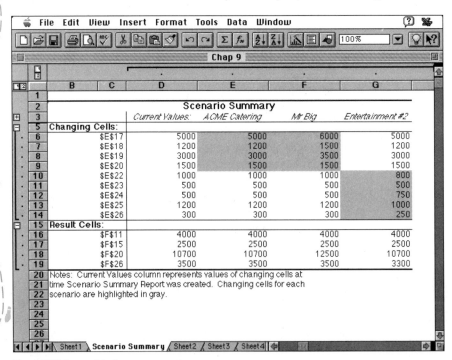

	B	C	D	E	F	G
1						
2				Scenario Summary		
3			Current Values:	ACME Catering	Mr Big	Entertainment #2
5	Changing Cells:					
6		$E$17	5000	5000	6000	5000
7		$E$18	1200	1200	1500	1200
8		$E$19	3000	3000	3500	3000
9		$E$20	1500	1500	1500	1500
10		$E$22	1000	1000	1000	800
11		$E$23	500	500	500	500
12		$E$24	500	500	500	750
13		$E$25	1200	1200	1200	1000
14		$E$26	300	300	300	250
15	Result Cells:					
16		$F$11	4000	4000	4000	4000
17		$F$15	2500	2500	2500	2500
18		$F$20	10700	10700	12500	10700
19		$F$26	3500	3500	3500	3300
20	Notes: Current Values column represents values of changing cells at					
21	time Scenario Summary Report was created. Changing cells for each					
22	scenario are highlighted in gray.					
23						
24						
25						
26						

Figure 9-11: A completed summary report.

Remember, you can rearrange worksheet pages by dragging the page tab. Excel may insert the Scenario Summary report page at the front of your workbook. You can move it to another location if desired.

Using Pivot Tables

A pivot table provides a way of viewing large amounts of information. Also known as a cross-tabulation report, a pivot table presents database information, such as statistical, financial, or marketing data, in a concise, readable summary. You can then manipulate the presentation by changing the emphasis placed on certain parts of the data.

For example, suppose your worksheet contains raw sales data for 1995. And suppose it shows sales volume related to two pieces of information: the product name and the store where the product was sold. The raw data consists of each sale made through out the year, which includes the two key variables plus one more critical variable:

- ◆ the product name of the item sold

- ◆ the store name where it was sold

- ◆ the dollar amount of the sale

To summarize this information, you may form a simple table showing the three pieces of information. Figure 9-12 shows the raw data and a table that summarizes the data.

As you can see, compiling raw data and displaying the results in table form is a natural way of gaining an overall view of your data. Rather than looking through the individual information, you can total the results in a nice presentation, as shown in the figure.

Now suppose you add another piece of data to the model. Rather than showing sales data for 1995 only, you now want to compare the 1994 and 1995 sales data. Instantly, your raw data will double. But the presentation table (or tabulation report) is hardly affected at all. You can simply add another layer to the table in one of several different ways, as shown in Figure 9-13.

Notice that the three presentations show the same data in different ways. One presentation emphasizes the comparison between the two years, while another one emphasizes how each of the sales outlets performed. The third tabulation calls attention to the product comparison. Each method of displaying these totals is useful for a different reason. An accountant may be more interested in the yearly comparison, while the sales manager may want to compare the sales outlets.

Topic 9
Analyzing Data in Excel

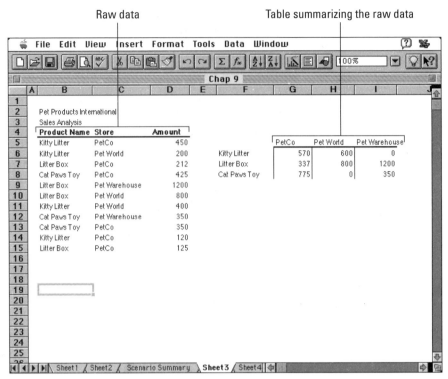

Raw data   Table summarizing the raw data

Figure 9-12: A simple presentation of two pieces of information.

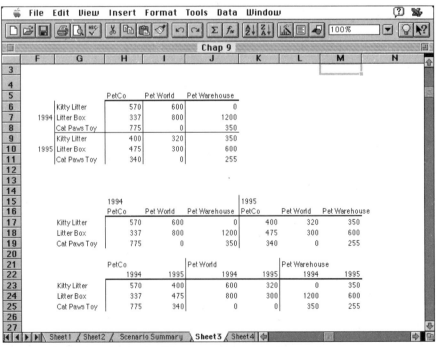

Figure 9-13: Tabulation tables showing different comparisions using the same data.

By adding a third element to the data (in this case, another sales year) you effectively increase the number of ways in which the data can be presented. If you were to add another piece of data to the example, the possibilities would multiply. Instead of three ways to display the totals, you'd have nine! Imagine adding numerous elements to the data, such as product color, store type, and salesperson. The possibilities are almost endless. Figure 9-14 shows a pivot table with many levels (pieces of data).

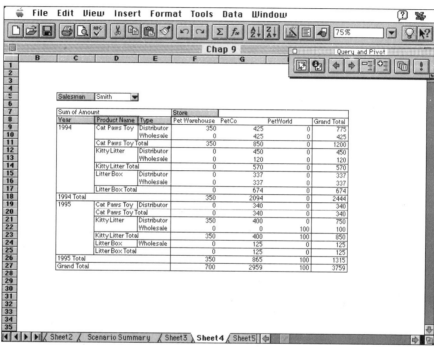

Figure 9-14: A complete, pivot table showing many levels of data.

An Excel pivot table lets you create and manage these data presentations. Using a pivot table, you can instantly change the emphasis of the presentation without having to recreate the table. With a pivot table you can make numerous comparisons using the same basic data and display different tables for different purposes. This capability makes pivot tables especially useful when you want to graph or chart the results of your data, because by displaying the data in different ways, your graphs or charts can make different visual comparisons.

Creating a pivot table

The easiest way to create a pivot table is to use the PivotTable Wizard. Note that your raw data will probably be in the form of a database or data list. Provided you have column headings (field names) above each column, you are ready to begin. For more information about database setup and management in Excel, refer to Topic 8.

Creating a pivot table

1. Open the workbook that contains the raw data you want to tabulate. If Excel is not the source program for your information, you can also create a pivot table from external data.

2. Choose the PivotTable command from the Data menu. The PivotTable Wizard dialog box appears on the screen (see Figure 9-15).

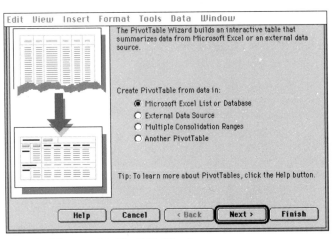

Figure 9-15: Step one of the PivotTable Wizard.

3. Choose the appropriate data source from the options provided. For data located in an Excel worksheet, choose the Microsoft Excel List or Database option. Click Next to continue to Step 2 of the PivotTable Wizard process.

4. Identify the data range containing the raw data. If your data is located in Excel, you can enter a reference to the data, such as a range reference or range name. If you want to, you can click the worksheet to highlight the range. (Choose the Browse button to open a different workbook or source file, such as a Microsoft FoxPro file.) Click Next to continue to Step 3.

5. Drag field names, which appear from your specified data range, into the ROW, COLUMN, DATA, and PAGE areas of the layout screen. This action creates the layout of the pivot table and determines what information from the database will be included. Details about this step of the process are covered in the following section. Click Next to continue to Step 4.

6. Specify the destination for the final table. You can click a worksheet tab to identify a separate page for the table and then add a starting cell location, such as B3. Click the Finish button when you are done. ♦

Designing the pivot table

In Step 3 of the PivotTable Wizard process, you can design the pivot table itself. Designing the table means that you choose what information (headings and totals) from the data range will be included in the table. In addition, you can determine what information is emphasized and what information is not. Because pivot tables are flexible, you can always rearrange the design after you create the table.

There are four primary areas of the pivot table — the ROW, COLUMN, DATA, and PAGE areas. The task is to drag the field markers (the field names) from your data block into these four areas to create a specific design. Figure 9-16 shows this step of the PivotTable Wizard.

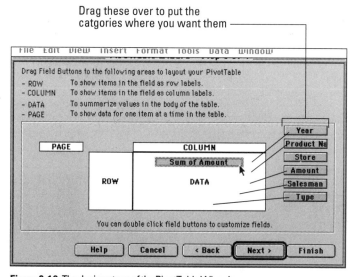

Figure 9-16: The design stage of the PivotTable Wizard process.

The dialog box shows the four basic areas of the pivot table and includes markers for each of the field names in your data block. Simply drag each marker into one of the four areas to determine its location. Here are some general guidelines to keep in mind:

◆ **COLUMN and ROW areas are typically used for descriptive headings.**
Generally you should drag the descriptive information into the column and row areas. Using the example, from Figure 9-13, you may drag the Year field into the ROW area and the Product and Store location fields into the COLUMN area.

- **Numeric data is generally displayed in the DATA area.** The DATA area is typically used for displaying the numeric data that applies to the column and row headings, such as sales figures. You cannot place a nonnumeric field into the DATA area, but you can place a numeric field into a ROW or COLUMN area.

- **Use the PAGE area to split the table.** You can use the PAGE area to create multiple *iterations*, or pages, of the table — where each page represents a new item. For example, you can display a separate table for each salesperson, store, or year. Your choice depends on how you want to emphasize the relationships among the data items. The PAGE area becomes a drop-down list in the actual data table. The list contains the various items within the field you placed there. For example, if you drag the Year field into the PAGE area, you can switch between the 1994 and 1995 tables by choosing the desired year from the drop-down list.

- **You can place numerous fields in each area.** Place as many of the items as you want within the various areas. If you place two fields in the ROW area, then you'll have a different relationship than if you place one of those items in the COLUMN area. Excel automatically arranges the data to fit your specifications.

- **Excel automatically includes subtotals in the pivot table.** Your finished data table will automatically include subtotals between the various fields. Therefore, you can eliminate the subtotals in Step 4 of the Pivot Table Wizard process.

Rearranging the pivot table

After the pivot table is created, you can still change the arrangement of information it displays by dragging the field heading markers that appear in the table. For example, you can move a field marker from the COLUMN location into the ROW location directly in the table itself. Excel then rearranges the table's data to fit your new conditions. You can move a PAGE marker into the ROW or COLUMN area to put all the information on the same table. Just drag the field markers into the desired locations to make these changes.

In addition, you can change the order of items that appear within the same area. For example, you may want to place the Year field below the Store location field in the ROW area (see Figure 9-17).

Change the order of the fields by dragging the fields to the locations shown in the figure. The beauty of a pivot table is that you can rearrange the fields at any time to view the data in a different way.

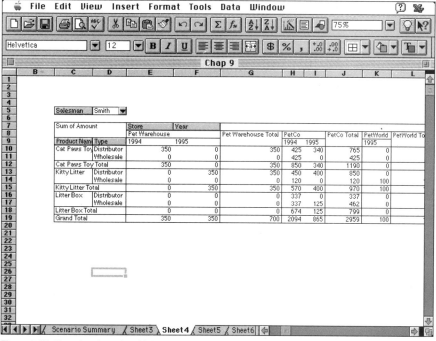

| File | Edit | View | Insert | Format | Tools | Data | Window |

Figure 9-17: Changing the order of fields in a pivot table is as easy as dragging the fields where you want them.

Working with Arrays and Array Calculations

An *array* is a special type of range (also known as an *array range*). Although an array resembles a normal range of cells that contains formulas or values, it differs in one major respect: the cells in the array range can only be edited as a group, not independently. You cannot change the formula or value in one of the cells of an array range; you must change the entire array together.

The values in array ranges are also created as a group through a procedure called an *array calculation*. You can use arrays in place of standard ranges, however, to save time and conserve memory in your worksheets. Although arrays and array calculations may seem complicated, they actually make worksheets simpler and can save you time in entering formulas.

Array calculations help you consolidate complex worksheet formulas and make simple array formulas. While arrays are not always necessary in your worksheets (that is, you can accomplish most calculations without array formulas), they help you reduce the amount of calculations required for certain tasks — tasks that involve blocks of worksheet cells. Arrays are most useful when your worksheets use formulas that repeat over a range of cells. If you feel comfortable with standard worksheet formulas and functions, you are ready for the next step — arrays.

Making basic array calculations

A basic array calculation takes the place of a series of individual calculations spread over a range. In Figure 9-18, the formulas in column C add the corresponding values in columns A and B.

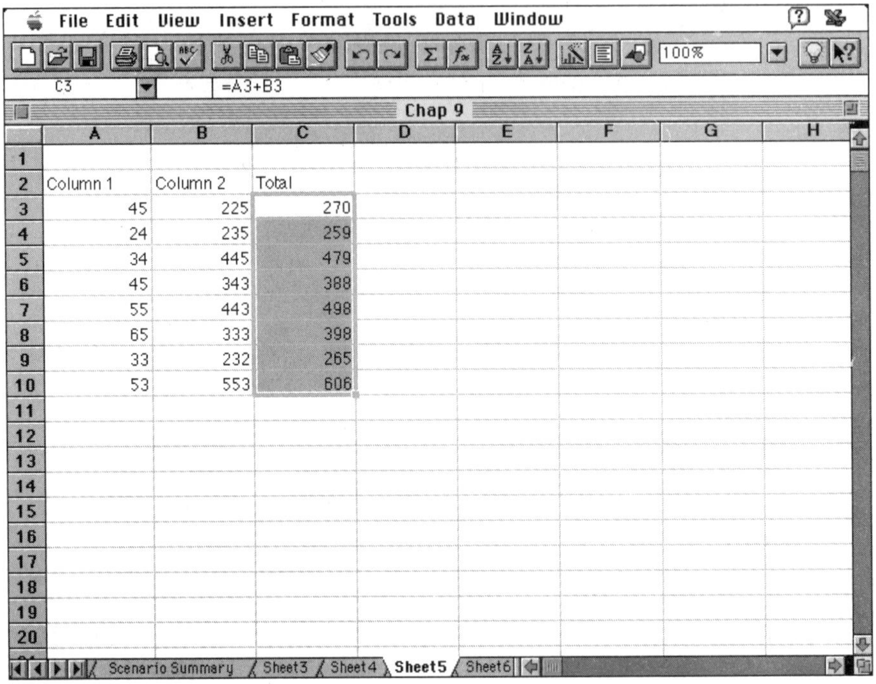

Figure 9-18: A basic array calculation.

Each cell in column C contains an individual formula, such as =A3+B3. An array formula can take the place of these formulas by adding the values in the range A3:A10 to the values in the range B3:B10. The result is the range of answers in cells C3:C10.

You enter the formula used for this calculation into column C as an array; Excel treats the other two ranges as arrays.

Entering array formulas

1. Highlight the range. For example, highlight C3:C10.

2. Type the formula. For example, type **=A3:A10+B3:B10.**

3. Press Command-Enter to accept the formula.

The result is a range of cells (an *array range*) containing the answers to the set of calculations. You cannot alter individual cells in this range; you must treat them as a single unit. Excel uses special array math to calculate these values, all of which are dependent on one another. Each cell in the array contains the formula surrounded by brackets, as the formula bar in Figure 9-19 shows.

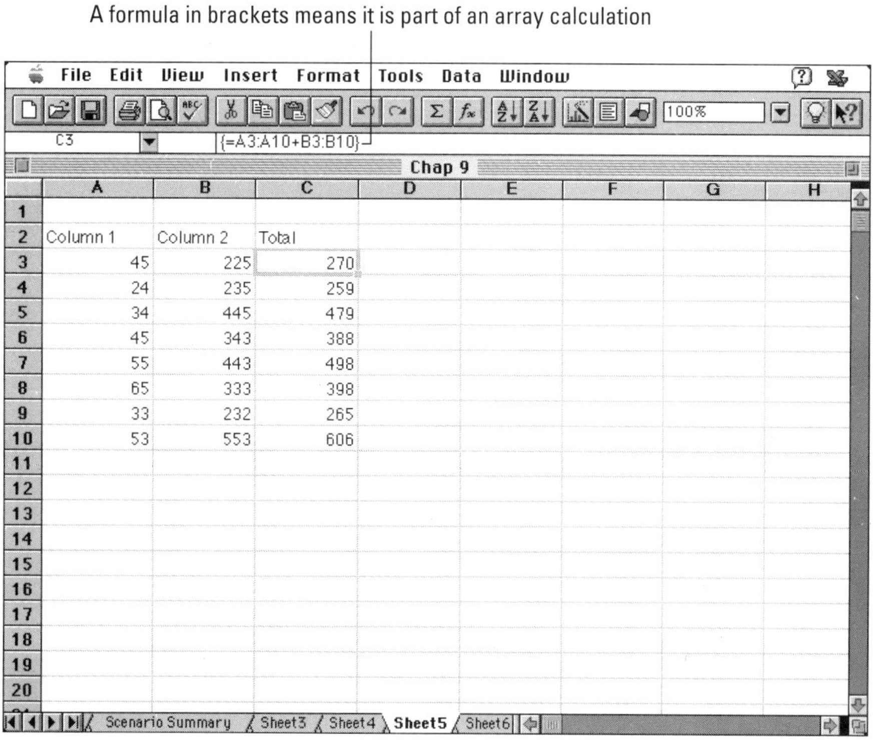

A formula in brackets means it is part of an array calculation

Figure 9-19: Each cell in an array range contains a formula in brackets.

You do not have to use two array ranges in the formula. Figure 9-20 shows an array produced with the formula =A3:A10+$B$3.

When you use this formula, Excel adds each cell in the range A3:A10 to the cell B3, producing eight values. You can replace the reference to B3 with a constant value, as in =A3:A10+2. You can even enter an array formula that contains no ranges, as in the formula =A3+B3. The result is a range of cells containing the same value, however.

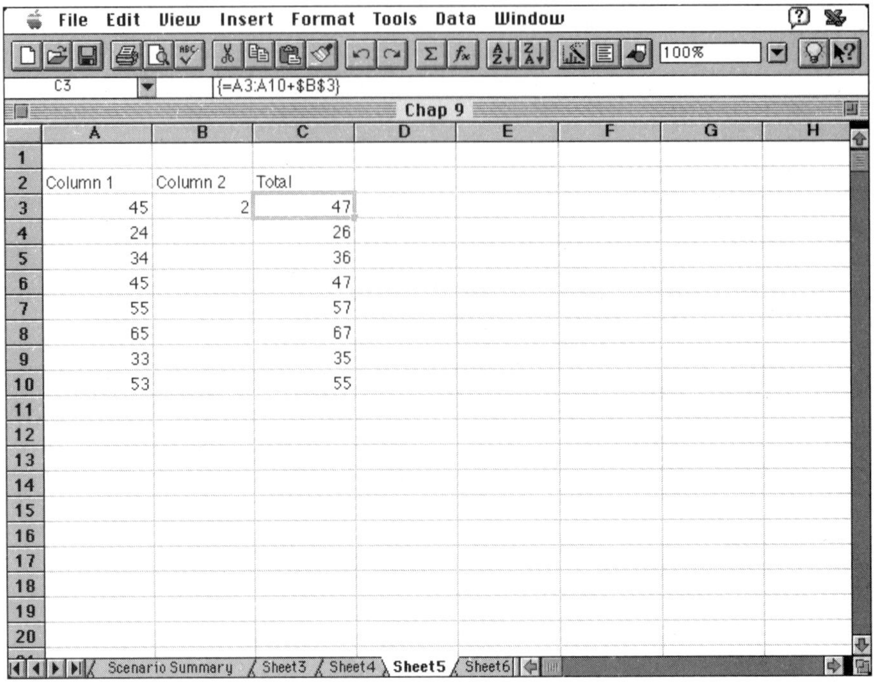

Figure 9-20: Arrays can add ranges to single cell references.

Normally, the *resulting array* (the array containing the results) must be the same size as the largest range referenced in the formula. In the previous examples, the resulting array contains eight cells because the ranges in the formula contain eight cells. If you highlight fewer cells, Excel completes the array calculation for as many cells as you highlight. If you highlight a range that is larger than the largest referenced range, Excel enters an error into the extra cells. If you highlighted ten cells in the previous example, for instance, the last two would contain errors.

Using functions in array calculations

When you use a function in an array calculation, keep in mind that there are three types of functions: those that have no arguments, those that have values or expressions as arguments, and those that have ranges as arguments. The following are examples of each:

◆ PI( ): No arguments

◆ SQRT(*value*): Numeric expression or value argument

◆ SUM(*range*): Range argument

Each type of function is handled differently in an array calculation. The simplest function is the one that has no arguments. You can use this function in an array calculation just as you would use any value or single cell reference. You can highlight the range C3:C10, for example, enter the formula **=B3:B10*PI( ),** and then press Command-Enter to create the array. The function is part of the array calculation. The result is a series of values in cells C3:C10, which are the values of B3:B10 multiplied by π.

When you use a function that requires values as arguments, you must enter the value as a range, thus causing the function to work on an array range rather than a single value. Again, you should highlight a range of equal size for the results. To calculate the square root of each cell in the range B3:B10, for example, highlight a blank range for the result, type the formula **=SQRT(B3:B10),** and press Command-Return. You also can use an expression in a larger array calculation, such as the following:

    =A3:A10+SQRT(B3:B10)

This formula takes the square root of each cell in the range B3:B10 and adds it to the corresponding cell in the range A3:A10.

The final type of function includes those with ranges as arguments, such as SUM, AVERAGE, and COUNT. Because these functions produce a single value from a standard range, they are single values in array calculations — like a cell reference, a constant value, or functions such as PI.

Because these functions use standard ranges for their arguments, however, they can be confusing. The array formula =SUM(A3:A10)*B3:B10, for example, multiplies the sum of the range A3:A10 to each cell in the range B3:B10 and places the eight results in the resulting array. In this example, the sum of the range A3:A10 is 640, which is then multiplied by each cell in the range B3:B10 to produce eight values.

Another way to use a range function in an array calculation is to make an array calculation in the argument of the function. Suppose that you have values in the ranges A3:A10 and B3:B10. You can enter an array formula such as =SUM(A3:A10*B3:B10). In this case, the result is a single value. You should highlight only one cell as the resulting array because the SUM function calculates a single value from a range — even an array range. The resulting range (one cell) still will be an array range. In this example, the formula multiplies each cell in the range A3:A10 by its corresponding cell in the range B3:B10 and then totals the values. You can express the formula like this:

    (A3*B3)+(A4*B4)+(A5*B5)+...+(A10*B10)

Editing arrays

You cannot insert new cells, rows, or columns into an array range; an error message appears if you try. Similarly, you cannot change individual cells within the array range. You can change the formula for an entire array at once, however. Just highlight the entire array range and change the formula. When you finish editing, press Command-Enter to establish the array again.

To convert array results into constant values, highlight the array range and choose Copy from the Edit menu to copy the range. Then use the Edit⇨Paste Special command and select the Values option to paste the values back to the worksheet. Click OK to complete the conversion. The values are placed into the cells that originally contained the array.

You also can turn an array range into a series of constant array references. Begin by highlighting the entire array. Then use the mouse to highlight the entire array formula in the formula bar. Press Command-= to convert the references and Command-Enter to place the new formulas into the range.

Finding Dependents and Precedents

Because worksheets can contain a tangled network of formulas that refer to one another, finding problems in formulas can be difficult. Excel provides some tools for locating incorrect values and problematic calculations. These tools can help you find the problems, although it's up to you to correct them.

A cell that contains a reference to another cell is dependent on that value for its own value. All cells containing references, therefore, are *dependent cells*. The precise cells they depend on, however, can be difficult to determine.

Suppose that cell A2 contains a reference to cell A1 and cell A3 contains a reference to A2. Cells A2 and A3 are dependent on cell A1. Cell A2 is a *direct dependent* of cell A1. Cell A3 is an *indirect dependent* of cell A1, but a direct dependent of cell A2.

Just as cell A2 is the dependent of A1, cell A1 is the precedent of A2. A *precedent* is a cell that is used (or depended on) by another cell. Precedents also can be direct or indirect. In the example, cell A1 is a direct precedent of cell A2 and an indirect precedent of cell A3.

Excel can locate any cell's dependents or precedents for you. This capability can be helpful in tracking down worksheet bugs across complex formulas.

Selecting dependents and precedents

1. Move the pointer to the cell whose precedents and dependents you want to track.

2. From the Edit menu, choose the Go To command and then click the Special button. The Go To Special dialog box appears as shown in Figure 9-21.

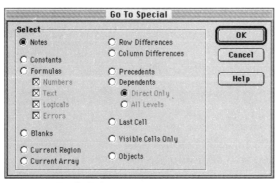

Figure 9-21: The Go To Special dialog box.

3. Choose the Dependents or Precedents option and click it.

4. Choose the Direct Only or All Levels option and click it.

   The Direct Only option finds only direct dependents or precedents. The All Levels option finds both direct and indirect dependents and precedents.

5. Click OK. Excel highlights the dependents or precedents of the cell in the actual worksheet.

*Q*uick Tips

Making good use of Go To Special

As you can see from the options in its dialog box, the Go To Special command does more than select dependent and precedent values for a cell. You can use it to select blank cells within a selected range, cells that contain notes, parts of a formula, and many other special values in a worksheet.

You can always change the pivot table later

Remember that you can change the order and position of the field in your pivot tables at any time. Just drag them from their current locations into other locations. You can move fields from the ROW area to the COLUMN area, for example or just change the order of items within a single area.

AutoFormating your tables

Try using the AutoFormat command to format your pivot tables and data tables. Excel includes several attractive formats for tables of data. The AutoFormat command is located in the Format menu.

Adding an Outline

Refer to Topic 10 for information about outlining your worksheets. You might find it convenient to add an outline to your pivot table applications.

Using the auditing toolbar to find precedents and dependents

The auditing toolbar (see below) provides a clear way to understand precedents and dependents. If you find yourself doing a good deal of searching for precedents or dependents, activate this toolbar — it has buttons for finding precedents and dependents.

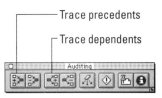

Trace precedents

Trace dependents

Working with Large Workbook Applications

Overview

Excel applications can get rather large and complex. To help keep larger applications from getting confusing, you can split them among several pages of your workbook — or even between several different workbooks — and then link them together. Other methods of managing large workbooks include creating outlines and consolidating information. This topic covers these and other Excel features that help you control large and complicated workbook applications.

Outlining Worksheets

Most worksheets have a natural progression, or hierarchy, of data. Individual cells are summed with formulas, those sums are summed into grand totals, and so on. This format gives your worksheets several *levels* of data. Excel's outlining feature finds these levels in your worksheets and lets you work with each level independently.

In a worksheet, the lowest level of information is a simple value entered into a cell. All these values are on the same level. Formulas that total these values are on the next level. Formulas that total the previous formulas are another level, and so on. Figure 10-1 shows a worksheet with this type of structure. As you can see, many worksheet applications follow this general structure.

When using such a worksheet, it can be useful to view only certain levels of data while the other levels are hidden. This capability is one of the main features of outlining; you can collapse and expand the levels to hide or reveal more detail about the worksheet. Figure 10-2 shows the example worksheet with some lower levels collapsed.

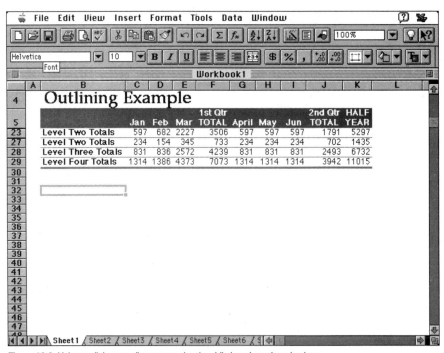

Figure 10-1: A worksheet with several levels of data.

Outlining Example

		Jan	Feb	Mar	1st Qtr TOTAL	April	May	Jun	2nd Qtr TOTAL	HALF YEAR	
6	Level One	45	66	112	223	45	45	45	135	358	
7	Level One	45	56	132	233	45	45	45	135	368	
8	Level One	56	87	131	274	56	56	56	168	442	
9	Level One	4	44	332	380	4	4	4	12	392	
10	Level Two Totals	150	253	707	1110	150	150	150	450	1560	
11	Level One	34	66	131	231	34	34	34	102	333	
12	Level One	23	87	134	244	23	23	23	69	313	
13	Level One	55	98	232	385	55	55	55	165	550	
14	Level Two Totals	112	251	497	860	112	112	112	336	1196	
15	Level One	76	11	131	218	76	76	76	228	446	
16	Level One	77	12	144	233	77	77	77	231	464	
17	Level One	68	23	322	413	68	68	68	204	617	
18	Level Two Totals	221	46	597	864	221	221	221	663	1527	
19	Level Three Totals	483	550	1801	2834	483	483	483	1449	4283	
20	Level One	34	44	111	189	34	34	34	102	291	
21	Level One	35	55	120	210	35	35	35	105	315	
22	Level One	45	33	195	273	45	45	45	135	408	
23	Level Two Totals	597	682	2227	3506	597	597	597	1791	5297	
24	Level One	78	65	110	253	78	78	78	234	487	
25	Level One	68	66	145	279	68	68	68	204	483	
26	Level One	88	23	90	201	88	88	88	264	465	

Figure 10-2: Using outlining to collapse some levels while keeping others in view.

Outlining Example

		Jan	Feb	Mar	1st Qtr TOTAL	April	May	Jun	2nd Qtr TOTAL	HALF YEAR	
23	Level Two Totals	597	682	2227	3506	597	597	597	1791	5297	
27	Level Two Totals	234	154	345	733	234	234	234	702	1435	
28	Level Three Totals	831	836	2572	4239	831	831	831	2493	6732	
29	Level Four Totals	1314	1386	4373	7073	1314	1314	1314	3942	11015	

Collapsing lower levels lets you view summary reports without copying or moving data to fit on a single page. You can print column headings and totals by collapsing all the levels of data between them. Also, when levels of detail are hidden, you can copy, paste, format, and generally manipulate the remaining totals more easily because the totals appear in adjacent cells instead of being spread throughout the worksheet. You can also create charts from the totals — without having to select multiple ranges.

You may find creating an outline on your worksheets useful at some point in the worksheet's development. The advantages you gain in formatting, charting, and report building are well worth the effort of setting up the outline.

Creating outlines

The easiest way to create an outline is to let Excel do the work for you. Excel can usually locate the levels in your worksheets and group them for the outline. If the data is organized properly, you don't have to do very much to create an outline.

Automatically outlining your work

1. Highlight the data and formulas you want to outline. To outline the entire worksheet, select only one cell.

2. Choose Group and Outline⇨Auto Outline from the Data menu. When you release the mouse, Auto Outline executes your request immediately. ◖

Excel outlines the worksheet and displays the outlining symbols on the side and top of the worksheet headings. See "Using the outline symbols and tools" later in this topic for an explanation of these symbols.

Adding styles to outlined data

If your worksheet contains data that can be outlined, it probably also fits into a standard pattern of formatting. For example, you may use boldface for all first-level totals, boldface and italics for grand totals, and a large font for column headings. The outlining example from figure 10-1 shows how you can apply the same formats to equivalent levels of data in an outlined range. You can format most table-oriented reports in the same manner.

Because outlined data is often formatted by using a pattern, Excel provides a special option that automatically adds a set of styles to the Styles list and attaches these styles to the various levels of your outlined data. To add these styles to the list, click the Apply Styles option in the Settings dialog box (choose Data⇨Group and Outline⇨Settings). You can apply these settings before or after you create the outline. You also may want to format the data before adding the styles by using one of the AutoFormats listed in the Format⇨AutoFormat command. This feature can save you some time in formatting data because you don't have to add styles yourself. Excel's automatic styles assume the names RowLevel_1 to indicate the grand totals at the bottom, RowLevel_2 to indicate the next level down, ColumnLevel_1 to indicate grand totals in the far right column, ColumnLevel_2 to indicate the next level down, and so on.

Because Excel adds these styles to the worksheet, you can reformat any level of data by updating the style as described in Topic 4. Here are some points to remember about applying styles to your outlined data:

◆ **Existing formatting is preserved.** If you already formatted your data, using the Apply Styles button does not change the formatting of the cells (provided that the Automatic Styles option is not selected). It assigns names to your formatting options and applies the same style to all equivalent levels of the outline, however. If you use the Currency [0] style on your grand totals, the Apply Styles command changes the style to RowLevel_1, but still displays the currency number format as before. If you do not apply the same formatting options to all similar levels of data, Excel uses the formatting from the first occurrence of the data level.

You can combine the outlining features with the automatic table formats listed in the AutoFormat command. Apply the Format⇨AutoFormat command to your data and then use the Formula Outline command with the Apply Styles option to turn the formatting options into styles that you can select from the Styles list.

◆ **Custom styles are not removed.** If you used custom styles on your data before outlining, Excel changes the styles assigned to the data, but it does not remove your custom styles from the Styles list.

◆ **You can modify the style of an entire level.** By changing one of the assigned styles, you can modify an entire level at one time. Refer to Topic 4 for details about changing a style.

◆ **The Automatic Styles option applies existing formatting.** If you check the Automatic Styles option in the Outline dialog box, the Apply Styles command replaces all your current formatting with the automatic formatting. You may prefer to use one of the formats in the Format⇨AutoFormat command instead, however, because the automatic formatting for outlines is rather rudimentary.

Using the outline symbols and tools

Excel adds outline symbols to the worksheet after creating the outline. These symbols provide information about the worksheet data and also give you control over which levels you can view at any time.

All formulas (or totals) in the outline are given a Group Collapse/Expand button. At first, this button appears as a square containing a minus sign and is displayed on the top and left side of the worksheet. The line attached to this button brackets the data that comprises the total. In Figure 10-3, cells C7, C8, and C9 create the total in cell C10. Row 10 contains the Group Collapse/Expand button and the attached line brackets rows 7, 8 and 9. All formulas on the same level are grouped together under a Row Level button that indicates the level. (Column Level buttons apply to column outlines.)

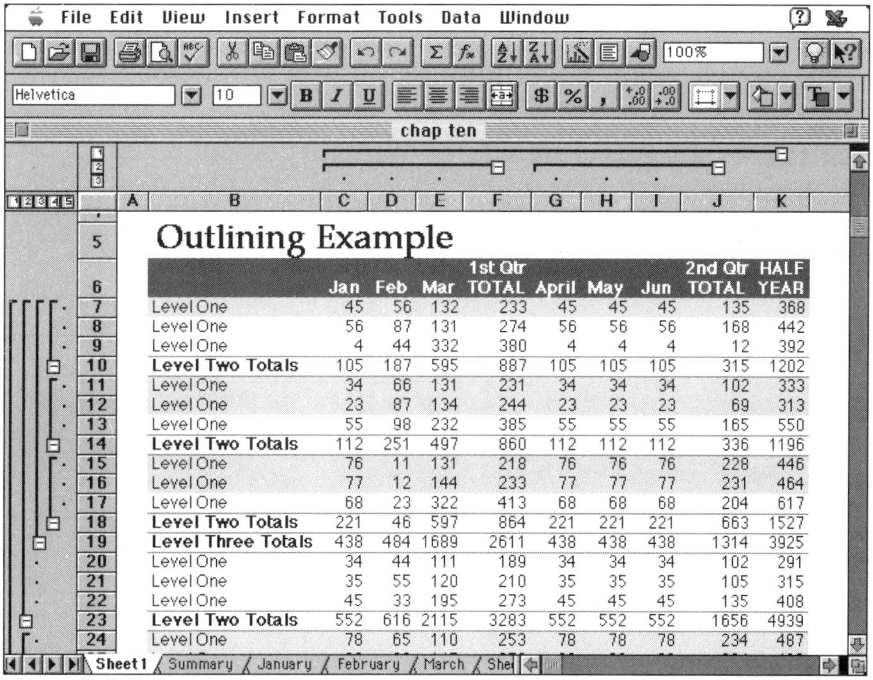

Figure 10-3: Outlined data.

If you click the Group Collapse/Expand button, Excel hides the data in that group and shows only the group total. The Group Collapse/Expand button beside the total changes to a plus sign to indicate that additional data is available by expanding the outline (see Figure 10-4).

Topic 10
Working with Large
Workbook Applications

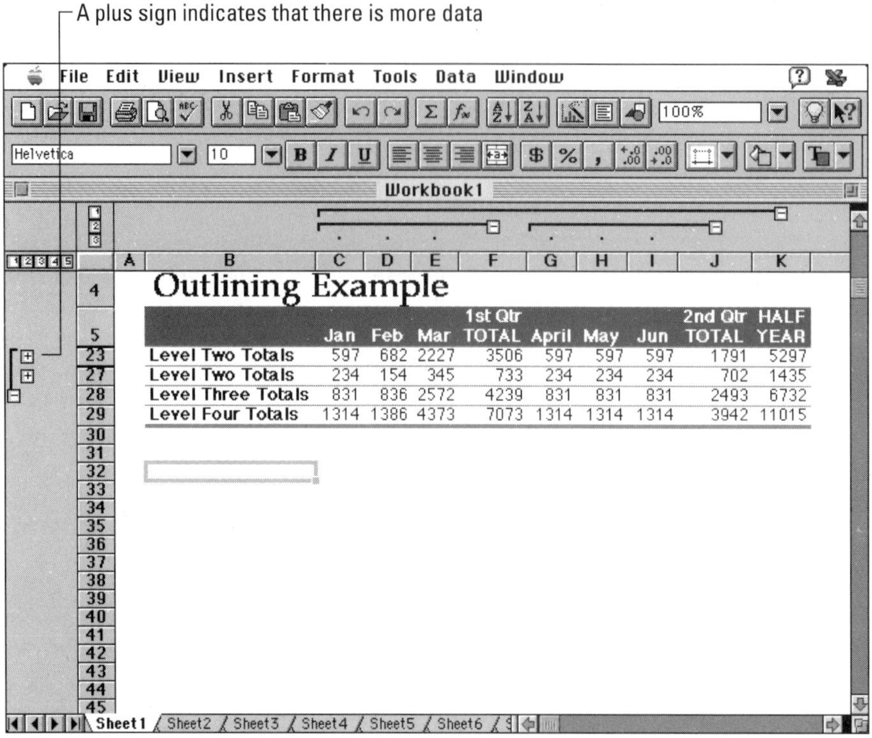

A plus sign indicates that there is more data

Outlining Example

		1st Qtr			2nd Qtr	HALF
	Jan	Feb	Mar	TOTAL	April	May	Jun	TOTAL	YEAR
23 Level Two Totals	597	682	2227	3506	597	597	597	1791	5297
27 Level Two Totals	234	154	345	733	234	234	234	702	1435
28 Level Three Totals	831	836	2572	4239	831	831	831	2493	6732
29 Level Four Totals	1314	1386	4373	7073	1314	1314	1314	3942	11015

Figure 10-4: Collapsing a group so that the total appears and the minus sign changes to a plus sign.

The plus sign indicates that you can expand the group to reveal the hidden data. To collapse or expand an entire level (all groups on the same level), use the Row Level buttons. Click the button indicating the highest level you want to show. To collapse level 3 data, for example, click the level 2 button. To show level 3 data, click the level 3 button.

The following list shows these buttons and the other outlining tools that you can add to your toolbars through the toolbar customization feature.

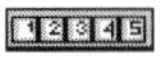

◆ **Row Level.** Indicates the level of each group in a row outline. Click the row level button that indicates the highest level of data you want to show.

 ◆ **Column Level.** Indicates the level of each group in a columnar outline.

 ◆ **Group Collapse/Expand.** Indicates what data makes up the group and whether the data is showing (collapsible) or hidden (expandable). Click this button to collapse or expand the data in that group.

 ◆ **Ungroup button.** Increases the level of the selected group. Select the cell containing the group total and then click the Ungroup button to increase its level. You can use this button if Excel does not properly outline the worksheet and you need to change the level of a particular total. You can also use the Ungroup button if you change the total so that it applies to a different level.

◆ **Group button**. Decreases the level of the selected group. Select the cell containing the group total and click the Group button to decrease its level.

 ◆ **Show/Hide Outline Symbols.** Displays or removes the outline symbols from the screen.

 ◆ **Select Visible.** Makes your highlighted range apply only to the visible cells in the worksheet. When you collapse levels of the worksheet, the remaining totals appear in adjacent cells.

 If you highlight a block of collapsed totals (which apply to collapsed data), you are also highlighting all the hidden data between the totals, which affects many procedures (such as copying, charting, and moving). If collapsing the worksheet causes rows 4 and 10 to be adjacent (because cells between them are hidden), for example, highlighting the cells A4 and A10 actually includes the entire range A4:A10 — including the collapsed cells.

 If you click the Select Visible Cells button after you highlight the totals you want, however, Excel uses only the visible cells in the worksheet as the highlighted range — eliminating the hidden data. You then can chart this data or copy it to another area.

Linking Worksheets

In Topic 7 you learn how one worksheet can reference information in a different worksheet in the same workbook through the use of external references. These references include the worksheet name in addition to the cell addresses you are referencing. Besides being able to link one worksheet to another, you can link cells between two entirely separate workbooks through external references that include the workbook name.

Table 10-1 shows the distinction between the references.

Table 10-1 Referencing Material in Excel	
Type of Reference	*Example*
Normal reference	=B5
Worksheet reference in same workbook	=Sheet1!B5
Workbook reference	=[Workbook1]Sheet1!B5

In an external reference to a workbook, the workbook that contains the external reference is called the *dependent* workbook because it depends on the other workbook for its information. The workbook that provides the data for the dependent workbook is called the *supporting* workbook.

To create an external reference, you can open all involved workbooks and then begin the reference in the destination sheet by typing an equal sign. Then you can point to the desired cell in the desired sheet of the source workbook — provided the workbook is open and on-screen. The external reference should include the name of the notebook, the worksheet name, and the cell address in the following syntax: [workbook]worksheet!range

You don't have to open the supporting workbook in order to create an external reference to it. You can specify the entire directory path to the workbook file on disk as part of the external reference. Use the syntax:

'disk_name:folder:folder:[workbook]worksheet'!range.

If you try to enter an external reference and Excel cannot locate the worksheet or workbook you specify, you are asked to locate the worksheet using a file selection dialog box.

Updating and repairing links

Whenever you open a dependent workbook, Excel updates any external references within it. In other words, Excel locates the supporting workbooks and updates the external references with the current data in those workbooks.

Excel stores the entire folder location associated with the external workbook. However, if you move, rename, or delete the supporting worksheet, Excel is unable to find it. Rather than show you potentially obsolete data on your dependent worksheet, Excel informs you that the supporting workbook cannot be located and gives you the chance to locate it. Assuming the worksheet was not deleted, you can reestablish the link by choosing the worksheet from the file selection dialog box.

Here are some guidelines for linking workbooks with external references:

◆ **Use names instead of cell addresses whenever possible.** The cell reference in the external reference formula can be a name applied to a single cell or group of cells of the supporting worksheet. Name the cell or cells and then use the name in the external reference. This practice helps eliminate confusion in linked worksheets.

◆ **If the name of the supporting worksheet contains spaces or special characters, enclose the name in single quotation marks.** This rule does not apply to names that contain periods or underscore characters. Remember to place the exclamation point outside the single quotation marks.

◆ **If the external references are entered properly, you do not have to open the supporting worksheet for the dependent worksheet to update its link.** Excel remembers the location of the supporting worksheet.

◆ **Whenever possible, save linked worksheets in the same folder.** Saving linked worksheets together is not necessary, but it is a good practice to follow. If linked worksheets must be in different folders, save the supporting worksheets by using the File⇨Save As command, not the File⇨Save command. Open the appropriate folders and type the worksheet name in the Save As dialog box; then click the OK button to save the worksheet. Do this step before you save the dependent worksheet.

◆ **Do not use the same name for two supporting worksheets referred to in the same dependent worksheet.** Excel cannot access information from two different worksheets that have the same name. (Although this rule may seem obvious, worksheets saved in different folders may have the same name, and you may make this error inadvertently.)

Linking is an important part of building custom applications in Excel. With these guidelines, you should be able to complete any linking operations required.

Linking data via pictures

Excel offers a special way to link data from one worksheet to another — or even between applications. This method involves creating a *picture* of the data that you want to reference. The picture is placed into the dependent worksheet and refers to data in a supporting worksheet. Several characteristics make this picture different from a normal external reference. First, the picture is an object that

Turning off links

You may want to stop (or deactivate) linking formulas within dependent worksheets. You can turn off the links in two ways. You can convert the linking formulas to their values, or you can deactivate remote references (ignore incoming data). To convert the linking formulas to their values, follow these steps:

1. If the linking formula has produced an array, highlight all cells in the array. If the formula is not an array, select the cell you want. If the link is to a picture, click the picture to select it. In all cases, the linking formula appears in the formula bar. For more information about arrays, refer to Topic 9.

2. Using the mouse, click and drag in the formula bar to highlight the entire formula. This procedure is described in Topic 2.

3. Press Command-= to calculate the highlighted formula and turn the formula into a value. Press Return when finished.

To leave the linking formulas intact and tell Excel to ignore incoming data from the supporting worksheet, follow these steps:

1. Choose the Options command from the Tools menu and select the Calculation page tab.

2. Click the Update Remote References check box to deselect the option.

3. Press Return.

If you turn off remote references, you can always turn them on again later. Therefore, this procedure gives you more freedom than converting linking formulas to their values, which is useful when you want to work on the source worksheet without having your changes affect the linked worksheet.

resides on the worksheet's object layer. The object layer is an invisible plane that rests on top of (in front of) the worksheet plane. Each object you draw rests on its own invisible layer and these layers stack on top of each other to create overlapping effects. You can move, size, copy, and overlap the picture like any other object. (You may want to refer to Topic 5 before continuing with this section.)

Secondly, the picture refers to an *area* in the supporting worksheet—not to individual cells. This subtle distinction has many ramifications. In particular, objects that appear in the area are part of the picture. All formatting applied to the original data is also part of the picture. Therefore, you cannot format the picture independently of its surrounding data.

You may wonder why you would use a picture instead of directly linking formulas. The following list offers several reasons:

◆ Pictures enable you to link formatting as well as data. When you alter the formats or values in the supporting worksheet, the picture changes.

◆ Pictures enable you to link any objects that reside in the original area on the supporting worksheet. If you move an object into the linked area on the supporting worksheet, that object appears in the picture. This feature is useful for linking forms or completing reports.

◆ You can move, size, group, and manipulate pictures as you can any object. If you change the size of a picture, you can achieve interesting effects.

◆ You cannot alter the data inside a picture (including objects that appear in the picture) by changing the data in the dependent worksheet; you can only alter the data by changing the data in the supporting worksheet. Because the linked values are placed in an object, the linked values do not occupy cells you can edit. This feature can be useful for protecting data.

Linking pictures between workbooks

Step-by-Step

1. Open the supporting and dependent workbooks.

2. Highlight the data in the supporting workbook that you want to copy (and link) to the dependent worksheet.

3. Click the Camera button. (This button appears in the Utility tools in the toolbar customize dialog box. Refer to Topic 5 for details on using the Camera button.)

4. Use the Window menu to make the dependent worksheet active.

5. Click anywhere on the dependent worksheet to place the picture. You can move and edit the picture after it is in place. ◀

Alternatively, you can copy data by choosing the Copy command from the Edit menu. Then press Shift as you pull down the Edit menu; choose the Paste Picture command to paste the data as a picture.

Linking Excel with other programs

You can access information contained in other programs and bring that information into Excel. Likewise, you can use Excel data as supporting data for another program, such as a word processing document. You can use two methods to exchange data between Excel and other programs: linking data and data exchange.

Linking data

You can link data between an Excel worksheet and data in another application in two ways. One method, commonly called Publish/Subscribe or "edition management," was devised by Apple for all versions of System 7, including the newest System 7.5. The other method, called *Object Linking and Embedding (OLE)*, was devised by Microsoft. Both methods require that you have System 7 running on your Macintosh and that the external application supports OLE or Publish/Subscribe, depending on which you decide to use.

If the external program does not support OLE or Publish/Subscribe procedures, you will be unable to create direct links between the program and Excel. Instead, consider using the data-exchange techniques described in the section "Exchanging data."

Applications that support the new Publish/Subscribe features of System 7 can link data and graphics to other applications by using an *edition file*. An application stores data in an edition file, and other applications access the edition to get the most recent data.

This procedure is different than copying and pasting between applications. Linking to an edition file gives you a "live link" to the original document that created the file. If you change the original document, the edition file and the file linked to the edition file change. Creating an edition file from your data is called *publishing*. Linking to an edition file to access the data is called *subscribing*. Publish/ Subscribe has the following advantages:

◆ Several different applications can link to (subscribe to) a single edition file.

◆ The edition file is stored on disk for permanent reference.

◆ Many Macintosh applications support Publish/Subscribe.

Topic 10
**Working with Large
Workbook Applications**

Creating an edition file

1. Select a range of cells (or a graph).

2. Choose the Edit⇨Publishing⇨Create Publisher command. The options in the Create Publisher dialog box enable you to select a name and location for the file. ◖

Your Excel range selection is now available as a published file. You can place it into files created with other programs through the Subscribe To features of System 7. The following is a step-by-step explanation of how to subscribe to an edition file from Excel. Other programs may have different procedures.

Subscribing to an edition file in Excel

1. Select the Edit⇨Publishing⇨Subscribe To command.

2. Use the Subscribe To dialog box options to locate and select the edition file. The information is brought into Excel at the location of the active cell. ◖

You may want to use Microsoft's OLE linking instead of the Publish/Subscribe features of System 7. OLE linking between applications offers the following advantages:

◆ OLE linking between applications is similar to simple worksheet linking between two Excel worksheets.

◆ Many Microsoft products support OLE, including the PC versions of their products. You also can use OLE between Macintosh computers and PCs.

◆ OLE requires no extra file to be stored on the disk. Links are direct references to data in other applications.

To use OLE linking, you must create links between your Excel worksheet and the external document. Creating direct links between programs is like creating links between Excel worksheets. To create direct links, follow one of these four procedures:

◆ In the dependent worksheet, enter a linking formula that contains an external reference to the other program and its document. This formula requires the following syntax:

=application | document!reference.

Application is the name of the program to which you are linking; *document* is the particular file name. *Reference* is the cell, field, or reference point in the document to which you are linking. Each program has its own standards to follow within OLE.

◆ Enter a linking formula by pointing to the information in the external program and file.

◆ Copy data from the supporting file and paste the data into the dependent file by using the program's Paste Link feature (an option in the Edit⇨Paste Special dialog box). If the program does not have a Paste Link feature, it does not support OLE.

◆ Copy the data from the supporting file and paste the data into the dependent file using the Paste Picture feature.

Exchanging data

Everyone wants to get a job done as quickly as possible, and exchanging data can help you accomplish that goal. Exchanging data with other programs enables you to use information directly with Excel, eliminating the need to perform one of the biggest money and time wasters in business today — taking data from one computer and manually entering it into another (or spending a great deal of time reformatting data organization).

In some cases, exchanging data enables you to create Excel documents that ordinarily wouldn't be possible with Excel alone. For example, you can include a graphic object created with Aldus PageMaker or a table of information created with Microsoft Word.

If you work alone and only use Excel, you can skip this information. On the other hand, if you work in a corporate or other type of environment where you need, or could use, data from sources other than what you or someone else enters manually, it's well worth your while to window-shop this section. Exchanging data is one of the Macintosh's less-publicized strengths, and it is a strength that you can tap into easily.

Sharing the wealth

You can access data from other sources in the following ways:

◆ Opening a file on disk

◆ Using the Clipboard

System 7 users can exchange data in the following ways:

◆ Using Publish and Subscribe

◆ Linking

◆ Embedding

Table 10-2 summarizes the Macintosh data exchange options and can help you decide which ones are right for you.

Table 10-2 Data Exchange Options							
Option	**Requirement**						
	Additional hardware/ software	**System 7**	**Network**	**More than one program per disk**	**More than one program open**	**Automatic updating**	**Access by other users**
Disk files: IBM to Mac	No	No	No	No	No	No	No
Disk files: Mac to IBM	Yes	No	No	No	No	No	No
Clipboard	No	No	No	Yes	No	No	No
Publish & Subscribe	No	Yes	Yes	No	No	Yes	Yes
Linking	No	Yes	No	Yes	Yes	Yes	No
Embedding	No	Yes	No	Yes	No	Yes	No

Each of these options has its own set of pros and cons. Sometimes one method is better than another. These methods are explored in the next section.

Opening a file on disk

You can read a variety of file formats directly in Excel by selecting Open from the File menu or by clicking the File⇨Open tool. Simply select the name of the file from the file's folder or subfolder from the File Open list box. Excel can read the following file formats, plus many more:

Program	**File format**
Excel for Windows 4.0, 3.0, 2.2	xls
MultiPlan	sylk
Lotus 1-2-3 1A	WKS

Program	File format
Lotus 1-2-3 2.01, 2.2, 2.3, 2.4	WK1
Lotus 1-2-3 3.0, 3.1, 3.1+	WK3
Lotus 1-2-3 for Windows 1.0, 1.1	WK3
Lotus Symphony	WRK, WR1
VisiCalc	DIF
dBASE	DBF2, DBF3, DBF4

You can also open text files with no formatting and text files with comma separated values (CSV) created by a DOS, Windows, or OS/2 program.

In addition, if a format file accompanies a Lotus 1-2-3 worksheet file (.ALL files for 1-2-3 2.01 and 2.2, .FMT files for 1-2-3 3.0, 3.1, 3.1+, or .FM3 files for 1-2-3 for Windows), Excel applies the corresponding formatting to the worksheet's contents. In other words, you can retain all the visual effects in your original files.

Opening a file created by another program is usually a quick and easy way to get data and applications into Excel, thereby eliminating tedious reentry of the data into Excel. The capability of computers to use the disk containing the file is another story, however, depending on whether you're transferring data from an IBM-PC or compatible computer to the Macintosh, or vice versa.

Converting a text file into Excel

1. From the File menu, choose the Open command.

2. Use the Open dialog box options to locate the text file you want. You may want to choose the Text option from the List of File Types drop-down list.

3. Double-click the name of the text file to open it. You are at the first step of the Text Import Wizard, shown in Figure 10-5.

4. Follow the steps of the Text Import Wizard to designate the type of text file you are opening. When finished, the file appears in Excel. ◊

Topic 10
Working with Large
Workbook Applications

Figure 10-5: The Text Import Wizard.

To save an Excel worksheet in one of these formats, use the Save As command, specify the file name you want, and click the Options button. Click the button next to the file type you want to specify.

Exchanging different file formats

If the file you want was saved to disk in your Macintosh or another Macintosh, you're home free. Any Macintosh can easily open the file you need. If you want to share data with friends who use an IBM-PC (or compatible), you'll need to navigate heavier seas.

Actually, moving data from a PC to the Macintosh isn't too difficult if the PC has a 3¹/₂ inch disk drive. Fortunately, the floppy drive in all Macintoshes that came out in the late summer of 1990 and later read 3¹/₂ inch MS-DOS disks. Consequently, in Excel you can choose Save As from the File menu and save an Excel document to a 3¹/₂-inch disk for the PC.

The Apple File Exchange application (in the Apple File Exchange Folder, which is in your System Folder), enables you to use files contained on a 3¹/₂-inch disk from an IBM-PC (normally, a dialog box appears asking you if you want to format the disk if you put it in the drive), and transfer the data to the folder of your choosing. Choosing Quit from Apple File Exchange's File menu ejects the disk from the Macintosh. Figure 10-6 shows the Apple File Exchange dialog box.

If you exchange files frequently, you should consider transferring data by connecting two (or more) computers together. For Macintosh-to-PC data transfer, this is your only option because PC disk drives unfortunately don't recognize the Macintosh floppy disk format. Several companies have cabling and communication software that enable you to move data from the Macintosh to the PC (and vice versa) with or without the use of a modem. Dataviz's MacLink Plus/PC and Traveling Software's LapLink/Mac contain everything you need to transfer files back and forth between the Mac and PC.

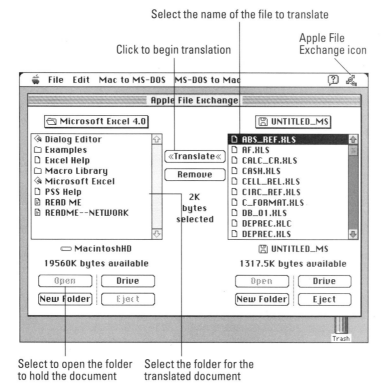

Select the name of the file to translate

Click to begin translation

Apple File Exchange icon

Select to open the folder to hold the document   Select the folder for the translated document

Figure 10-6: An example of the Apple File Exchange dialog box.

Another option is to share files via a network. Adding a LocalTalk expansion board to the PC, and file-server software (Tops or AppleShare) to the Mac, enables both camps to talk to each other quickly and conveniently.

If you'd like to learn more about transferring files between the Macintosh and PC, read Jim Heid's *Macworld Complete Mac Handbook Plus Interactive CD*, published by IDG Books, 1994.

Using the Clipboard to exchange data

If you cannot link data directly between programs, you may be able to exchange data using the Clipboard. This process is a simple matter of using the copy and paste procedure between the different programs and their files. Almost all Macintosh programs support Clipboard copy and paste procedures. The resulting data is not linked to its original document but is merely transferred to the new document.

Consolidating Worksheet Data

You may think of external references as an excellent way to consolidate the information across several worksheets. Consolidation is the process of combining the data from several different worksheets into one summary worksheet. The summary worksheet is the total of all the other worksheets in the workbook. (You can also consolidate data across different workbooks.) Figure 10-7 shows a Consolidate dialog box.

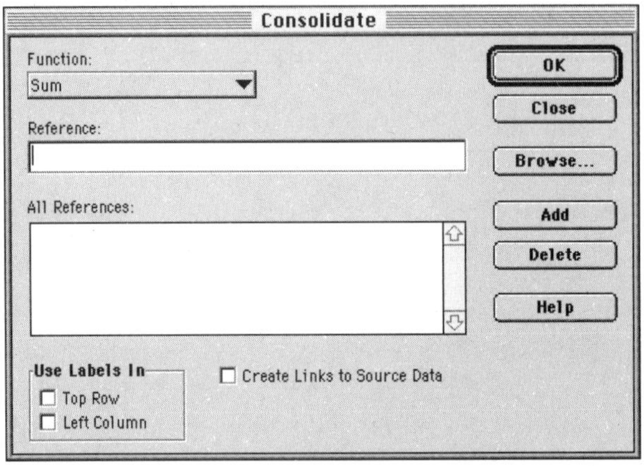

Figure 10-7: Using the Consolidate dialog box to consolidate worksheets.

Suppose you use separate worksheets to calculate monthly sales for your organization. Each quarter, you need to prepare a quarterly total worksheet that consolidates the data from the previous three months. You can set up a consolidated worksheet to help you compute the quarterly worksheet.

The monthly worksheets all use the same format as the totals worksheet—they just contain different data. You may think that external references between the worksheets is a good way to consolidate this data. However, you will probably find the formulas like the following to be time-consuming to enter:

='January!C5+February!C5+March!C5

You have to enter a lot of external references to complete the task! Excel provides other ways to consolidate worksheets. The following sections describe three methods for data consolidation.

Consolidating with the Copy and Paste Special commands

One way to consolidate several worksheets onto a summary sheet is to copy the data from the individual worksheets and paste it into the summary worksheet—adding each new set of values to the previous ones. You can consolidate several worksheets with the Edit⇨Copy and Edit⇨Paste Special commands.

Consolidating by copying

1. Activate the worksheet to be included in the consolidation and highlight the cell or range you want to consolidate.

2. Choose the Edit⇨Copy command.

3. Activate the Summary worksheet and move to the upper-left cell of the range into which the data is to appear.

4. Select the Edit⇨Paste Special command and choose the Add operation from the options in the Paste Special dialog box. Click OK when finished.

5. Repeat these steps for the next worksheet you want to consolidate — pasting and adding the new data over the existing data in the Summary worksheet. ♦

Each time you copy data from one of the source worksheets and paste it into the same range in the Summary sheet, Excel adds the new data to the existing data in the Summary sheet. The advantage to this method of consolidating is that you can quickly combine two or three worksheets by using simple copy and paste procedures. Unless you have more than three or four worksheets to consolidate, this is the fastest method. However, the final summary worksheet contains no direct links to the source worksheets. Therefore, if you update the source worksheets, the summary sheet does not reflect the changes, and you'll have to repeat the consolidation process using the updated workbook.

Consolidating with the Consolidate command

Excel's consolidation feature provides a convenient way to combine the data in several worksheets. Simply tell Excel which ranges on which worksheets you want to combine by pointing to the ranges with the mouse or keyboard. After indicating the source ranges, click the OK button, and Excel combines the data across the worksheets you specified. You can even tell Excel to create links from the summary worksheet to the individual worksheets, so that when you update the worksheets later, the summary will automatically update itself.

Consolidating worksheets

1. Open the workbook containing the worksheets that you want to consolidate.

2. Activate the Summary worksheet and position the cell pointer in the upper-left corner of the range that will contain the consolidated data.

3. Select the Data⇨Consolidate command. The dialog box shown in Figure 10-7 appears.

4. Press Tab until the cursor appears in the Reference entry box.

5. Activate the first worksheet and highlight the cell or range to be consolidated. The Consolidate dialog box remains on the screen as you highlight this range, so you may want to move it aside. As you highlight the range, it appears in the Consolidate dialog box as an external reference.

   You can also consolidate from external workbooks by clicking the Browse button to open the desired workbooks and pointing to ranges on the appropriate sheets within them.

6. Click the Add button to add the specified range to the list of worksheets in this consolidation procedure (see Figure 10-8).

This is a range added to the Consolidate dialog box

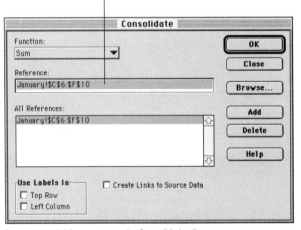

Figure 10-8: Adding a range to the Consolidation list.

7. Repeat this procedure for all ranges on the other worksheets to be included in the consolidation. These ranges do not have to be in the same place on each worksheet but they probably always will be.

8. Excel assumes that you want to sum the data in the indicated ranges, but you can specify a different mathematical operation by selecting from the Functions list in the Consolidate dialog box.

9. If you want to establish links from the source worksheets to the Summary sheet, click the Create Links to Source Data option.

10. When all the options are complete, click OK to consolidate the data using the mathematical function you selected.

When you complete the operation, Excel fills the appropriate number of cells with the consolidated values. If the source ranges are all the same size and shape, then all inserted values represent totals from the source worksheets. However, if you highlight ranges of different sizes and shapes on the source worksheets, only the overlapping cells are consolidated.

You can highlight the exact range into which the consolidated data should be placed on the Summary worksheet, rather than just moving to the upper-left corner. Excel fills whatever range you specify and leaves out any data that does not fit into the range. If your destination range is a single row, Excel expands the range downward to display the consolidated data. If your range is a single column, then Excel expands the range to the right to fit the data. If you highlight a block, then Excel fills only that block.

If you choose to establish links between the Summary worksheet and the source worksheet, be aware that Excel inserts rows into your worksheet to accommodate the link references. A new row that contains an external reference to that sheet is then inserted for each source worksheet. The inserted rows are not visible at first on the Summary sheet because Excel hides them in an outline structure. However, you can expand the outline to see the references.

Consolidating selected data

By using a variation of the Data⇨Consolidate procedure, you can summarize specific items rather than entire ranges from the source worksheets. For example, you may want to consolidate specific products from the monthly sales worksheets — rather than all products in the source ranges. By including the row and column headings in the consolidation ranges (and in the summary range), you can single out specific items in the source ranges. When you've looked at those entries, just change the items you want to consolidate to get a different set of summary values. You don't have to repeat the consolidation setup; the consolidation Summary worksheet is flexible and changeable.

Consolidating data

1. Set up the Summary worksheet with row and column headings that indicate the items you want to consolidate. Figure 10-9 shows an example. Note that these labels must match the row and column headings in the source worksheets.

2. Highlight the category names in the left column, the top row, or both.

3. Choose the Data⇨Consolidate command.

4. Add the first source range to the list by highlighting the data range on the first worksheet, including the row and column labels that match those on the Summary worksheet (see Figure 10-10).

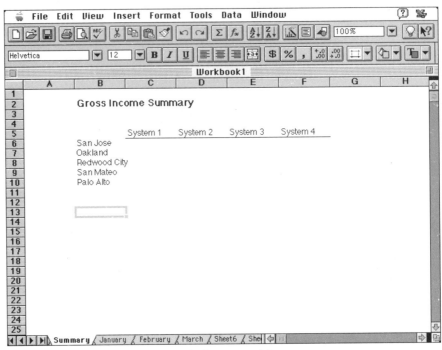

Figure 10-9: Add row and column headings to the Summary worksheet.

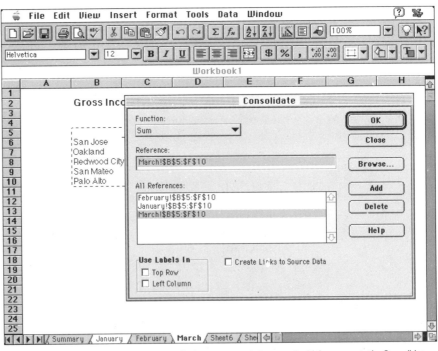

Figure 10-10: Highlight data and the headings in the source worksheets and add the ranges to the Consolidate box.

5. Click the Add button to add the range and then add other source ranges and their headings.

6. Click OK to consolidate.

The important point is that you can now change the row and/or column headings in the Summary worksheet and re-consolidate the data with the Data⇨Consolidate command (the source ranges are already established in the Consolidate dialog box). Changing the headings gives you a new set of data.

Here are some important points to remember about consolidation:

◆ If the highlighted destination range is smaller than the source ranges, Excel fills as much as possible, but it won't consolidate all the data you selected. If the destination range is larger than the source ranges, Excel skips extra cells. Excel presents a message explaining what it does in these cases.

◆ The source ranges do not have to be located in the same positions in the worksheet. As long as you highlight the ranges you want, consolidation takes place.

◆ The source ranges do not have to be the same size or shape. Excel consolidates the information that overlaps within the source ranges.

◆ Excel does not replace formulas or formatting in the destination range. Number formats, however, are copied from the source ranges.

◆ If you highlight a single row as the destination, Excel expands the range downward to accommodate the number of rows being consolidated. Excel consolidates only as many columns as you highlight, however — even if the source ranges contain more columns. If the source ranges each contain four columns and ten rows, for example, and you highlight three cells in a row for the source, Excel fills three columns and ten rows in the destination. Similarly, if you highlight a single column, Excel expands the destination to the right to accommodate the number of columns being consolidated.

◆ If you highlight a single cell for the destination range, Excel automatically makes the destination range match the size of the consolidated data.

◆ You can choose from several worksheet functions for consolidation, including AVERAGE, COUNT, COUNTA, MAX, MIN, PRODUCT, STDEV, STDEVP, SUM, VAR, and VARP. Normally, you use the SUM function to add all the source data together.

◆ You can create automatic links (external references) between the source data and the destination range. This procedure makes the relationship between the worksheets more permanent. When you change data in a source worksheet, the destination changes accordingly. To establish links, choose the Consolidate command from the Data menu, and then check the Create Links to Source Data option. For more information on linking, see "Linking Worksheets," earlier in this topic.

◆ Within source ranges, you can consolidate specific information rather than all the data.

Quick Tips

Creating an outlining toolbar

If you find that you outline data often, you might want to create an outlining toolbar that contains the various custom toolbar buttons applicable to outlining. Refer to Topic 3 about creating custom toolbars.

Using Microsoft's file translators

If you are moving data between the PC and Macintosh versions of Excel, use the File Í Save As command to save your Excel file in the opposite format. Microsoft has built into Excel the ability to translate Excel files between the PC and Macintosh and this capability exceeds that in Apple File Exchange.

Using outlining for charts

You can use outlining to chart the totals of a chart worksheet. When various totals are spread across many rows and columns of data, use outlining to bring those totals together for your chart. This way, you can simply highlight a range of cell containing the totals — rather than trying to locate the totals throughout the worksheet.

Creating many links

If you have the need to link your workbook to many other workbooks, you might find it easier not to open all the related workbooks, but let Excel locate them for you. Just enter a linking formula with a reference to a workbook that does not exist. Excel will automatically present the Find File dialog box where you can locate the desired workbook for the link.

Exchanging database data

If you want to import your database data into Excel from a different database program — such as 4-D, you might find it easiest to use the Microsoft Query feature rather than importing the data. This is especially true if you are not converting from the database program to Excel, but intend to continue using the database program to manage the data. Perhaps you are using Excel for some special charting or data analysis. By using the Query feature, you can keep the data linked between the two programs.

Part IV:
Creating
Informative Charts

2nd Edition

Macworld Excel 5 Companion

Creating Charts

Overview

Charts, or graphs, are visual representations of numeric data. Charts provide powerful messages and can help you draw conclusions from raw numeric data. Excel offers a comprehensive set of charting tools, including 14 different chart types and numerous ways to customize your charts.

This topic examines the initial procedures for creating charts, including setting up and selecting chart data, drawing a chart onto the worksheet, and making changes to the chart type, data, and orientation. You learn about the following:

◆ Selecting data for your chart

◆ Drawing the chart onto the worksheet

◆ Using the ChartWizard to build a chart

◆ Modifying the chart data after you create the chart

◆ Changing a chart's data orientation

◆ Choosing the right chart from Excel's chart types and built-in AutoFormats

◆ Creating a chart on a separate worksheet page

The Basic Charting Process

The charting procedure is simple. Excel provides tools that do most of the work for you. The ChartWizard is the primary charting tool; it takes you through five simple steps for building a chart. The following is the basic procedure:

1. Highlight the chart data. (The chart data is the range of cells that contains the chart titles and numeric data.) For best results, the chart data should appear in a single, contiguous range of cells. However, you can have chart data located in different ranges. More information about selecting the chart data appears in the following section.

2. Click the ChartWizard and then click and drag on the worksheet to draw the chart onto the sheet. This drawing procedure determines the initial size, shape, and position of the chart on the worksheet, although you can change these attributes at any time. You can also create a chart on a special Chart Worksheet, as described later in this topic.

3. Follow the five ChartWizard steps to specify the various aspects of the chart. In these steps you establish (or confirm) the chart's data range, select a chart type, select a specific chart AutoFormat, set the data orientation, and add chart titles and a legend.

4. Customize the chart by using the charting commands and options available through the Format and Insert menus. (Chart customization is discussed in Topic 12.)

Notice that the preceding procedure is not the only way to create a chart. Rather than going through the five ChartWizard steps, you can quickly create any of the basic charts (line, column, pie, and so on) by using the tools on the Chart toolbar. (See "Creating a Chart without the ChartWizard" later in this topic.)

Selecting the Chart Data

The first step in creating a chart is highlighting the chart data. Chart data consists of the chart's labels and numeric values and usually appears in a table format, as shown in Figure 11-1. This figure shows the chart data and the resulting bar chart. (Excel calls this a *column chart*). Chances are that your worksheet data is already set up in this way. If so, all you have to do is highlight the table.

But your data may not always fit this model, and you may not want to use all your data for the chart. The following are some considerations for selecting chart data that do not fit the perfect table-oriented mold:

◆ **Don't include totals in the data range.** If you want to chart a table of values, you should probably exclude row and column totals from the data range. Stacked charts show these totals for you, and other types of charts are not effective if they mix totals and individual values. If you want to chart the totals, create a chart that includes only the totals as the data range (see next point).

◆ **You can highlight specific parts of the data range.** You don't have to select an entire table for charting; you may want to chart just the totals or just certain items from the table. You can limit the items by making a multiple-range selection as shown in Figure 11-2. You can compare just the items you want to see in the chart and keep the chart data to a minimum for better readability.

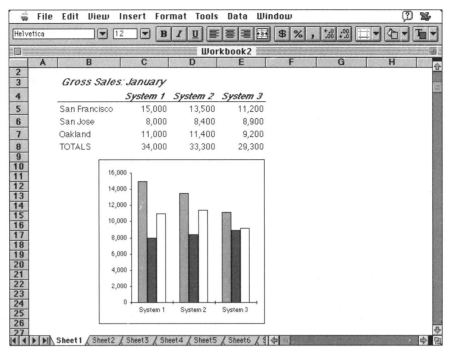

Figure 11-1: A typical data range for a chart.

◆ **Labels are not required.** Your data range does not have to include row and column labels; however, you will probably want to include at least one set of labels. If your data does not include any labels, you should pay particular attention to the ChartWizard Step 4 to make sure that the data orientation is correct.

◆ **All numeric data should be in the same ballpark.** Charts are most effective when the numeric data does not include vast differences in values. If your data includes such variations, try grouping the data into value ranges and creating a separate chart for each range.

After you create the chart from the selected data, the chart and data are linked together. You can then change any or all values in the chart data range, and the chart will reflect those changes immediately. Your charts use "live" links to the data you select.

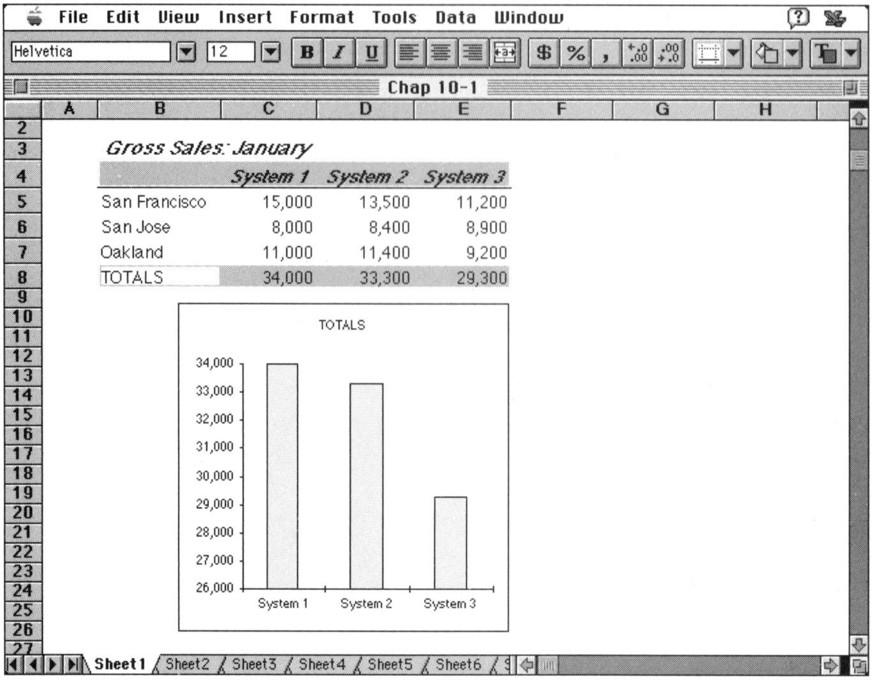

| File | Edit | View | Insert | Format | Tools | Data | Window |

Helvetica | 12 | B | I | U |

Chap 10-1

	A	B	C	D	E	F	G	H
2								
3		*Gross Sales: January*						
4			*System 1*	*System 2*	*System 3*			
5		San Francisco	15,000	13,500	11,200			
6		San Jose	8,000	8,400	8,900			
7		Oakland	11,000	11,400	9,200			
8		TOTALS	34,000	33,300	29,300			

TOTALS

```
34,000 ┤   ███
33,000 ┤   ███    ███
32,000 ┤   ███    ███
31,000 ┤   ███    ███
30,000 ┤   ███    ███
29,000 ┤   ███    ███    ███
28,000 ┤   ███    ███    ███
27,000 ┤   ███    ███    ███
26,000 ┤   ███    ███    ███
         System 1 System 2 System 3
```

Sheet1 / Sheet2 / Sheet3 / Sheet4 / Sheet5 / Sheet6 /

Figure 11-2: You can highlight portions of a data range for charting.

Creating a Chart with the ChartWizard

After selecting the chart's data range, you're ready to draw the chart onto the worksheet by using the ChartWizard tool that appears on the Standard toolbar. The basic process is simple: Just click the ChartWizard tool and then click and drag on the worksheet to draw a box. Your screen should look something like the one in Figure 11-3. When you reach the desired size and shape of the box, release the mouse. Excel then presents you with the first of five ChartWizard steps.

You can also access the ChartWizard's steps by choosing the Chart⇨On This Sheet command from the Insert menu. Then draw the chart onto the worksheet.

You can draw the chart box to fit exactly within a range of cells on the worksheet by holding down Command as you draw the chart box. The box adheres to the worksheet cell borders.

You can draw a perfectly square chart box by holding down Shift as you draw the chart box. Be sure to release the mouse button before you release Shift.

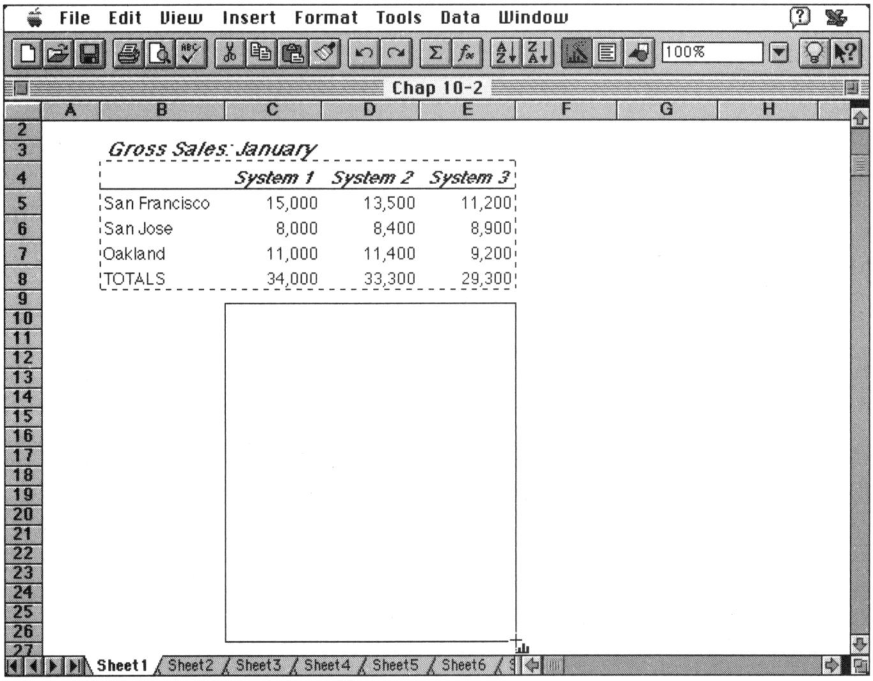

Figure 11-3: Draw the chart onto the worksheet as if you're drawing a box.

Notice that the chart box you draw contains the chart after you finish the five ChartWizard steps. The chart box is a worksheet object, which means that it behaves like all other worksheet objects. Here are some of the ways a chart object behaves (a more detailed discussion of objects appears in Topic 5):

◆ **Charts float over the worksheet.** Charts and other worksheet objects appear on the object layer, or plane. This layer keeps all objects above the actual chart data and cells. Hence, objects can overlap, or cover up, the worksheet data as Figure 11-4 shows.

◆ **You can move charts around the page.** All worksheet objects can be moved around at any time. Usually, you just click the object and drag it to another location. For more information on moving charts, see "Moving and Sizing Charts" later in this topic.

◆ **You can modify the size and shape of the chart box.** You're not stuck with the original chart box you draw; you can change its size and shape at any time. For more information on modifying the size and shape of a chart, refer to "Moving and Sizing Charts" later in this topic.

◆ **Charts are saved with the worksheet.** When you save the worksheet, all worksheet objects are saved, too.

◆ **You can format the chart box.** Just as you can change the color and border of a box, you can change the attributes of the chart's box container, or *chart frame*. For more information on formatting chart frames, refer to Topic 12.

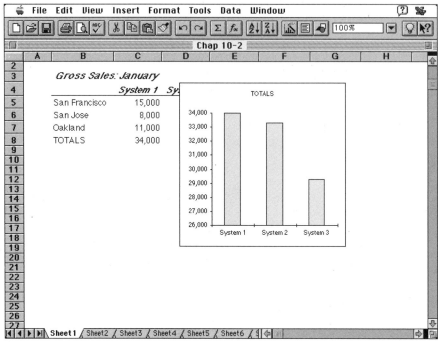

Figure 11-4: Charts can overlap worksheet data.

Before examining the five ChartWizard steps, take a moment to review the ChartWizard controls. These controls are found on each of the five steps:

◆ **Cancel.** Cancels the chart and places you back on the worksheet. Use this control if you change your mind about creating the chart.

◆ **|<<.** Takes you back to the first step. Use this control in any of the five steps to start over again.

◆ **< Back.** Takes you back one step. Use this control if you want to review or change your preceding step.

◆ **Next >.** Moves you to the next step. Use this control when you are finished with the current step and want to continue. You can also press Return to move to the next step.

◆ **Finish.** Moves you to the end of the procedure. Use this control if you want to skip the remaining steps and add the chart immediately. You can use this control at any time during the procedure. Excel uses default selections for any steps you skip, which can be useful for quickly finishing a chart.

Step 1: Choosing data

If you highlighted the desired chart data before starting the ChartWizard procedure, the first step is probably already done for you. Step 1 lets you specify the chart's data range. If the data range is already entered into the dialog box (see Figure 11-5), you can simply press Return to continue to the next step.

Figure 11-5: The first step of the ChartWizard procedure.

However, if you want to change the data range, just move the dialog box aside and then click and drag on the worksheet to highlight the desired range. You can also type the range reference — including a range name, an external range reference, or a 3-D range reference — into the dialog box. Table 11-1 lists some examples of range names:

Table 11-1	
Example Range References	

Name	What It Refers To
SALES	Specifies the range SALES on the active worksheet.
'[Workbook]Page'!Range	Specifies a range from a different page of the current workbook or any other workbook specified. Be sure to include the entire pathname of the workbook file.
Worksheet!Range	Specifies a range from an external worksheet. Be sure to specify the entire location of the worksheet file.

Refer to Topics 5 and 7 for more information about external and 3-D references. When the data range entry is correct, press Return to continue to the next step.

You can actually draw the chart onto a different worksheet than the one containing the chart data. Just click the page tab to move to the desired worksheet before drawing the chart.

You can change an existing chart's data range by double-clicking the finished chart to select it and then clicking the ChartWizard tool. After using the dialog box from Step 1 to change the data range, you can then move on to Step 4 to set the orientation for the new data range.

Step 2: Selecting a chart type

The next step of the ChartWizard procedure is simple: Just click the image representing the chart type you want to use — you have 15 chart types from which to choose. Figure 11-6 shows the chart types available in this step. Be sure to read up on the various chart types later in this topic under "Changing Chart Types."

If you double-click a chart type tool, Excel automatically moves on to the next step. Otherwise, press Return to continue or click Next >.

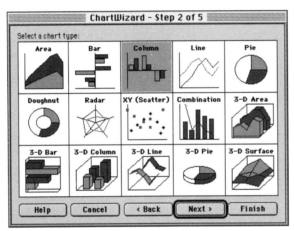

Figure 11-6: Step 2 of the ChartWizard presents chart types from which you can choose.

Step 3: Selecting an AutoFormat

The next step involves choosing one of Excel's built-in chart formats for the chart type you selected in the preceding step. Each chart type comes with several built-in formats (or AutoFormats) from which you can choose. Figure 11-7 shows the formats available for Column charts.

Many of the AutoFormats include stacked, unstacked, and 100 percent versions of the chart. In addition, you may see some variations on gridlines and interior labels in these built-in formats. You can change or modify the chart's formats at any time, so don't worry about making the wrong choice here. For more information on customizing chart formats, refer to Topic 12.

```
┌─────────────────────────────────────────────┐
│        ChartWizard - Step 3 of 5             │
│  Select a format for the Column chart:       │
│     1       2       3       4       5        │
│  [chart] [chart] [chart] [chart] [chart]     │
│     6       7  8    8       9      10         │
│  [chart] [chart] [chart] [chart] [chart]     │
│                                               │
│  [ Help ] [ Cancel ] [ < Back ] [ Next > ] [ Finish ] │
└─────────────────────────────────────────────┘
```

Figure 11-7: Step 3 provides the chart AutoFormats.

You can access Excel's AutoFormats and select a new AutoFormat even after you've created a chart with the ChartWizard. Just double-click the finished chart and choose the AutoFormat command from the Format menu. Chart types are listed along the left side of the AutoFormat dialog box.

Step 4: Setting the data orientation

Data orientation is an important part of charting. When you create a chart, it's important to know whether the rows or the columns are used to represent the data series in the chart. A *data series* includes the items plotted in the chart and is represented in different ways, depending on the chart type you select. Line charts show each data series as a separate line. Column charts (commonly known as bar charts) show each data series as a set of bars — all using the same color or pattern. If you have two data series in a column chart, you may have a set of red bars and a set of blue bars. The chart in Figure 11-8 shows how the rows of your worksheet data range become data series on a column chart. Notice that there are two data series in this chart — each data series consists of three bars. The two data series come from the two rows of data, and the three bars for each series come from the three columns of data (three cells in each row). The columns are known as *categories*.

But this chart could easily use the columns as data series and the rows as categories. In this case, you would see four different data series with two bars in each. Figure 11-9 shows this reversed row/column orientation.

The difference between these two charts is dramatic and has a profound affect on how the chart is interpreted. You need to search for an appropriate data orientation for your data and the message that you want to convey.

Step 4 of the ChartWizard process lets you reverse the data orientation and see the effect on the sample chart. Click either Rows or Columns to make your choice. You can also determine how Excel uses the first row or column. If you have both row and column labels in the data range, you should probably select the first item in each option.

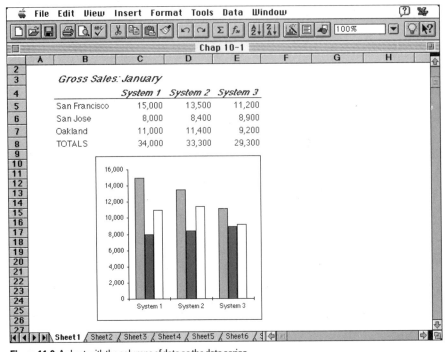

Figure 11-8: A chart with the columns of data as the data series.

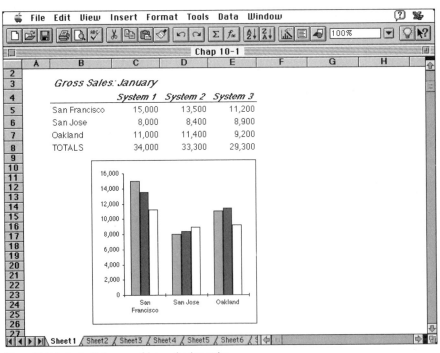

Figure 11-9: A chart with the rows of data as the data series.

You can change a chart's orientation after you've completed the five ChartWizard steps. Just click the chart and then click the ChartWizard tool. You'll see the Step 1 dialog box allowing you to change the data range. Press Return to continue to the Step 4 dialog box that lets you change the orientation.

Step 5: Adding a legend and chart titles

In the final step of the ChartWizard procedure, you can add a legend and other text to the chart. Most of the options in this dialog box are self-explanatory, as you can see in Figure 11-10. Select Yes or No to add a legend from the chart's data series. Excel takes the legend entries from the first cell in each series — assuming that you have specified that these cells contain the legend text (see Step 4).

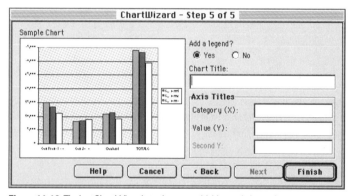

Figure 11-10: The last ChartWizard step lets you add titles and a legend.

You can enter a chart title into the space provided, and Excel automatically places it at the top of the chart. You can change the formatting of this title, and you can also add titles by using *floating* chart text, as described in Topic 12. Floating text gives you more control over the placement of the title.

The category axis title appears at the bottom of the chart (except on rotated bar charts), and the value axis title appears next to the value axis along the left side. If you have added a second value axis on the right side (as described in Topic 12), you can enter a title for that axis in the Overlay entry box.

After you are finished with this step, press Return, and the complete chart with all its effects appears in the chart box that you drew.

After you draw a chart onto the worksheet and complete the ChartWizard steps, the chart appears and is automatically selected. When a chart is selected, the Charting toolbar, containing buttons for modifying and formatting the chart, automatically appears. Details on the Charting toolbar can be found in the next section.

Creating a Chart without the ChartWizard

Although the ChartWizard provides a quick and easy way to create charts from scratch, you are not required to use it. You can create a chart more directly by "drawing" the chart onto the worksheet when you use the Chart Type button in the Charting toolbar.

Drawing a specific chart type

1. Activate the Charting toolbar. Choose Toolbars from the View menu and select the Charting toolbar from the list. Then press OK.

2. Highlight the desired chart data on your worksheet.

3. Choose one of the chart types from the Chart Type button in the Charting toolbar.

4. Click and drag on the worksheet to draw the chart. ◖

This procedure creates a chart by using the chart type you selected from the Chart Type button. Using this method, you can instantly create any type of chart from your highlighted data. And remember, you can change the chart type and customize any element in the chart at any time. So you're never stuck with your decision.

The Chart Type button is also useful for modifying an existing chart when you want to change its type. Just double-click the chart that you want to change and then choose the desired chart type from the palette of choices. For more details on changing chart types, see "Changing Chart Types" later in this topic.

Creating a Chart on a Chart Worksheet

Rather than insert a chart alongside other data in your worksheet, you can create a chart on a worksheet of its own. A *chart worksheet* is a special page in a workbook that holds only one chart — the chart fills the entire screen. Figure 11-11 shows an example of a chart worksheet.

Reasons for using chart worksheets to hold your charts include the following:

◆ You can automatically fill the entire screen with your chart.

◆ You can produce more effective on-screen presentations of charts.

◆ The larger charts are easier to read.

◆ You can move directly to any chart by clicking the appropriate page of the workbook.

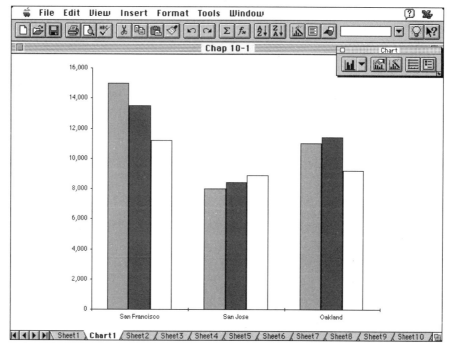

Figure 11-11: A chart worksheet.

◆ You can move and copy chart pages between workbooks.

◆ You can create slide shows from your chart pages via the Slide show add-in.

Using a chart worksheet

1. Highlight the desired chart data in your workbook.

2. Press Control as you click the current page tab. The shortcut menu for manipulating worksheet pages appears.

3. Choose the Insert command from the shortcut menu.

4. Choose Chart from the list that appears.

5. Follow the ChartWizard steps (see the steps explained earlier in this topic). ◀

When you're finished with the ChartWizard steps, the chart automatically fills the screen on a new page of the workbook. You can move this page around the workbook if desired. (See Topic 3 for details on manipulating workbook pages.) You can also place each chart on its own page of the workbook for easy access.

Another way to create a chart on a new page is to use the Chart⇨As a New Sheet command in the Insert menu.

Use the Sized With Window command in the View menu to view a chart worksheet at full-screen capacity. This command automatically fills the screen with the chart by choosing exactly the right zoom magnification factor for your system.

If you decide you no longer want the chart on its own worksheet, you can copy or move the worksheet chart onto any other worksheet page as a floating chart. Just move to the chart worksheet and click the edge of the chart to select the entire chart area (see Figure 11-12). Now press Command-C to copy or Command-X to cut the chart. Finally, move to the desired chart page and paste the chart with Command-V. You may now have to move and resize the chart to fit its new location. For further details on moving and sizing charts, see the next section.

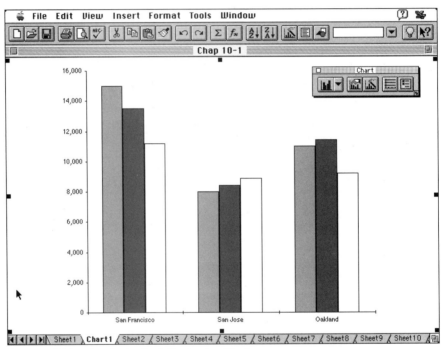

Figure 11-12: Select the entire chart by clicking the edge of the chart area.

Moving and Sizing Charts

After you have completed the ChartWizard procedure, your chart appears on the worksheet where you originally drew it. However, you can move the chart box at any time. Just click the mouse on the chart and drag it to another location.

If you're moving the chart a great distance, you may find it easier to cut and paste the chart by using the Edit⇨Cut and Edit⇨Paste commands. Remember that you should move to the new location and paste the chart immediately after you cut.

If you want to change the size and shape of the chart, just click the chart to highlight it. A highlighted chart displays small black boxes, called *size boxes*, around its edges. (You can double-click the chart to produce the size boxes, but this also activates the charting options.) After the chart is selected, just click and drag on any of the size boxes. For more information about sizing and moving worksheet objects (including charts), refer to Topic 5.

You can remove a chart from the worksheet by clicking the chart and then pressing Delete or Command-X.

Changing Chart Types

In Step 2 of the ChartWizard procedure, you select a chart type from the 15 main chart types. You can then go on to Step 3, in which you select the AutoFormat for the chart type you selected. Excel provides several preformatted charts in each of the 15 types so that you can quickly and easily choose a chart that's perfect for your needs. This section describes how to access the AutoFormats after you have finished creating the chart so that you can change to a different AutoFormat at any time. You then learn about the different types and subtypes of charts available so that you can choose the best AutoFormat chart for the occasion.

Choosing a built-in chart format (AutoFormat)

1. Double-click the chart that you want to reformat.

2. Choose the AutoFormat command from the Format menu. If this command does not appear, then you have not double-clicked the chart. This command appears only when a chart frame is activated or a chart page is activated.

3. Under the Formats Used option, make sure that the Built-In button is selected.

4. Choose one of the 15 basic chart types from the Galleries list box. When you click a chart type in this list, a gallery of built-in formats appears in the dialog box (See Figure 11-13).

5. Choose one of the formats in the gallery by clicking its picture.

6. Click OK to apply the selection to the chart. ◖

If you can't find a format in the AutoFormat dialog box that suits your needs, choose one that comes close and then turn to Topic 12 for information about manually customizing charts. Doing so gives you control over every detail in a chart's design, thereby giving you the power to build spectacular chart effects.

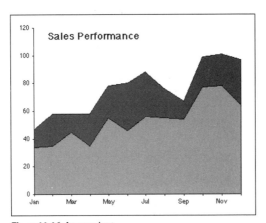

Figure 11-13: The AutoFormat option presents a gallery of built-in formats.

Area charts

Area charts are used primarily to show how the total of several elements changes over time. The category labels are usually time values and are evenly spaced. The more plot points you include in an area chart, the more effective the chart is in showing the trend. For example, an area chart would be useful for showing the relative volume of product sales over time — where the chart shows two or three products and how they combine to form the entire sales volume.

Remember that the top of the area chart shows the total of each data series, and the layers of color (or shading) show how each data series contributes to the total over time. When you look at an area chart, examine the change in heights among the individual layers and the change in the top line. Figure 11-14 shows an area chart.

Figure 11-14: An area chart.

 Normal area charts plot each data series on top of the preceding one, so that the data is stacked. Hence, the top line of the chart shows the total of all the data. However, Excel provides a 100 percent area chart format. A 100 percent area chart is a stacked chart that shows each data series as a percentage of the total, which is useful for charts that show market saturation or segmentation over time.

Bar charts

Bar charts are used much like column charts, but they emphasize competition and distance achieved. They are often used to show race results, such as the status of a vote or survey. Generally, a bar chart uses only one or two data series and often only one category. Figure 11-15 shows some examples of bar charts.

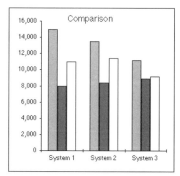

Figure 11-15: Bar charts are most effective when they use a minimum amount of data, such as one or two comparisons (data series).

 Excel's bar chart AutoFormats consist of three primary subtypes. The stacked version plots each data series on top of the preceding one to show how the parts make up the total. Stacked bar charts compare the totals of several data groups. An unstacked bar chart plots each value from the baseline — rather than from the top of the preceding value. And a 100 percent bar chart is a stacked chart that shows each data series as a percentage of the total.

Column charts

Column charts are generally used to show quantity comparisons among several items — or to show how one or more items differ for different categories. Hence, you may plot one item in several different categories; several items in only one category; or several items in several categories (see Figure 11-16). As shown in the figure, column charts are commonly used for business comparisons, such as sales statistics.

 Some of the built-in AutoFormats include gridlines, interior labels, or overlapping effects; others use stacked or 100 percent variations. A stacked column chart plots each data series on top of the preceding one, showing how the total of all data series compares across the categories. Also, you can see how each data series contributes to the total. An unstacked column is a normal column chart, as shown in Figure 11-16. And a 100 percent column chart is a stacked column chart that shows each data series as a percentage of the total. The total of each column is 100 percent.

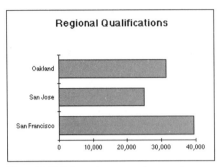

Figure 11-16: Column charts can make several types of comparisons, depending on the number of columns and rows in your data.

Line and high-low charts

Line charts are used to show how data fluctuates over time. Like area charts, the more data points you plot on a line chart, the more revealing the trend. Generally, the category axis of the line chart shows time or date values in even increments. These charts are commonly used for tracking stock prices on a regular time schedule, such as every day. If you must show uneven time or date values, use an XY chart instead.

Line charts plot individual points along the category axis markers. You can then "fill-in" between these points by using lines, or you can just leave the points. If you plot two sets of points (two data series), you can add horizontal lines between them, called high-low lines. Instead of high-low lines, you can use a box to connect two sets of points. Figure 11-17 shows a standard line chart.

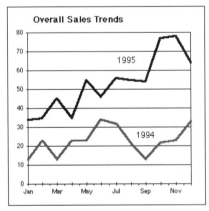

Figure 11-17: A standard line chart showing comparisons over time.

Note that the high-low-close chart offered in Excel's AutoFormat charts requires that you plot exactly three data series (columns of data). The first column is used for the high, the second for the low, and the third for the close. Also note that AutoFormat requires that you plot four data series. The vertical axis in AutoFormat is measured on a Logarithmic scale for applications that show data changing exponentially.

Pie and doughnut charts

Pie charts show how individual elements make up a total of 100 percent. A pie chart is similar in purpose to a 100 percent column or bar chart that has only one bar. It is also similar to a doughnut chart. Each pie chart plots only one data series, so the point is to make comparisons within the series, not among two or more series. To create a pie chart, just highlight a data range consisting of data labels and one data series. Figure 11-18 shows a pie chart and a doughnut chart.

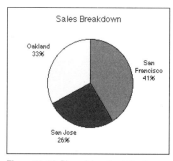 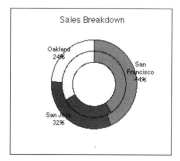

Figure 11-18: Pie and doughnut charts.

A doughnut chart can display more than one data series by showing each series as a "ring" on the chart. The outer ring, but not the inner rings, can include exploded segments. A doughnut chart is a good alternative to a 100 percent column chart.

 To explode a pie or doughnut segment (that is, to separate the segment from the rest of the chart), double-click the chart frame to select the chart. Then click the desired pie slice twice. Click slowly (not a double-click), or you will activate a dialog box. When the desired slice is highlighted, drag it away from the center of the chart to "explode" it.

Radar charts

A radar chart plots a series of values along several axes and creates a *wheel and spokes* effect with the center as the baseline. Each value axis uses the same scale, and the number of categories in the data series determines the number of axes.

After the data points are plotted along the axes, you'll see a "ring" around the center of the graph. Each data series plots another ring (see Figure 11-19).

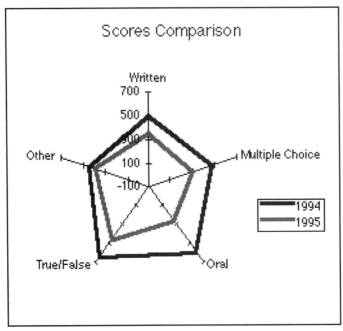

Figure 11-19: A radar chart plots data series as "rings" around a center hub.

Radar charts offer many ways of formatting the axes. You can add gridlines around the axes points, include data markers along each plot point, or remove the axes altogether. Finally, you can display the axes in a logarithmic scale for data that increases geometrically. All built-in radar formats are just variations of these effects.

XY charts

XY or scatter charts plot data points along two value axes. Both the horizontal and vertical axes are numeric values that progress in a positive direction from the corner point. A data point is plotted by locating an intersection of an X-axis and a Y-axis value. You can create a simple XY chart by highlighting exactly two columns of data. The first column is used for the category axis values (X-axis values), and the second is used as the data series for the graph. Each point is plotted along the X-axis values created by the first column.

XY charts are similar to column or line graphs, in which the first column of data contains the category axis labels — in this case, the labels are values. Figure 11-20 shows an example of an XY chart.

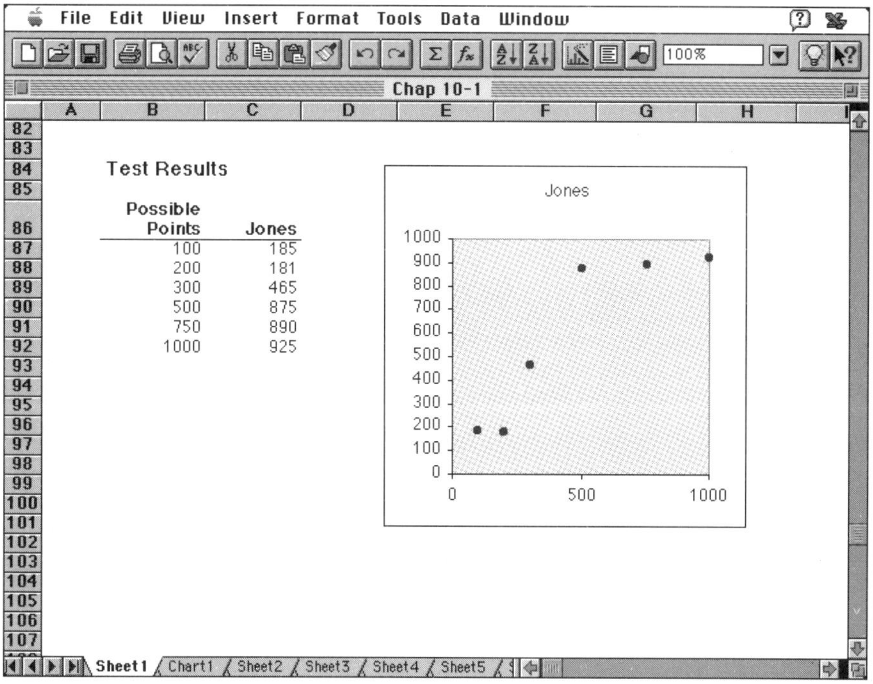

```
 File   Edit   View   Insert   Format   Tools   Data   Window        ?  %
```

Chap 10-1

	A	B	C	D	E	F	G	H
82								
83								
84		Test Results						
85								
86		Possible Points	Jones					
87		100	185					
88		200	181					
89		300	465					
90		500	875					
91		750	890					
92		1000	925					

Jones

(XY scatter chart plotting Jones values from 0 to 1000 on Y-axis against 0 to 1000 on X-axis)

Sheet1 / Chart1 / Sheet2 / Sheet3 / Sheet4 / Sheet5 /

Figure 11-20: A simple XY chart.

If you include more than one data series, each new series will be plotted against the same X-axis values from column 1 of the data range. Hence, you'll find that plot points line up on common X-axis values.

X-axis values can be dates. Because dates are just numbers displayed as dates, you can use dates as X-axis values for an XY graph. The dates don't have to be evenly spaced in XY graphs — as long as the dates progress in a chronological direction. (By contrast, a line graph can be misleading if X-axis dates are not evenly spaced.)

You can also use an XY graph to plot data pairs, in which each point is plotted by using two unique values — as opposed to one unique value and one common X-axis value. This kind of graph creates a true scatter graph in which each point plots a pair of values. To create this paired XY graph, you must start with only two columns of data and create the standard XY graph as described and then add each new data pair by highlighting two columns of data.

Creating a paired XY chart

1. Start with the basic XY graph showing one set of values.

2. Highlight two columns of values representing the X and Y values for each new point.

3. Copy the two columns using the Edit⇨Copy command.

4. Double-click the chart to activate the chart window.

5. Choose Edit⇨Paste Special.

6. Click the Categories (X Values) in First Column option to enter a check beside it.

7. Press Return.

8. Repeat these steps for any other data series. ◖

Figure 11-21 shows a paired XY chart with its corresponding data sets. Notice that each data series in the chart is displayed with a different marker and corresponds to two columns from the data.

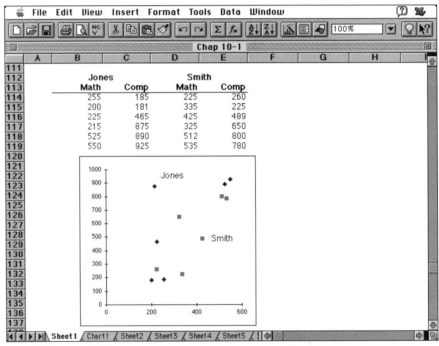

Figure 11-21: A paired XY chart uses two columns of values for each plot point.

The built-in XY formats offer various combinations of gridlines, marker styles, and logarithmic axes. The logarithmic axes (charts 4 and 5) are useful when the values increase geometrically.

A common addition to an XY graph is the regression line, or *trend line*. Excel has several methods for calculating trends. And you can calculate several different types of trends, depending on the need. Excel's new Add Trend feature provides all the options you'll ever need: Just highlight the data series for which you want to plot a trend line and then choose the Trendline command from the Insert menu. The dialog box shown in Figure 11-22 appears.

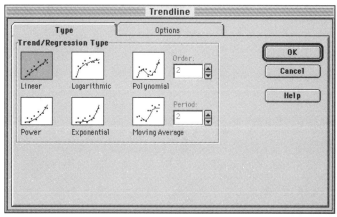

Figure 11-22: Adding a trend line with the Insert⇨Trendline command.

Choose the desired trend function from those available and click OK. Excel automatically adds the appropriate trend line to the chart. Figure 11-23 shows a chart with two different trend lines added.

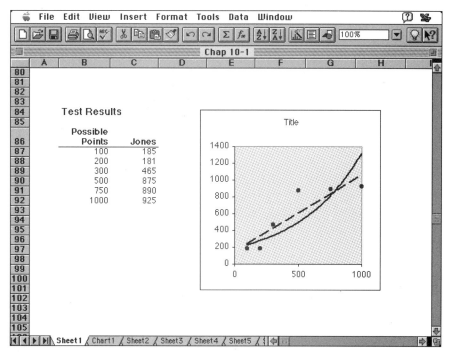

Figure 11-23: Two different trend lines added to an XY chart.

Combination charts

Combination charts show two or more data series using two different overlaid chart types. Combination charts allow you to examine two different sets of values for possible relationships. The two sets of values may require two completely different chart types, or they may use the same chart type but completely different scales along the value axis. Figure 11-24 shows these variations.

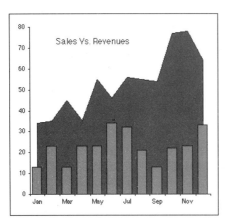 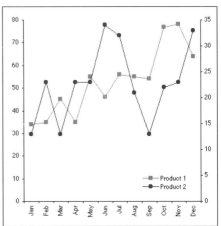

Figure 11-24: Combination charts can use contrasting chart types or the same chart type with two contrasting axis scales.

When you choose a combination chart from the available chart types, Excel automatically splits the data series in half: Each half is displayed with a different chart type (depending on the combination you select), and each half is called a *group*. For example, a combination chart may have a column group and a line group. If you add a data series, Excel adds the extra series to the first half. You have control over the chart type used for each data series in a combination chart. Refer to Topic 12 for details on this and other combination chart formatting.

Several of the built-in combination charts use two value axes — a right and a left. Notice that in these combination charts, the second half of the data series is plotted along the right-hand value axis, and the first half is plotted along the left-hand value axis. In Topic 12, you learn how to change the axis scale for either of these axes.

3-D charts

3-D charts come in two flavors: charts with a depth axis (or Z-axis) and charts without a depth axis. 3-D charts that include a depth axis plot each data series behind the next one on the depth axis. Therefore, these charts can never offer stacked formats — because each data series is split from the rest and plotted from the zero-line, or *baseline*. 3-D charts without the depth axis simply add a three-dimensional "effect" to the data series. These charts can be stacked. Figure 11-25 shows these two types of 3-D charts using 3-D column charts.

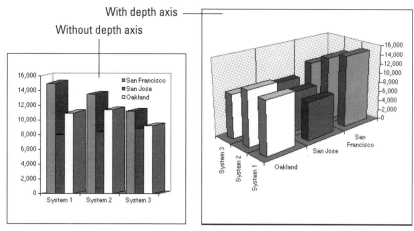

Figure 11-25: 3-D charts come in two primary types, those with depth and those without.

Built-in 3-D AutoFormats include area, bar, column, line, pie, and surface charts. Within each of these main chart types, Excel offers variations on formatting, including stacked, unstacked, 100 percent, and depth versions. Stacked 3-D charts show data series plotted on top of each other, rather than plotted from the baseline. These charts are identical to their 2-D counterparts, except that they add a 3-D effect to the plot points. One hundred percent 3-D charts are, again, identical to the corresponding 100 percent 2-D charts. These charts, however, include a 3-D effect on the data series. Finally, 3-D depth charts plot each data series on a depth axis providing a true 3-D perspective.

Quick Tips

Adding data to a chart

To add a new data series to an existing chart, simply copy the data (including the heading) from the worksheet and paste it into the chart by double-clicking the chart frame and pressing Command-V.

Arranging values in bar charts

You should arrange the values in a bar chart so that the largest bar appears at the top of the chart — usually, this means that the largest number in the data series appears at the top of the column or in the first column of the chart's data range.

Using box plot charts

The box plot chart, which appears in the line chart AutoFormats, is useful for plotting four values: a high, a low, and two quartile values. If the first quartile value is larger than the second, the box appears with a solid color; otherwise it appears empty. The quartile values (the values forming the box plot) should appear as the first and last data series in the data range.

Evaluating XY charts versus line charts

XY chart formats that include lines connecting the "dots" are not the same as line charts. XY charts should always use numeric or date values for the X-axis data; whereas, a line chart uses text values. In an XY chart, the numeric X values do not have to be evenly spaced, although they should be in ascending order. The numeric horizontal axis of the XY chart accounts for unevenly spaced values; whereas, using numeric values for the horizontal axis of a line chart can create a misleading chart.

Making charts with drag and plot

You can add data to an existing graph by simply highlighting the desired data and dragging the range over to the chart. As you drag onto the chart, the chart will become selected and you can "drop" the data on the chart for instant plotting.

Customizing Charts

Overview

If you have read the preceding topic, you know the value of charting your numeric data in Excel. But you may be wondering how you can add or modify elements in a chart *after* you've created it. In addition, you may be interested in changing or customizing Excel's AutoFormat charts to better suit your needs. For example, you may want to add special descriptive text inside your chart.

Well, you're not stuck with the AutoFormat charts offered by Excel. After you create a chart, you can customize it to meet your needs. Excel provides numerous customization options to enhance charts, including ways to display the charted values as pictures, to change the colors within the chart, to add descriptive text and labels to the chart, and so on. This topic explains Excel's flexible chart formatting powers so that you can develop charts that fit your needs. You also learn how to save your chart creations as your own custom chart AutoFormats so that you can repeat your customizations over and over again.

Selecting Chart Elements

Before you can perform chart customization options, you need to know how to select the various parts of a chart. Like most activities in Excel, customizing charts is a matter of "select then do." That is, select the element first and then perform the command. This section discusses the various elements in a chart and how you can select them. First, refer to Figure 12-1 for an overview of a chart's elements.

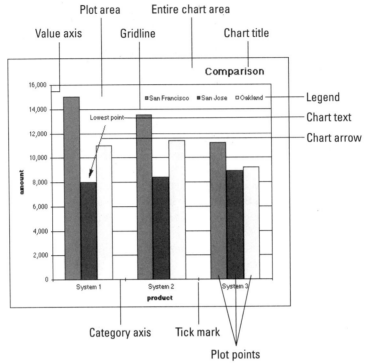

Figure 12-1: The elements of a basic chart.

Table 12-1 provides descriptions of several chart elements.

Before you can select a chart element, you must first activate, or select, the chart by double-clicking the chart frame within the worksheet. This action does two things: it changes the Excel menu bar and menus, and it brings up the Chart toolbar. You can now select individual elements within the chart frame. The easiest way to select chart elements is to click directly on the element (one click) with the mouse. When the element is highlighted, it has small boxes around its edges. If you click a bar, line, or other plot point, you select the entire data series in which that point appears. Figure 12-2 shows a data series selected in a column chart.

Table 12-1
Chart Elements and Descriptions

Element	Description
Axis	In 2-D charts, the horizontal line (X-axis) displays categories of data; the vertical line (Y-axis) displays the range and increments of data. In 3-D charts, the X-axis displays categories of data; the Y-axis displays data series; and the Z-axis displays the range and increments of data.
Chart	All items in the chart window, including the chart, axes, legend, and titles.
Chart text	Labels that identify items in a chart. Text can be unattached (movable) or attached (unmovable) to an object in a chart.
Data marker	Symbol that represents a value in a worksheet, such as a bar, dot, or pie wedge.
Data series	Symbols that represent the values of a row or column of data in a worksheet.
Gridlines	Lines that you display for easier identification of the values in a chart.
Legend	Information that identifies a marker's data series.
Menu bar	The pull-down menu bar that is available when a chart window is active.
Plot area	The region of the chart that contains the axes lines and the data markers.
Tick mark	The small lines on the axes lines that separate data categories or indicate value increments.

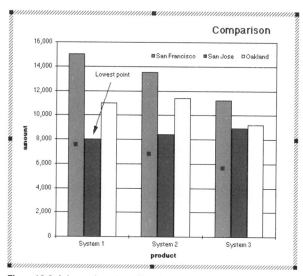

Figure 12-2: A data series selected in a chart.

You can now choose commands that affect the entire data series. If you want to select an individual plot point, you must first select the data series and then click the desired plot point within the series. Figure 12-3 shows one of the plot points selected in the preceding chart example. You can now perform actions that apply to the individual data point.

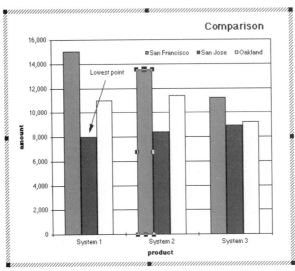

Figure 12-3: An individual plot point selected in a chart.

You can make individual data points reflect new values. In a column chart, you can drag on any selected column to increase or decrease the height of the bar. Changing the bar's height actually changes the value linked to that bar in the chart's data range. If you increase the bar's height, you consequently increase the value in the cell. You can manipulate column, bar, and line charts this way.

Some elements can be tricky to select with the mouse. To select the entire chart, for example, click just inside the chart window's border — in the white space between the chart frame and the chart. If you click too close to the frame, nothing happens; if you click too close to the chart, you may select the plot area or another element. Therefore, Excel offers another way to select chart elements. You can use the four arrow keys to *rotate* your selection within a chart. First, double-click the chart frame; then use the keys described in Table 12-2 to select individual elements.

Table 12-2
Chart Element Selection Keys

Key	What It Does
Up arrow	Moves forward through the elements.
Down arrow	Moves backward through the elements.
Right arrow	Moves to the next like element. For instance, to the next gridline if a gridline is selected or to the next plot point if a plot point is selected.
Left arrow	Moves to the preceding like element.

When the chart window is closed and the chart appears normally on the worksheet, it can be manipulated like any object on the worksheet. Commands like Edit⇨Copy and Edit⇨Paste apply to the chart box containing the chart. For details about manipulating objects (including charts), see Topic 5.

Try placing objects *behind* charts. You can manipulate the chart frame as you would any object. One suggestion is to make the interior area of the frame transparent, rather than its usual white. Do this by clicking the chart frame to select the chart object without activating the chart. Then choose the Format⇨Object command and select the desired patterns from the dialog box provided. You can stack the chart frame over other worksheet objects to have those objects appear behind the chart.

The charting menus appear when a chart frame is active — or a chart worksheet is active. You can activate any chart frame by double-clicking the chart. Activate a chart worksheet by clicking the worksheet's page tab.

The various options are discussed in the charting menus throughout this topic. For now, keep in mind that all commands in these menus act on the chart, or on a highlighted element in the chart. The Insert and Format menus, in particular, contain commands that apply specifically to selected chart or chart elements.

Customizing the Chart Type

Excel lets you change a chart's type at any time. You can instantly turn a column chart into an area chart. You can plot your data with different chart types to see which type best conveys your message. The simplest way to change the chart type is by using the Chart Type button located in the Chart toolbar. The Chart Type button provides a tear-off palette that you can keep available, if desired. (See Topic 1 for information about tear-off palettes.)

To change the chart type, simply activate the chart (double-click its frame) and then click the desired chart type button within the palette.

The Chart type palette does not give you the full spectrum of choices regarding chart type formatting. For example, if you want a stacked column chart, you should use the Chart Type command in the Format menu. This command gives you access to many different chart type formats.

Customizing the chart type

1. Select the chart by double-clicking the chart frame.

2. Choose the Chart Type command from the Format menu. The Chart Type dialog box appears.

3. Click to select the Entire Chart button under the Apply To options.

4. Click 2-D to view a palette of 2-D charts or click 3-D to view the 3-D charts.

5. Click the desired chart type in the palette (or gallery).

6. Click Options.

7. Select from the various options presented on the pages of the dialog box.

8. Click OK to apply your settings to the chart.

The Options button in the Chart Type dialog box presents a dialog box with chart type options that vary depending on the type of chart you selected from the gallery. The following sections discuss the various options that you encounter within this dialog box.

Chart subtypes

Many of Excel's chart types are available in two or more variations, known as *subtypes*. A subtype is more than just a different way of formatting the chart—it involves a different way of displaying the data. For example, a column chart can be displayed in three ways: unstacked, stacked, and 100 percent (see Figure 12-4). The stacked column chart displays data much differently than the unstacked subtype and would be used for completely different charting needs. To access the chart subtypes, choose the Format ⇨ Chart Type command and click the Options button. Figure 12-4 shows the subtypes for column charts.

The AutoFormats you select in the Chart Wizard procedure or by using the Format ⇨ AutoFormat command include variations on the basic subtypes provided for each chart. For example, of the ten built-in formats for column charts, you get six unstacked, two stacked and two 100 percent charts.

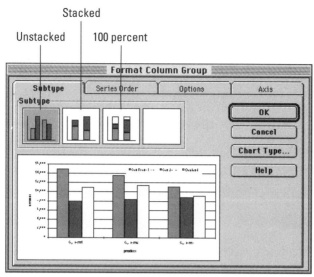

Stacked

Unstacked   100 percent

Figure 12-4: Column chart subtypes include unstacked, stacked, and 100 percent.

Select the desired chart subtype from those provided. Some chart types, such as pie charts, offer only one subtype, while other types offer several subtypes. Table 12-3 provides a summary of subtypes you'll encounter.

Table 12-3
Chart Subtypes and Descriptions

Subtype	Description
Unstacked	Unstacked charts, the normal view for most charts, plot each value from the baseline so that each plot point is relative to the value axis.
Stacked	Stacked charts plot each data series from the top of the preceding series, showing you the total of all data series over each category. Individual data series comprise portions of the total.
100 percent	This data view is a stacked chart in which the data series are displayed as percentages of their totals. The total of each stacked column (for column charts) is 100 percent. Therefore, the height of all the columns is the same.
Depth	3-D charts offer the depth view, which plots each data series on a different depth of the Z-axis, or depth axis. Because data series are plotted on a third axis, charts that use this data view can never be stacked.

The subtype you select for the chart influences the remaining settings in the Format Group dialog box. For example, stacked charts automatically set the Overlap value (which appears on the Options tab of the dialog box) to 100 percent. Details on these options follow.

Chart formatting options

When you use the Format⇨Chart Type command and select Options, you have access to many chart formatting options. Note that you must double-click a chart in order to select it and have the apropriate formatting options available in the Format menu. If you don't have the chart selected, you won't find the options discussed here in the specified menu, dialog box, or tab. Where appropriate, you also must select an item you wish to format such as a data series, a gridline, or an axis.

The following sections discuss all the remaining options you may discover as you format your chart type. These options may appear on different *pages* in the Format Group dialog box.

Overlap

The Overlap option appears on the Options page of the Format Group dialog box. It controls the overlap of data series within each category on the chart. It applies only if you have more than one data series in the chart and you have selected a bar or column chart type. Overlap can be used as a simple graphical device to add interest to column or bar charts. Note that an Overlap value of 100% places each data series directly over the other and is generally used only for stacked charts. Figure 12-5 shows (from left to right) a stacked and unstacked chart with Overlap values of 50%.

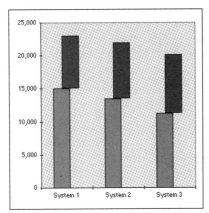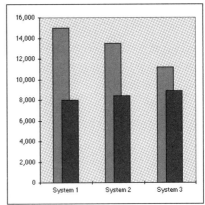

Figure 12-5: The Overlap value overlaps the data series within each data category. Use it for stacked or unstacked charts.

Gap Width

Another option for bar and column charts is Gap Width. This option controls the amount of space between each bar. Gap Width is expressed as a percentage of the bar width; hence a Gap Width value of 100% widens the gap between each bar to the width of each bar. If necessary, Excel shrinks the bar width to accommodate your Gap Width request. You may end up with skinny bars if you use a large Gap

Width value because Excel does not change the size of the chart window but fits everything into the current chart proportions. Use a Gap Width setting of zero to create step charts, which are column charts without any space between the columns.

Series Lines

The Series Lines option applies to stacked column and bar charts only. By checking this option, you tell Excel to connect each data series with lines as a way of emphasizing the change in values. Notice that you can add series lines to a chart that has only one data series by turning it into a stacked chart with the stacked subtype.

Vary Colors by Point

The Vary Colors by Point option applies primarily to column and bar charts that plot only one data series. It lets you display a data series with different colors and patterns in each category. In other words, a column chart can use a different color for each bar — even within the same data series. Normally all the bars in the same data series receive the same color or pattern. Checking the Vary Colors by Point option lets you format each bar independently.

Drop Lines

The Drop Lines option adds thin lines that extend from the baseline line and area charts to each plotted point. Drop lines are available only for area, line, 3-D area, and 3-D line charts and are useful for emphasizing the plot points and their heights above the baseline.

When adding extra elements to a chart, such as drop lines, make sure that the chart is not too cluttered. Consider removing portions of a chart to simplify it. Also notice that Drop Lines are most effective when your area or line chart plots only one data series. Figure 12-6 shows two examples.

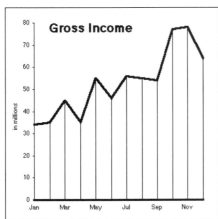
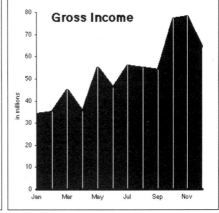

Figure 12-6: Drop lines added to line and area charts.

In the area chart in Figure 12-6, the drop lines have been reversed from the plot area. You can format drop lines by double-clicking any of the lines after you add them. The Patterns dialog box appears for the drop lines where you can select a color and pattern for the lines. You can be creative with various combinations of drop lines and marker styles. If you remove the lines from a line graph and use only markers, you can have effects such as those shown in Figure 12-7.

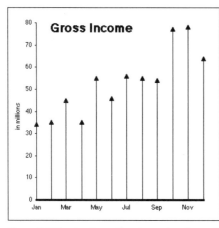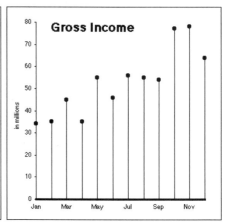

Figure 12-7: Use drop lines with series markers for special effects.

You can remove the line associated with a line chart's data series by double-clicking the line and selecting the None option in the Patterns dialog box under the Line options.

High-Low Lines

The High-Low Lines option inserts lines that extend between pairs of data series on 2-D line charts. High-low lines are used primarily to create high-low graphs, which plot two data series and uses only high-low lines to show them on the chart. All series lines and markers are removed. You can emphasize the top and bottom points of a high-low chart by adding the markers to the data series by using the Patterns dialog box. Figure 12-8 shows an example of a high-low chart.

A high-low-close chart plots a third data series in addition to the two series that create a high-low chart. The third data series creates a mark — usually between the high and the low points — that indicates a closing figure, as in stock prices.

Up-Down Bars

The Up-Down Bars option is like the High-Low Lines option. Up-down bars apply to line graphs and extend between pairs of data series. The advantage that up-down bars have over high-low lines is that they can show positive and negative changes between the first and second data series — not just the span value between them. An increase shows up as a light bar, and a decrease appears as a dark bar. Figure 12-9 shows an example of an up-down bar.

Figure 12-8: High-low charts use a combination of series markers and high-low lines for various effects.

Figure 12-9: Use Up-Down bars to show increases and decreases between points.

Remember, to use up-down bars, you must start with a line chart. However, you can use column charts for similar purposes.

Radar category labels

Radar charts show each category of data as a separate *spoke*, or axis, on the chart. These axes are normally labeled with the values that appear along the category axis of a column or line chart. Excel takes these values from the chart's data range.

Normally you can remove the category axis labels on a chart by double-clicking the axis and setting the Tick Labels value to None. But because radar charts have no category axes, Excel provides the Radar Axis Labels option in the Format Chart dialog box so that you can add or remove the labels. For more information about radar charts and when to use them, refer to Topic 11.

Angle of First Pie Slice

Pie and doughnut charts normally start with the first data point at the 12 o'clock position — or the top of the pie. You can determine where the first pie slice should start by using the Angle of First Pie Slice option. Enter a value indicating the degree of angle from the vertical position. For example, a value of 90 puts the first slice at the 3 o'clock position.

The angle setting is useful for solving problems with pie labels that overlap on the chart. Often, changing the angle of the slices allows text to fit more easily on the chart without overlapping. You can also use the angle setting to position exploded slices in the upper-right quarter of the pie, the optimum location for visual appeal.

Gap Depth

3-D charts let you control the space between data series on a 3-D depth chart. Although you can use this setting with any 3-D data view, it's most effective with the depth data view. The Gap Depth setting sets the amount of space between data series on the depth axis. The setting is measured as a percentage of the depth of the data series markers (for example, the depth of the bars in a column chart). Therefore, a setting of 200% increases the gap to twice its normal size — twice the depth of the bars. Because Excel expands the chart size to make this increase, it provides the extra depth space by decreasing the depth of the data series markers. Therefore, increasing the Gap Depth value decreases the depth of the data markers.

Chart Depth

The Chart Depth setting is similar to Gap Depth. Chart depth affects the depth of the chart base itself. The Chart Depth setting effects the depth of the data markers, too. You may want to play with the Gap Depth and Chart Depth settings for a combined effect. Use combinations of the Gap Width, Gap Depth, and Chart Depth settings to view their various effects on 3-D charts (see Figure 12-10).

Series Order

The Series Order setting affects the order in which data series appear in the chart. This option has a dramatic effect on area and column charts. For example, you can place the smallest column in the first position of a column chart by rearranging the series order. Click the desired data series and use the Move Up and Move Down buttons to change its position. The sample chart in the dialog box will reflect your changes.

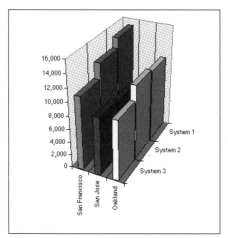

Figure 12-10: Combining Gap Width, Chart Depth, and Gap Depth settings.

Customizing combination charts

Combination charts use two or more chart types on the same chart. You can split the data range into groups and apply a different chart type to each group. To split a chart, you simply choose the desired data series and then use the Chart Type dialog box to set the desired chart type for that data.

Creating a combination chart

1. Double-click the chart frame to select it.

2. Click the data series you want to display as a different chart type.

3. Choose the Chart Type command from the Format menu.

4. Click the Selected Series option in the Apply To options.

5. Select one of the desired chart types from the gallery.

6. Click OK or use the Options button to select from additional options.

Repeat this procedure to set the desired chart type for other data series in the chart. After you have created a combination chart, you can change an entire data group by choosing the Group option in Step 4.

When you create a combination chart, the Axis page tab in the Options dialog box becomes active. You can add a second axis to the chart by using these options, if you want.

Customizing Data Series

Double-click a data series to change the colors and other settings for the data. Notice that the options in the Format Data Series dialog box (see Figure 12-11) may vary slightly, depending on the element you select.

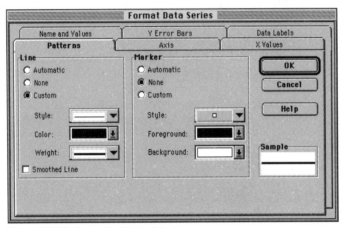

Figure 12-11: The Format Data Series dialog box.

Data series options include tools for changing all aspects of the data series. The following sections discuss these options.

Changing colors and patterns

Use the color and pattern selection tools to modify the internal color and pattern of the data series, the appearance of lines on a line chart, and the marker styles for line and XY charts. Most of these options are self-explanatory: you can choose to customize the colors and patterns, use Excel's automatic choices, or remove the color or pattern altogether. Notice that if you select a data series in a line chart, you can choose the Smooth Line option to create a bell curve (see Figure 12-12).

The Invert if Negative option appears for column and bar charts whose baseline is below zero (that is, negative). You can use the Invert if Negative option to show the zero line in addition to the baseline (see Figure 12-13).

Adding a second axis

The Axis tab of the Format Data Series dialog box lets you establish the axis on which the data series is plotted. Normally, all data series are plotted along the primary axis, which is the left-hand vertical axis. You can add a second vertical axis along the right side of the chart, resulting in a combination chart. Use the options in the Axis tab to determine which axis the data series is plotted on.

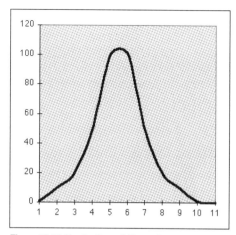

Figure 12-12: Use the Smooth Line option to create a bell curve.

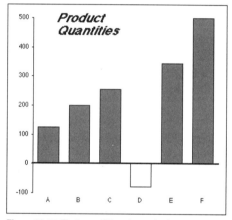

Figure 12-13: The Invert if Negative option lets you reveal negative values on the chart.

Changing the X Values

The X Values tab of the Format Data Series dialog box lets you specify or change the range of cells that contain the X-axis values. Normally, these appear as the top row — or possibly the first column — of the data range. But you can use a completely different range of cells for this information. Your X-axis labels don't have to be the same cells used for your column headings. Just enter a range reference or range name into the space provided and click OK.

Displaying data labels

Data labels are the numeric values of each plot point in the chart. You can tell Excel to automatically display these values beside any chosen data series. Depending on the type of chart you are formatting, you can display this information as values, category labels, percentages, or labels and percentages. Figure 12-14 shows an example of data labels added to a pie chart and a column chart.

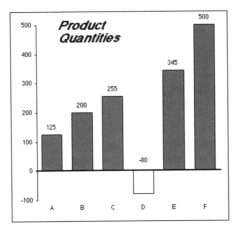

Figure 12-14: Data labels added to charts using the Data Labels options in the Format Data Series dialog box.

You can also display data labels by using the Insert➪Data Labels command, which appears when you double-click the chart frame.

Adding error bars

With the Y Error Bars tab, you can add error bars to your graphs by using a fixed amount of error, a percentage of error, a standard deviation, or custom error formula. Error bars are useful for graphing applications that call for displaying a *margin of error* in the values being plotted. Figure 12-15 shows error bars applied to a data series.

You can choose to show values plus a margin of error, minus a margin of error, or both. Then choose the type of error amount you'd like to display from the Error Amount options provided.

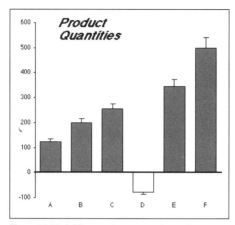

Figure 12-15: Adding error bars to your data series.

Changing the series name and values

The Name and Values tab of the Format Data Series dialog box lets you change the data range that identifies the data series values and legend entry. Enter a cell reference in the Name box to specify the cell containing the legend entry for the data. Enter a range reference in the Y Values box to specify the range that contains the data series values.

Customizing Axes

Double-clicking a chart axis brings up the Format Axis dialog box shown in Figure 12-16. The options in this dialog box vary depending on whether you are formatting a value (vertical) or category (horizontal) axis.

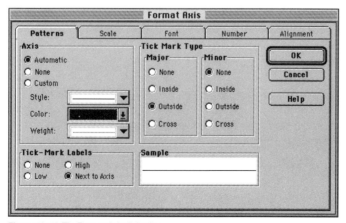

Figure 12-16: The Format Axis dialog box.

Changing axis color and pattern

To change the color and pattern of an axis, double-click the axis line and choose the Patterns tab of the Format Axis dialog box. The Patterns tab lets you change several elements of the axis. You can change the color and thickness of the axis line (including removing the line completely), the appearance of the axis tick marks, and the position of the axis labels. Use the color options to choose Excel's automatic color for the axis or any other color of your choice. Use the None option to remove the axis line completely.

You can also add or remove axes using the Insert⇨Axes command, which is available when you activate the chart by double-clicking it.

Tick Mark Type

You can change the style of the major and minor tick marks of the selected axis. Major tick marks correspond to the incremental axis values, and minor tick marks are the smaller subdivisions of the incremental values. Tick Mark Type options let you select the type of tick mark that appears for these values — including removing the tick marks completely. Notice that you can change the axis values themselves on the Scale tab of the Format Axis dialog box.

Tick-Mark Labels

Tick-Mark Labels options set the style for the labels, not including the axis title, that appear along the axes. You can remove the labels, place them next to the axes, or move them to the top (High) or bottom (Low) of the chart. The High and Low options are useful for charts that plot negative values or values on either side of the axes.

Changing the value axis scale

To change the scale of the value axis (or Y-axis) of the chart, simply double-click the axis to bring up the Format Axis dialog box and then select the Scale tab. The following sections describe each option in this dialog box.

Minimum

Minimum determines the lower limit of the axis. Any value lower than the minimum is plotted off the chart and is not visible. If you check the Auto box beside this option, Excel chooses the minimum value based on the lowest value in the chart.

Maximum

Maximum determines the upper limit of the axis. Any value greater than the maximum is plotted off the chart. If you check the Auto box beside this option, Excel chooses the maximum value based on the greatest value in the chart.

Major Unit

Major Unit determines the number of intermediate values that appear between the minimum and maximum values. You should make sure that the Major Unit values divide evenly into the minimum and maximum values. For example, if your maximum value is 79 (with a minimum of zero), you should change the maximum to 80 so that you can set the Major Unit value to divide evenly into 80. You may use 1, 2, 4, 5, 8, 10, 16, 20, 40, or any other number by which 80 is divisible. The Major Unit values are displayed as values along the axis.

Minor Unit

Minor Unit determines the number of incremental units that appear between each Major Unit. For best results, the Minor Unit should divide evenly into the Major Unit — otherwise, the axis displays two separate scales. Notice that the Minor Unit tick marks appear on the chart only after you use the Format/Patterns command to make them appear. Normally, Minor Unit tick marks are not displayed. Minor Unit tick marks are not labeled on the chart; they can be displayed only as tick-marks.

Category (X) Axis Crosses at . . .

The category axis determines where the category axis crosses along the value axis. Normally, the category axis meets the value axis at the zero point, but you can change this intersection to show a unique baseline limit by using the Category (X) Axis Crosses at option. Values that extend below this limit can be displayed in a special color or pattern by using the Invert if Negative option in the Format Data Series dialog box (see Figure 12-17).

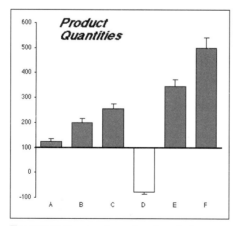

Figure 12-17: You can set a new baseline value to emphasize values that extend below a certain point.

If the category axis crosses at the same value used as the Minimum scale value, the two axes meet at the bottom-left corner of the chart — commonly used as the zero point. However, you can make this point any value you want by setting the value Minimum axis value and using the same value for the Crosses At entry.

Logarithmic Scale

The logarithmic scale displays the value axis in a logarithmic scale, which can be useful when your values increase geometrically. When you use a logarithmic scale, it's a good idea to include horizontal gridlines to emphasize the special treatment.

Values in Reverse Order

Values in Reverse Order displays the value axis in reverse order, with the highest value at the bottom and the lowest at the top. You may use this option for plotting negative values above the baseline when the entire chart shows negative values — such as debt. You can also use this feature to show an increase in speed, where the tallest column represents the fastest unit (see Figure 12-18).

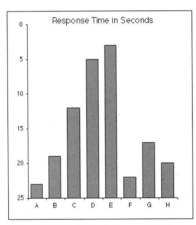

Figure 12-18: Use Values in Reverse Order to chart negative values above the baseline, such as when showing speed.

Category (X) Axis Crosses at Maximum Value

This feature moves the baseline to the top of the chart (unless Values in Reverse Order is checked — in which case, the maximum value is at the bottom of the chart). This feature is useful for charts that plot all values below the baseline.

Changing the category axis scale

The Scale settings for category axes differ from those for value axes. If you double-click a chart's category axis and then choose the Scale tab in the Format Axis dialog box, you see the options shown in Figure 12-19.

Format Axis
Patterns	Scale	Font	Number	Alignment

Category (X) Axis Scale

Value (Y) Axis Crosses
at Category Number: `1`

Number of Categories
between Tick-Mark Labels: `1`

Number of Categories
between Tick Marks: `1`

☒ Value (Y) Axis Crosses between Categories
☐ Categories in Reverse Order
☐ Value (Y) Axis Crosses at Maximum Category

OK
Cancel
Help

Figure 12-19: The category axis Scale options.

Value (Y) Axis Crosses at Category Number

This feature sets the placement of the value axis along the category axis. You can choose which category to use as the intersection point, which can be useful for showing a significant date along a date-oriented category axis (see Figure 12-20).

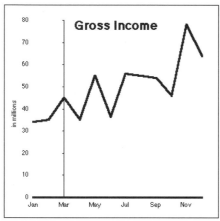

Figure 12-20: Change the point of intersection between the axes to show a cut-off date.

Number of Categories between Tick-Mark Labels

This feature sets the number of labels along the category axis. By increasing the Number of Categories between Tick Mark Labels, you effectively decrease the number of tick labels on the chart. A setting of 2 removes every other tick label. Use this option to eliminate crowding of category axis labels.

Number of Categories between Tick Marks

This feature sets the number of category groupings on the chart and actually changes the category groupings so that you can combine categories. For example, you may group 12 monthly categories into quarterly groups by setting the Number of Categories between Tick Marks value to 3. Even though you have plotted 12 categories of data, the chart will display them in groups of 3. Use the X Values tab of the Format Data Series dialog box (double-click the data series) to relabel these groups. Figure 12-21 shows this feature in action.

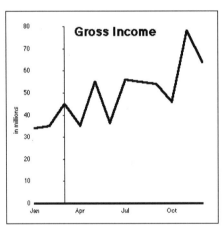

Figure 12-21: Use the Number of Categories between Tick Marks setting to group several points into a single axis label.

Value (Y) Axis Crosses between Categories

This feature determines whether the value axis crosses between categories or through the middle of categories. This can be useful for area and line charts to determine whether data series contact the edges of the chart.

Categories in Reverse Order

This feature displays the category axis in reverse order, which can be useful for line and area charts that use a date-oriented category axis. This option can be used to display the latest date at the front of the chart.

Value (Y) Axis Crosses at Maximum Category

This feature makes the value axis appear on the right-edge of the chart — at the maximum category. You can achieve this with the Value Axis Crosses at Category Number setting, as well.

Setting the font of axis values

You can set the font of the values along the vertical and horizontal axes. These fonts can match other text you add to the chart. When you double-click the desired axis, you receive the Format Axis dialog box. Click the Font tab to view the standard font-selection settings for this text.

Setting the numeric format of axis values

When your axis values are numeric, you may want to control the format of the numbers to display dollar amounts, percentages, or other values. You can do this through the Number tab of the Format Axis dialog box. Choose any of the numeric code categories in the Category list provided and then choose a numeric format code. Refer to Topic 4 for more information about formatting numbers.

Aligning axis value text

The Alignment tab of the Format Axis dialog box provides four basic text orientations for the axis values. You can use these options to squeeze more text into the chart area or to make the axis values easier to read. Experiment with these options for best results.

Customizing the Plot Area

Double-click the chart's plot area to produce the Format Plot Area dialog box. This dialog box provides the color and pattern selection tools that you can use to modify the chart's plot area. Choose from the Border and Area options provided or remove them altogether. Figure 12-22 shows a chart with the plot area's interior and border removed.

Notice in the figure that the plot area has been moved. It is not in the usual centered location within the chart area. You can move and resize the plot area by dragging its size boxes. You can make room for a legend, chart annotations, or descriptive text. You can also change the proportions of the plot area by dragging on the size boxes. For example, you can emphasize the columns in a column chart by making the plot area taller.

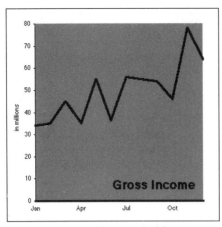

Figure 12-22: A chart with a customized plot area.

Customizing the Chart Area

Double-click the chart area to set the color, pattern, and font for the chart's main background. The Format Chart Area dialog box provides options for changing patterns and fonts for the chart area. The Patterns tab lets you change the border and interior settings, and the Font tab lets you change the font used throughout the chart. If you change the Font settings, all attached chart text, such as axis labels and data labels, change to your new setting. Unattached text does not change. For more information about adding and formatting chart text, refer to the section "Customizing Chart Text" later in this topic.

Note that the chart area is not the same as the chart frame. You can change the pattern and border of the chart frame by clicking the chart frame (don't activate the chart) and using the Format⇨Object command. Figure 12-23 shows a chart with the chart frame and the chart area formatted to include a shadow.

Customizing Gridlines

Determining the value of a plot point can be difficult on some charts. Rather than display data labels, which places the actual chart values alongside the plot points, you may just want to extend the gridlines from the value axis across the entire chart. Excel lets you display two types of gridlines for both the value axis (Y-axis) and category axis (X-axis).

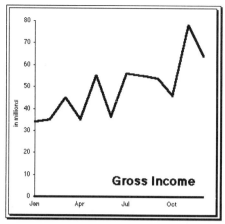

Figure 12-23: The chart area can be formatted separately from the chart frame.

If you choose the Gridlines command from the Insert menu (the chart frame must be active first), the Gridlines dialog box appears. Horizontal gridlines are displayed if you choose one of the Value (Y) Axis options, and vertical gridlines appear when you select one of the Category (X) Axis options.

You can add any number of gridlines to your chart depending on the level of detail you want to show. If your charts are relatively simple, the Major Units option is probably sufficient. More complex charts may need Major and Minor Units.

You can change the placement of the Major and Minor Units for the value axis by double-clicking the value axis to produce the Format Axis dialog box. Establish the desired Major and Minor Unit scales from the Scale tab. You can also change the placement of the units and even control the color and pattern of the gridlines through the Format Gridlines dialog box. Just double-click any one of the gridlines to produce this dialog box.

Use the Gridline button in the Chart toolbar to quickly add or remove the gridlines from the chart.

Customizing the Legend

A legend provides a bridge between the data in your worksheet and your chart's data series. A legend identifies a range of data and its corresponding data series, so in most cases, it's a good idea to include a legend in your chart.

Adding a legend to a chart is simple: Just double-click to activate the chart frame and then select the Legend command from the Insert menu. The legend automatically appears along the right edge of the chart.

You can move the legend around the chart area by dragging the legend box or by double-clicking the legend and using the Placement options in the Format Legend dialog box.

Use the Legend button in the Chart toolbar to quickly add or remove the chart legend.

After double-clicking the legend to produce the Format Legend dialog box, you can use the Font options to change the font of the legend text and the Patterns option to change the style of the legend box. Figure 12-24 shows a customized legend that has also been moved to a unique location.

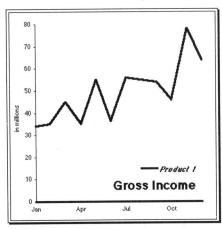

Figure 12-24: A chart with a customized legend and text.

Customizing Chart Text

There are two types of text you can add to your charts: titles and random text. Chart titles are specific labels on the chart, such as the axis titles and the main chart title. In Topic 11, you learn about the ChartWizard procedure. You may remember that you can add titles in Step 5 of the ChartWizard procedure, including the two axis labels and the main chart title.

Random text can be added to your chart via the Text Box button on the Drawing toolbar. You can add a text box to your chart as you would add it to any area of the worksheet. The text box becomes part of the chart and is useful for annotating elements of the chart. You are more limited in the formatting and manipulation of chart titles, so you may prefer to use text boxes for all your chart text. The following sections explain the details.

Adding chart titles

As mentioned earlier, you can add some attached titles to a chart through the ChartWizard. Step 5 of the ChartWizard procedure lets you add a main chart title, in addition to titles for the two axes.

To add attached text to a chart after the ChartWizard procedure is complete, simply choose the Titles command from the Insert menu after double-clicking the chart to activate it. Then click to select the desired title and press Return. After you press Return or click OK, Excel adds the title to the chart but uses a place-holder to mark the position. You can change the text placeholder to your own label by dragging inside the text area to highlight the existing text placeholder. Then type your new text. For more information about text editing commands, refer to Topic 2.

Adding random text

To add random text to a chart, begin by displaying the Drawing toolbar. Then use the text box button to draw a text box inside the chart frame. Edit the text place-holder using the following editing procedure.

Using text boxes in your charts

1. Double-click the chart frame to activate the chart.
2. Use the View⇨Toolbars command to display the Drawing toolbar.
3. Click the Text Box button in the Drawing toolbar and drag inside the chart window to create the text box.
4. Begin typing the desired text inside the text box.
5. Click outside the text box to accept your text. ◖

After you complete this procedure, you can return to the text box to change its size and shape. Just click the text box inside the active chart and drag the corners of the box to change its shape. Text can also be moved around the chart; just click the text and drag it to the desired location. To change text, highlight the text inside the text box. Text can be added or removed from a text box at any time.

Removing chart text

To delete a text box from a chart, click the text to highlight the text box and press Delete. The only text that you cannot delete are the axes labels.

Formatting chart text

After chart text is entered properly, you can format the text and the box in which the text appears. Text formatting includes changing the font, color and style of the text. You can change individual words or characters or all the text at once.

Begin by clicking the text box to select it. Then click and drag inside the box to highlight the desired text. You can highlight all the text or a portion of it. Now choose the Format⇨Selected Object command. You are presented with options for changing the font, color, and style of the selected text.

Often, you'll want to alter the text box or display the text in a unique font. To format the text box itself, double-click the text box. You may want to click the text first to highlight the text box and then double-click an edge of the box. Either the Format Chart Title dialog box or the Format Object dialog box appears, depending on whether you selected a chart title or random text. Figure 12-25 shows the Format Object dialog box for a text box.

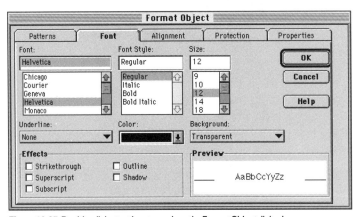

Figure 12-25: Double-click a text box to produce the Format Object dialog box.

Use the Patterns, Font, and Alignment tabs to change the attributes of the text box. Note that the Patterns options apply to the text box itself, not the text inside the box.

You can format the text used throughout the chart at one time by double-clicking the chart area and using the Font tab of the Format Chart Area dialog box. All text in the chart adheres to your selections. This is a useful shortcut. You can then return to individual text boxes to change specific elements.

Adding Graphics and Annotating Charts

Excel 5 offers the new feature of letting you draw inside a selected chart frame. By using the buttons on the Drawing toolbar, you can add all sorts of annotative elements to a chart. The drawn objects become part of the chart object on the worksheet. Figure 12-26 shows an example of annotations added to a chart frame.

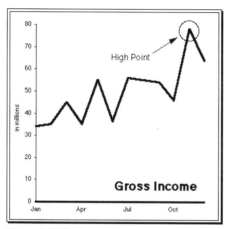

Figure 12-26: Use the Drawing toolbar to help you annotate a chart.

To add a graphic object to the chart, as shown in the figure, choose the Insert⇨Picture command after selecting the chart frame. Now locate the desired picture file on disk. Excel brings the picture into the chart. Notice that all inserted pictures appear in front of the chart data and may cover up other chart elements.

You can have more control over the relationship between the inserted picture and the chart by copying an illustration from another program and pasting it into the Excel worksheet, thus placing the picture in the worksheet and not inside the chart frame. Overlap the picture and the chart frame to achieve different effects. For example, you can place the picture behind the chart frame to create a background for the chart. If you do this, be sure to remove the pattern from the chart frame by clicking the frame (don't activate the chart) and using the Format⇨Object dialog box to remove the fill pattern from the frame.

Notice in the figure that annotative text is used outside the chart frame, along with an arrow pointing into the frame. These objects (a text box and an arrow) were drawn onto the worksheet with the Drawing toolbar and then moved into relationship with the chart frame. They are not part of the chart itself. If you want to move the chart, you should move all the associated objects, too.

Any line, column, bar, or XY chart can become a picture chart in Excel. A picture chart uses pictures as the individual plot points on the chart. To create a picture chart, begin with a normal chart and then insert the desired picture from its disk file.

Turning a normal chart into a picture chart

1. Copy the picture onto the Clipboard from any desired graphics program.

2. Double-click the chart window to activate the chart.

3. Click to select a data series on the chart. For example, click a column of a column chart to select it.

4. Choose the Paste command from the Edit menu.

When finished, Excel turns the data series into a series of pictures using your selection. Figure 12-27 shows some charts that use pictures as data series.

If you start with a column or bar chart, you can choose to stretch the picture to the size of the bar or stack multiple pictures to produce the bar. To make this choice, just double-click the data series after pasting the picture. Table 12-4 shows you the options you'll see.

When using picture charts, be careful not to use a complex image. Keep the images simple and direct. Use images that have only one or two colors in them. Picture charts are useful if the pictures you use help communicate something about the data. Otherwise, they may distract the reader from your intended message.

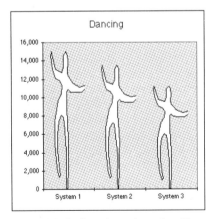

Figure 12-27: Replace a data series marker with a picture through the Edit ⇨ Paste command.

Table 12-4
Picture Chart Options

Option	What It Does
Stretch	Stretches the picture to fit the bar height.
Stack	Stacks the picture to fit the bar height.
Stack & Scale	Stacks the picture at specific increments. Each picture can represent a specific value of the bar. For example, to make each picture represent units of 10, enter 10 into the space provided.

3-D Charts

In the preceding topic, you discover that you can build 3-D charts by selecting two or more data series and choosing one of the built-in 3-D chart types from either the ChartWizard or the Format⇨Chart Type command. If you select any 3-D chart to display your data, you have the option of manipulating the perspective of the chart.

Perspective involves the view angles at which the chart appears and is easier shown than explained. Therefore, look at Figure 12-28 for two different view angles of a 3-D chart.

In the chart on the left, the view angle appears to be above and to the left of the chart; whereas, the view angle of the right-hand chart is below and to the right.

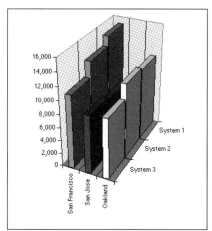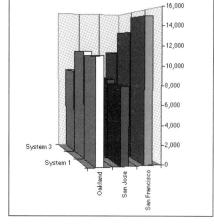

Figure 12-28: Two different 3-D angles.

To change the view angle of a 3-D chart, just activate the chart window and click the chart's plot area to select it. Then click any of the corner points of the chart's plot area; these points should be displaying selection boxes. When you click a corner point, the boxes change into solid selection boxes.

Now click and drag any of the solid selection boxes to rotate the angle of the chart. You can change the *elevation* of the view angle and the *rotation* of the chart.

If you hold down Control as you drag the selection boxes, you can view a more detailed representation of the chart. Try it and experiment with changing a 3-D graph view.

You can change a third view angle for 3-D charts that are formatted with a depth main format. Just activate the chart window and select the Format⇨3-D View option to see a dialog box of view options. Here you can change the elevation and rotation of the chart (as you can by using the mouse). In addition, you can change the chart's perspective. Experiment with these settings to see their results.

Note that you can enter values for the elevation, rotation, and perspective of the chart. You can use the arrows to change these values in increments. The sample chart shows you the results of your changes.

Quick Tips

Selecting a single data marker

To select a single data marker, press Command as you click the data marker.

Specifying major and minor units

When using the Scale options in the Format Axis command, entering the same number for both the major and minor units makes tick marks invisible. When specifying a Minor Unit, be sure to use a number that can divide the Major Unit evenly.

Using menu commands to replace double-clicking

Rather than double-clicking an element to produce the Format dialog box, you can click the element and choose the first command in the Format menu, which reads Format⇨*element*, where *element* is the name of the selected element.

Creating "what if" scenarios

You can play "what if" games by clicking and dragging a data marker. The corresponding data in the worksheet changes accordingly.

Displaying major tick marks in combination charts

In combination charts that have two value axes, use the Format Axis dialog box to display major tick marks for the left Y-axis and minor tick marks for the right one.

Part V:

Macros and Customizing Excel

2nd Edition

Creating and Running Macros

Overview

Excel comes with one of the most complete and powerful macro capabilities of any Macintosh program. But don't let that scare you off; macros can be very simple to create and use. This topic shows you the basics of creating and using macros in Excel. You learn how to record your own macros, what macros are useful for, and how to run macros in various ways.

How Macros Work

A macro is a set of instructions for Excel to carry out automatically. Excel reads the instructions and performs the actions indicated — you never have to touch the keyboard or mouse.

A macro can perform the same action over and over again, which is useful for automating complex or repetitious tasks. In addition, a macro can perform its actions faster than you can. For these two reasons, macros instantly increase your productivity and accuracy.

But macros can do more than perform routine menu commands and options quickly and repeatedly. Some macros can actually accomplish tasks that you cannot otherwise accomplish manually. For example, you can build a macro that adds a customized command to one of Excel's menus. The following are some of the ways you can use macros in your worksheets:

◆ **Automate complex or repetitive tasks.** Use a macro to automate any task that you perform over and over again. For example, you can create a macro that quickly enters a set of criteria entries for a database range and then extracts records that match the criteria. Another macro may change the worksheet by removing gridlines, changing the color of the worksheet, and activating the Drawing Toolbar — all at once. Any time you must combine several commands to perform a task and then repeat that task over and over, you can save time by creating a macro.

◆ **Customize the environment and user interface.** When your worksheet will be used by other people in your workplace, you may want to customize the Excel environment and user interface. Using macros, you can create your own menus that perform specific actions within a workbook. For example, in your financial analysis worksheet, you may create a Reports menu that includes the commands Balance Sheet, Income Statement, Trial Balance, and so on. Each command prints the appropriate report from the worksheet by performing a macro that activates the appropriate worksheet and invokes the File⇨Print command. Besides creating custom menus, you can create custom dialog boxes and custom tools for your toolbars. A good user interface protects your worksheets from inexperienced users and helps them perform actions without having to read the Excel documentation.

◆ **Create custom functions.** Macros can be used to add worksheet functions to Excel. For example, you may want to create a custom SUM function that adds values other than numbers. Suppose you have a column of values that represent cards in a deck. The face cards Jack (J), Queen (Q), and King (K) represent 10 points each, the Ace (A) card 15 points, and all other cards their face values. Your custom SUM function can automatically add the following to receive a sum of 49:

5

7

2

J

J

A

◆ **Control other programs from within Excel.** When you're ready for more advanced macro uses, you can try controlling other applications from Excel. Macros can switch to another program, perform some actions, and then return to Excel. Macros of this nature are outside the scope of this book.

You may already have several ideas for macros. But before you jump right into your special macro creations, take a moment to review some general information about macros and the various methods for creating macros in Excel.

Macro Essentials

Macros consist of sets of macro instructions that are entered on a special page of your workbook, called a module. Excel automatically stores your macro instructions onto the module page when you use the macro recorder to create a macro.

At first glance, macro instructions look like gibberish, but after a while, you'll find them pretty easy to decipher. The instructions often give you clues to their purpose. The particular name for this gibberish is *Visual Basic for Applications*. Visual Basic for Applications is the language used for macro instructions in Excel and other Microsoft products. The Visual Basic for Applications language is quite extensive and offers many options and features. For more information about programming in Visual Basic, look for *Visual Basic For Dummies*, published by IDG Books Worldwide.

A module sheet is very much like a normal worksheet but is especially designed for macros. It does no good to enter macro instructions into a normal worksheet. Fortunately, when you record a macro, Excel automatically takes care of placing the instructions onto a module sheet. Recording a macro is the easiest way to create one. You simply turn Excel's recorder on and then perform the actions that you want the macro to perform for you. Turn the recorder off. That's it! You have created a macro and Excel automatically stored the instructions onto the module sheet. Details about recording macros are covered later in this topic under "Recording a Macro."

You can record several macros on a single macro module if you like. Excel takes care of separating the macro instructions for each of your creations.

You'll want to combine macros onto the same module when all the macros relate to the same worksheet. In other words, if you create some macros for use with a particular worksheet and its data, these macros may not apply to other worksheets. These macros should all be stored in the macro module of the desired workbook.

On the other hand, you may want to create some macros that can be used with any worksheet. These generic macros may perform actions like setting up the workspace or adding special commands or tools to Excel. To make some macros available to all your worksheets, you can record them on the special *Personal Macro Workbook*. Macros stored in the Personal Macro Workbook are available to any open worksheet — at all times.

You shouldn't have to open the Personal Macro Workbook because it should already be open, albeit as a hidden file.

You can view the Personal Macro Workbook by using the Window⇨Unhide command. The Personal Macro Workbook is invisible because it has been hidden with the Window⇨Hide command. Just use the Window⇨Unhide command to display the sheet again so that you can edit the macros on the Personal Macro Workbook. If the Window⇨Unhide command does not appear, then the Personal Macro Workbook is not open because it doesn't contain any macros.

Creating Macros

There are two ways to create macros. The first is to use the macro recorder to record your keystrokes and mouse movements so that you can replay them again as a macro. The second method is to enter Visual Basic instructions onto the macro module sheet by hand. The second method requires some familiarity with Visual Basic and is not covered in this book.

The macro recorder is the easiest method of creating simple macros. You don't have to remember complicated macro functions — just turn the recorder on and then perform any actions you want to store in the macro. These actions will be repeated when you run the macro later. All you have to do is start and stop the recorder at the proper times, and Excel translates your actions into the proper macro instructions and stores them onto the macro module for you.

Although the macro recording procedure is ideal for beginners, even macro experts find it useful for quickly determining which macro functions relate to specific actions. By recording the action, you tell Excel to produce the action-equivalent function; when finished, you can examine the results in the macro module sheet.

The disadvantage to this method of creating macros is that it limits you to Excel's action-equivalent and command-equivalent macro functions. In other words, only actions that you can perform with the keyboard and mouse can be recorded using this procedure. Visual Basic includes many features that do not reflect actions you can perform in Excel.

Therefore, more advanced macro users may prefer to enter macro instructions by hand. Doing so provides the most control over the macro and gives you access to the entire library of macro functions. The disadvantage is that you must find and correctly enter the instructions before the macro will work. Typing errors and errors in macro logic can render the macro useless.

Recording a macro

Suppose you want to create a macro that removes the gridlines from your worksheet and sets the default worksheet font to Times 12 point. Rather than locate the functions that perform these actions, just turn on the macro recorder and perform these actions to the active worksheet. Then stop the recorder. You can then repeat these commands whenever you want by running the macro. You can run a macro using a sequence of commands that activates the desired macro. Details about running macros appears later in this topic.

Using the macro recorder

1. Select the Record Macro ⇨ Record New Macro command from the Tools menu. The dialog box in Figure 13-1 appears on the screen.

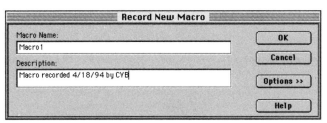

Figure 13-1: The Record New Macro dialog box.

2. Enter a name for the macro into the space provided. Do not include spaces or special characters in the name.

3. Enter a description of the macro into the Description box.

4. Click Options to view additional macro record options. These options are discussed in the section "Macro recorder options" later in this topic.

5. Click OK. At this point, everything you do in Excel is being recorded.

6. Perform the actions that you want recorded in the macro. For example, you may remove the worksheet gridlines by using the Tools ⇨ Options command or change column widths on the worksheet.

7. Select the Record Macro ⇨ Stop Recorder command from the Tools menu or click Stop. ◖◗

You have now recorded your macro. Excel creates a new macro module and enters all the appropriate Visual Basic instructions onto that module worksheet for you. You can now repeat the recorded activities by running the macro on a different worksheet in the workbook. Later in this topic, you learn various ways to run your recorded macros, including how to assign activation keys (or hotkeys) to the macros.

Using toolbar buttons to record macros is easy. You can use the buttons inside the Visual Basic toolbar to start, pause, and stop the macro recorder. You can also run your finished macros through the Run button. Figure 13-2 shows these buttons.

Figure 13-2: The visual Basic toolbar and its buttons.

Choosing macro recorder options

When you begin the macro recorder, you can select Options in the Record New Macro dialog box to view some recorder options. Figure 13-3 shows the extended dialog box with recorder options.

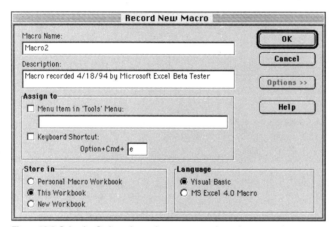

Figure 13-3: Selecting Options shows the macro recorder options.

The Assign To options let you establish two simple ways to run your macro after you have finished recording it. To place a special menu command into the Tools menu which, when selected, runs your macro, click to place an X in the Menu Item in Tools Menu option. After checking this option, enter the desired menu name into the space provided under the option, as shown in Figure 13-3, to make your macro commands available in the Excel menu structure. The disadvantage is that you may want to record so many macros that you'll make this feature somewhat impractical. Too many custom commands in the Tools menu can be difficult to manage; avoid using more than six or seven custom commands in the Tools menu.

You can place an X in the Keyboard Shortcut option to run your macro by pressing Control (or Option-Command) along with another key that you specify.

Enter the desired shortcut key in the space provided under the option. For example, you may use the key "g" for a macro that removes the worksheet's gridlines. When you want to use this macro, you can press Control-g.

Excel uses both uppercase and lowercase letters for macro shortcut keys, so be sure to note which you use. The macro shortcut Z can apply to one macro and z to another.

The Store In options determine where you want the macro instructions to appear. Normally, Excel assumes that you want them stored in a macro module in the current workbook. However, you can tell Excel to store the macro instructions in a new workbook or in the Personal Macro Workbook. Storing macros in the Personal Macro Workbook makes them available in any workbook you use in Excel.

The Language options let you record the macro as Visual Basic instructions or as Excel 4 macro functions. Saving the macro in Excel 4 format tells Excel to use the older-style macro functions, rather than the new Visual Basic macro language. This option is included for those upgrading from Excel 4 who have not yet mastered the new Visual Basic language. Unless you have a specific reason for using the Excel 4 functions, always use the Visual Basic standard.

Examining the finished macro

When you record a macro, Excel opens a new macro module. You can examine the finished macro by switching to the module worksheet at the end of the workbook file. Just move to the last page of the workbook file by clicking the paging buttons. Click the page tab of the Module1 sheet to view the macro. Figure 13-4 shows the module containing the macro example recorded earlier.

You can see that the macro reflects your movements via its commands. You'll find that it's not too difficult to understand macro commands that were produced with the macro recorder because they remind you of the action you performed. You can make changes to the macro if desired, and you can remove the commands that appear from any mistakes you made while recording the macro. For example, while recording a macro, suppose you select the wrong command. Select Edit⇨Undo to fix the mistake. This error and the undo command used to correct it will both appear in the macro and the macro will faithfully repeat the error and undo correction each time you use it. By removing these commands from the macro, you can *clean up* the macro's performance.

Viewing the Personal Macro Workbook

If you want to examine a macro on the Personal Macro Workbook, first unhide the workbook with the Window⇨Unhide command. The Personal Macro Workbook appears in the list of open sheets under the Window menu. When you

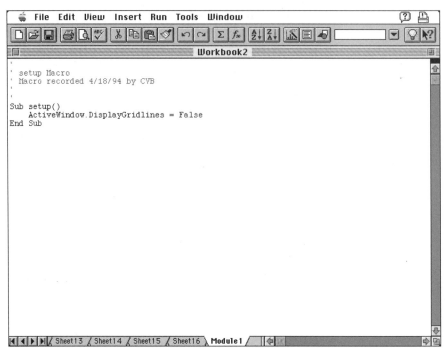

Figure 13-4: Viewing the macro module.

are finished viewing the Personal Macro Workbook, be sure to hide the sheet again by using the Window⇨Hide command. When you exit Excel, you will be given the option of saving the changes you made to the Personal Macro Workbook; you should almost always select Yes.

Running Macros

You've already seen that you can run your macros by pressing Control along with the macro's shortcut key or by selecting a custom menu command from the Tools menu. Both these options are available from the Options button in the Record New Macro dialog box. But there are many other ways to run your macros. The following sections explain several ways to run your macros.

When you run macros, remember that the macro repeats the commands you recorded, exactly as you recorded them. Therefore, you should be sure that the macro will run properly from the current worksheet when you invoke it again. For example, if you record a macro that removes the worksheet gridlines and sets the global worksheet font, then you should always run the macro from a new worksheet that contains the gridlines. Running the macro on a worksheet that already has its gridlines removed has no effect.

Running macros with a shortcut key

The easiest way to run a macro is to invoke its shortcut key. You determine each macro's shortcut key when you first record the macro. Select Options from the Record New Macro dialog box and enter the shortcut key into the space provided.

To run the macro using the shortcut key, just press Control along with the shortcut key. Remember that Excel distinguishes between upper- and lowercase letters for these shortcut keys.

You don't have to provide shortcut keys for all your macros. If you omit the shortcut key, you can still run the macro using another method.

Note that you cannot give two macros in the same workbook identical shortcut keys. Excel applies the key to the last macro you define. However, you can use the same shortcut key on two macros in two different macro workbooks.

Running macros from the Tools menu

Another way to run your macros is to add them to the Tools menu. You can choose a command name for the macro and assign the command to the Tools menu in Excel by using the Record New Macro dialog box options, as explained previously.

To run the macro from the Tools menu command, just choose the Tools menu and select the command at the bottom of the menu. Figure 13-5 shows an example of a custom command.

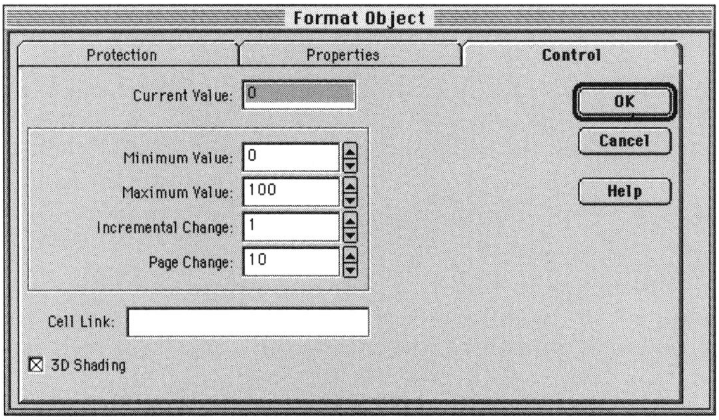

Figure 13-5: A macro command that was attached to the Tools menu manually.

Running macros with the Tools⇨Macro command

You can run macros by using the Macro command in the Tools menu and selecting the macro's name from the list that appears (see Figure 13-6). Note that this list shows you all available macros in all the macro modules and in the Personal Macro Workbook. Preceding each macro's name is the macro's shortcut key. To run one of the macros in this list, just double-click its name.

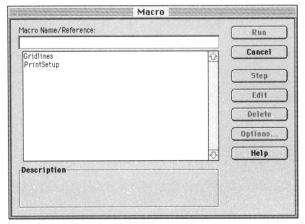

Figure 13-6: The Tools⇨Macro command provides this list of macros.

One advantage to this method is that you can run either of two macros that have the same shortcut keys. You can also see each macro that's available at any given time — including all macros on the Personal Macro Workbook. You can also view the macro descriptions by clicking the macro name and viewing the Description information at the bottom of the dialog box.

Running macros from custom toolbar buttons

Another way to run macros is to attach them to custom toolbar buttons. In Topic 3 you learn how to create your own toolbars or customize an existing toolbar using Excel's palette of buttons. But you can also create your own custom buttons and add them to an existing toolbar — or a toolbar you've created from scratch.

A custom button is simply a device for running your macros. You can attach macros to these buttons so that when you click the button, Excel runs the macro that you've attached to it. Because custom buttons and toolbars are available at all times through the View⇨Toolbars command, you'll probably want their macros available at all times, too. Therefore, you should store your custom toolbar button macros in the Personal Macro Workbook.

Attaching a macro to a toolbar button

1. Display the desired toolbar to which you will add the custom button by using the View⇨Toolbars command. If desired, you can use a custom toolbar. For details about creating a custom toolbar, refer to Topic 3.

2. With the desired toolbar on the screen, press Control. Click any button and select the Customize option from the shortcut menu that appears. Alternatively, you can choose View⇨Toolbars and select Customize.

3. Click Custom at the bottom of the category list. The dialog box now displays a selection of custom button faces (see Figure 13-7). If you don't like any of these designs, you can create your own — or copy the face of any other button in Excel. Details on creating your own button designs appear in the next section.

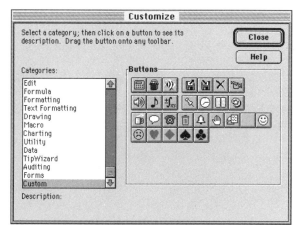

Figure 13-7: The Custom buttons in the toolbar Customize dialog box.

4. Drag any button from the selection of custom buttons onto the desired toolbar that you opened in Step 2. When you finish moving the tool onto the toolbar, Excel displays the dialog box in Figure 13-8. This dialog box displays the macros currently available in Excel and asks you to choose one for the button.

5. Double-click the macro that you want to attach to the button.

6. Repeat the process to add other custom buttons or click OK to return to the worksheet.

Figure 13-8: Assigning a macro to the custom toolbar button.

Notice that the Assign Macro dialog box contains a Record button so that you can record your tool macro on the spot if it does not appear in the list of available macros. Click the Record button and begin the macro as usual. Select Record Macro ⇨ Stop Recorder command from the Tools menu when you finish with the macro.

Remember, it's a good idea to store macros onto the Personal Macro Workbook if you plan to use them with custom toolbar buttons. Toolbar buttons are available in any workbook, so the macros assigned to those buttons should also be available in any workbook. Storing the macro on a module sheet in a particular workbook leaves it unavailable for other workbooks. However, as you learn in Topic 3, you can store custom toolbars with specific workbooks, so that each time you open the workbook the toolbar is also activated. In such a case, it would be appropriate to store the button macro on a module page of the workbook.

Customizing a toolbar button

If you don't like the graphic image on any of Excel's custom buttons, you can customize a button to suit your needs. There are three main ways to get a graphic image onto a custom toolbar button:

◆ **Copy a different button face.** You can copy the image from any other button face onto the button you are designing. While inside the Customize dialog box, click the button whose face you want to copy and then choose the Copy Button Image command from the Edit menu. Then paste the image onto your custom button to replace its current design with the one you copied.

◆ **Copy any graphic object into Excel.** You can copy any graphic image into Excel and paste it onto a button. Be sure to copy an image that is of the appropriate size to fit onto a button face. With the image on the clipboard, move into the toolbar customize dialog box and use the Paste command to paste the image onto a custom button.

◆ **Use the button editor to draw your own button design.** While the Customize dialog box is active, you can press Control (or Command-Option) and click any toolbar button to view a special shortcut menu. Selecting the Edit⇨Button Image command produces the Button Editor dialog box shown in Figure 13-9. Edit the pixels inside the Picture image to change the design.

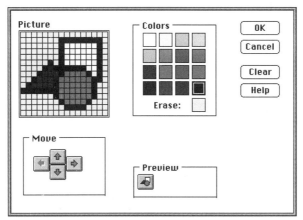

Figure 13-9: The Button Editor dialog box is available through the toolbar shortcut menu that appears when the Customize dialog box is in view.

Running macros from worksheet buttons or objects

Another way to run macros is to attach them to worksheet buttons. Similar to custom tools, worksheet buttons can run any macro when you click them. By attaching macros to buttons, you can make the macros available within worksheets without having to use the macro's shortcut key or toolbar buttons.

Worksheet buttons differ from toolbar tools in that they appear on the worksheet itself and are saved with the worksheet. Because the buttons appear on the worksheet, they scroll along with the sheet; in other words, worksheet buttons appear in a particular location on the worksheet and stay there when you scroll around in the worksheet. Therefore, worksheet buttons are used primarily for macros that apply to specific areas of a worksheet. For example, you may use a worksheet button to quickly display a graph of a certain data range on the screen. Another button may print that area. Worksheet buttons are useful for manipulating the data and values inside a database or table of data. Figure 13-10 shows some examples. Note that these buttons apply to the area in view.

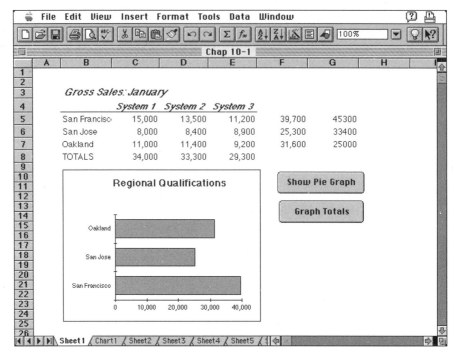

Figure 13-10: Using worksheet buttons to manipulate specific data on the worksheet.

You can add a worksheet button to any worksheet by drawing the button onto the sheet. Refer to Topic 5 for more information about drawing objects onto the worksheet. Buttons, like all other worksheet objects, cover up the worksheet cells over which they are drawn.

To draw a button, first activate the Drawing toolbar using the View⇨Toolbars command. Click the Button tool and then click and drag to draw the button. When you release the mouse, Excel presents a dialog box listing all available macros. To attach one of the macros to the button, double-click its name in the list. You can now run the selected macro by clicking the button.

Creating a worksheet button

1. Choose the Toolbars command from the View menu and activate the Drawing toolbar.

2. Click Create Button and then drag to draw a button object on the sheet. Refer to Topic 5 for details about drawing. When you are finished drawing the button, Excel presents the Assign Macro dialog box.

3. Double-click the name of the macro that you want to assign to this button or choose the Record option to record the button's macro.

4. To move the button around the page, click the Drawing Selection button on the Drawing toolbar and drag the object. Alternatively, you can hold down Command as you drag the button. ◖

Once a button is drawn and a macro attached to it, you can still change its size, shape and position on the screen as you would any object. Just hold Command down as you click the button. With the button selected, release the Command key and drag the button to another location or size the button by dragging on one of the *handles* around its edges. Click anywhere on the worksheet when finished and the button returns to normal. If you click the button without holding down Command, you simply activate the attached macro.

Because a button applies to a specific worksheet area, you should probably store the button's macro on a module in the same workbook — not in the Personal Macro Workbook.

You can turn any worksheet object into a button that runs a macro when clicked. Just click the object to select it and then choose the Tools⇨Assign Macro command. Even a graph frame can be turned into a button. Try copying some graphic images into Excel from other programs and turning them into buttons. There are many creative ways to apply this feature.

Quick Tips

Interrupting a macro recording

If you need to take a break and stop recording a macro, choose Record Macro⇨Stop Recorder from the Tools menu. When you're ready to get rolling again, choose Start Recorder from the same menu.

Learning about Visual Basic

You can gain a better understanding of macros by viewing the Visual Basic Help screens available through Excel's help system. Refer to Topic 1 about accessing the help system.

Creating a Custom Application

Overview

A custom application is any workbook (or enclosed worksheet) that you create with the goal of having others use it to perform certain tasks. When you create worksheets for use by other people, you'll find it helpful to add a *custom user interface*.

A custom user interface provides interaction between the user of the worksheet and the information inside the worksheet. A custom user interface can reduce the errors or unintentional mistakes created by inexperienced users who play with your system. By removing potentially damaging (or just plain unnecessary) commands from Excel's menus and then adding your own custom menus and commands, you can make your workbook applications easier to use. This topic shows you several ways in which you can improve the interface in your custom applications. (Notice that the terms "custom workbook" and "custom application" are used interchangebly throughout this topic.)

What Are Custom Applications?

A custom application can be as simple as a Travel Expense workbook used by your sales staff or as complicated as a full-blown accounting package that is sold commercially. In other words, a custom application can be created for a just few people in your office or for professional and commercial use. Whatever your needs, Excel's application building tools make your workbooks friendly and easy to use. The following are some elements that you can add to your custom Excel applications.

Customized toolbars

Customized toolbars are an excellent way to make an application easier to use. By providing point-and-click buttons on custom toolbars for specific activities in your application, you reduce the amount of Excel know-how required to use your workbook. With button controls, someone can perform complicated tasks in your application with a simple click. For example, suppose you create a job estimate worksheet. You can add a button that automatically prints a customer's job estimate report. Anyone using your application would be able to print this report without any knowledge of Excel's printing procedures. The button does all the work. Custom toolbars and toolbar buttons are discussed in Topics 3 and 12.

Worksheet buttons and controls

Worksheet buttons, discussed in Topic 12, are similar to custom toolbar buttons, except that they appear right on the worksheet page — along with your data and charts. Worksheet buttons are excellent for controlling specific data on your worksheet. For example, you can add a button that instantly changes a line chart to an area chart or a monthly chart to a quarterly chart.

In addition to worksheet buttons, Excel provides a host of worksheet controls that are useful for manipulating worksheet data. Controls include custom scroll bars, list boxes, check boxes, and much more. For example, you can attach a scroll bar or spinner control to the value in a cell and easily change that value by using the control. Details about creating and using worksheet controls appear later in this topic.

Customized menus

In Topic 13 you learned how you can attach a macro to the Tools menu to make it easy to locate and run your macros. Excel offers even more custom control. You can create your own custom menus or change any of Excel's menus. You can add custom commands that run your macros — or just rearrange the existing commands and options. For example, in your Sales Tracking workbook, you can add a menu called "Reports" that contains commands for printing and viewing various sales reports based on the data inside the workbook. Instead of making the salespeople learn how to create and print reports, you can perform all the required actions through macros that are attached to your custom menu commands.

Documentation

Your custom applications will be much easier to use if you add some simple documentation elements. One idea is to take advantage of Excel's cell notes and text boxes. Cell notes can hold vital information about the kinds of information a user should enter into your application. Text boxes can offer brief suggestions for using the application. Beyond these tools, you may consider adding custom help screens to your application. You can do this with the Visual Basic macro language. (For more information, refer to *Visual Basic For Dummies*, published by IDG Books Worldwide. Even though this book describes Visual Basic in a Windows environment, it is an excellent beginning guide to the program's concepts.)

Customized dialog boxes

Excel lets you build custom dialog boxes that you can attach to your custom menu commands. You can also make your dialog boxes available through toolbar and worksheet buttons. Dialog boxes provide various options regarding the information in your application. In a few minutes, this topic explains the basics of adding custom controls to your worksheets.

Worksheet protection

Because you'll want to protect the data and formulas that make the application work properly, worksheet protection often accompanies custom applications. Preventing users from changing your formulas and worksheet structure keeps the integrity of your application. In addition, protection prevents accidental changes, such as users typing over cells that contain important formulas.

Good design and layout

When you create a custom application that will be used by other people, you may consider paying special attention to the visual appeal of the application. Spending a little time designing an attractive worksheet can go a long way in making the application easier to use. This topic discusses some of the key ingredients in a well-designed custom application.

Designing Your Application

Before you attempt to create that large custom application for your company, take some time to plan the application in advance. Good planning answers such important questions such as

◆ "How many sheets will I need?"

◆ "What types of reports will be necessary?"

◆ "What data is required for these results?"

Answering these questions up front will save a lot of time that could be lost if you have to restructure the workbook later. The following sections discuss some of the planning steps you can take to better cover all the bases before you start creating the application.

Start at the end

When designing a large application, consider its overall purpose. Consider what types of reports and output you want from the application. These issues should start you thinking in the right direction. You can then start to determine what information and formulas will be required to produce the desired reports by evaluating questions like these: "What happens to the data that you enter for these reports to be possible?" and "What Excel features will be required to manipulate the data in this way?"

Many people don't think about printing reports until the end of the design process and end up having to *force* the workbook into creating the types of reports they want. Starting at the end is a good way to keep the application on track. You may even design the actual report forms you want. For instance, if you are creating a job estimation workbook, you can sketch how the customer's job estimate sheet should look and what information should be in it. If your system will be used to send invoices to the customer, create a sample invoice and consider the data you want in it. Will you want to store this information as an historical accounting of each customer's activity? If so, then you'll need to consider what features (probably database features) will be required.

Imagine the application in use

Once you plan the reports and outcome of the application and have an idea about the Excel features required to produce these reports, you can begin to imagine the application in use. In your mind, run through every conceivable scenario for the application. You can even run through some actual examples from your company. For example, when designing your job estimation workbook, pull out some old estimates and see what types of problems arise when entering these examples into your Excel application. Ask yourself these questions:

◆ "What types of scenarios must the application be able to control?"

◆ "What types of limitations are you willing to place on the system?"

◆ "How much can proper documentation help prevent unforeseen scenarios from happening?"

View the structure on paper first

When you have the ingredients of your application, including the data, the Excel features you'll use, and the resulting reports produced, you may want to design the application on paper before diving into a blank workbook file. When looking over your custom application, consider the following:

- "How many pages will you need and what will be on each page?"
- "How will the data on these pages be connected?"
- "How will you store data permanently?"
- "How will data flow through the application?"
- "How will the user get around in the application?"

Figure 14-1 shows an example of planned application sketched on paper.

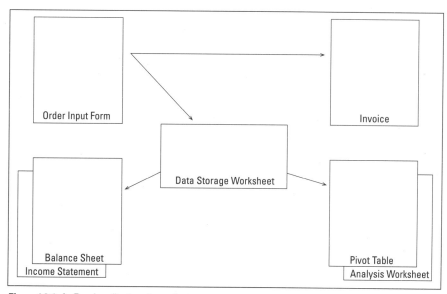

Figure 14-1: An Excel application planned out on paper.

Document as you go

When you begin creating the application in Excel, consider adding cell notes and other documentation elements that clearly explain important formulas and procedures. You may also want to keep your application notes on a documentation page of the workbook. The user can then turn to this page for complete instructions. Another advantage to documenting your work is that you can go back through and locate errors more quickly — a process known as troubleshooting.

Test the first draft

Enter test data into the application to uncover any errors in your formulas or procedures. Use simple data that you can quickly check for problems. Run through various scenarios and examples to test how the system handles each one. Make corrections as needed.

Add automation and a user interface

Once the application is working properly, it's time to consider the types of user interfaces and automation elements you can add. Consider these questions:

◆ "Will a custom menu or toolbar help?"

◆ "How about macros to automate certain tasks?"

◆ "How much automation will be required for the people using the system?"

◆ "Will automation help prevent user errors in key areas?"

◆ "How much time and effort are you willing to spend on automation?"

These are important questions to ask yourself at this final stage of planning.

Custom Interface Controls

To build a custom Excel application, you need a user interface. To build a user interface, you need tools, which Excel calls controls. Excel provides many controls to help you build a custom user interface, including custom menu commands, custom buttons, and many more.

Controls for your custom user interface can be added to your worksheet by *drawing* them onto the page. After accessing the Forms toolbar (View⇨Toolbars), you can draw several different types of controls onto the worksheet.

Drawing a custom interface control

1. Access the Forms toolbar through the View⇨Toolbars command.

2. Click the desired button, such as the Check Box button.

3. Click and drag the worksheet to create the check box.

4. Edit the text associated with the control, if applicable. Figure 14-2 shows some controls added to a worksheet. ◖◗

What gives a control its power in the worksheet is the *link* you make between the worksheet and the object by using the Format⇨Object command. Each tool returns a value to the worksheet cell you specify. You can act on this value to suit your needs.

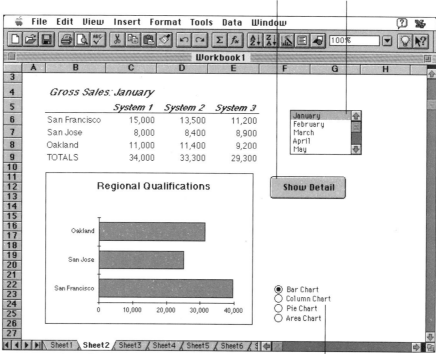

Figure 14-2: A worksheet with custom user interface controls added.

Option buttons

Linking a control to the worksheet

1. Press and hold Command and click the control object to select it.

2. Choose Object from the Format menu. The Format Object dialog box appears.

3. Click the Control page of the dialog box.

4. Click on Cell Link entry box and enter the desired cell address to which you want the control linked. You may also click the Cell Link box to activate it and then click the worksheet to point to the desired cell.

5. Click OK. ◊

The value associated with the control object now appears in the specified cell. Depending on the type of control, this may be a numeric value or a TRUE/FALSE value. You can use these values in your worksheet application or link the controls to cells in a remote area of the worksheet (or a special page used just for these links). Then you can act on the values through IF formulas and macro procedures. The following sections discuss the various controls that are available in your worksheets and how they can be used to manipulate information in the worksheet.

Like any object on the worksheet, you can move and copy user interface tools. Refer to Topic 5 for more information about manipulating objects and changing their properties. After you have drawn a control onto the worksheet, you can select it again by holding Command while you click the object.

Once you have drawn a user interface object, such as a check box, you can edit the text associated with the object by holding Command and clicking the object to select it. Release Command and click inside the text area of the object. You can now edit the text.

You can view the shortcut menu associated with control objects by pressing Command-Option as you click the object, which is also a handy way of producing the Format Object command.

Check boxes

Check boxes are useful for providing a series of options for the user. Because the user can select one or more of the check boxes at the same time, these options are *and/or* options. In addition, check boxes are useful for presenting "check all that apply" types of options. You can draw a series of check boxes onto the worksheet to cover as many items as you like. Although check boxes usually come in a group, they actually act independently of each other — each one returning an individual value.

To act on the selections made through check boxes, link each text box to a cell in the worksheet by selecting the check box control (hold Command and click the object) and choosing the Format⇨Object command. The Format Object dialog box appears with a special Control page, as shown in Figure 14-3.

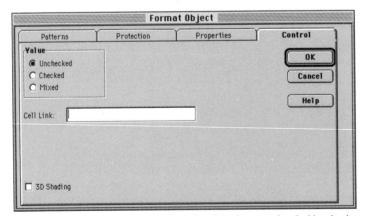

Figure 14-3: The Control tab of the Format Object dialog box associated with a check box control.

Click the Cell Link entry box and type the address of the cell to which you want the check box linked. The linked cell can be in a remote area of the worksheet. The cell you specify will contain the value TRUE when the check box is checked, FALSE when the check box is unchecked, and N/A when the check box is mixed. Using a simple IF formula, you can act on the value contained in this cell. For example, the following formula adds $12 if the check box is checked:

=IF(Z12=TRUE,12,"")

In this formula, cell Z12 is linked to the check box and contains the value TRUE, FALSE, or N/A. This formula may, for example, appear inside an order form to add $12 for special shipping instructions. Add a formula like this to evaluate each check box.

Option buttons

Option buttons are like check boxes, except that they are *either/or* options. Use option buttons when only one out of several options applies. When you click an option button, other option buttons in the same group are unselected. Therefore, only one cell link is required for all the option buttons in a group. The cell you link to the button group contains the number of the button you select.

For example, if you have four buttons in the group and link the group to cell Z13, then cell Z13 contains a number from 1 to 4 to indicate which of the four option buttons is selected. You can then act on the value in this cell using IF statements or macros. To link an option button group to a cell, select any one of the buttons and choose the Format⇨Object command; this will link the entire group to the linked cell you specify. Enter the desired cell into the Cell Link entry area on the Control page of the dialog box. (Refer to Figure 14-3.)

If you require two separate groups of option buttons, you can separate the groups by placing them inside group boxes. Just draw two group boxes onto the page and drag each option button into the appropriate group box. The options instantly separate themselves based on the box in which they appear. When you are finished separating the groups, you can link the groups to separate cells on the worksheet.

List boxes

A list box is useful for presenting a series of options from which a user can choose, such as a list of products or names. When you link a list box to a cell on the worksheet, that cell contains the number of the item in the list that is selected. In other words, a list box returns a numeric value that represents the number of the item in the list (numbered in order of appearance) to its linked cell. Therefore, if you have a list of months in the list box and the user selects March, the linked cell will contain the value 3.

To link the list box to a cell, select the list box control and choose the Format⇨Object command. The Input Range is the range of cells on the worksheet that contains the actual items you want listed in the box. Enter or point to a range containing the desired list. The Cell Link option specifies the cell that contains the number of the chosen option from the list. Figure 14-4 shows an example of the list box Control page.

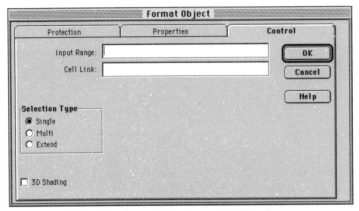

Figure 14-4: A list box Control page showing input and cell link references.

With the numeric value of the selected item listed in the linked cell, you can now act on that information through IF functions or macros on the worksheet.

Drop-down lists

A drop-down list has the same basic qualities as a list box, but takes less room on the page. It displays the selected item in the box and presents more items when you click the arrow associated with the box. Like a list box, the drop-down list can be linked to a cell on the worksheet that contains the numeric value of the selected item in the list. The controls offered for the drop-down list include an Input Range, a Cell Link, and Drop Down Lines. The Drop Down Lines option specifies the number of lines in the list. If your Input Range includes more items than the Drop Down Lines values allows, the list scrolls.

Scroll bars and spinners

Scroll bars and spinners can be used to select values from a range, or scale. When you click the arrows of a spinner tool, you move forward or backward through numeric values. You can use a scroll bar in the same manner. With the Format⇨Object command, you can set the upper and lower value limits for the scroll bar and the spinner. Figure 14-5 shows the Control page of the Format Object dialog box for a scroll bar object.

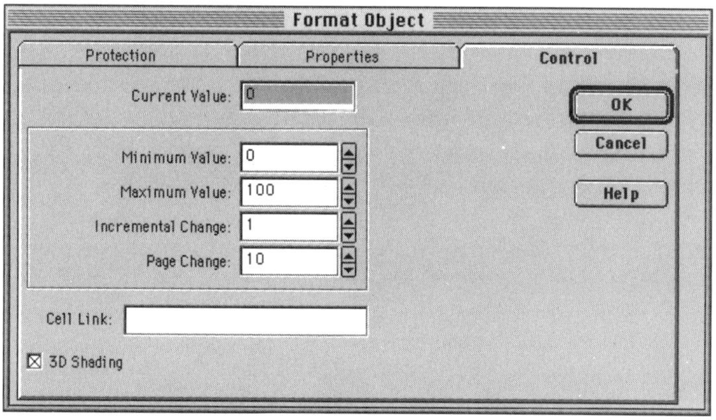

Figure 14-5: The Control tab for a scroll bar.

The spinner Control properties are identical to the scroll bar's, except that the Page change option is unavailable. Table 14-1 provides a summary of the spinner control options.

Table 14-1
Spinner and Scroll Bar Control Options

Option	What It Does
Current Value	The value currently showing on the scroll bar or spinner
Minimum Value	The lowest value available through the scroll bar or spinner
Maximum Value	The highest value available through the scroll bar or spinner
Incremental Change	The amount of change (increase or decrease) in value when you click the arrows of the scroll bar or spinner
Page Change	The amount of change in value when you click the bar of a scroll bar (not available for a spinner)
Cell Link	The cell to which the value is linked

The cell you specify as the Cell Link contains the value you choose on the scroll bar or spinner. One example of using a spinner control is to select a year date for a calendar; by clicking the arrows of the spinner control, you can move forward or backward through the years.

Creating Custom Menus

Excel lets you modify its menu structure for your custom applications. You can add or remove commands from Excel's menus, create your own custom commands and options for menus, remove menus from Excel, and even add entirely new menus from scratch.

Changes you make to Excel's menu structure apply to the active workbook and are saved with the workbook. Therefore, you can have different menu structures for different custom applications. For example, if you don't want the users of a custom application to edit anything within the application, you can completely remove the Edit menu. You can also insert a custom menu of your own design to add commands for the application.

Your custom menu commands are used to invoke (or run) macro procedures. It's a good idea to create your macro procedures first and then think about attaching these procedures to custom menu commands. Refer to Topic 13 for information on creating macro procedures.

Menu customization is accomplished through Excel's Menu Editor, a special dialog box that gives you access to each menu bar, menu, and command in Excel. You can add your own custom menus and commands with the Menu Editor.

Viewing the Menu Editor

1. Display the Visual Basic toolbar by using the View⇨Toolbars command.

2. Click the Menu Editor button. The Menu Editor dialog box appears, as shown in Figure 14-6.

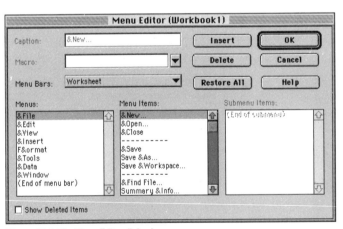

Figure 14-6: The Menu Editor dialog box.

3. Choose the desired menu bar from the Menu Bars drop-down list. ⁍

Excel has several different menu bars that appear at different times during your operation of Excel. For example, when you select a chart, the Charting menu bar appears. The Worksheet menu bar is the standard bar that appears during most of your normal worksheet operation.

Removing built-in menus and commands

You can modify Excel's built-in menus by removing entire menus or individual commands. If you want to eliminate certain options from certain applications, you can simply remove the command or menu from Excel. You don't have to worry about damaging Excel's menu structure; you can easily restore the original menus if you want to return to normal.

Removing menus and commands is useful for custom applications whose users know little about Excel. You can eliminate commands and options that may let them change or damage the application — and make the application simpler at the same time.

Deleting a menu or command

1. Display the Menu Editor using the Menu Editor button on the Visual Basic toolbar.

2. Using the Menus list in the Menu Editor, click the menu that you want to remove — or which contains the command that you want to remove.

3. Select the menu you want removed and click Delete. Or click a command listed in the Menu Items list and then click Delete. ◀◀

You can restore the menus to their original state by clicking Restore after selecting the menu in the Menus list. If you have deleted an entire menu, click to place a check mark in the Show Deleted Items list. Then click the desired menu and choose Restore.

Inserting a menu or command

If you have a macro procedure that you want to attach to custom menu commands, you'll want to insert a new menu and/or command. You can insert a command into an existing Excel menu or create a new menu to hold your command. For example, you may want to add a menu called Reports to your application. This menu could contain several types of reports you can print, and each command in the menu could invoke a macro that prints the specified report.

Adding a new menu or command

1. Display the Menu Editor using the Menu Editor button on the Visual Basic toolbar.

2. Choose the desired menu bar from the Menu Bars drop-down list.

3. Click the menu into which you want to insert a new command. Or click the menu above which you want to insert a new menu. If you want to insert a new menu at the end of the menu bar, click the End of Bar item.

4. Click Insert to insert a new menu. If you want to insert a new command, click the command in the Menu Item list above which you want the new command to appear. If you want the command to appear at the bottom of the menu, choose the End of Menu option. Click Insert when you are ready to insert the new command. A blank space appears in the menu.

5. Type the name of the menu or command in the Caption space provided.

6. Select the macro that you want to attach to this menu command from the Macro list.

Quick Tips

Creating a submenu

You can attach a submenu to any custom command you create. Just insert an item into the Submenu Items list in the Menu Editor dialog box using the same basic procedure described in the steps concerning adding a new menu or command.

Using custom dialog boxes

In Excel, you can add all the custom interface controls discussed in this topic and more to your custom dialog boxes. Attach these dialog boxes to your custom menu commands so that the command automatically calls up the dialog box. Or attach them to buttons or other tools. You can create a dialog box by inserting a Dialog page into your workbook through the page tab shortcut menu. Calling up the dialog box from a control or menu command requires a macro procedure.

Naming controls

You can name your controls and other objects in the workbook by selecting the object and then choosing the Name command in the Insert menu. The name can then be used in macro procedures to address the object.

Formatting controls

You can format the appearance of your worksheet controls through the Patterns page of the Format Object dialog box. Add a gray or colored background to your controls, for example, to make them stand out. You have no control over the font used in the controls, but you can combine text boxes with your controls for various results.

Why forms?

Adding controls to your worksheets is especially useful for creating interaction with input and output forms. For example, you can add check boxes to your order input form to let the user select product options or shipping options. The toolbar containing these controls is called the Forms toolbar. The cell gridlines toggle button also appears on this toolbar, adding another feature to your customization repertoire.

Part VI:
Excel Reference

2nd Edition

Macworld Excel 5 Companion

Installing Excel

Excel's installer program makes installing Excel 5 a no-brainer. The Installer, however, does give you a few choices about what you'd like to install and where. So it's worth your while to review this appendix if you (or another user) haven't installed Excel or want to install a missing Excel capability.

Getting Started

Before you begin installation, you should make sure your Macintosh has adequate disk space and memory (RAM) to install and use Excel. At a minimum, you'll need 5.8MB of hard disk space to install Excel. To fully install Excel, you need more than 14MB. You can determine the amount of available hard disk space by double-clicking the hard disk icon on your desktop. The directory window that appears will show you the space available in the top-right corner. You can verify the amount of RAM by selecting About This Macintosh from the Apple Menu.

To get adequate performance, especially if you plan to use Excel for some heavy-duty applications, you should probably at least have 8MB of memory. Fortunately, the price of memory is pretty reasonable these days.

Installing the Software

Before you begin installing, close any open applications on your Mac. Also, you may want to make backup copies of the installation disks. To begin installation, place the Disk-1 Setup disk in the Macintosh's disk drive. After a few seconds, the contents of the disk appear in a window (just as if you'd chosen Open from the File menu). Double-click the Microsoft Excel Setup icon, and the window shown in Figure A-1 appears.

When you are ready to begin installing Excel, click OK. Next, you are presented with the window shown in Figure A-2, in which you are asked to type your name and the name of your organization. Enter your name and the name of your organization (if any) and click the OK button or press Return. (Please note that the name and organization you enter will be displayed on all subsequent installations of Excel.) At this point, Excel asks you to confirm what you just entered (see Figure A-3). If you need to make a change, click Change, make the corrections, and then click OK (twice).

Figure A-1: Click OK to begin installing Excel.

Type your name and your organization's
name in these boxes

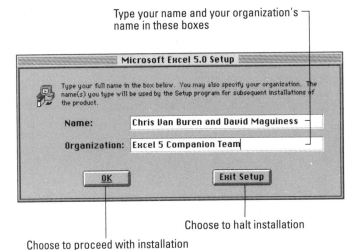

Choose to halt installation

Choose to proceed with installation

Figure A-2: Enter your name and the name of your organization here.

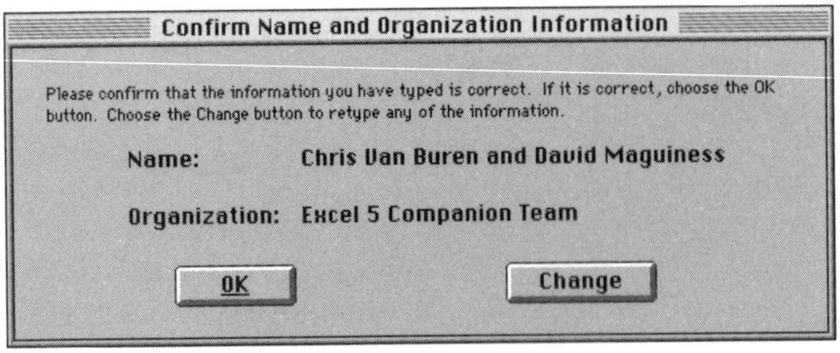

Confirm Name and Organization Information

Please confirm that the information you have typed is correct. If it is correct, choose the OK
button. Choose the Change button to retype any of the information.

Name: **Chris Van Buren and David Maguiness**

Organization: **Excel 5 Companion Team**

OK   Change

Figure A-3: Confirming your name and organization.

After you click OK (to accept the name and organization you entered), you are asked to specify a folder in which you want to place the Excel files. The Installer automatically places the Excel files into a folder called Microsoft Excel unless you specify a different name for the folder. You can locate this folder anywhere on your hard drive by using the dialog box shown in Figure A-4. Just choose the desired folder from the list that appears by double-clicking the folder's name. If you do not wish to place the Excel folder in another folder on your hard drive, simply click on Setup to preceed with installation and the folder containing Excel will be loaded directly onto your hard drive.

The example shown in Figure A-4 occurs when you are upgrading. Excel warns you that a previous version of Excel has been found and asks if you want to install Excel 5 over the earlier version. If you do, then click Setup. If for some reason you would like to save your old version of Excel, click New Folder, enter a name for the folder, and click OK. Then click Setup. In Figure A-5, the new folder is called Microsoft Excel 5.

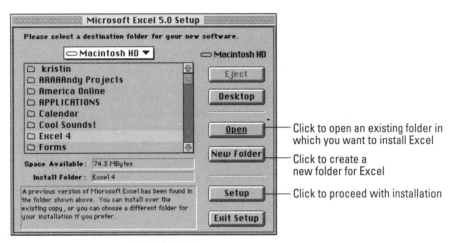

Figure A-4: Entering a destination folder for Excel 5.

The window in Figure A-6 should now be on your screen. This window enables you to choose the type of Excel installation that's right for you. Choose Typical if you want the most common Excel program files and example files copied to your hard disk; choose Complete/Custom if you'd like to have the complete Excel package installed, or if you wish to pick and choose what gets installed or choose Minimum if you want only the essential Excel files installed. If you are concerned about space on your hard drive, your best bet is to choose Minimum or to choose Custom and install as much of Excel as you can fit onto your hard drive.

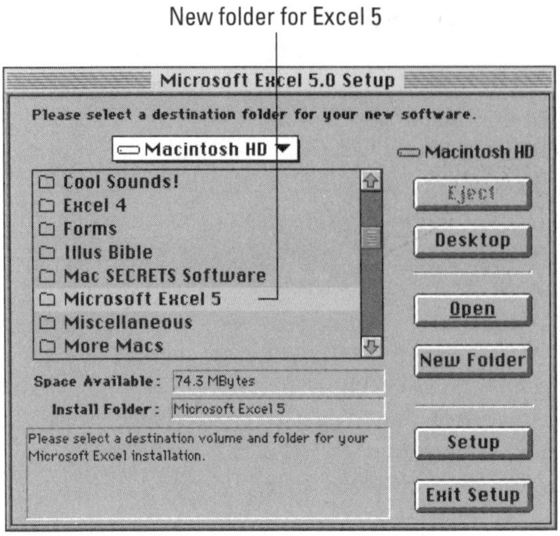

New folder for Excel 5

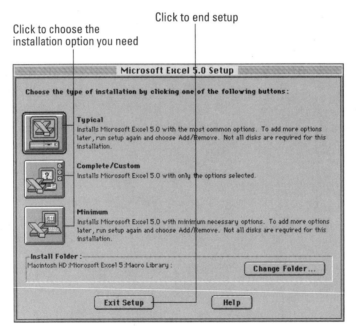

Figure A-5: Creating a new folder, called Microsoft Excel 5.

Click to choose the
installation option you need

Click to end setup

Figure A-6: Click Typical, Complete/Custom, or Minimum to choose the type of installation that you want.

If you choose Custom or Minimum, don't worry that you might miss out on some of Excel's capabilities — you can go back and install additional Excel options at a later date. Just run through the installation procedure again, making sure that you choose Custom. If you do choose Custom (during an initial or subsequent installation session), the dialog box shown in Figure A-7 appears.

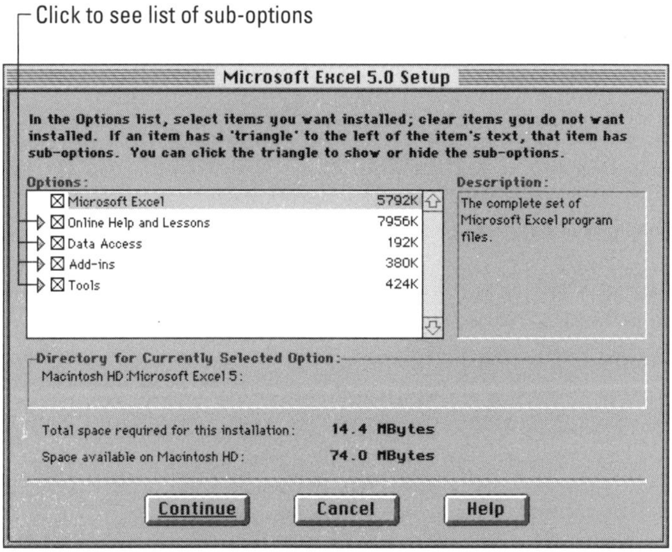

Click to see list of sub-options

Figure A-7: Choose which Excel options you want to install by clicking the check box next to the option.

The options with an X in their check boxes are the ones that are to be installed. If you want to remove an option from the list of those to be installed, then click the check box to remove the X. As you can see in Figure A-7, all options are selected, making this a complete installation of Excel. Please note that the items that have a triangular arrow next to them have suboptions. Click the triangle to reveal a list of files (suboptions). You can deselect those options that you do not want installed. For example, if you click the triangular arrow next to Online Help and Lessons, you receive the list shown in Figure A-8.

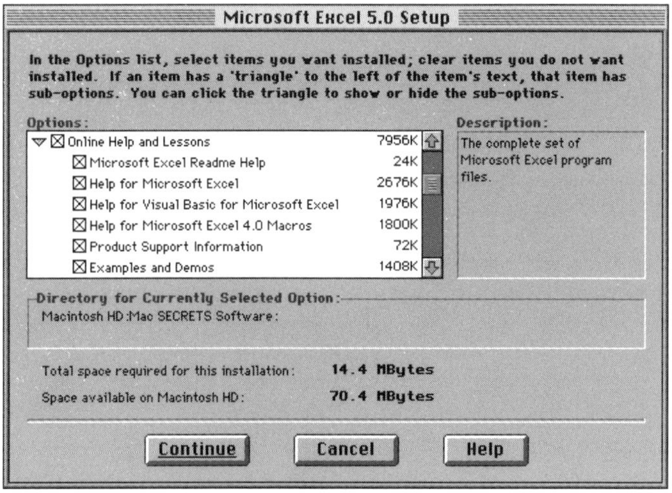

Figure A-8: Choose which Online Help and Lessons options you want.

You may want to leave out the help for Excel 4.0 Macros, for example, if you do not plan to use the old macro system. Doing this will save you about 1.8MB of disk space.

The disk space required by a Custom installation depends on the options you select. And remember that by installing some of the options (such as Help, which is a suboption of Online Help and Lessons), those options automatically become part of your working set. The more options you select, the more memory Excel occupies on your hard drive. You can always rerun the installation procedure at a later date and remove any options that you no longer want, need, or have disk space for.

If you need to save disk space, use the Minimum option.

After you have selected the installation option, you will see a dialog box that is new to Excel 5 — the Setup dialog box that asks whether you are installing Excel on a Power Mac or other Macintosh model. Choose the appropriate option (see Figure A-9).

After you choose that option, the installation begins and the Mac displays a window indicating the status of the installation progress and prompts you to remove and load disks as necessary.

Figure A-9: Excel 5 added a new option to accommodate the next wave of Macintosh technology—the PowerMacs.

As a user-friendly feature, Excel presents colorful and informative messages as the instllation is taking place. The messages range from suggesting that you register your software to telling you some of the features of Excel 5 (see Figure A-10).

When installation is complete, the window in Figure A-11 appears. Click OK to close the window and return to the desktop.

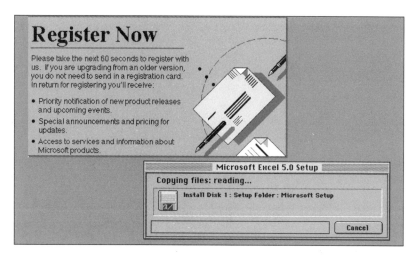

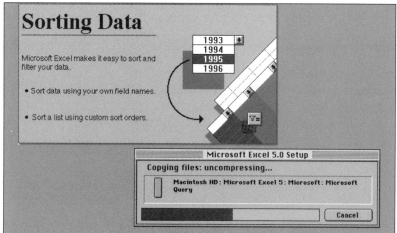

Figure A-10: Friendly messages flash across your desktop as Excel works through the installation process.

Figure A-11: Installation of Excel is complete. Click OK to return to your desktop.

After you've successfully installed Excel, make sure you store the installation disks in a secure, easy-to-remember place that is dry, away from magnetic fields, and has a moderate temperature.

Worksheet Examples

This appendix provides some actual worksheet examples that use many of the techniques and procedures discussed throughout this book. You can use the steps and explanations to duplicate these worksheets and receive practical experience in creating Excel applications.

The examples in this appendix cover a range of personal finance needs, including income and expense analysis and tax planning. You learn how the following tasks are performed:

- ◆ Using workbooks to store several linked worksheets
- ◆ Using database lookups between worksheets
- ◆ Using database statistical functions
- ◆ Using logical functions, such as the IF function

The first example involves several worksheets in a workbook. The four worksheets in this application work together to provide income and expense analysis for personal or small business use. This application helps you keep track of your income and expense records and produces summary reports for your taxes and personal income analysis. Summary reports show totals for each income and expense category (for example, total spent on utilities, rent, or office supplies) and totals for each month or period. You can also produce yearly totals for each income and expense category, which helps you prepare a personal financial statement. The yearly summary will be valuable for preparing your taxes.

The LOG Worksheet

The LOG worksheet is primarily used for data entry. It contains a database into which you enter your income and expense transactions. The column headings for the database (field names) are an important part of the worksheet because they determine what information is stored. Other worksheets in this application pull information from this LOG sheet using external references. Figure B-1 shows the LOG worksheet.

To create this worksheet, begin by entering the labels across the top of the columns. These appear in row 9. Use the formatting buttons, Boldface and Italic to format these labels. Also, use the Format/Border command to create the vertical and horizontal lines. The skeleton should look just like the example in Figure B-1.

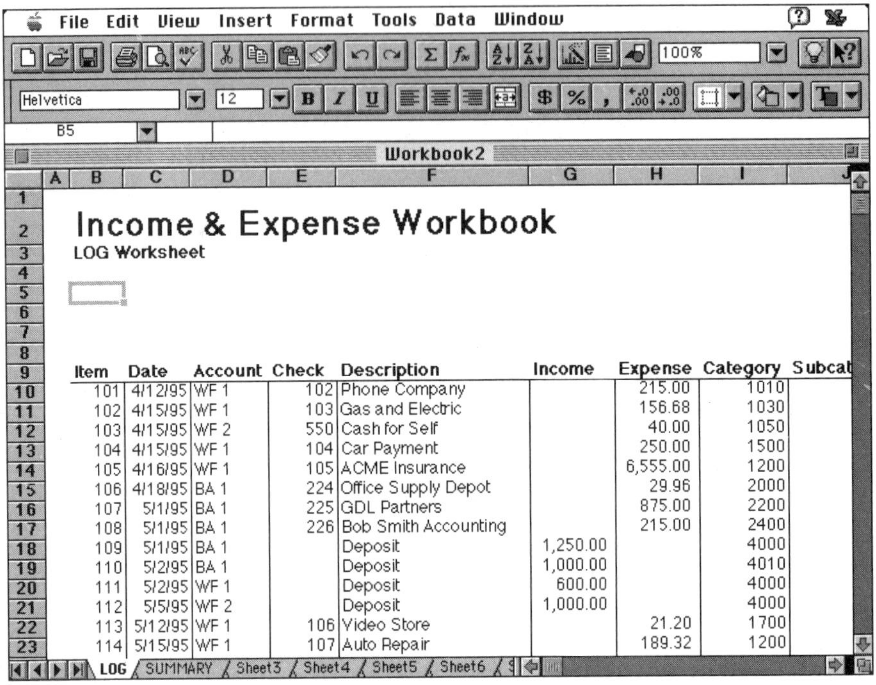

Figure B-1: The LOG worksheet holds your transactions.

Automatically entering the current date

The only other formula in this worksheet appears in the Date column. It automatically enters the current date into the column whenever you enter a value into the Item column. It uses the function ISBLANK to determine if the adjacent cell in column B contains a value. The ISBLANK function uses the following syntax:

ISBLANK(*reference*)

Enter the reference of the desired cell into the *reference* argument. This function returns the value TRUE if the cell is blank and FALSE if it's not blank. When you use this function with the IF function, you can make decisions based on the result of the ISBLANK test. The IF function works as follows:

IF(logical test,value_if_true,value_if_false)

Enter a logical expression into the *logical test* argument. A logical expression is one that results in a logical value of TRUE or FALSE. Generally, logical expressions require that you use a logical operator between two values or references. Logical operators include the following:

> Greater than

< Less than

= Equal to

>= Greater than or equal to

<= Less than or equal to

<> Not equal to

For example, the expression C5>25 results in the value TRUE if cell C5 contains any value greater than 25. Besides these expressions that use logical operators, you can use a host of logical functions provided by Excel.

The entire formula in cell C10 is =*IF(ISBLANK(B10),"",TODAY( ))*. This tests for a blank cell in column B and enters the current date if it's not blank. Note that the null string "" is used as the *value_if_true*; this string enters nothing into the cell.

Using the LOG worksheet

When you enter data into the LOG worksheet, select the Data/Form command to bring up the data form. Enter all information into the data form, and Excel automatically enters your records into the database range. Refer to Topic 8 for information about using the data form. The following is a description of the data you should enter into each column of the database and how you can account for various activities:

◆ **Item.** Enter a unique number for each new transaction into this column. A simple sequential numbering system works fine. However, you may need to use two or more rows for a single transaction. In these cases, be sure to use the same Item number for all the entries. You need to use multiple rows if you split a transaction into two or more categories. For example, a check written for two different expense categories must be split into its individual amounts. Enter each amount as a separate entry, but include the same Item number for each. Chances are these entries will have the same date, check number, and other elements, too.

◆ **Date.** This cell automatically enters the current date based on its formula. In the data form, you are unable to enter a value into this field because it's a calculated field.

◆ **Account.** If your transaction is an expense involving a check, enter the checking account number into this cell. If desired, you can just enter a code for the account, rather than entering the entire account number. This is just a method of tracking several checking accounts for the check register worksheet.

◆ **Check.** Enter the check number used for the transaction. If you want to track the check numbers of your income, you can enter those check numbers here also.

◆ **Description.** Enter a description for the transaction. If desired, you can split the entry onto two lines by using Alt-Enter. Be sure to format the cell with the Text Wrap alignment if you do this.

◆ **Income.** Enter the amount of income transactions into this column. No single transaction should have both an Income and Expense entry.

◆ **Expense.** Enter the amount of the expense transactions into this column. No single transaction should have both an Income and an Expense entry.

◆ **Category.** Enter the number of the income or expense category into this column. Categories are described more fully in the SUMMARY worksheet.

◆ **Subcategory.** If you want to categorize your transactions further (in more detail than the simple account codes), enter your own code into this column. As a rule, you should list these codes so you can repeat the same ones over and over when applicable. Using a coding system makes it easy to perform data analysis on groups of data. For example, you may want to enter invoice numbers for expense items into this column. Or you may list specific vendors from which you purchase supplies so that you can calculate totals for each vendor.

◆ **Notes.** Use this column to enter any informal notes about the transaction.

The SUMMARY Worksheet

The SUMMARY worksheet provides totals of each expense and income category in your LOG worksheet, which is useful for end-of-month tallies and for year-end totals for your tax records. The SUMMARY worksheet uses database statistical functions to draw information from the LOG worksheet. It uses a separate function for each income and expense category, so you can see the current totals for each category. Figure B-2 shows the main area of the SUMMARY worksheet.

Begin by entering all the category descriptions and code numbers in columns C and D. The Income and Expense Summary heading was created with text boxes.

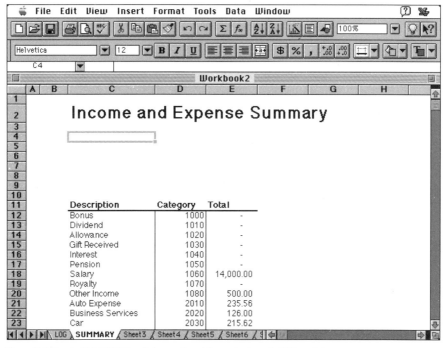

Figure B-2: Use the SUMMARY worksheet to draw information from the LOG worksheet.

Creating the criteria ranges

Each DSUM function in column E of this worksheet requires a unique criteria range because each of these functions searches the database for a different type of information. Cell E12, for example, searches the LOG database for bonus income and returns the total of all bonus income activity. To locate the bonus income, this DSUM function must identify a criteria range that specifies that the Category of the database must contain the code 1000. If the Category column contains 1000, then include the transaction amount in the total; otherwise, skip it.

You need a criteria range for each total in column E. Follow these steps to quickly create these ranges.

Creating criteria ranges

1. Enter the formula **=D12** into cell F12.

2. Select cell F12 and drag the corner down to cell F84.

3. Select the range F12:F84, which should contain all the codes from column D.

4. Select the Edit⇨Replace command. In the Find What entry box, enter **D**. In the Replace With entry box, type **D**. Click the Replace All button to make the change.

5. Copy the range F12:F84 by pressing Control-C.

6. Move the cell pointer to cell M102.

7. Select the Edit⇨Paste Special command and choose the Transpose option. Then choose OK.

8. Type **Category** into cell M101 and copy it across the row above each of the code entries. ⟨⟨

You have now set up the criteria range for the DSUM functions. Each one specifies the correct code number for the Category field of the database. If you want, you can copy the code descriptions into row 100 above each of the code numbers to help clarify which code is which. Also, you can now remove the formulas in column F.

The reason for copying the codes in this manner is to link the criteria entries to the list of codes in column D. Therefore, if you change any of the code categories or code numbers, the criteria ranges automatically reflect the changes.

Entering the DSUM functions

Each total in column E comes from a DSUM function that totals a specific category of data from the LOG worksheet. The DSUM function uses the following syntax:

DSUM(database,offset,criteria)

Enter the database range into the *database* argument. In this case, enter an external reference to the LOG worksheet. As the *offset* argument, enter the column from the database range that you want to sum. In this case, you want to sum column 6, which is the Income column, and column 7, which is the Expense column. As the *criteria* argument, enter the name of the criteria range used for the database lookup. In this case, identify the criteria range that corresponds to the category for the total. Here are a few examples from the worksheet:

◆ E12:=DSUM(LOG!Database,6,M$101:M$102)

◆ E13:=DSUM(LOG!Database,6,N$101:N$102)

◆ E32:=DSUM(LOG!Database,7,AG$101:AG$102)

◆ E33:=DSUM(LOG!Database,7,AH$101:AH$102)

Notice that the cells showing expense totals refer to the *offset* column 7.

You should also enter formulas for the Income and Expense items. These appear in cells F29 and F84:

- ◆ F29: =SUM(E12:E29)
- ◆ F84: =SUM(E32:E84)

These two formulas provide you with totals for income and expenses during the current month.

Using the SUMMARY worksheet

The SUMMARY worksheet always contains current totals from the LOG worksheet. You can turn to the SUMMARY at any time to view the breakdown of income and expense. At the end of a month, you can closeout the SUMMARY by copying the entire column of values (column E) to columns L through W. First, use the Edit/Copy command to copy the range E12:E84; then use the Edit⇨Paste Special command with the Values option to paste the values into the destination column.

After copying the values into the storage area, just leave the information in column E as it is. To clear the values in column E, begin a new LOG worksheet by removing the entries from the current LOG. Of course, you should use the File⇨Save As command to store the current values under a special name, in case you need the data later. Your new, cleared-out LOG worksheet automatically clears the current information in the SUMMARY worksheet.

If you want to view year-to-date totals, sum columns L through W in column X. You can use the values in this column for tax estimation purposes.

Enhancing the Basic Application

This appendix has outlined the basic skeleton of an income/expense tracking worksheet. It gives you the general principles used in linking worksheets and performing database search and extract functions. You can enhance the application in many ways. Here are a few ideas:

Filtering

Using database filtering features, you can establish automatic data filters to show you totals for any data category you like. For example, you may want to view the total of a specific category by filtering out all other categories. Set up your standard filters and return to them over and over. You can add DSUM and other functions to calculate database statistics based on your filtered list.

Data form

Use the data form to insert and edit records in your LOG worksheet. You will find it a convenient way to update your database.

Data analysis

You can perform all types of data analysis on your financial data, including creating a pivot table. This can show you how your income and expenses compare. Also, you can chart the specific results of the pivot table or even the raw data. Try adding database subtotals to view the totals for each category. There are many data analysis features that Excel offers for an application such as this one. Refer to Topics 9 and 10 for more information.

Macros

You can automate specific procedures in this application through macros. For example, try automating the filtering process so that, at the push of a worksheet button, you can view a specific set of records, such as all transactions on a specific date.

Additional Topics to Explore

Excel has more features and options than you will probably ever use. Chances are, you'll use only about 50 percent of Excel's capabilities. This book presents the features that you're likely to use most often. However, you may occasionally find a need for a feature contained in this appendix. These features are separated from the rest of the book so that you can progress more quickly through the topics.

Excel Functions

This book contains a list of commonly used functions for your formulas. Functions such as SUM, AVERAGE, and IF will become second nature to you as you build spreadsheet applications. But Excel contains many more functions for specific purposes — including special functions that are especially useful for advanced macros. For example, Excel offers a bunch of functions that tell you the status of specific elements of your worksheet or selected cell, such as what numeric format is being used in a specific cell. These functions can be useful information for your macros.

If you want specific information about a function, try the Function Wizard first. You can look for more help by using the Function Help screens offered in Excel 5. If you are still at a loss, look for an advanced book about Excel or an Excel function reference.

Excel 4 Macros

Excel 5 introduces a new macro system, called Visual Basic for Applications. If you are familiar with Excel 4 or previous versions, you'll discover that the new macro language is virtually nothing like the old language. You will probably have to relearn macro programming from scratch. If you are already adept at using Excel 4 macros, or if you have worksheets that include Excel 4 macros that you want to use in Excel 5, you're in luck. Excel 5 contains a special feature that lets you run, create, and even record Excel 4 macros. You can use this feature to edit and update your older worksheets while you learn the new macro system. Although Excel 5 does not include an automatic version-4-to-5 translator, you can continue to use the Excel 4 macros.

To switch Excel's macro system to the older style from Excel 4, choose the Tools⇨Record Macro⇨Record New Macro command and click the Options button. The Language options include Visual Basic or Excel 4.0 Macro.

Visual Basic

This book does not go into great detail about the Visual Basic language. To get a proper understanding of this language, you should pick up a book about Visual Basic for Applications — or even a general Visual Basic book will do. Even a basic book for the IBM-PC version of Visual Basic will serve you. (Take a look at *Visual Basic For Dummies*, from IDG Books.) As a complete programming language Visual Basic offers many features that are beyond the scope of this book, such as the ability to control and manipulate other programs with Excel.

If you don't plan to write advanced macros for your applications, you can probably get by with the Visual Basic information in this book — especially the information about automatically recording your macros with the Excel Macro Recorder. If you outgrow this information, look for a book written specifically about Visual Basic programming.

External Databases

Excel has the ability to read and process information from external database files. In other words, you can use Excel to chart or analyze data from a FoxPro, Access, dBASE, Paradox, or other database file. You can possess the powerful charting and data processing features of Excel on top of the database features of the originating program. Reading data from an external database is a feature offered in two ways by Excel.

First, you can access information from external data sources through the Macintosh clipboard by copying information from the source program and pasting it into Excel. If you require more direct links between Excel and the source program, try using the Publish and Subscribe features of System 7 or Microsoft's DDE features, if applicable. These are described in Topic 10 of this book.

If your database file is not even located on the same computer (that is, it's available through a networked computer), the Microsoft Query add-in can give you access to the data directly from Excel. Query is a network agent that locates and searches databases across a network and pulls desired information into Excel. You can create an Excel database from the resulting network query. For more information about the Microsoft Query feature, refer to your user's guide or the Microsoft Help system.

Goal Seeker and Solver

Excel provides two tools that let you solve problems in reverse. Rather than starting with specific values and making calculations to get a result; the Goal Seeker and the Solver let you design a formula or calculation model and specify a result. Then the Goal Seeker and the Solver can calculate the values that produce that result. In effect, these tools let you process a problem backward, starting with the result.

The Solver lets you take complex data models — which include as many calculations as you like — and calculate values to produce specific results. For example, suppose you want to determine the quantities of raw materials that will be needed to produce a specific amount of finished products. Based on a spreadsheet model that you design you can enter the desired number of products you want to produce and then "Solve" the question of raw material quantities in reverse.

For details about Excel's Goal Seeker and Solver features, refer to the Excel Help screens or your Excel user's guide.

Add-Ins

Excel has a wide range of features for everything from the most common tasks to the most obscure. Excel provides a worksheet function that adds up a column of numbers and another function that performs a Z-Test on a data population. You will probably use the SUM function in every worksheet you create, but you may never need Excel's advanced statistical analysis functions. So rather than build every feature directly into Excel, Microsoft made some of the less frequently used functions available on an "as needed" basis.

By activating special modules of Excel, you can make additional commands, functions, and options available for your special needs. Microsoft calls these modules *add-ins*. Add-ins are special macros that add features to Excel itself and extend the natural feature set of the program. Add-ins can place extra commands on an Excel menu or add an entirely new menu. They can also add special worksheet functions to the normal list of functions available in the Function Wizard.

Locating and opening Add-Ins

You can open any add-in using the File⇨Open command. Just locate the desired add-in file in the Microsoft Library folder of the Microsoft Excel folder. Add-ins included in this folder include Crosstab, Auto Save, Data Access Macro, Slide Show, and View Manager. Others may also appear.

When you open an add-in file, you may not see anything happen. But the add-in is working. Usually, an extra command appears in one of Excel's menus. You can open as many add-in files as you like. When you quit Excel, the add-ins are removed and must be opened again the next time you need them.

To close an add-in that you opened, you cannot use the File⇨Close command. You must use the Add-Ins Manager available through the Tools⇨Add-Ins command (see the following).

Installing Add-Ins into Excel's feature set

Some add-ins are so commonly used that the installation procedure assumes you want to make them auto-load add-ins. Auto-load add-ins are active each time you start Excel, so you don't have to open them individually with the File⇨Open command or the Add-Ins Manager. One such add-in is the View Manager. Auto-load add-ins are essentially part of Excel's standard feature set.

You can opt to make any of the auto-load add-ins optional by eliminating them from the installation. If you have already installed Excel, you can use the Excel Setup Maintenance program to remove them. In addition, you can make any add-in an auto-load add-in if you copy the add-in file to the Excel Startup folder located in the System folder of your Macintosh.

The Add-Ins Manager

The Add-Ins Manager is a tool that helps you manage add-ins. With it you can open new add-ins, close add-ins that are currently running, or just view the add-ins that you are using. Select the Tools⇨Add Ins command to view the manager screen (see Figure C-1).

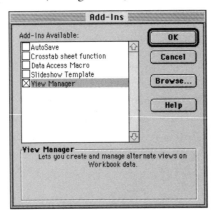

Figure C-1: The Add-Ins Manager dialog box.

The dialog box contains a list of all add-ins currently active in Excel, in addition to other add-ins that you can activate. You can add or remove the check mark (or X) from any add-in to change its status. Place a check mark beside the add-ins you want active in Excel.

Upgrading from Excel 4

If you have upgraded to Excel 5 from the previous version or if you are considering the upgrade, you will find this appendix useful. It contains a summary of the new features in Excel 5, plus some useful information about switching from Excel 4.

Menus and Dialog Boxes

Perhaps the most visible change in Excel 5 is the organization of commands and options in the menus and dialog boxes. Excel 5 presents an entirely new menu system with more intelligent grouping of commands and options. The Insert menu, for example, contains many of the commands previously found in the Edit and Formula menus of Excel 4.

Dialog boxes are also enhanced. Excel 5 presents new *tab dialogs*. Tab dialogs combine many dialog boxes into a single box. The tab dialog has multiple "pages," each with a page tab, that you can view for various options. A good example of this is the Page Setup dialog box, which now contains many different page tabs for setting options like page margins and headers. Previously, you were required to progress through more and more layers of dialog boxes to find all these options. A single tab dialog makes Excel 5 significantly easier to use.

Using Excel 4 Menus

If you have trouble switching to Excel 5's menu system, you can continue to use the Excel 4 system for awhile. When you are ready, you can return to the Excel 5 menus.

Switching to Excel 4 menus

1. Choose the Tools⇨Options command.

2. Click the General tab of the dialog box.

3. Choose the Microsoft Excel 4 Menus options to place a check mark next to it.

4. Click OK. ◖

Switching to Excel 4 menus may leave some of the new version 5 commands and options out of your menus. However, features for which Excel 4 commands apply will operate as new version 5 features.

Help Features

As described in Topic 1, Excel 5 contains a slew of help features to make your spreadsheet journey easier. Every button on every toolbar contains a *tooltip*, a simple button description that appears when you rest the mouse over a button. Tooltips often provide as much information as you need to remind you of the purpose of a particular button. However, if you need more information, Excel's on-line help features are available for detailed steps.

In addition to on-line help, Excel provides a special function help system that includes detailed information about every function offered. Turn to the function help if you need details about the purpose or use of a function. However, if you simply need a reminder of a function's syntax (the specific way to type it), turn to the new Function Wizard, which provides the syntax for each function in Excel.

Wizards are a significant help in Excel 5. They guide you through processes that are otherwise complex, such as creating charts, importing data, and consolidating worksheets. Tip wizards are available through toolbar buttons.

Finally, the new Tip Wizard provides on-the-fly advice and tips for using Excel. The Tip Wizard, when activated, senses your movements and provides information about the actions you are taking. For example, if you copy data in your worksheet, Excel's Tip Wizard may provide two or three tips on copying. You can display or hide these tips as desired.

Workbooks

Another very visible difference in Excel 5 is the workbook structure. While Excel 4 allowed you to combine individual worksheets in to a workbook file, Excel 5 is designed around the workbook structure. Every new file you open is a multiple-page workbook, and you can flip among the pages or worksheets at will. You can also add or delete pages from your workbooks if desired.

When you open an Excel 4 workbook file, Excel 5 automatically turns it into a new workbook with multiple pages. Each worksheet in your workbook becomes a page in the new workbook file. If your old workbook contained unbound sheets, these will be turned into separate workbook files in Excel. An Excel 4 worksheet automatically turns into an Excel 5 workbook containing a single sheet. An Excel 4 chart file automatically turns into an Excel 5 workbook containing a single chart worksheet. An Excel 4 macro sheet automatically turns into an Excel 5 workbook with a single macro module.

Creating Workbooks

Excel has many new features that help you create your workbook files. This section contains a brief overview of each new feature.

Custom AutoFill

Excel 5 has an addition to the old AutoFill command, which is useful for creating a series of values automatically. You can now create your own, custom series and apply them to the AutoFill command. For example, if you want to be able to create a series of store locations — where the same series of locations appears frequently on your worksheets — you can add the series of names to the custom AutoFill command. Then by starting with the first two names in the list, you can complete the entire series using the AutoFill feature. For details about this new feature, turn to Topic 2.

In-cell editing

In-cell editing lets you change the contents of a cell directly in the cell itself and removes your dependence on the old formula bar method of editing. In addition, as you enter information into Excel, you see it appear in the cell as you type — rather than having to wait until you press Return to complete the formula. In-cell editing makes the formula bar almost obsolete (but it still contains some other useful tools).

Range name tool

Excel adds a list of your worksheet's named ranges to the formula bar. At any time, you can turn to a named range to locate the range for a formula or macro. The range name list is updated as you add or remove range names from your worksheets — and each worksheet contains its own list.

AutoSum subtotals

The AutoSum command in Excel 5 has a new capability. It automatically senses when you are creating a subtotal or grand total and can create the SUM formula for you. For example, suppose you have a series of three values with a total at the bottom. Below these four cells is another set of three values and a total, like this:

value	5
value	25
value	12
total	42

value	10
value	13
value	9
total	32

You can automatically place a grand total at the bottom of these series of values using the AutoSum button. Place the cell at the bottom and click the AutoSum button to get the total of the two totals.

Format parts of a cell

Along with the in-cell editing features of Excel 5, you gain the ability to format pieces of a cell's data. This lets you highlight a specific word within a cell. Just highlight the desired portion of the entry and use the formatting commands desired. Of course, you can still make changes to the entire cell at one time by simply clicking the cell without highlighting a portion of the entry.

Tear-off palettes

New tear-off palettes leave frequently-used choices in view while you work. Palettes of options, such as border styles, colors, and patterns can be "torn off" the toolbar and placed on your worksheet for repeated use as you format your work. You can remove the palettes at any time.

Default font

Excel lets you quickly and easily change the default font used in all your worksheets. This is a new option in the Tools⇨Options command dialog. No more tricky ways to get that default font changed!

Making Better Charts

Excel 4 contains some of the best charting features on the market. Now Excel 5 makes those features even better and easier to use. The following sections describe the new charting capabilities in Excel 5.

Annotate charts

You can now add drawing and annotations directly to your chart frame — and the annotations become part of the chart itself. You can move and size the chart within the chart frame, and make room for annotations if you like. In addition, you can import pictures and place them in your chart frame for permanent use with the chart. Of course, you can still format the chart frame itself — making it transparent or colored or whatever.

Chart AutoFormats

Chart AutoFormats provide numerous preformatted charts that you can use for your data. AutoFormats offer examples of each chart type — and show the different ways that you can create these charts. For example, AutoFormats for column charts provide versions with gridlines, overlapping columns, stacked columns and more. You can create your own AutoFormats for repeated use.

Besides the AutoFormats, you can customize any part of a chart by double-clicking the chart element. Each chart element then displays a dialog box with customization options.

Floating text

All chart text is floating text, except for axis labels. That means you can move all titles, axes titles, legends, and other text anywhere within the chart frame. And remember … you can resize the chart within the frame to make more room for text and other annotations.

Trendlines and error bars

Excel 5 offers new trendline features that automate the process of calculating and charting trendlines (or regression lines) on your charts. The new trendline feature offers several different trendline additions to your XY or line chart and you can add the lines with a simple click of the mouse. No more calculating trend functions. Trends include simple linear, moving average, and many others.

You can also add error bars to your charts to point our "margins of error." Error bars can be added as a percentage, a straight value, or a range of values. Excel 5 automatically plots the error bars onto the chart.

Managing Databases

Excel's new database management features make the old way of handling data seem ancient. Excel now rivals stand-alone database products for flat-file database management tasks. The following changes provide most of the new functionality.

Filtering databases

One of the most significant changes to Excel is its database management features. You can now perform most database searches without the need for a criteria range. In fact, you can visually filter your entire database list down to specified data to get a subset of the list. This feature also makes database extraction features of Excel 4 nearly obsolete.

Database filtering is a process of selecting criteria from lists that Excel automatically generates from your data. By selecting values from lists, you can create subgroups of the overall list. You can also create custom filters to group records by more complex sets, such as all those records between two values.

Subtotals

Excel can now create subtotals in your databases automatically. A simple subtotal command tells Excel to look through your database file and subtotal a specific field. You can even subtotal filtered lists.

Customizing Excel

The most significant feature of Excel customization is the new Visual Basic for Applications macro language. This language adds significant powers to Excel for customization and application building. For details about Visual Basic, refer to your Excel Visual Basic manual or *Visual Basic For Dummies*, published by IDG Books Worldwide.

Glossary

This glossary contains definitions of words associated with spreadsheets and terms related to Excel. The glossary also includes definitions of the italicized words found throughout the 14 Topics of this book. The index and step-by-steps index show you where you can learn more about each term.

absolute cell address

A cell address that has a dollar sign preceding both the column letter and the row number of the address. The address is not changed when copied.

active cell

The cell that is selected; it is surrounded by a border. The active cell's address is displayed in the reference area of the formula bar.

add-in

A macro or custom program that enhances or extends Excel's functionality. Add-ins that come with Excel are located in the Macro Library folder. Macros you create can be saved as an add-in by choosing Options from the Save As dialog box and then selecting Add-in from the File Format pull-down list.

application

A software program, such as Excel, or a file created by a software program, such as an Excel worksheet application.

argument

A unit of information that a worksheet function needs to calculate a result. An argument can be a value or calculated value, referenced by a name or cell address. Some arguments are optional, but most are required to calculate properly.

area chart

A chart used to show how the totals of several elements change over time.

array

A special type of range that resembles a normal range that holds values or formulas, except that the cells in an array can only be edited as a group. Also called an array range.

array calculation

Takes the place of a series of complex formulas in an array range. Array calculations allow you to create array ranges.

array formula

See array calculation.

axis

The vertical or horizontal scale of a chart. Chart values are plotted against the axes. In Excel you can change the scale and appearance of the axis.

bar chart

A graph that compares the performance or progression of items, such as the results of an election. Bar charts are like column charts turned sideways.

baseline

The point on a chart's value (Y) axis at which the category (X) axis crosses. This is the line from which all values are plotted. It is usually the zero line.

border

A line around at least one side of a cell or range.

box plot chart

A chart that shows two points for each plotted value — a high and a low. The order in which the points are plotted determines whether the box plot appears as a negative or a positive span.

calculated criteria

Criteria on which a database search or extract procedure is based and which are created through calculations or formulas. Calculated criteria are able to produce complex searches.

CSV

An acronym for Comma Separated Value. A text file that contains only values, where each value is separated by a comma.

category

A group of plot points on a chart that represent a single element on the category (X) axis. Often, these values relate to the column headings in your chart's data range.

cell

The intersection of a row and column of the worksheet. A cell can hold text, a value, a worksheet function, or a formula.

cell address

The location of a cell on a worksheet, as a result of the intersection of a column and row. The cell's address is comprised of the column letter and row number.

cell format

The attributes you apply to the contents of a cell or range. Formatting can be as simple as aligning the cell entry or as thorough as coloring, shading, bordering, and bolding. Formats affect what appears on screen as well as on paper.

cell pointer

The rectangular border that highlights the active cell.

cell reference

A code that identifies the location of a cell in a workbook.

chart

Worksheet data displayed in a picture format. Excel can display data in eight two-dimensional, six three-dimensional, or several combination chart types, also known as graphs.

chart frame

The border that surrounds the chart object on the worksheet. The chart frame can be manipulated like any other object in Excel.

chart worksheet

A worksheet in the workbook that is designed to hold a chart. A chart worksheet is especially useful for on-screen presentations (slide shows).

choose

The process of picking a command from a pull-down menu or closing a dialog box. Commands can be chosen with the mouse or a keyboard shortcut. See *close* for dialog box options.

circular reference

A series of formulas that cannot calculate a result because they rely on each other for their results.

clicking

Pressing the mouse button.

Clipboard

An area of the Macintosh's memory that is set aside to hold information that you've cut or copied.

close

To remove a window or dialog box from display. Close windows by clicking the close box or by pressing Command-W. Close dialog boxes by clicking Open or Cancel, or by pressing Return or Esc.

column

A vertical range of cells beginning in Row 1 and extending to Row 16,384. Columns are normally identified by a letter, ranging from A to IV.

column chart

In Excel, a column chart is a series of data markers (bars) that make comparisons among the values of items over time.

combination chart

A chart that uses two different formats (chart types) to plot two or more data series. Alternatively, a combination chart can use two different value (Y) axes to plot two or more data series — whether the chart types are different or not.

combination reference

A range reference that includes multiple ranges. The ranges or cells of the combination reference are separated by commas, as in C5:C10,A5,G23:J100.

command

An instruction you issue from an Excel pull-down menu, shortcut menu, or tool. The task is normally carried out on the selected cell or range.

criteria

Formulas in the criteria range that act as filters so that you can find, extract, or delete records that meet the criteria conditions.

criteria range

The range in the worksheet that you've specified to hold criteria for your database searches and extract procedures. Criteria ranges are also required for database statistical functions. The criteria range contains formulas that represent conditions you want met during a database find, extract, or delete operation.

data

Text and/or values that have meaning to you. Excel uses data to compute other values (results). Data can be entered manually from the keyboard, by opening a file stored on disk, or by transferring files from another computer.

data form

A dialog box that you can use to enter, edit, find, or delete records in a worksheet database. You can view the data form by placing the cell pointer inside your database range and selecting the Data⇨Form command.

data marker

A symbol that represents a value on the worksheet, such as a bar, dot, or pie wedge.

data series

The symbols that represent the values of a row or column of data in the worksheet.

data table

A table of values produced by calculating a series of variables in a formula. This produces a matrix of results — each result representing a different combination of variables for the formula.

database

A range of continuous cells on an Excel worksheet. Each record (row) of the database is made up of fields (cells) that contain unique information. Each field (column) of the database contains the same type of information in each record. Databases can be sorted, printed, queried, and charted.

date serial number

Also called the julien date, which is the number of days elapsed since January 1, 1904.

default

An action or setting automatically performed unless changed by the user.

delimiter

A separator character between items of data in a row of text in text files. The character can be a tab, comma, space, semicolon, or other character.

dependent worksheet

A worksheet that depends on another (source) worksheet for data.

destination worksheet

A worksheet receiving information. See source worksheet.

direct dependent

A cell that contains a formula that refers to another value. If a formula refers to another cell for a value, the cell containing the formula is dependent on the cell being referenced.

document

An Excel worksheet, macro sheet, or chart that you create.

doughnut chart

A chart that displays one or more data series in a circular format where each section of the doughnut represents a percentage of the total of all the values.

drag

Sliding the mouse while the mouse button is depressed.

drop lines

Lines extending from the plot points of a line or area chart to the baseline.

edition

A file created by publishing and used by subscribing. An edition file contains data and information about the file.

embed

An object that is placed on a worksheet. Embedding an object enables you to receive information from another open program.

export

Saving a document in a format other than an Excel format for use with another program.

expression

A piece of a formula that can calculate to a value.

external reference formula

A linking formula that resides in a cell of a dependent worksheet that refers to a source worksheet. *See* dependent worksheet *and* source worksheet.

extract range

The range in the worksheet you've specified by choosing Set Extract from the Data menu. Database records that meet the criteria specified in the criteria range are copied to the extract range. *See* criteria range.

field

A vertical range of information in an Excel database. The same field in each record contains the same type of data.

file

Information stored as separate units on disk. You create a file when you choose Save or Save As from the File menu, which copies the information in memory as displayed on screen in a worksheet, macro sheet, or chart file.

file format

The way a program arranges data as a unit on disk. Excel can read file formats from most popular software programs.

floating chart text

Text placed on a chart that can be moved anywhere within the chart frame. All text in Excel 5 charts is floating text — except for axis values.

floating toolbar

A toolbar that is positioned over the worksheet and contains a title bar and close box.

font

A complete collection of characters (letters, numbers, punctuation marks) in a specific design or typeface.

font family

A group of fonts that are of the same type but have different sizes and other attributes.

footer

Information, such as date, time, or page number, that appears at the bottom of each printed page. Choose Page Setup from the File menu to specify footer information.

formula

A mathematical expression you create with arithmetic operators, worksheet functions, values, text, cell or range references, or names. Each formula must begin with an equal sign, and there is a limit of one formula per cell.

formula bar

The rectangular area between the menu bar and the worksheet's title bar. The formula bar enables you to enter new or edit existing cell contents.

function

A built-in formula provided by Excel. Functions need arguments to calculate but calculate faster and more accurately than a formula counterpart. Excel has over 200 worksheet functions and over 350 if you install the Analysis ToolPak add-in.

freezing panes

The process of holding a pane in place on screen. Freezing a pane is helpful when you need to see row text or column text displayed continuously while another pane scrolls.

group

A series of worksheets in a workbook that are grouped together for synchronous editing and formatting.

handles

Small squares that surround objects or chart items when selected. Objects with black handles can be moved or sized, but objects with white handles cannot.

header

Information, such as date, time, or page number, that appears at the top of each printed page. Choose Page Setup from the File menu to specify header information.

high-low chart

A chart that plots two points for each value — a high and a low point. See also Box Plot Chart.

import

Opening a file created by a program other than Excel. Importing text files requires that you parse the data to make it usable in Excel. *See* parse.

indirect dependent

A cell that contains a formula that depends on a particular cell, but which is once removed from that cell. For example, if cell A1 is used in a formula in cell A2 and cell A2 is used in cell A3, then cell A3 is an indirect dependent of A1.

key field

A field by which data is sorted.

line chart

A chart that plots a series of values over time and is expressed as a line.

linking

The process where one worksheet depends on another for information, or where an Excel worksheet is linked to another Macintosh application program or vice versa.

logical value

A value of TRUE or FALSE. Usually the result of a logical test, which is an expression that uses a logical operator, such as A4>A5.

macro

A list of commands in a continuous range down a column of a macro sheet. Macros can be created by Excel's macro recorder or entered manually. A macro sheet must be open to use the macros with a worksheet. Macros can be as simple as keystroke reducers or as complex as custom dialog boxes.

marquee

The counter-clockwise moving dashed line that surrounds selected cells when they are cut or copied.

menu bar

The narrow rectangle at the top of the Macintosh display that contains Excel's pull-down command menus, as well as the Apple and Finder menus.

mixed address

A cell address that has a dollar sign preceding the column letter or the row number of the address, but not both. Only the portion of the address that does not have a dollar sign (the relative portion) changes when copied.

multiple range reference

See Combination Reference.

note indicator

A small box appearing in the upper-right corner of a cell that contains a note. You can hide or display the note indicator using the Tools➪Options command.

object

A graphical item placed on a worksheet or chart. You can create an object by using the Drawing toolbar or embed an object from another open program. You can add arrows and lines to charts, as well as move and size objects.

open

To retrieve a copy of a worksheet, macro sheet, or chart saved on disk to memory and display it on screen.

page break

The dashed lines displayed on the worksheet indicating where printing of the next page begins. Page breaks do not print and can be set automatically by Excel or manually.

palette

The group of sixteen colors available in Excel documents. The palette can be customized, copied among documents, or substituted with a palette from the Custom Color Palette add-in.

pane

A worksheet window segment. A worksheet window can have two horizontal, two vertical, or four window panes.

parse

The process of taking a text file and making it usable by Excel. Text files normally contain many rows of information, one row per cell in Column A. Parsing separates each data item in the row into its own cell in the same row. Choose Parse from the Data menu or use the Flat File add-in (Smart Parse) to parse text files.

pie chart

A chart that shows one series of values as percentages of the total.

pointer

The symbol displayed on screen that moves as the mouse is moved. The pointer changes shape as you move it to different areas of the Excel display. The pointer can resemble, among other things, a black pointer, white cross, and black cross hairs. The pointer enables you to select commands, ranges, and objects, and to move and resize windows.

precedent

A cell that is used or depended upon by another cell. Precedents can either be direct or indirect.

print titles

Text in rows and/or columns that are printed along the left side and top of the paper, respectively.

publish

To create an edition file from a selected range of the worksheet for use by others on a network.

RAM

An acronym for random-access memory. The Macintosh's main memory that interacts with its central processing unit. Information stored in memory is lost when power is turned off, so save to disk frequently.

range

A group of cells on a worksheet. A range can be as small as a single cell or as large as an entire worksheet. A selected range can be comprised of contiguous or noncontiguous cells. You must select a cell or range before carrying out most Excel operations.

radar chart

A chart that plots values along many axes that meet at the center.

record

A horizontal range of information in an Excel database. Each field in the record contains a different type of information.

reference area

The small rectangle to the left of the formula bar. The reference area displays information about a task in progress, such as the size of a selected range, percent of add-in loaded, and so on.

relative address

The address of a cell that changes when copied.

row

A horizontal range of cells from Column A to Column IV in the worksheet. Rows are numbered from 1 to 16,384.

sans serif

A font without the short line at the ends of the strokes of each character.

scenario

An alternative set of values for a worksheet. You can create and store several scenarios for your worksheets and switch among the different value sets by using the Scenario Manager.

scroll bars

The narrow bar on the right side and along the bottom of a worksheet window. The vertical scroll bar enables you to move the screen display up or down, and the horizontal scroll bar enables you to move the screen display left or right.

select

To use the mouse (or Shift and arrow keys) to mark a cell, range, object, chart item, or other Excel item for editing, formatting, or other action.

serif

A font with a short line at the ends of the strokes of each character.

Single-step mode

A macro running one command at a time, rather than at full speed. Single-step mode helps you spot and correct errors in macros by seeing problems you wouldn't ordinarily see because the macro is running at full speed.

source worksheet

A worksheet furnishing data to another (dependent) worksheet.

split bar

The black box at the top and to the left of the vertical and horizontal scroll bars, respectively. Dragging from the split bar creates two worksheet window panes.

status bar

The rectangle along the bottom of the Excel display, directly below the worksheet window. The status bar displays Excel's current mode (Ready, Edit, Help), and whether SCROLL, CAPS, or NUM is on.

style

A combination of fonts, borders, shading, and other format attributes. Styles can be created and named for repeated use in any worksheet.

subscribe

To include information contained in an edition file in a worksheet.

supporting worksheet

A worksheet that provides values for a dependent worksheet. A worksheet on which another worksheet depends for one or more values through external cell references.

syntax

Rules that a worksheet or macro function contains to calculate properly.

text

Characters entered into a cell using the keyboard; used primarily to describe values and results of functions and formulas.

text file

A file that contains only text characters and no formatting. When opened in Excel, each line of text is an entry in Column A. A text file must be parsed to be of any use in Excel. *See* parse.

time serial number

The number of increments elapsed since 12:00 midnight. An increment is a decimal fraction of a 24-hour period, such that .5 is 12:00p.m.

toggle

To change the status of a two-way (toggle) option, such as an on/off option.

toolbar

An on-screen rectangle that holds tools. Toolbars can be displayed, hidden, and customized. The Standard toolbar appears by default between the Command menu and the formula bars.

toolbar dock

One of the four areas of the Excel display where you can position a toolbar. Toolbars can be docked between the Command menu and formula bars, above the status bar, and along the left and right sides of the screen.

trend line

A line that is produced by a trend formula that calculates a relationship among values. Often, trend lines are plotted on a line or XY chart.

type face

The visual characteristics of a font.

unattached text

Chart text that you've added and can move.

value

A number entered into a cell in a worksheet from the keyboard, or as a result of a worksheet function or formula calculation.

virtual memory

The capability of using a portion of a computer's hard disk as an extension of random access memory.

wildcard

A character that takes the place of a character or several characters so that you can locate groups of records that share common naming conventions. Examples include * and ?.

workbook

A file that can contains worksheets, charts, and macro sheets.

working set

The add-ins that automatically load into the computer's memory when you start Excel.

XY chart

A chart that plots points along two numeric axes — an X and Y axis. XY charts are also called scatter charts.

Part VI
Excel Reference

Step-By-Steps™ Index

Topic 1: Excel's Basic Concepts

Topic 2: Creating Worksheets

Topic 3: The Excel Environment

Topic 4: Formatting Your Work

Topic 5: Drawing and Annotating

Topic 6: Printing

Topic 7: Formulas and Functions

Topic 8: Using Excel as a Database

Topic 9: Analyzing Data in Excel

Topic 10: Working with Large Workbook Applications

Topic 11: Creating Charts

Topic 12: Customizing Charts

Topic 13: Creating and Running Macros

Topic 14: Creating a Custom Application

Appendix B: Worksheet Examples

Part VI
Excel Reference

Index

Symbols

Index

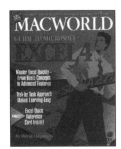

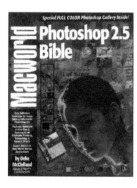

Order Form

Order Center: (800) 762-2974 (8 a.m.-5 p.m., PST, weekdays) or **(415) 312-0650**

For Fastest Service: Photocopy This Order Form and FAX it to: **(415) 358-1260**

Quantity	ISBN	Title	Price	Total

Shipping & Handling Charges

Subtotal	U.S.	Canada & International	International Air Mail
Up to $20.00	Add $3.00	Add $4.00	Add $10.00
$20.01-40.00	$4.00	$5.00	$20.00
$40.01-60.00	$5.00	$6.00	$25.00
$60.01-80.00	$6.00	$8.00	$35.00
Over $80.00	$7.00	$10.00	$50.00

In U.S. and Canada, shipping is UPS ground or equivalent.
For Rush shipping call (800) 762-2974.

Subtotal _____

CA residents add applicable sales tax _____

IN and MA residents add 5% sales tax _____

IL residents add 6.25% sales tax _____

RI residents add 7% sales tax _____

Shipping _____

Total _____

Ship to:

Name _____

Company _____

Address _____

City/State/Zip_____

Daytime Phone _____

Payment: ❑ Check to IDG Books (US Funds Only)   ❑ Visa   ❑ Mastercard   ❑ American Express

Card# _____ Exp._____ Signature_____

Please send this order form to: IDG Books, 155 Bovet Road, Suite 310, San Mateo, CA 94402.

Allow up to 3 weeks for delivery. Thank you!

IDG BOOKS WORLDWIDE REGISTRATION CARD

Title of this book: MACWORLD EXCEL 5 COMPANION, 2E

My overall rating of this book: ❑ Very good [1] ❑ Good [2] ❑ Satisfactory [3] ❑ Fair [4] ❑ Poor [5]

How I first heard about this book:

❑ Found in bookstore; name: [6] ❑ Book review: [7]

❑ Advertisement: [8] ❑ Catalog: [9]

❑ Word of mouth; heard about book from friend, co-worker, etc.: [10] ❑ Other: [11]

What I liked most about this book:

What I would change, add, delete, etc., in future editions of this book:

Other comments:

Number of computer books I purchase in a year: ❑ 1 [12] ❑ 2-5 [13] ❑ 6-10 [14] ❑ More than 10 [15]

I would characterize my computer skills as: ❑ Beginner [16] ❑ Intermediate [17] ❑ Advanced [18] ❑ Professional [19]

I use ❑ DOS [20] ❑ Windows [21] ❑ OS/2 [22] ❑ Unix [23] ❑ Macintosh [24] ❑ Other: [25]_____
(please specify)

I would be interested in new books on the following subjects:
(please check all that apply, and use the spaces provided to identify specific software)

❑ Word processing: [26] ❑ Spreadsheets: [27]

❑ Data bases: [28] ❑ Desktop publishing: [29]

❑ File Utilities: [30] ❑ Money management: [31]

❑ Networking: [32] ❑ Programming languages: [33]

❑ Other: [34]

I use a PC at (please check all that apply): ❑ home [35] ❑ work [36] ❑ school [37] ❑ other: [38] _____

The disks I prefer to use are ❑ 5.25 [39] ❑ 3.5 [40] ❑ other: [41]_____

I have a CD ROM: ❑ yes [42] ❑ no [43]

I plan to buy or upgrade computer hardware this year: ❑ yes [44] ❑ no [45]

I plan to buy or upgrade computer software this year: ❑ yes [46] ❑ no [47]

Name: _____ Business title: [48] _____ Type of Business: [49]

Address (❑ home [50] ❑ work [51]/Company name: _____)

Street/Suite# _____

City [52]/State [53]/Zipcode [54]: _____ Country [55]

❑ **I liked this book!** You may quote me by name in future
IDG Books Worldwide promotional materials.

My daytime phone number is _____

IDG BOOKS

THE WORLD OF COMPUTER KNOWLEDGE

❏ **YES!**

Please keep me informed about IDG's World of Computer Knowledge.
Send me the latest IDG Books catalog.